A Year in the Life of a Film Critic
1968-1969

# A YEAR
# IN THE DARK

## RENATA ADLER

A BERKLEY MEDALLION BOOK
PUBLISHED BY
BERKLEY PUBLISHING CORPORATION

*To ARTHUR GELB and A.M. ROSENTHAL*

*Published by arrangement with Random House, Inc.*

BERKLEY MEDALLION EDITION, APRIL, 1971

SBN 425-01977-2

*BERKLEY MEDALLION BOOKS are published by*
Berkley Publishing Corporation
200 Madison Avenue
New York, N. Y. 10016

BERKLEY MEDALLION BOOKS ® TM 757,375

Printed in the United States of America

## ·········· CONTENTS

Being film critic for the *New York Times* for a year (fourteen months, really) was for me a particular kind of adventure—with time, with tones of voice, with movies, with editing, with the peculiar experience it always is to write in one's own name something that is never exactly what one would have wanted to say. The job came to me at an odd time. I had begun at *The New Yorker* as a book reviewer, until I no longer saw the point of reviewing other people's books unless the books themselves were so important that one would want to make them known. There were not at that time enough books to explain a regular critic's job, and I do not believe in professional criticism anyway, as a way of life. I turned to reporting, and it seemed to make more sense. Selma, Harlem, Mississippi, the New Left, group therapy, pop music, the Sunset Strip, Vietnam, the Six-Day War—I wanted very much to be there and accurate about these things. I particularly detested, and detest, the "new journalism," which began, I think, as a corruption of a form which originated in *The New Yorker* itself. After a genuine, innovating tradition of great *New Yorker* reporters (A. J. Liebling, Joseph Mitchell, St. Clair McKelway, Lillian Ross, Wolcott Gibbs) who imparted to events a form and personal touch that were truer to the events themselves than short, conventional journalism, determined by the structure of the daily news, had ever been, there sprang up almost everywhere a second growth of reporters, who took up the personal and didn't give a damn for the events.

There began, apparently, to be a taste for this. The facts dissolved. The writer was everything. It is hard enough to define hard fact, but we were starting to get, in what looked like quite respectable contexts, a new variant of sensational or yellow journalism—that corroding thing, the news or some distortion of the news, as entertainment. I remember particularly a reporter for the then "lively," dying *Herald Tribune* who would charge up to people in Alabama with extended hand, introduce himself, and beginning "Wouldn't you say . . . ?" produce an entirely formulated paragraph of his own. Sooner or later somebody tired or agreeable would nod, and the next day's column—with some intimate colloquialisms and absolute fabrications thrown in—would attribute its quotes and appear, as a piece of the new journalism.

The finest reporters I met at the time were *Times* men in the South. While others were rushing frantically about, desperate and verbal about deadlines, dangers, reputation, the problems of safely reaching a telephone, Paul Montgomery, Gene Roberts and Roy Reed more or less sloped from place to place, getting the story with true ear and straight into the next edition of the *Times*. They were entirely free of self-importance or punditry, rather like great short-order cooks. The harassed ones are never any good. It seemed almost a question of making it look easy. My idealization of the *Times* in this respect was much later modified, in the Paris disturbances of May. (The bureau, with one exception, was always in a terrific huff. They were normally shallow and about a day behind events. And they seemed always trying to recoup, with stories headlined "Parisians Have Second Thoughts About . . . ," some particularly inadequate story of the day before. All such a headline ever meant was that the reporter himself had changed his mind.) But most *Times* reporters still seem to me the best I know.

In October, 1967, when the *Times* suddenly, almost incidentally, offered me Bosley Crowther's job, Mr. Crowther had been reviewing for twenty-seven years. Anything one man has done in his own way for that long becomes unoccupied in a truly vacant sense. People form strong ideas about how it should not be done; yet it is not at all clear what the job, apart from the man who has done it almost as long as it exists, might be. Like nearly everyone, I had always gone to the movies a lot and liked to go to them. It so completely blotted out the content of much of life and yet filled the days, like dreaming. (It later turned out that my favorite screening time was eight in the morning, when the change to the movie world was entirely smooth.) I had done a few movie reviews before, at *The New Yorker* for a month, and once for *Life*, but I had never read much film criticism—except by writers who interested me on other grounds. Reviewing movies seemed not at all like reviewing books, more like writing about events, about anything. And although there was wide access in the *Times* (a lot of people seem to read movie reviews), there was not, except in foreign films, the seriousness of making or ruining a film, as there can be with plays or books. I trusted my judgment enough to think I would know what distinction there was, and try not to harm it.

I bought quantities of film criticism in the months before the job began, Agee, Arnheim, everybody: the angry trash claimers (writers who claim some movie they have enjoyed is utter trash, and then become fiercely possessive about it); the brave commercialism deplorers (writers forever saddened that some popular movie has failed to realize the high aesthetic possibilities they might have envisioned for it); the giddy adjectivalists, stunned, shattered or convulsed with hilarity every other day by some cinema experience; the severe traditionalists, usefully comparing any given film to one which had gone before; the cement solid positivists, whose essays were likely to begin, "The screen is a rectangle," and, although the exposition rarely got much deeper, seemed to feel most comfortable with formulations about the Medium. The best criticism I read was still by writers who simply felt moved by film to say something about it—without reverent or consistent strategies, putting films idiosyncratically alongside things they cared about in other ways.

In those months, I also began to go to the movies all day long, drive-ins, Spanish theaters, Chinese, Forty-second Street, museums, etc. and then I stopped. It began to produce a sensation of interior weightlessness, of my own time and experience drifting off like an astronaut's. It was not at all the private reading binges that take place at

11

home. It was more like travel, dislocating, among strangers, going into public dark for dreams and controversy. On January 1st last year, the job began. Or more accurately, on Friday, December 29th, when the Sunday piece for January 7th was due. This was the first indication I had of the absolute exigencies of scheduling. From that moment, it was like catching your sleeve in a machine. The final, immutable deadline for Sunday pieces turned out to be the small hours of Tuesday morning—which created occasional disastrous coincidences, like a piece on violent suffering written just before Senator Robert Kennedy was shot and published the Sunday after he died. But the grinding calamity could be the daily pieces, whose simple mechanics were these: a screening, perhaps the day of the opening, perhaps a few days before, copy due at six in the afternoon, to appear when the paper is printed at 9:30 P.M. The pieces were typed with nine carbons, and edited in hurdles. The idea at the *Times* is that reviews are not edited at all, but the reality was a continual leaning on sentences, cracking rhythms, removing or explaining jokes, questioning or crazily amplifying metaphors and allusions, on pieces that were not that good in the first place. The first hurdle was the young editor of what was called the Cultural News Department, whose major contributions were to divide paragraphs in unlikely places, losing the sense (there is an ancient newspaper tradition that paragraphs more than one or two sentences long "look terrible"), and to point to as many sentences as possible and ask what I meant by them. I fell for this every time, would explain at length, and then receive that absolute nightmare of editorial replies, "Well, why don't you come right out and say it?"

After a few months, this transaction became untenable and I was permitted to submit pieces directly to the second hurdle, the Obituary and Culture Desk (Obit), where all culture pieces are edited. Here, sentences were often reversed (there was rarely the conception that in doing sentences a writer chooses among options), the timing of remaining jokes undone, and meanings "clarified." Little things could occur on Sundays: "unavailing work"

12

one week became "unavailable work"—quite a difference, after all—and a movie's reference to Jean-Sol Partre was helpfully explained in a parenthesis to be "a pun on the name of Jean-Paul Sartre." But the Sunday section, under a kind, harassed, intelligent editor, Seymour Peck, was edited slightly and for good reason. In the daily, after regular, protracted and yet tentative argument (one is never, even in the face of pure inanity, that certain about editing), there would be spasms, for days on end, of drastic changes whose source was never clear. At one point, lower echelon editors were coming over the hills like the Chinese, with queries and suggestions, until it occurred to me that I could complain. That worked. It stopped. The only defense against the sourceless spasms, though, was to keep a vigil on editions of the paper until 1 A.M., call the Obit Desk and quarrel, threaten to resign (on February 11, 1968, I did resign; nobody paid much attention), or to ask for the intercession of a major editor. Arthur Gelb, Abe Rosenthal, Clifton Daniel, all the major editors of the *Times*, were, and are, after all writers themselves and very patient about writers' problems, but it seemed hardly possible—the importance of other things in the world considered—to ask them often to intercede in prose and culture wars. In the end, I just stopped reading the paper, in order not to know.

The spatial context of writing at the office was peculiar. I sat, for the first few months, at a desk among rows of desks in what is called the culture pool. Looking up from my typewriter to think, I would often be staring directly into the eyes of Hilton Kramer, who was thinking too. Phones rang incessantly on every side. When it was possible, I wrote at home. On a particularly grumpy day, several months after Bosley Crowther had left the *Times* for Columbia Pictures, I decided, out of pure grumpiness really, that it was time to move into his office. All first-string critics' offices at the *Times* are glass enclosed, and late one night, working on a Sunday piece—with Grace Glueck, who also worked late, typing nearby—I began to scrub the words Movie News off what had been Mr. Crowther's door. The letters had always looked unseemly to me. I tried to slide them around into Movie Snew, but that didn't work, and I finally removed them altogether and felt fine.

From the first, the job had sides I had not quite anticipated. For one thing, it turned out to be extremely public, more like a regular, embarrassed, impromptu performance on network television than any conception of writing I had ever had. The film reviewer writes more frequently than anybody else at the *Times* except Clive Barnes, who did theater and ballet, and who writes gladly, naturally. I don't; one of the reasons for trying daily journalism was to see whether it would get any easier. The Movie News staff at the time consisted of three other reviewers, Vincent Canby, whom I liked and admired a lot, and Howard Thompson and Abe Weiler, whom I liked too. In principle, I had the choice of which movies to review, but for a while I reviewed them all, sometimes two or three in a day, trying to get the rhythm of the job. The paper thought it important that I should establish a position vis-à-vis Mr. Crowther at the start so that readers would have some context for what they were reading then. That led to the first long piece on violence, and later, to one about *The Graduate*. I thought it a bad idea, supposing that what shift there was from Mr. Crowther might be clear without returning to specific issues at once for differences. Near strangers were always telling me whether they agreed or disagreed with me. (This usually produced an evening of doubt, with a particular violence of tone in the review of the following day.) Conversations around me hardly ever seemed to be about anything but films any more.

Some odd, incidental things began to happen in my life outside. On February 17th, for example, there was the awards dinner of the Directors' Guild. Normally, I tried to stay clear of occasions of that kind, but a friend was getting an award, and he had invited his friends. For some days before the event, a lady from the Guild kept calling alarmingly, demanding to know who my escort for the evening would be. It turned out this was only for place cards—which were little gilded director's chairs with each guest's name engraved on them. The dinner itself, 700 people at the Americana, was not alarming in any way. We sat next to the director of "Dark Shadows," a television soap opera about vampires, which I happened to watch from time to time, and we later moved to a table of close friends. Then, without having drunk very much or anticipated it in any way, as soon as the presentation of the awards began, I became completely hysterical with giggles, very high, hee hee, and very loud. A speaker would no sooner begin to praise a nominee, or to thank all the people who had made his award possible, than I was off again. The speeches became very brief. I couldn't leave the room either. It would have seemed an even greater fuss. It went on for more than a hour, part mirth, part crack-up. I wondered whether I would have to be led away.

An early surprise was the number of utterly deadly films that came out, tolerable to sit through, nearly impossible to discuss. I enjoyed reviewing the spiritedly awful ones, *The Power, Dr. Faustus, Survival 1967, Broken Wings,* and I kept returning compulsively to the ones I liked. But a news event of comparable insignificance to, say, *The Impossible Years,* would receive no coverage in the *Times* at all. I felt we should simply mention that such a movie had opened, and let it go at that, or perhaps, as somebody suggested, appraise in some very practical consumer way the movie's proper price: first half hour worth fifty cents; second hour, minus four dollars; net loss in going, three-fifty plus baby sitter. Another solution was to try to broaden the context a little, move as far and as fast away from consumer service inventories as possible and, except for the plot (it is very difficult to discuss a film at all without telling what it is "about" in the narrative sense), skip performance, direction, choreography, and so on, unless they *meant* something—and try to go on to details or tangents that did. I tried that sometimes.

For some reason, "the industry" was continually upset. This was puzzling. In all of 1960, Hollywood produced scarcely any movies of any value, scarcely anything that moved people, captured their fantasy lives, made them laugh, or even diverted them a little. It seemed to have lost

15

even the knack of making artful trash. "The industry," as compared to other characteristically American industries, was bewildered, inefficient, antiquated, also not much in touch with art. (I suspect, with all the talk of audiences under twenty-five, children are beginning to lose the movie-going habit entirely.) But I was certainly not costing them any money. People, including me, will apparently still go to movies no matter what. Although I am now convinced that the old movie factory is going to lose its audience and become a mere feeder for unindustrialized countries and television, while the movie audience fragments, becomes more particularized, and attends only the films of artists in control of their work, I did not think so then. I rather liked the industry. It was not enough. The producer of a creaky leviathan wanted not only his own millions but François Truffaut's reviews. The third-generation, imagination-depleted moguls wanted to be treated like auteurs.

There began to be constant rumors that I was fired or had quit, that the industry had applied pressure. The pressure rumors were silly. The *Times* might be besieged, unhappy at moments, conciliating, but certainly unpressurable. They seemed rather glad about controversy. They did not give a damn about the industry. I got a memo from Abe Rosenthal once, asking me to use the words "very" and "boring" less often. Arthur Gelb once or twice reminded me that readers see reviews before and not after films. Members of the bull pen, another editing hurdle, whose function I never did quite understand, often loathed what I was doing. But the major editors were unfailingly steadying. There were lots of cheery memos, and after the twelfth week, a call from Mr. Gelb to say that the trial period was over and it was all right. I guess we all knew I wasn't going to do it for a hundred years. As for the early quitting rumors, they probably had to do with a certain cycle of misery—particularly at low points, like a piece on Music, or the Death piece, which I never did get quite right—when the articles themselves were so bad I got desperate. At other times, there were cycles of fun.

There was once a full-page ad in the *Times* not liking the reviews, and *Variety* used to point out as factual errors things that often were and occasionally were not factual errors I had made. Strom Thurmond once denounced the *Times* in Congress for my review of *The Green Berets*, which he read into *The Congressional Record*, along with Clive Barnes's review of *Hair* (I was a liberal Republican, I think, when Senator Thurmond was still a Southern Democrat). But the only direct contacts I had with the industry (since the *Times* said I could avoid contact with public-relations people if I liked) were two, one over *Star!* one over *Funny Girl*. The *Funny Girl* episode was a drink, at which the producer complained—about the distinction of his film, about the execrable quality of the *Times* review. I made as many sympathetic noises as I could. In a while, a box arrived, containing a gilded broccoli. I had written that William Wyler's attitude toward Barbra Streisand in *Funny Girl* seemed to be simultaneously patronizing and grand-standing, as if he were firing off a gilded broccoli. I was touched by the gift, although (since I had twice postponed this apparently unavoidable interview) it was a few days old and rather smelled. I laughed. Then the producer, apparently quite seriously, asked me why I had implied that Miss Streisand was a whore. Nothing had been further from my mind, and I asked him wherever he had gotten that idea. "You called her a broccoli," he said. I said that whoredom and broccoli were truly not associated in my mind. He said they were in his and, as though there could be no doubt whatever about this, in the reader's. It seemed to me the interview was not going well and I asked him, out of courtesy really, whether I might keep the gift. "On one condition," he said. I asked what the condition was. He asked why I didn't trust him. I said I did, but that it would be nice to know what the condition was. We discussed this a while. Finally, he said the condition was a kiss. It seemed unsporting to say no, and I said all right. It turned out the kiss had to be right there, at Sardi's, in the drinking hour. I said that the *Times* kissing a producer at Sardi's might be bad form. He lost all interest in the matter after that. Normally a private anecdote, except that it would have been so clearly public had it gone the other way.

At the screening of *Star!*, in the first act, I went to the ladies' room and was sick. No fault of the film's. Flu. Back in the screening room, not wanting to step over many feet, I took up a different seat, near the aisle. A *Times* reviewer, out of fairness, is never supposed to walk out of anything, but when I started to be sick again, I decided it was ridiculous to stay. I particularly waited until after the intermission, so that when the house lights went on, and then off again, I would still be clearly in my seat (one of the myths of the *Times* film reviewer's power is that if the *Times* looks unhappy at something, the other reviewers will hate it). I waited a half hour more, and then tiptoed out. I saw the rest of the film at the last preview. A terrific fuss ensued. The P.R. man from Fox, finding himself at the end without the *Times'* elbow to grasp or fanny to pat, called and asked for an explanation. I explained. Suddenly, a deluge of letters from Darryl Zanuck to the *Times*. I had left, for no reason, before the intermission. Therefore my review was short and, he felt, unkind. Mr. Daniel patiently replied. Mr. Zanuck wrote again. It went like that. Outrage. Patience. That was all.

The people I did hear from a lot were readers—about six letters a day. "Our reader," particularly as conceived by the culture editor, was a hypothetical, highly serious person, hanging from a subway strap, who had never read a book or seen a movie, used an obscenity or slept with anyone, but who was desperately anxious that every character, however minor, involved in any way with the making of a film should be identified by some parenthetical reference to his prior work. I began to throw in such identifications maniacally for a while, referring to winners of the Silver Arena at Pula or supporting roles in films like *Three*, but nobody seemed to find that funny except me, and so I stopped. "Our readers" came up a lot, particularly in truisms about good writing being simple writing and so forth, until one day I said, rather mildly I thought, that I didn't give a damn about our reader, and the crisis passed. Speaking of damns and who gave them, there was always a little compulsion—shared by most writers for family publications I think—to sneak a little obscenity into the *Times*. Once, in reviewing *The Killing of Sister George,* I tried to say that it had some

18

good Anglo-Saxon expletives ending in "off" and meaning "go away." An editor who was always fair in these matters did make me give up the "ending in off." It was some similar, though awful compulsion, I think, that made me put in some really grotesque errors in matters I knew perfectly well: type in an extra name, for example, in just copying the letters off a creditsheet, or write of the moments when the earth moved in *The Bridge of San Luis Rey*. It was like planting mines for oneself when one is feeling guilty about expressing so many opinions about everything.

The readers I guess I was writing for, and whom I presumed I had been hired for, were people fairly like myself, or specific friends I had had somewhere along the way. It varied a bit, depending on whom I had seen or lately read. I don't think it is possible to write for people completely unlike yourself. I tried not to be completely negative, except about films I considered reprehensibly rotten, and the readers I heard from were often kind—although certainly not always. After the *Green Berets* review, among highly imaginatively obscene or physically threatening mail, there was an anonymous soul who sent me each week, addressed to Red Renata Adler, his losing tickets from Aqueduct. After several pieces attacking the Left, there were similar letters from the other side. And of course, there were always highly intelligent critical letters as well—and eleven humorous ones after the San Luis Rey debacle. I tried to answer all of them, although, being fairly messy with bills and papers, I lost a few. There was naturally some crazy mail, which I tried to answer seriously too. Just once, at a low time, I used the senatorial gambit for writing to weird vituperative constituents: "Dear Sir, I think I ought to inform you that some preliterate lunatic has been writing me letters and signing your name." Inevitably, I chose the wrong case. I got an immediate reply. The reader answered that, though he had perhaps been a bit harsh, he was certainly no lunatic, and he hoped that I bore him no ill will. The nicest mail was from people who wrote as though they thought I was having a hard time.

In a way, I guess I was. What I wanted to do with the

job was to try, as a just-under-thirty person then, of fairly contemporary experience, to review films in earnest (or in fun, depending on the film) with a bit more tension and energy than the traditional paper way. I was trying to shorten and tighten the daily pieces, from what they had been before, and expand the range sometimes. In particular, I wanted drastically to change the redundancy of the Sunday articles. (It seemed absurd to rephrase every Sunday the reviews I had done on weekday afternoons.) None of this quite worked out. One continual problem was control. I was forever trying to do in a line something that should have been a piece, and making a piece out of what might have amounted to a line, and frazzling tone. I never seemed able to get it right. There was a special complication with what I can only call the easy victories. That is, I have a personal suspicion of critical writing that comes easily, of felicitous accidents. In criticism, I think there ought to be evidence of time taken, trouble ironed out, of a kind of American Gothic zeal for suffering. It makes the doing of criticism have some risks of its own and it seems more fair. Yet what would happen is that the dashed-off pieces, the unearned lines almost always worked out best. It was like being told, as people often are, that a shoddy piece of work is the best thing they have ever done. It leaves one somehow off-stride with fate. And often, I did wind up recapping in Sunday pieces, either because it was late Monday night and I did not have a thought in my head, or to go back to films and try to get the proportion right, or because repetitions somehow became inadvertent rest stops in my mind.

Some of the nicest times were when events in the outside world were allowed to impinge—the strikes in Paris and Cannes, the Evelyn Waugh disturbances in Venice, meeting the Czech directors, their doubts in the spring, their absolute despair in France and Italy in summer, meeting artists in those weeks, following them about and doing criticism of some films that mattered a bit. The little dramas of solid *Times* reporting came up then too: having to cross borders in hired cars to phone stories for deadlines during strikes; barricades; and, when I knew I couldn't possibly face another Sunday piece, Cuba—

where, though it turned out the international desk had been banned for a year, the culture desk was not. It was in travelling too that I discovered that, in newspaper terms, the culture copy desks have been treating me, when I was at home, with their own version of restraint. A story of marathon private strike meetings in Paris, on which the desk really got its chance, was rewritten top to bottom, with mistakes. The Cuba pieces presented problems of their own. Since regular *Times* reporters were still banned, the stories got treated a little as though they were news (the first piece, for instance, appeared on the front page), and it was a kind of writing I was only trying to learn about. But politics at other times (in a year when notoriety and power, media performance and political act, were becoming confused from Washington to Columbia) seemed to occur in writing about movies anyway.

In time, in just struggling with the pace and form, I think there began to be a kind of continuity—not the continuity exactly of criticism or prose, but a record of what movies come out in the course of a year, what movies there actually *are,* and what it can be like for somebody to go to nearly all of them. With all the truisms about the glamour and vitality of the medium, reviewing it daily turned into a kind of journal, with spells of anger, friendliness, ideas, just being tired—the movies themselves coming over the hills in swarms, so many of them nearly undistinguishable, some of them really fine. I have cut little except the purest redundancies, and left some of those. I thought I'd like to record the balance of films just about the way it was for one year, from Elke Sommer and Norman Mailer through festivals, George C. Scott, Truffaut and theaters like the Lyric and the Amsterdam. About a film every other day. I guess I believe things now, about film sex, horror, plot, satire, empathy, foreign languages, old prints, criticism, audio-visual aids, inter-generational dirty jokes, cinémathèques, color films, the reviewable quality of TV commercials and so on, that I hadn't thought about before, but they are in here somewhere without any logic except that of newspaper space and time. I am still taken with a thought about plotless absurdism and its relation to a new value system in which the quality of events is

21

regarded as neither desirable nor undesirable—in which it is desired only that *something* should happen, no matter what. The happening as a value. I think it runs deeply counter to existentialism, and that it is dangerous to life. It occurred to me at the end of my first review of *Faces*—a film which, incidentally, because of schedulings, I reviewed four times. But a year in the dark consisted far more truly of stories and actors, directors and theaters, and seeing them to write really entailed about 160 collisions of one's own experience with Doris Day's, Jean-Luc Godard's, Kahlil Gibran's or Sidney Poitier's. And here it is, not an encyclopedia of movie statistics, or selected critical essays, but the whole peculiar year.

Some pleasant things happened near the end: a screening of *Yellow Submarine* at which so many of the under-forty reviewers were resolutely seeing it through once with pot that a police raid would have seriously diminished the number of reviews next day; a movie desk memo saying that Roberto Rossellini's *Axe of the Apostles* would be screened that afternoon; and a meeting of the New York Society of Film Critics, for the annual awards. I had never gone to its meetings before. (I had seen most of the critics at screenings throughout the year, of course.) This was different. As the voting went from what I thought was mediocrity to mediocrity, as it began to be clear that criticism is everybody's personal word and certainly not a court or a democracy, I decided to walk out. I had never done anything remotely like walking out of something to resign and I didn't do it very well. Stefan Kanfer of *Time* and Richard Schickel of *Life* whispered kindly that I should sit down again, since they were planning to walk out too, and had a statement prepared. I sat down and sent a note to Vincent Canby, who agreed. The statement, Mr. Schickel's, I think, was read. There were expressions of outrage, and of regret. Joseph Morgenstern of *Newsweek* said he had walked out once, but discovered that it made no difference. It seemed to me, though, that if *Time*, *Life* and the *Times* walked out, there would be, in effect, no New York Society of Film Critics. In the end, we all settled for a change of rules, and thought we might resign later, one by one, more quietly. I did realize that a lifelong member of a society of film critics was not something I would like to be. I had known for some time that a year at the movies—at a time when I was at the end of a tether of some kind, wanted to drop out of life for a bit and yet try to cope, about as audibly as some new journalist, with things I cared about—was fine for me, but that it was about enough.

RENATA ADLER
March, 1969

*1-4-68*

Even if your idea of a good time is to watch a lot of middle-aged Germans, some of them very fat, all reddening, grimacing, perspiring, and falling over Elke Sommer, I think you ought to skip *The Wicked Dreams of Paula Schultz*. This first film of the year is so unrelievedly awful, in such a number of uninteresting ways. The plot concerns an East German Olympic star (Miss Sommer) who escapes from a lecherous East German propaganda minister (Werner Klemperer) by pole-vaulting over the Berlin Wall in her black-lace underthings. She is ultimately bethrothed to a reformed American black-market operator (Bob Crane), who had previously tried to sell her to the East Germans and to the C.I.A. The real story, however, is a bit of bumbling, color pornography, a little nude film that lost its way on Forty-second Street and drifted on over to the Astor.

It seems to view the cold war as a vast conspiracy to get people undressed, as clumsily and joylessly as possible. In various scenes, Miss Sommer has her sweatshirt removed by the weight of some medals on her front, her bathrobe drawn off by a vacuum cleaner, her black-lace underthings reeled in by some fishermen on a riverbank, her dress split by a climb up the wall of a hotel, and so on. For the special interest groups, there is a moment when Miss Sommer tears the skirt off a rather substantial matron in uniform, and another in which (still in her underthings) she runs a gantlet of machine-gun fire. Many other characters are unbecomingly disrobed as well.

The movie neglects no opportunity to be gross (everyone's pudgy hands, for example, are constantly on someone else, and there are two burps in the script, for high comic effect), and yet it can't quite relax and be porcine. In some scenes and complications of the plot, there is a perceptible strain toward heavy-breathing whimsy, which—since no one involved in the film has any comic talent whatever—becomes grotesque.

. . . The Movies Make Heroes
of Them All

*1-7-68*

The motion picture is like journalism in that, more than any of the other arts, it confers celebrity. Not just on people—on acts, and objects, and places, and ways of life. The camera brings a kind of stardom to them all. I therefore doubt that film can ever argue effectively against its own material: that a genuine antiwar film, say, can be made on the basis of even the ugliest battle scenes; or that the brutal hangings in *The Dirty Dozen* and *In Cold Blood* will convert one soul from belief in capital punishment. No matter what filmmakers intend, film always argues yes. People have been modeling their lives after films for years, but the medium is somehow unsuited to moral lessons, cautionary tales or polemics of any kind. If you want to make a pacifist film, you must make an exemplary film about peaceful men. Even cinema villains, criminals and ghouls become popular heroes overnight (a fact which *In Cold Blood,* more cynically than *The Dirty Dozen,* draws upon). Movies glamorize, or they fail to glamorize. They cannot effectively condemn—which means that they must have special terms for dealing with violence.

I do not think violence on the screen is a particularly interesting question, or that it can profitably be discussed as a single question at all. Every action is to some degree violent. But there are gradations, quite clear to any child who has ever awakened in terror in the night, which become blurred whenever violence is discussed as though it were one growing quantity, of which more or less might be simply better or worse. Violence to persons or animals on film (destruction of objects is really another matter) ranges along what I think is a cruelty scale from clean collision to protracted dismemberment. Clean collision, no matter how much there is of it, is completely innocent. It consists, normally, of a wind-up, a rush, and an impact or series of impacts; and it includes everything from pratfalls, through cartoon smashups, fistfights in westerns, simple shootings in war films, multiple shootings in gang films, machine gunnings, grenade throwings, bombings, and all manner of well-timed explosions. Most often, thorough and annihilating though it may be, a film collision has virtually no cruelty component at all. It is more closely related to contact sport than to murder, and perhaps most nearly akin, in its treatment of tension, to humor. I am sure that such violence has nothing to do with the real, that everyone instinctively knows it, and that the violence of impact is among the most harmless, important, and satisfying sequences of motion on film.

Further along the cruelty scale, however, are the individual, quiet, tidy forms of violence: poisonings and stranglings. Their actual violence component is low, they are bloodless but, as any haunted child knows, their cruelty component can be enormous. The tip-off is the sound track; abrupt, ingratiating, then suddenly loud, perhaps including maniacal laughter—the whole range of effects that the radio-and-cinema-conditioned ear recognizes as sinister—to approximate the nervous jolt of encounters with violence in reality. Further yet along the scale are the quick and messy murders with knives or other instruments (some uncharacteristically ugly impact scenes also fall into this category) and finally, the various protracted mutilations.

I do not know whether scenes of persons inflicting detailed and specific physical sufferings on other persons increase the sum of violence in the world. There are probably saints who dote upon amputations, and certainly

27

sadists who cannot stand the sight of blood. But I think the following rules are true: violence on the screen becomes more cruel as it becomes more particular and individual; and it is bad in direct proportion to one's awareness of (even sympathy with) the detailed physical agonies of the victim. What this amounts to, of course, is a belief that films ought to be squeamish. In life, it is different: awareness of the particular consequences of acts is a moral responsibility and a deterrent to personal cruelty.

The difference between film and life on this point, I suppose, is this: that an audience is not responsible for the acts performed on screen—only for watching them. To be entertained by blasts, shots, blows, chairs breaking over heads, etc., is not unlike being entertained by chases, bass drums, or displays of fireworks; to be entertained by their biological consequences is another thing entirely. An example, again from *The Dirty Dozen*: in one scene, a demented soldier, rhythmically and with obvious pleasure, stabs a girl to death; in another, a château full of people is blown up by means of hand grenades dropped down gasoline-drenched air vents, and nearly everyone else is mowed down by machine-gun fire. In real life, or in ethics seminars, one person dying slowly is less monstrous than a hundred blowing sky high. Not so, I believe, on film, for none of the deaths was real, and only one was made cruel and personal. The style of the Armageddon was most like the style of an orchestra; the style of the stabbing was too much like violence in fact. And while I don't suppose that anyone will actually go out and emulate the stabbing, I don't think dwelling on pain or damage to the human body in the film's literal terms can ever be morally or artistically valid either. Physical suffering in itself is not edifying, movies celebrate, and scenes of cruel violence simply invite the audience to share in the camera's celebration of one person's specific physical cruelties to another.

*1-8-68*

Norman Mailer's first film, *Wild 90*, is more or less continuous with the rest of his work. It runs on. It features Mailer. It leans quite heavily on the assumption that lack of form liberates—that time, impulse, spontaneity, a willingness to risk personal embarrassment, above all, a constant unrestricted play of energy will sooner or later yield a breakthrough into something fresh. It relies also upon the indulgence of an audience that must be among the most fond, forgiving, ultimately patronizing and destructive of our time. There seems to be so much riding for so many on the fragments of value that always (or almost always) appear in Mailer's quantities of free association; it seems unlikely that the permissive school, which treats Mailer as an endearing protagonist in a Peter Pan adolescent struggle to free and find himself, would ever welcome a formed, compressed, and unapologetic piece of work.

*Wild 90*, which opened yesterday at the New Cinema Playhouse, is certainly not it. It arose out of a few evenings Mailer and two friends (Buzz Farbar and Mickey Knox) spent drinking together and pretending to be Mafiosi, trapped, somewhat as the Gallo brothers were in 1961, in hiding from a rival gang. Mailer thought their improvised conversations might make an interesting movie. After a few moments, one longs for the Gallo brothers.

What the conversation turns into almost at once is a subsurface contest for the attention of the camera. In this, Mailer has an enormous advantage, not because he is a public figure or because of anything he has to say, but because he has become, over the years, such an accomplished continuous actor. Speaking nasally, affecting as he does the accent and the cauliflower mannerisms of a stumblebum, he seems paradoxically structured and wary. His whole posture is insulated against spontaneity or surprise. He is constantly watching for the effect of his own words on the other two, and he looks more guarded than the most courtly formalist.

What the three of them do, with occasional welcome interruptions by other characters, is to cast aspersions on one another's manhood. For ninety minutes. A minute or two of this is funny. There is, for example, a sequence when Mailer, who has been barking words intermittently at the other characters, barks barks at a German shepherd, who has a brief walk-on with José Torres, a former light-heavyweight champion. The dog barks back. They bark at each other. After a few seconds, however, one becomes aware that the dog, after all, is being held tightly in check by Torres, and that, being unaware of who Mailer is, the animal is becoming really frightened. It does not seem such good sport to be casting aspersions on the manhood of a dog after all.

There is also a moment when Farbar, a little out of control, seems as though he might spit his drink at Mailer. But real outbreaks are not in the cards, and Farbar changes his mind and swallows. Knox tells an old French fable about the fate of a bird in a meadow, which is funny enough; but most people have probably heard it before. Finally, Mailer, using a few words of his own coinage or abbreviation (paying attench, anticipating the fyooch), is funny—just because he delivers a line so well. The camera, run by D. A. Pennebaker (who did the photography for *Don't Look Back* and other good documentaries), has nothing to do and no place to go. The photography is, on the whole, intensely boring.

In an article in *Esquire,* pre-reviewing *Wild 90,* Mailer implies that truck drivers laugh at his film, while the higher-brow middle classes are offended by it. This seems unlikely—though consistent in questioning the manliness of those who dislike the movie. There is an enormous amount of profanity in *Wild 90;* but it seems strangely uncool and ill-used. This may be because, thanks in part to Mailer, a whole generation now swears so easily and without self-consciousness. In the movie, there is too much brouhaha, compulsion and fanfare about it.

In the end, *Wild 90* faces a problem that now confronts Mailer's work as a whole. The frontier has shifted. The

battle against dead forms, useless conventions, and pointless inhibitions is over, or no longer interesting; the break-
throughs are now in terms of limit, live forms, tighter
economies. The very urgency that Mailer has always tried
to communicate makes it impossible to wade through so
much rambling for so little art.


........ *China Is Near:*
A Mother Is Like a Flower


*1-9-68*

*China Is Near*, the second film by the young Italian director Marco Bellocchio (whose first work, *Fist in the
Pocket,* won Italy's Silver Ribbon award), is all right for
people who go to the movies a lot and who like to see
every film with any talent or sincerity in it which comes
out. The film is a rather heavy social and political satire
(the word-game in the film's Italian title, *La Cina e
Vicina,* is an example of the sort of not exactly sparkling
thing that amuses Bellocchio), but it has, as they say,
some good things in it.

The story, written by Bellocchio, concerns a rather dolt-
ish Italian aristocrat, who is a professor of political
science and who has been, by his own account, a member
of "all four parties of the Italian center-left"; his sister,
who is mainly occupied with her love affairs; and their
younger brother, who is a church acolyte and a Maoist.
Another young Maoist, a student who is having an affair
with the professor's secretary, expects to be nominated for
the county council by the Socialists; but because the professor is rich, the Socialists nominate him instead.

The professor hires the cynical student as a campaign
assistant and they tour the countryside, addressing sparse
groups of toothless and vacant old men and bicycle packs
of delinquent boys. They are set upon by Stalinists, and
nearly blown up by a time bomb placed in their headquarters by the Maoists. The professor is at first indignant,

31

then exhilarated. The student begins an affair with the professor's sister; the student's former girl becomes involved with the professor. And the two young people of the Left, having grown more fond of money and social position than of each other, resolve to marry the two aristocrats. Sex, religion, and politics thereafter become mixed up, as the film wavers in tone from farce to dead earnest.

Despite these shifts of tone and despite interminable dull stretches in the film, the acting is competent, and Bellocchio directs with a certain authority. After two films, he seems to be establishing trademarks of his own: piercing, ethereal music to accompany the opening credits, which flash all over a bleak and otherwise empty screen; people using the cellophane covers of other people's portraits as mirrors in which to see themselves. There are constant cross-references to other films, and Bellocchio seems to consider carrying props from one of his own films to another, as a kind of cross-index to his work. (The bathroom in both his films is the same, although the houses in which it supposedly appears are completely different; and fists, or at any rate hands, in the pockets are referred to in the *China* script as a kind of subliminal ad for the first film.)

Finally, there are a few funny scenes: choirboys singing, very flat, to a bedridden old prelate; the professor contemplating the ethics of voting for himself; a Socialist reading to one group of party members a telegram announcing the presence of a bomb in the room, and a Maoist reading to another a tract recommending the rape of working-class girls to alienate them from the system. Both readings are in the normal political monotone of the party line. There is also one bright interchange when a really emancipated radical makes an uncomplimentary reference to another radical's mother: a less-emancipated radical remarks that his mother is not to blame, and a priest who has overheard begins, "A mother is like a flower . . ."

*1-11-68*

*Venom,* a Danish film that was awarded a grant for "artistic daring" by the Danish State Film Foundation, was censored—with great slashing white X's, which block out quite a bit of the action—by the Danish State. It wears its X's rather as Hester did her scarlet letter, proudly; but it shows a really interesting seaside confrontation of generations and ideologies.

The film begins with some shots of a worn, middle-aged couple asleep in a nice house, some waves and a Danish beach marked "Privat" and "Forbudt." (It is one of those foreign movies in which a combination of extremely good sub-titles and foreign-English homophones makes the script perhaps more entertaining to follow than it was in the original.) A fine family—mother, father, daughter, maid—inhabit the house, in a row of similar houses, along similar beaches. The fathers in all the houses come out for horrible invigorating morning swims at about the same hour each morning.

One summer day, as she is lying on the beach studying for her exams, the daughter is picked up by a young man passing by in a motorboat. They begin an affair; and as the summer progresses, he manages to convince her by degrees that one purpose in life is physical pleasure, and the other is filming. He films their affair and whatever other sexual interludes he can find; he projects the films for her and, later on, for her mother. (This is where the X's mostly are.) He crashes a party given for the girl by her family, and makes her a present of a book of pornography, which her family ultimately burns in the fireplace. In retaliation, after a long mock-Messianic speech, the young man burns the Bible. (This is somehow the most genuinely shocking moment in the film.) The father, struggling to regain the offensive in some way, invites the young man to live with his daughter in the house.

The young man accepts, and finally, very nearly seduces the mother.

What is interesting about *Venom*, aside from some incidental photographic effects (like the filming of a fine gluey, under-cooked dessert in a tense dinner-table scene), is that it presents its case absolutely straight. The young hedonist is neither rugged nor poetic looking; he moves and talks with completely charmless insolence. The jowly father is no model of squaredom either; before the young man's arrival, he has been shown lusting after his own daughter, approaching the maid and propositioning his secretary. The young man's argument is the weakest and least winning that can be made for youth. He does not speak of love or sentiment (in fact, in a fine scene of some young people gathered on the beach, he delivers another mock-Messianic speech to a girl whom he suspects of being a romantic, then sexually parodies the laying-on of hands and runs his camera); and he does not pretend to have been disillusioned by any moral failing of his elders. He is that product of affluence—the completely useless, full-time nihilist—and he simply challenges society to continue to afford him. The film's soundtrack even denies him the support of the best argument for his generation: the distinction of its music. There is hardly any rock in it at all.

The father's situation in this conflict is quite clear; he cannot win until he finds something the young man wants, and within himself, the power to withhold it. The young man has the daughter (although not that unambiguously either: one of the sub-themes of the movie is the failure of men to protect their women and the social framework within which they can be loved). There are intimations that the young man is accessible in one sense: he has ambition. He would like, through his films, to be famous, to be rich in the new currency—publicity, which measures wealth in terms of the number of people who have access to one's name. The father can deny him money to distribute his films. But in the end, the older man, the representative of order, has only two weapons: love of his daughter and the moral nerve to commit violence. But the need for violence is, in itself, a defeat, and that is the stand-off between them. Youth is inert, and the older generation is compromised.

There is some fine comic acting by Judy Gringer as the maid (creator of the ill-fated dessert), and some nice, understated acting on the part of Grethe Morgensen as the secretary. It would have been really interesting to see the film (written and directed by Knud Leif Thomsen) uncensored because then it would have turned, in part, into the film the young man was making. But that, presumably, will be some months yet.

........Our Monuments to
How It Was

*1-14-68*

It is not surprising that so many of what we call classics were not recognized in their own time, because one of the main functions of art is to speak out of its own time, not to its own time but to others; and the love of art is necessarily in large measure the love of old things. The artist at work, of course, is a man concerned with the new, but the work itself always casts its lot with the past, dragging its feet against all innovation, and trying to endure as the representative of its time when that time and all its inhabitants will have been long dead. In this sense, an audience that follows the new as though it were all a question of fashion is doomed to pass along with last year's hemline; fashion only tries to kill the past and dies before what follows. An audience aware of its own ultimate stake in the past places its bets more carefully, choosing to survive in the truest selection of its monuments to how it was.

In this sense, too, the movies are an art and a death cult like none that have gone before. Nearly everything about us, how we looked, what we did and said and wore, is gradually accumulating in the cans of celluloid. More people each day take to making films at home, as naturally as well-bred young ladies of the past made samplers, or learned piano or spinet (or other what they used to call "accomplishments"). Everyone can now film himself a tomb, as elaborate and self-expressive as the pyramids.

What the film does that is unprecedented is to turn an event into an object, which can be preserved through time. It used to be that we had, on the one hand, objects, paintings, sculptures; on the other hand, events, plays, symphonies; between them, objects written of events—books. But books could be turned away from, returned to, read at one's own pace; they never imposed the pace of the events themselves. Films do. They freeze events in time and make it possible for parts of lives to be replayed.

It therefore seems no accident that the more serious a film cult is, the more likely it is to be preoccupied in all sorts of ways with death. The cult of Bogart, the cult of W. C. Fields, even the teenage cult of James Dean some years ago, or the high-brow obsession, immediately after her death, with Marilyn Monroe—and James Agee as well. These grew not only out of the fact that these figures spoke, in various ways, to our time, but also, preeminently, out of the fact that they were dead. And death is so well suited to the medium. A sense in which film differs from plays, of course, is that it is not "live"; the audience cannot affect or influence what happens on the screen, as it can by responding to a living cast. Film stars on celluloid are inaccessible. Death redoubles that inaccessibility.

There is also the intense tradition-consciousness of movie fans; in everything from the current courses in film history at the Museum of Modern Art, through the showing of old films on television and the success of theaters devoted exclusively to old movies, film seems to carry its whole history with it at every step. This does not reflect only the relative newness of the medium, or the need of television to play something at all times. It is a matter of replaying what is dead and gone.

Films themselves constantly assimilate and reintegrate elements out of the cinema past. One is continually startled by shots in new films which deliberately include elements of older films. Sometimes this is strongly

36

emphasized and overt. There is, for example, the famous sequence in *Breathless*, when Jean-Paul Belmondo stands contemplating the Bogart poster; in *China Is Near*, there were brief shots of a poster for *Alfie*—a double reference to *Alfie* and to the *Breathless* scene. Reaccumulation of the past is common in all the arts in various ways, of course. But only in one other current medium—recorded pop music—is reassimilation as plain and as common as it is in film.

What films and pop records have in common, of course, aside from being the two most distinctly contemporary arts of our time, is that they normally record performances that never happened. They make use of cutting, splicing, dubbing and all the other electronic aids to produce performances that, not only did not, but could not have happened live. For film, in comparison with theater, this has another re-doubling effect: if the theater is a performance of fiction, the movies, as a performance which never really took place, is double fiction. But fact or fiction, the action on films has already taken place and ended well before the film is run. This, too, would help to account for film's special affinities with the arts of death.

. . . . . . . . . . . Mann's
*Tonio Kröger*

*1-16-68*

If one had to film Thomas Mann's *Tonio Kröger* and be quite faithful to the text, then *Tonio Kröger* would be the way to do it. But the project seems somehow worthy and unrewarding—like a film of "If," or "Indian Love Call," or the *Symposium*. Not every written thing aspires to be a movie.

The problem is that hardly anything actually happens in *Tonio Kröger*. The young poet Kröger, son of a German merchant and what Mann describes as an "exotic" mother, travels to Italy, Germany and Denmark, where certain changes are brought about in him by the climate and by philosophical discussions with his Slavic mistress. The changes are all interior, psychological. What this amounts to on film is a series of close-ups within a travelogue.

The plot, such as it is, is dreamily episodic. Kröger, who had been since childhood somewhat different from the blond, blue-eyed, ordinary children whom he at once loves and holds in contempt, is shown walking home from class; in dancing school; in bed with an Italian lady of the street; in conversation with his mistress in Munich; at home in Lübeck; en route to Denmark, and at sea with an inarticulate bourgeois who longs to express his thoughts about the infinity of stars and the littleness of man. By the end, Kröger has reconciled his middle-class and exotic origins in himself as a poet. This is hardly *The Guns of Navarone*.

The shots of Munich, Lübeck spires, Italian courts, and Danish mists—all stills, essentially—are very handsome and stylized. The text by Thomas Mann, a good part of which is read by a narrator, is beautiful. ("After all, I am not a gypsy in a green wagon" is a lovely line, even in subtitles; so are many others.) Jean-Claude Brialy's face, in a Comédie Française beard, registers suitable expressions of sensitivity, irony, and alienation (although the fact that he, speaking French, must be dubbed into German, is rather distracting). Gert Frobe has a good, huffing walk-on as the police inspector who suspects Kröger is a thief who is also rumored to be on his way to Denmark.

There is a nice shot of a train pulling out of a station, but the happy affinity of movies for trains has been quite thoroughly explored in other contexts. There are some boys who—presumably to avoid the miseries of child-overacting—say all their lines as though they had memorized them for class. And there are some awful improvements on the original. When Kröger goes downstairs to retrieve a poem that has drifted from his room into a courtyard (and comes upstairs again with a woman he has met), it is tolerable; but when, in a later scene, his poems blow out the window and turn into sea gulls, it is, along with other misbegotten lyric touches, a bit much.

*1-18-68*

*The Biggest Bundle of Them All* begins like one of those really bad movies that are unintentionally funny. Then it becomes clear that it intends to be funny, and it isn't. The film lasts 106 minutes, of which the last fifteen are worth seeing if you are really intent on going to a movie. The afternoon price of admission at the Selwyn Theater on Forty-second Street, where the film opened yesterday, is only eighty-five cents; and although the theater is perhaps not the best ventilated in New York and the audience is not the most reverent, the movie is worth the price of admission, as long as the first ninety-one minutes are skipped.

The story concerns five amateur crooks (Robert Wagner, Raquel Welch, Godfrey Cambridge, Davy Kaye, Francesco Mule) who kidnap one semi-retired old professional (Vittorio De Sica) at a Mafia funeral in Naples. When it turns out that he cannot afford the ransom, even with the aid of relatives in Chicago, the old crook is so humiliated that he enlists the help of a colleague (Edward G. Robinson) to redeem his honor. They all go off to steal five million dollars in platinum ingots from a train, by means of a tank, a military truck and a surplus military airplane. They bungle several holdups and other minor crimes quite boringly along the way. After one of these holdups, I understood De Sica to say, rather interestingly, of a victim, "He was taken by a mustard!" It turned out to be only De Sica's version of "He was taken by a master."

Robert Wagner, who might be well cast as the recording secretary of a campus fraternity, is badly miscast as a leading man; Raquel Welch seems, quite simply, stronger. She has some unfortunate dancing sequences, however.

Godfrey Cambridge, whose form and comic style became continually more gross, keeps his mouth open and his eyes half shut—like a frog or an inflated guppy. Francesco Mule resembles Cambridge. By the time Edward G. Robinson appears, his wrinkled countenance, flat eyes, and generally turtlish appearance make it seem everyone might be on location for *The Wind in the Willows*.

There is a lot of pointlessly dizzying camera work, and an opening song that is off-key. There are a lot of broad, tired jokes. When Davy Kaye gets himself locked in an outhouse, there even has to be a bee in it. The final robbery, however, has a nice absurdist quality. The tank plays particularly well. Godfrey Cambridge sticks what looks like an enormous wad of chewing gum on the wall of a railroad car and ignites a fuse. The ingots are dropped on an improbable canvas assembly line like dishes in a cafeteria. Robert Wagner, who has vanished for a time, reappears abducting a plane. A convergence of policemen, a helicopter landing, even some lines by Raquel Welch, are funny. It becomes all right.

There ought to be a rule, though, that all shaky comic films should have a happy ending. Presumably out of fondness for plot twists that are too heavy for them, they seldom do. It might be just as well to leave *The Biggest Bundle of Them All* a moment or two before the end.


. . . . . . . Cartooning and
*Animations: Zagreb*


*1-20-68*


*Animations: Zagreb,* a series of programs being shown this weekend at the Museum of Modern Art, is a selection of cartoons from the work of Yugoslav animators over the last ten years. It uses a technique the Zagreb school calls reduced animation—a minimal number of frames drawn to suggest each movement. As a result, the cartoons (mostly well and imaginatively drawn) seem oddly choppy, almost in the manner of the early silents. All seven films in yesterday's program (there will be another one today, and a special children's program tomorrow) mix water-colors, oils, photographs, line drawings and Disney-like characters in collage. They frequently verge deliberately (and quite perilously for the kind of illusion cartoons normally depend on) upon the actual—adult fables, political satire, allegories.

In this country, the animated cartoon, in the great Disney tradition, is almost never used for any high serious purpose. To burden Tom and Jerry with ideology would be too much like sending Moonbird on a man's errand. But there are important Disney propaganda cartoons from World War II (Minnie Mouse conserving bacon grease was memorable). And there is a whole philosophy of life implicit in the way the cartoon world customarily operates: everything is arbitrary, violent, anarchical. Anything can collide with, flatten, frazzle or destroy any other thing. But everything is reversible. As the film can run backward, the harm done to any cartoon creature can be undone in an instant. An eternal chase can begin again. The cat, sleeked down if he's been frazzled, restored to his third dimension if he's flattened out, returns to health and resumes his pursuit. But that's it. No moral. No dead earnest. Even the cartoons shown on television, which contain some of the most sophisticated puns and allusions to draw children over their heads into the world of adult conversation, never try to make a point.

In Europe, particularly in the Eastern countries, it is different. Cartoons deal with everything from politics to the human condition. Perhaps charm and whimsy in animation are the perfect disguises for messages, since no one can be sure when and whether a message is there. The cartoon after all is the most abstract, least real of movies (in this sense, it is the opposite of a documentary). The problem is that the charm and whimsy do not always survive.

The Yugoslav cartoons try to mix whimsy and message, not always successfully. In *Concerto for Sub-Machine Gun*, Dusan Vukotic (who won an Academy Award for cartooning in 1961) has an enormously sleek-looking

Capitalist in tails who constantly eats and disgorges dollars as people fire machine guns at one another through perforated line-drawn streets. This film also has the first cartoon character I can remember who, once maimed, stays maimed—a dismal, frayed, brown paper tab dragging himself along. The problem is that even a frayed tab is too representational; it looks documentary, without having access to any of the feelings a real documentary would arouse. But it is interesting. In *Diogenes Perhaps,* Nedejko Dragic has created a little figure, squat, dressed in a blue shirt and hat, and carrying a bundle at the end of a stick. He is sweet, rather like Chaplin in spirit, but he wanders through a lot of Steinberg situations (threatening letters of the alphabet looming over him, for example) and he distinctly resembles a character in the work of *The Village Voice* cartoonist, Jaf.

In *Little and Big* by Zlatk Grgic, a little person undergoes incredible anarchical contretemps (his balloon is broken, his parachute is cut, his hide-out is revealed) at the hands of a big person, who is having problems of his own (the earth falling out from under him, a pair of shoes sprouting hands to attack him with). It is clearly a highly unreliable world, but once again it is disturbingly adult. Nothing is elastic, nothing really bounces back. There is something very real and topical about it, which is not quite resolved. At the end of this "animation," clearly about persecution, the little person keeps asking in a variety of languages, "What is the message of this film?" Finally, he answers his own question in Serbo-Croatian and the big person repeats—suddenly in Russian—after him: "No message."

# Love Song of Two Paragons:
## Questions of Geography,
## Mass Production and
## Personal Hygiene

*1-21-68*

Among the 12,000 reels of the 3,000 different films, which are now on file at the main office of the Bureau of Audio-Visual Instruction of the New York City Board of Education, there are thirty-three separate How To films ("How To Get Cooperation," "How To Say No," "How To Prepare a Grapefruit: Grapefruit Sections," "How To Catch a Cold"); twenty-one just plain How films ("How Seeds are Scattered," "How Billy Keeps Clean," "How Do You Do?", "How Do You Know It's Love?"); one snuggly, statistical How's film ("How's Chances?"). And an old favorite, "The House I Live In."

There are also thirteen burbly Let's films ("Let's Be Clean and Neat," "Let's Have Fewer Colds," "Let's Give a Tea"); twenty epic Story Of Films ("Story of King Midas," "Story of the Modern Storage Battery," "Story of Potatoes"); seven gregarious We films ("We Plan Together," "We Explore the Beach," "We Discover the Dictionary"); twenty-five bewildered What films ("What About Drinking?" "What Is Art?" "What To Do on a Date"); and twenty-three presumptuous You and Your films ("You and Your Friends," "Your Cleanliness," "Your Friend the Soil: Keep It or Lose It"). The L section alone contains movies ranging from "Lentil" to "Learning About Your Nose."

In a current list of deletions from the supply of films on loan at the Bureau, there is evidence that educators are trying to keep up with events. "How to Bake Bananas: Banana Cream Pie," "How to Boost Interest in Breakfast: Banana Quickbread," and "Journey to Bananaland" will not circulate in the New York City schools this year; nor will "Arab Village," "Arabian Children" ("Israel" will), any of the twelve films in the "Are You Ready for (Military) Service" series, "Rhythm is Everywhere," or

"Care of the Feet." There is also evidence that the advertising films which used to form the core of most audiovisual aid programs of the fifties and early sixties have been phased out or subdued. The Bureau still accepts contributions of movies from companies or special interest groups, and brand names are still featured prominently in many films bought from regular educational distributors. But an audio-visual aid is no longer necessarily an extended commercial disguised as a text for the school assembly.

The philosophy of life put forth in these movies suggests that the human condition turns mainly on questions of geography, mass production and personal hygiene. A large number of the films fall into one or more of these categories; and it seems that the audio-visual superhero might be a young man who brushes his teeth every minute when he is not out digging an oil well or rushing off to tour a developing continent in eleven minutes. But there is another category, a personal advice-social pressure kind of film, which manages to give as clear an idea of the quality of life in modern America, or the quality of education anyway, as any adult film or specific study of the generation gap. An example, produced in 1948, reissued in the fifties and still circulating in 1968, is "Are You Popular?" (a Coronet Films release).

"Popularity," the narrator reflects, as the ten-minute black-and-white movie opens with some gray scenes of high school students at lunch in the school cafeteria. "What is it made of?" With that somber question, the students at one table begin a conversation about "that new girl in our class," Carolyn. Someone remarks that she is swell, and that she dresses well, and someone else agrees. "Especially," he says, in one of the film's moments of hip, "when you look at some of the weird cats around here."

The narrator returns. "Here comes Ginny," he says. "She goes parking with the boys at night. Is she welcome to join this group?" Ginny, carrying a tray and looking wary, comes over to the table to chat. It does not look as though she is welcome to join the group at all. "No," the narrator says. "Girls who park in cars are not really popular."

Carolyn is very welcome though, because, as the narrator explains, "She seems as interested in girls as in boys." We eavesdrop on a conversation of this paragon with a boy who is prop collector for a school theatrical production. "You sound like you need a helper," Carolyn says. "Can I lend a hand?" There is more talk of this sort, and then we cut to Carolyn at home, where her phone rings incessantly. Wally, the first boy who calls, asks her out for Saturday night, to a skating party. The narrator approves. "Wally has implied his price range," he says.

Carolyn approves also. "Oh, the skating sounds like lots of fun," she says. "Carolyn keeps a date calendar," the narrator goes on. "That's a good idea." Under Saturday, Carolyn writes, "Do Fingernails." The narrator approves the entire phone call. "Well," he says, "that phone call didn't go on for hours."

The paragon has just embarked on a conversation with her girl friend Ellie ("Take my advice," Ellie is saying, "before you start going steady"), when the phone rings again. It is Gerry, the prop boy, asking for a date that very night. He is turned down. "Can you imagine, Ellie?" Carolyn marvels. "He wanted a date for *tonight*."

Date night arrives, and Wally, in his earmuffs, arrives too. On time. Another paragon. Carolyn introduces him to her father, who has been reading the newspaper. "I was just looking into the world of events before we go to dinner," the father says. He puts the world of events aside. Carolyn's mother enters and is introduced. Then Carolyn tactfully leaves Wally alone with her parents for a little while. Her mother offers Wally a brownie.

The narrator is pleased. "Carolyn and her mother have found one way a girl can repay a boy for entertaining her," he says. Wally eats his brownie. There is a bit more of this, and the movie finally ends. One wonders if there is any part of this city, or the country for that matter, where this sort of smug, dated, utter falseness can have any meaning—other than that the system is a bore and a hypocrite. Of course, the phrase "audio-visual aid" is itself a kind of prose atrocity.

*1-25-68*

"The Burn, the Gouge and the Mangle" (its screen name is simply inappropriate) must be the most expensive, pious and repellent movie in the history of its peculiar genre. If Forty-second Street is lined with little pushcarts of sadism, this film, which opened yesterday at the Trans-Lux 85th Street and the DeMille, is an entire supermarket. The plot—and in their eagerness to mutilate someone, the writers continually lose track of it—seems to run as follows: A man whose pseudonym is Bill Carson, and who owns a clam-shaped snuffbox, knows the whereabouts of $200,000. Three characters—Burn (Clint Eastwood), Gouge (Lee Van Cleef) and the Mexican, Mangle (Eli Wallach), whose names in the film are Joe, Setenza and Tuco, respectively—are anxious to get hold of it. Ultimately, Clint Eastwood gets it. The action takes place in the West during the Civil War. That is all. It lasts two and a half slow hours.

The movie entitled *The Good, the Bad and the Ugly* forgets all about Bill Carson for an hour. Then, he makes a brief appearance, rolling his one eye (any number of characters in the movie have lost an eye, or an arm, or a leg, or two legs), and dies, covered with blood and flies and making rasping noises, in incredible agony. Before expiring, he divulges the location of the cemetery in which the money is buried to Mangle, and the gravesite to Burn.

The sole purpose of the snuffbox is to enable Gouge to jam Mangle's fingers quite painfully in it. Gouge himself is missing a joint of a finger on his gun hand. The camera dwells on this detail lovingly. Eli Wallach, as the Mexican, has a wound over his left eye, which heals and reopens throughout the film for no apparent reason. He is throttled three times, sun-scorched, and once so severely beaten by Van Cleef that anyone who would voluntarily remain in

46

the theater beyond this scene (while he might be a mild, sweet person in his private life) is not someone I should care to meet, in any capacity, ever.

Wallach rolls his eyes, makes hideous gastro-intestinal noises to convey shades of emotion, and laughs incessantly. Among his feldspar teeth, there is one capped with what looks like a molten paper clip. He also forgets, from time to time, what sort of ethnic part he is playing; and, particularly when he is called upon to shout, his Mexican is laced with Riverdale. Van Cleef's acting consists of displaying a stubble of beard and narrowing his eyes. Aside from various other shootings and beatings he administers, he shoots one man through a salad bowl (although most of the movie takes place in arid country, there are an awful lot of salads and vegetables) and another through a pillow. In the end, he is shot.

There is scarcely a moment's respite from the pain. Most of the scars and wounds are administered about the face, and even Eastwood, as the hero, spends a good part of the movie with his face blistered. His face and voice are expressionless throughout. Several of the actors are Italian, and their voices are dubbed. There are some irrelevant battle scenes, as though, near the end of the movie, the writers and the director, Sergio Leone, hoped that it might pass for antiwar. "Never so many men who were wasted so badly," Eastwood says. And there is a completely meaningless sequence with a bridge—as though it might pass for *San Luis Rey* or *Kwai*. Sometimes, it all tries to pass for funny.

The film is the third of a trilogy (*A Fistful of Dollars* and *A Few Dollars More* preceded it). In the special context, there are immortal lines. One, just when it appears there is going to be a nonviolent moment in the film, from an officer who is preaching against brutality: "Sergeant," he begins, "gangrene is eating my leg away. Also my eye." Another, when Eastwood surprises Wallach in the bathtub: "Put your drawers on and take your gun off," he says.

47

*1-25-68*

*Sebastian,* which opened yesterday at the 68th Street Theater and other houses, is what might be called a medium saturation put-on. A high saturation put-on would be a film like *Modesty Blaise,* in which plot, dialogue and decor feature an invention a minute in the hope that something will work. A really low saturation put-on would be any of the films of Andy Warhol, in which the invention is at absolute zero, and the complete put-on is that there is really nothing there to be put-on by.

Sebastian (played by Dirk Bogarde) is an Oxford mathematician and master decoder for British Intelligence. He has a large staff of young women working for him at rows of desks, which he can see through the picture window of his office one flight up. He is in the habit of chanting with his female staff, responsively:

"And when we finish?"
"Everybody goes home!"
"And when do we finish?"
"Never!"

This is chanted with enormous hilarity, as though everyone were having such good fun. And one of the problems with this sort of movie is the enormous pressure that it puts on the audience to have a good time over almost nothing. The music, in particular, becomes hysterically jaunty at moments when absolutely nothing is going on on the screen. Sebastian has a middle-aged leftist assistant (Lili Palmer) who objects to the Vietnam war, and a dipsomaniacal Saturday mistress (Janet Munro), who, in the service of a foreign power, freaks him out on LSD. These are the two with-it contemporary touches. For the rest, he is pursued to his bedroom by Susannah York. She ultimately has a baby by him—a very interesting looking, not at all soap-commercial baby, whose rattle helps him break a Russian satellite blip code. He also has some scenes with Sir John Gielgud, as Head of Intelligence.

The put-on, of course, consists in never really letting the audience know what level of seriousness the film is at, and the movie itself sometimes seems unsure. Miss York gets slapped once, Miss Munro twice. (The put-on as a form is almost always extremely hostile to women.) Miss York does quite well as the sort of against-his-will, healthy seductress she is meant to play; but some scenes in which she has to fight Bogarde physically (and he has lines like "Don't rupture yourself") would be impossible for anyone. Bogarde plays his usual dry, reserved, slightly sinister part, which is so ill-suited to comedy. Gielgud's part is really a walk-on.

It is unfortunate to be hard on this sort of British product which is so much better, funnier, and more articulate than its American equivalent (the latest bumbling Dean Martin extravaganza, *How to Save a Marriage—and Ruin Your Life,* comes to mind). The decoding idea, for instance, is a good one, although absolutely nothing is made of it; and some of the lines are lovely. Of Sebastian's LSD experience, Gielgud says, "Well, we all need taking out of ourselves from time to time." The opening scene, in which Bogarde is racing around Oxford in his academic robes until he meets Miss York and asks her to spell her name backward, has a fine White Rabbit/Alice in Wonderland quality, which is immediately abandoned, too. If only people wouldn't try to spoof everything at once, but concentrate on doing a thought-out funny thing or two.

. . Cold Blood, Cheap Fiction

*1-28-68*

The film *In Cold Blood* is probably as faithful in spirit to its original novel as any movie has ever been. And it reveals by what it finds necessary to explain, and paper over, and underscore, just what sort of book Truman Capote's much publicized non-fiction novel was.

The book's accretions of falsely illuminating detail

("Double-mint, Dick's favorite flavor; Perry preferred Juicy Fruit") are gone. Its two genuine bits of Americana (the little boy and his grandfather living on soda bottle refunds; the fat death-row homicidal prodigy pasting food pictures into his scrapbook) remain. So do the character outlines and the time structure of the book. *In Cold Blood*, in both media—unlike non-fiction novels by the real originators of the form (Gibbs, Ross, Mitchell, McKelway)—does not structure the facts for any truth beyond the scope of conventional journalism. It structures details to arrive at nothing deeper than an elaborate tease.

It begins with two killers converging upon four stereotypes: apple pie daughter, neurasthenic mother, salt of the earth father, fine young son. The Clutters might comfortably inhabit any aspirin or mouthwash commerical. They are set up as coldly and two-dimensionally as in a shooting range, with infinitely less reality than the people of Gasoline Alley. Despite the author's familiarity with the diaries, files, and correspondence of these dead (who could not present themselves to him in person, or, for that matter, sign his releases), one knows virtually nothing about them. On the screen, they are unactable, as in the book they were uninteresting. They are there to die. Perhaps they satisfy some East Coast idea that people in Kansas are two-dimensional. Or perhaps one tends to regard all objects of such a hunt as stereotypes.

For the movie, like the book, is a thriller with a single fact withheld. We know who is going to die. We know who is going to kill them. We know the killers will be caught. And we know what will happen to them. But *In Cold Blood,* in both media, uses every technique of cheap fiction—every cut, every shift, every flashback—to put off the actual murder scene. "I promise you, honey," Dick says early in the film, "we'll blast hair all over them walls." It is a promise to the audience, really. They will be present at the murders, know how they were done, what was said, how it looked and felt. After some delay (in the book it was 263 pages), everyone wants to know.

At Cinema I, where *In Cold Blood* is now playing to sell-out crowds, this is very clear. Throughout the first ninety minutes of the movie, the audience is relaxed, talking, laughing with the killers, waiting. Then, long after the crime has been disclosed, long after the killers have completed their travels and been arrested in Las Vegas—in fact, long after everything but the last pitch of morbid interest has gone by—Detective Alvin Dewey's car stops before the Clutter homestead in the night. The audience perceptibly draws its breath. This is it. They know what is coming. Perry will re-enact the crime.

There is no real reason why it should happen at this moment. With all its "No. No. No's" and "Oh, please don't's," and jerked back heads, and exposed blades, and tied ankles, and twitching feet. It should have occurred—in terms of the movie's actual time sequence—about an hour ago. Not too much blood, after all. No hair. This is not the Grand Guignol, but a serious study of violence in American life that sold over 600,000 copies and now lines them up around the block. There follows an absolutely dead interval of film: the trial, the prison, more homey jokes and delay. After a little rest, the audience is primed again: for the hangings. More twitching, some physiological detail, the drop. Everyone can go home. A serious study of violence, etc., and a treatise on capital punishment. A liberal intellectual double feature.

It is, of course, nothing of the kind. The soundtrack, for one thing, is among the most crudely exacerbating ever put on film. Everything is treble, an inexcusably high volume: guitar squeaks, paper cracklings, knuckle crackings, zipper slides, shotgun checks, sirens, brake squeals, train shrieks, stairs creaking, a scream. The "s's" alone of John Forsythe, who plays detective Alvin Dewey, are so sibilant they amount to a speech impediment; they become excruciating. The sound of a map being folded, an arm entering a sleeve, a cigarette being tamped, an intake of breath, even coffee being poured is tuned so high on the treble that it is a constant irritation, like a man sitting beside you whistling through his nose. When it is not a high-frequency agony. This is the level at which the direction is nervy.

The dialogue, where it diverges from the book, is largely impossible: cheap jokes, an aura of false cool, dime-store philosophy and psychiatry ("I'm glad you don't hate your father any more." "But I do. I hate him and I love him"), gold-plate journalistic pretension ("Mr. Jensen, what is your interest in this case?" "A violent, unknown force destroys a decent honorable family . . ."). But it is interesting where the book's own lines are virtually undeliverable. The "yellow bird" of Perry's imagination, never quite realized in the book, sounds in the movie like an advertisement for an airline. The line from the confession, "I thought he was a very nice gentleman. Soft spoken. I thought so right up to the moment I cut his throat," sounds completely false, like an interviewer's plant ("Did you like Mr. Clutter?" "Yes." "Did you think he was a nice man?" "Yes." "And yet you cut his throat," etc.).

It is interesting that the most severe criticism the book *In Cold Blood* received at the time of its publication came from England, where Kenneth Tynan accused the author of not having tried hard enough to keep Perry and Dick from capital punishment. It was a curious criticism. In the first place, Capote did try. In the second, there was no earthly reason why he should. And in the third, if there ever were two persuasive arguments for capital punishment, they were Dick Hickock and Perry Smith. It is true that Dick studied law in his prison cell, and Perry read and drew pictures; but hobbies acquired late in life hardly constitute an atonement for the taking of four lives. True, hanging takes twenty minutes, and the book might be taken to argue that, out of the same fastidiousness which led Perry to put Mr. Clutter out of his misery after his throat was cut, the state ought to do away with people more humanely. But nothing in the book explained that split second when Perry used his knife (the movie tries to paper this over by having his father appear to him). One gets the feeling it might have happened to anyone to be killer or victim at that time. For the rest, one believes in capital punishment or one does not. The book and the film do not constitute an argument either way. (Indeed, if they have any moral at all, it is that it is unwise to hire ex-convicts if they are prospective repeaters and gossips as well.)

What was curious was that it was exploitation of the

*killers,* not the victims, that worried the critics. The pacing of the book (and now of the movie) has been set up in such a way that only the killers have any reality at all. The book, the movie, the killers, the audience are stalking the family together. It was not the graves of Hickock and Smith that the Beautiful People—in the party that probably marked their overdue end as an American infatuation—were dancing on. It was the graves of the Clutters. Who, in the book's own terms, were never really alive. And who, in the movie, are set up in two dimensions six times a day, to be killed pointlessly again.

> . . . . . . The Bright Side of
> *Poor Cow*
> and Things Lost
> Track Of

*2-1-68*

*Poor Cow,* which opened yesterday at the Murray Hill and other theaters, begins with some shots of the real birth of a baby, and goes on to become one of those ringingly false, technicolor British films about working-class life in London. It is not very good; but January has been, in general, a poor month for movies, and it might be a good idea to look at the bright side—which, since the quality of the color makes England look like April in Disneyland, is very bright indeed.

Carol White, who plays Joy, the young mother (and Poor Cow of this title), is very pretty and natural in a part that amounts to Mrs. Alfie. People who liked *Alfie* will probably like *Poor Cow.* Joy is married to a burglar, played by John Bindon (a former seaman whose first film role this is). When he goes to jail, she falls in love with a gentle, sensitive friend of his, played very well by Terence Stamp. When he also goes to jail, she becomes a bar girl and photographer's model for middle-aged amateurs. She has a lot of affairs and divorces her husband; but she is really waiting for the return from jail of the man she loves.

The film's similarity to *Alfie* lies in its idea of the working-class young, freed by a period of prosperity from any hard need to work, leading empty lives absolutely permeated with Mod, until their attractiveness ends and they are left, without any real resources, to themselves. The difference is that Joy can keep her baby. And one of the movie's really excellent scenes occurs when the child is briefly lost, in a section of London where demolition and reconstruction are going on. As Joy searches for him (and Carol White plays this scene beautifully), there is a moment's sense of things lost track of, of life—for an instant's lapse of attention—turning unalterably bleak. There is also some rather nice musical accompaniment by Donovan.

One odd thing: despite Joy's many lovers, the camera turns quite skittishly away from love scenes. It seems, in this context, a mistake. An argument must certainly be made for sex in movies that try to approach seriously the problems of the young; and this one, which begins so frankly with maternity, seems to have become quite nervous about things physical right after the credits came on.


. . . . . . . . . Today's Stars,
and the Point Where
the Quiet Center Tilts


*2-4-68*


The real stars of our time are probably the actors who look least like the cosmetic stars of the past and most plainly real in themselves: Anouk Aimée in *A Man and a Woman,* Simone Signoret in *Ship of Fools,* Jeanne Moreau in *Jules and Jim* (but not in *Mademoiselle* or *Viva Maria*), Julie Christie in *Darling,* Charles Aznavour in *Shoot the Piano Player,* Jean-Paul Belmondo in *Breathless* (but not in *That Man from Rio*), Oskar Werner in *The Spy Who Came in from the Cold,* Brando in almost anything. It is not entirely a question of acting ability. Many fine actors do not seem to have any quiet, unruffled, real center at all.

In the gilt fantasy years of Hollywood, star quality was almost entirely flamboyance, pretense, ostentation; today it is a matter of naturalness, of cool. There is a sense in which modern actors can be real—uncompromised in their essential dignity by the business of acting—as some of the old stars, made up, falsified, and preserved for Hollywood or Forest Lawn, never were and never would have wanted to be.

Until recently, it was part of the essence of stardom to be extravagant, ungenuine. Even the screen's girl next door—June Allyson, Debbie Reynolds, Doris Day—was compounded of freckles, steel, noise, artifice and peppermint. The fact that old movies tend to acquire a certain grainy cool with age only confuses the issue; in modern terms, they tried too hard. There were always exceptions of course, a sense of real personality, inner repose, an honestly pitched voice and human quality of motion—Ingrid Bergman. Humphrey Bogart and Lauren Bacall, in other ways. But screen sirens, great lovers, swashbuckling heroes, even comedians (most comedy requires a pose), or participants in musicals were all, almost by definition, stars of the unreal. The authentic, grainy star, inhabited by a serious, intelligent and breathing person, is relatively new.

Hardly any Americans belong, except Steve McQueen and Patricia Neal. An essential real quality—the refusal to dissolve one's personality in order to endear oneself to crowds—is not characteristically American. Not since John Dewey, anyway. There is another quality—a matter-of-factness about one's physical presence. One has only to compare Rock Hudson with Tom Courtenay on this score, or Natalie Wood with Ingrid Thulin. The quality in question is often described as maturity (in the sense in which foreign movies about love affairs are always called "mature"); whatever it is, the American box-office stars seem not to inhabit their physical forms at all, or to use them in any recognizable way. Despite their smaller audiences, it is the authentic characters from abroad who are really speaking to the times.

55

Not that success is incompatible with the sense of the real in a star. Richard Burton and Elizabeth Taylor, debatably, still have it; and so, to a somehow diminished extent, does one of the original heroes of it—Marcello Mastroianni. And, of course, McQueen. Fame can reinforce the sense of a real personality in the same way that the aging of film does. Color, for some reason, is uncongenial to it, but David Hemmings in *Blow-Up* had it, and so did Michael Caine in *The Ipcress File*. That authentic quality which need not have much to do with talent at all. It is usually associated with quiet intensity, restraint, with not over-extending energy to the point where the quiet center tilts, but David Warner had it in *Morgan*, where he raced about, and so did Vanessa Redgrave. (His *cinéma vérité* complexion helped.)

It is certainly not a matter of beauty, or even of playing character parts. Rita Tushingham, Lynn Redgrave and Dustin Hoffman, good as they are, do not have the flat, understated, resigned adult presence. Children sometimes do; Jean-Pierre Léaud in *The 400 Blows* and Patricia Gozzi in *Sundays and Cybèle*. Though cool, it is deeply antithetical to camp, fashion, Pop, or any of the essentially homosexual forms. Tinsel, color, hard surface, do not coexist with it at all. Warren Beatty and Faye Dunaway don't have it. Joan Baez and Bob Dylan, of course, do. Hippies do not.

It has elements of the old British mystique of the unflappable, unsurprisable, as well as elements of the uncombative resignation of Camus. It has a certain economy of effort and it looks in some way private. It comes from all over Europe, Antonioni in *L'Avventura* and *La Notte*, Fellini in *La Dolce Vita* (though not in *Juliet of the Spirits*), Truffaut, Godard, Bergman, Richardson (in *The Loneliness of the Long Distance Runner*, certainly not in *Tom Jones*). It has to do with the least facile forms of alienation and boredom.

But most of all it comes, after all, from America. From the old cowboy with his narrowed eyes, laconic speech, and his natural instinct for understatement, and from the Negro idiom—where the ideas of cool and doing one's grainy personal thing originate. No Negro actors seem to have it just now, except perhaps Jim Brown, a rather special case. (The subject of what parts now exist for Negroes is another matter.) Basically, it is a style which consists in inhabiting one's own body, not trying too hard, being straight and somehow uncompromised at the center, and not making an ass of oneself. It runs directly counter to behavior that movies have always advertised; and as personified in any number of actors in the modern style, it is probably one of the sounder trends.

. . . . . . . *Doctor Faustus:*
Mr. Burton and Miss Taylor
Half in Tamburlaine

2-7-68

*Doctor Faustus,* starring Richard Burton, Elizabeth Taylor and members of the Oxford University Dramatic Society, is of an awfulness that bends the mind. Born of a theatrical performance that the Burtons gave at Oxford in 1966, the movie (which had its premiere last night at the Cinema 57 Rendezvous, and which opens tonight at the Baronet) presents itself as being as faithful as cinematically possible to the play by Christopher Marlowe.

But either Richard Burton, who plays Faustus, wished himself, understandably, in some other part, or Nevill Coghill, Merton Professor of English at Oxford, who adapted the play, was anxious to improve the text a little. Because at one point Faustus unaccountably begins the beautiful "Is it not passing brave to be a king / And pass in triumph through Persepolis?" speech from *Tamburlaine.* And at another, he grimly speaks the "Back and side go bare, go bare" song from *Gammer Gurton's Needle.* The whole enterprise has the immense vulgarity of a collaboration (almost Faustian, really) in which academe would sell its soul for a taste of the glamour of Hollywood; and the stars are only too happy to appear a while in academe.

The Burtons, both of whom act themselves as carried

over from *The Comedians,* are clearly having a lovely time; at moments one has the feeling that *Faustus* was shot mainly as a home movie for them to enjoy at home. One or the other of them is almost constantly on camera—in various colors, flavors, and shades and lengths of hair. Miss Taylor, who never speaks a word, plays almost all the female parts, from Faustus' devil wife through Helen of Troy and Alexander's Paramour. In this last role, she is, for some reason, frosted all over with silver—like a pastry, or a devaluated refugee from *Goldfinger.*

Burton, who has almost all the lines (the play has been quite badly cut) is worse. He seems happiest shouting in Latin, or into Miss Taylor's ear. The play's most famous lines sound like jokes in the context of so much celebrity: "Was this the face that launched a thousand ships / And burnt the topless towers of Ilium?" Well, no, one wants to say, but all the same. . . . The movie (directed by Burton and Coghill, and produced by Burton and Richard McWhorter) is full of all sorts of cinematic rococo touches (screens within crystals, and eyeglasses and eyes of skulls), which should be appropriate to the necromantic aura of the text, but are not. There is some horrible electronic Wagnerian theme music by Mario Nascimbene. There is also one fine, very pious performance as Mephistopheles in friar's robes by Andreas Teuber, an Oxford student.

. . . . . . *Sweet November:*
Twelve Affairs
at the Music Hall


*2-9-68*


*Sweet November* must be the most sentimental and sinister fantasy about contemporary love in years. One can't help leaving the theater sniffling and furious with oneself, which makes the movie a little hard to criticize. When Radio City Music Hall, where *Sweet November* opened yesterday, runs a movie about a girl—not a siren or a villainess, but a nice, fairly ordinary girl—who takes a different lover every month, there must be something very serious going on. And there is. A new myth that is deep and probably durable. A young manufacturer of boxes (Anthony Newley) falls in love with a Brooklyn Heights girl (Sandy Dennis) who sublets apartments and likes to paint in her spare time. Now, the cliché and the reality are likely to be that he wants to have an affair and she wants to get married.

What the movie does is reverse the terms of the modern urban argument: he wants to get married, and she, for her own special reasons, wants to have an affair. Brief, no regrets, perfect—just as it would be in the mind of the young man from *Playboy* in his struggle on the way to the altar with the determined young woman from *Cosmopolitan*. There is only one possible resolution for all this perfection. True romantics have always seen it, and the movie quite mawkishly presents it. Tragedy attends promiscuity at the Music Hall, still.

Sandy Dennis is very good. Her stammer, particularly if one has just seen *The Fox,* is a bit nerve-racking; but again—with a kind of awkwardness and Katharine Hepburn flatting of the voice—she gradually takes over her part. Anthony Newley, hardly clowning at all and playing quite softly, is good, too. Theodore Bikel, as a kind of vegetarian friend of the family, has to handle most of the mawkish part, and there is not much he can do with it. The music by Michael Legrand is not very noticeable—except for one song, "Sweet November," by Leslie Bricusse and Anthony Newley, which is ghastly.

The dialogue, by Herman Raucher, is extremely solid and witty. There is everything from standard two-liners ("There's not been a rape there in years." "Well, maybe things will pick up in the spring.") to very complicated routines with unlikely punchlines, such as "No one writes 'No handball playing' in the sky, Charlie." Unfortunately, Newley is supposed to be afflicted in the picture with a neurotic sense of haste that everyone keeps referring to as "Hurry, hurry, ding, ding." This is even more annoying than it reads.

...... *Planet of the Apes*

2-9-68

*Planet of the Apes,* which opened yesterday at the Capitol and the 72nd Street Playhouse, is an anti-war film and a science-fiction liberal tract, based on a novel by Pierre Boulle (who also wrote *The Bridge on the River Kwai*). It is no good at all, but fun, at moments, to watch. A most unconvincing spaceship containing three men and one woman, who dies at once, arrives on a desolate-looking planet. One of the movie's misfortunes lies in trying to maintain suspense about what planet it is. The men debark. One of them is a relatively new movie type, a Negro based on some recent, good Sidney Poitier roles—intelligent, scholarly, no good at sports at all. Another is an all-American boy. They are not around for long. The third is Charlton Heston.

He falls in with the planet's only human inhabitants, some Neanderthal flower children who have lost the power of speech. They are raided and enslaved by the apes of the title—who seem to represent militarism, fascism and police brutality. The apes live in towns with Gaudí-like architecture. They have a religion and funerals with speeches like "I never met an ape I didn't like," and "He was a model for all of us, a gorilla to remember." Some of them have grounds to believe, heretically, that apes evolved from men. They put Heston on trial, as men did the half-apes in Vercors' novel, *You Shall Know Them*. All this leads to some dialogue that is funny, and some that tries to be. Also some that tries to be serious.

Maurice Evans, Kim Hunter, Roddy McDowall and many others are cast as apes, with wonderful anthropoid masks covering their faces. They wiggle their noses and one hardly notices any loss in normal human facial expression. Linda Harrison is cast as Heston's Neanderthal flower girl. She wiggles her hips when she wants to say something. None of it is quite up to a single episode of "Star Trek," but it is all right.

.... *Winter Kept Us Warm*
at Colleges

*2-9-68*

Despite the growing importance of the college years in American life, there has been very little attention paid in books or films to college students. Not to what they say (a great deal of attention has been paid to that, and it is normally not very interesting), but to what happens to them, what their days are like. Few attempts have been made to convey the quality of their lives. *Winter Kept Us Warm*, which opened yesterday at the New Cinema Playhouse, is a Canadian movie about college students. Made on a budget of $8,000 by a group at the University of Toronto, it tells a kind of grasshopper and ant story about two boys, one a popular senior economics major (it is strange how seldom one refers to young people in terms of what they are actually studying), the other a shy freshman in history and literature. They become friends, more dependent on each other than they know. Ultimately, they desert each other in various ways and become estranged.

But there is a lot more to the movie than its simple story line. There is a camera amateurishly but painstakingly following young people about. It is surprising, for example, how very bleak are the rooms of college students, even in their modern affluence. One becomes aware that our society expects only students, criminals, the sick, and the military to live in dormitories—with desks, beds and the shape of the rooms themselves so depressingly alike. Only a blanket crocheted by the shy boy's mother and a difference in posters (the urbane boy has one advertising Sebring, the shy boy one for Calder) make it possible to tell their rooms apart.

Henry Tarvainen plays the introvert—intense, honest, almost cross-eyed with sweetness and sensitivity. John Labow is the older boy, combining casualness and love in a very difficult part. Joy Tepperman and Janet Amos, who play their respective girls, are excellent. The film was shot in 16-mm., and David Secter, who wrote, produced and directed, settles down—after a slow start with some rather flashy tracking shots—and does extremely well. The title of his gentle, honest little film is from a line in "The Wasteland": "Winter kept us warm, covering the earth in forgetful snow."

.... A Brilliant Breakdown

*2-11-68*

Seeing *The Graduate* is a bit like having one's most brilliant friend to dinner, watching him become more witty and animated with every moment, and then suddenly becoming aware that what one may really be witnessing is the onset of a nervous breakdown. After a perfect start and in spite of keeping every minor touch and detail perfect all evening long, the movie suddenly begins to exercise a series of basic, totally implausible options. As though the screenplay itself had lost its mind.

The script is quite faithful to the novel of the same title by Charles Webb. The difference is that the book is written quite clearly from the viewpoint of the Graduate, his perspective, his distortions, his caricatures of his elders and of himself. One can adjust to that perspective, make allowances for it, figure out more or less automatically what the reality was. What, in particular, the seduction meant to Mrs. Robinson, why she subsequently behaved as she did, what was really going on. Readers can project from the information there is.

Movies are a more autocratic form; and when *The*

*Graduate*, after beginning as a straight, beautifully made Mike Nichols satire, takes on almost imperceptibly the viewpoint of its major character—becomes afraid with him, for example, of Anne Bancroft and begins to see her as a villainess in a melodrama—it is, in conventional movie terms, very puzzling. Particularly since the acting is so good. Everyone becomes as the Graduate sees him, and only people who share his view of the world can really be completely satisfied with the film after that. Or people who are so delighted with sheer professionalism that they don't care too much about messages. Those who expect the movie to maintain the clear external focus with which it began become exasperated, do not understand the claims that are made for it, and suspect the film—for quite a long interval—of cracking up.

The breakdown, such as it is, knocks a few times before it occurs in force. The first intimation is when we are asked to believe that Dustin Hoffman is a track star named Benjamin Braddock. That is what the script says. But it is implausible. It is not the part Dustin Hoffman plays, or the one Mike Nichols directs him in, or the person the movie is about. Hoffman's whole situation in the movie, his whole interest really, is as a shy, inhibited intellectual (probably Jewish) who has never played on any team in his life. That is clear from the first. The beginning of the movie, however, inspires confidence in so many other ways—Hoffman and his suitcase advancing through the credits along an airport conveyor belt, the cocktail party, the man who has the single word, plastics, to say to him—that one is willing for a time to believe almost anything. Hoffman himself, with his stare and his nervous bipping noise, acts his real part so well that one forgets his nominal part for a while, in absolute trust.

The second knocking comes when Anne Bancroft throws his car keys to him and they land in the fishbowl. It is off-key. It is broader than anything that has gone before. Such great things are continually done, however, with shots of water throughout the film—Hoffman's agonized face photographed through the fishbowl, his descent into the pool in his diving gear, his floating on the pool all summer, and the wonderful cut of his leaping onto a raft in the pool and being borne along by Anne Bancroft in bed—that we forget this, too. Perhaps it is necessary, perhaps his hand plunging in after the keys is symbolic. Anyway, it is funny.

But in the Robinsons' house, it knocks again. Why is she coming on like such a monster? Why is he behaving like such a buffoon? Well, it is all right: some of the movie's frequent uses of words like "upset," "neurotic," and "mixed up" occur here and they seem to explain a lot. The humor has become quite broad and Mrs. Robinson is too grotesque. The whole movie has begun to share his fear of her, and to complicate matters she seems for a moment (with a Jewish inflection on, "Now if you won't do me a simple favor I don't know what") to be sharing the film's ethnic schizophrenia. But the arrival of Mr. Robinson, the perfect dialogue, and his strong acting soothe Benjamin and stabilize the movie again.

There follows a completely reassuring, very funny, absolutely controlled run of film. In the book, Benjamin calls Mrs. Robinson only after he has been on the road for a few weeks, fighting fires, hitching rides, sleeping with prostitutes in cow pastures. This is clearly not the movie Benjamin's sort of thing. It is wisely left out. The first hotel scenes are wonderful, the reception, the bar, the lobby, the phone calls, his hand on the room clerk's bell, brushing his teeth, her rubbing the spot from her dress. When he kisses Anne Bancroft in the bedroom before she has time to exhale her cigarette, it is one of the most hilarious moments on film. The seduction is right because this is how it was, or the way it might happen to anybody. They are both still human at this point.

It is in the bedroom scene where they argue that trouble starts in earnest and the movie's early symptoms return. Benjamin, whom the film had earlier alternately mocked and treated kindly, becomes cruel, boorish and stupid. He begins baiting Mrs. Robinson. In terms of the book's track star, this makes a certain amount of sense. He is a lout. He is not aware. But Benjamin in the movie has been, until this point, sometimes a jerk but essentially a sensitive young man. Even the alienation and sense of guilt he is supposed to be acting from would not make him behave as he does. Suddenly, everything about him seems wrong. His still calling Anne Bancroft Mrs. Robinson seems a tired joke in the script. His flat stubborn baby voice and the relentless stupidity of his remarks throughout the film force themselves upon one's attention. It becomes clear that he has never been a very interesting character, and that, unless this scene is being shot entirely from his own self-mocking, awry perspective, he is unreal.

And the options chosen for Anne Bancroft are really strange. There are, after all, some reasonable objections she might have to permitting the young man she has been sleeping with to take her daughter out. But from this moment on, Benjamin and the script choose to regard her objections as purely venomous and insane. She makes no further sense. Even the photography collaborates: none of the older people make a plausible move or are ever photographed as other than really ugly again.

Suddenly, her whole previous behavior is cast in doubt. It was presumably out of kindness, or desire, or affection, or some human thing that she slept with Benjamin in the first place; and it might be human for her to regard his dating her daughter as obscene. (And she is given one tragic-looking moment under Benjamin's interrogation in bed, as though the film were about to relent and make her plausible.) But it isn't treated that way, and for a while she and Benjamin and the entire *Graduate* go haywire.

The business of the dancer with the separately rotating breasts is too strong, mother and lover would not race to confide the affair to Mrs. Robinson's daughter, jokes like Benjamin's dialogue about his intention to marry (Father: That sounds to me like a half-baked idea. Benjamin: Oh, no. It's completely baked) simply emphasize the wavering focus upon him, and the "How could you rape my mother?" fiction simply makes Elaine Robinson unreal for a moment, too. It is almost all that way in the book and—literal truth or not—it doesn't work there either. It is not realism, or absurdism, or satire. It is out of control.

But the movie continues to surround everything with details of immense intelligence, competence and care (Mrs. Robinson and Ben's mother looking so much alike,

Benjamin's new smoking habit, all the comedy routines that work) that watching the film for a while is like observing a loved and meticulous lunatic.

As soon as Elaine comes to his boarding house, though, to kiss him, everything becomes right again. This scene is so convincing and well done that a whole new reservoir of trust is established, and all the succeeding absurdist touches seem simply fine absurdist touches. That is all. The movie reasserts control just about the time Benjamin begins taking initiatives, and by the time his car is racing across the Oakland Bridge, with the familiar Simon and Garfunkel song, "Here's to you, Mrs. Robinson. Jesus loves you more than you can know," the film is at top speed again. The perspective makes no further demands upon one's preconceptions about old and young. And one is certainly in the hands of the most brilliant, if rather unstable, movie in quite some time.

........ Albert Finney's
*Charlie Bubbles*

*2-12-68*

*Charlie Bubbles*, which opened yesterday at the Sutton Theater on East Fifty-seventh Street, is the first really fine movie of the year. It starts off with a slow, intensely boring conversation about business matters among three men at lunch. Then it becomes clear that the director, Albert Finney (who also plays Charlie), really wants it that way, that he knows what he is doing, and that he has something on his mind. There is one early unfortunate scene with food—as though Finney, with a loyal gesture toward the past, could rid himself of any debt to the fatuous enterprise, *Tom Jones*, which made him famous. Then the movie gets underway, and it becomes a completely honest and original thing.

The movie is about writing and celebrity. Finney plays a famous writer, Charles Bubbles, from a bleak industrial

66

town; and Shelagh Delaney, who wrote the screenplay, has caught all the insinuating reminders, all the uninvited conversations, all the corrosive nonsense, all the noise, that are likely to surround such a man when he is not working, and when he is looking for a little warmth or credible flattery from somewhere.

Bubbles is divorced. His former wife, played very quietly and bitterly by Billie Whitelaw, lives on a farm he has bought for her near his old home town, where she is "cultivating a beautiful compost heap" and trying to bring up their eight-year-old son—played, with a lack of hypocrisy unusual in child actors, by Timothy Garland. Bubbles lives in an immense house in London, where he is waited on by a couple called the Noseworthys and where he can watch, on television screens in his study, whatever takes place in every other room in the house. For a novelist this is perfect. One imagines that God observes his own universe by some similar arrangement.

Bubble's secretary and mistress is one of those shrill, hard, baby-adult and yet not quite detestable American girls who writes. Liza Minelli does this part, wide-eyed and with her voice pitched to set the teeth on edge. She is always talking about the "contributions" she sends to her home-town newspaper, and whether she ought to devote herself more fully to her novel. She takes pictures of everything, her energy is inexhaustible, her hairpiece comes off on the pillow, and she speaks of Charlie as "a wonderful person." The movie is partly about just this sort of thing, which the briefest exposure to the world or the arts teaches people—suddenly and for no apparent reason—to regard as too square to say, or to do, or even to think.

"Do you just do your writing now or are you still working?" a waiter who knew Charlie's father says to him; and a hitchhiker he picks up late at night refers to writing as a "knack." "I can relate a story, but I can't write it down," he says. Journalists, secretary, strangers, people who knew Charlie when—all treat him with superficially harmless cliché, deeply rooted in malice toward someone who has made a lot of money at something anyone can do. Since he is not working, he is left to his own boring irony.

Charlie has one friend, with whom he gets drunk; and

Finney and Colin Blakely (who plays the friend) do some of the most convincing drunken scenes to be found on film. They are disgusting. Their color is terrible. Yet they are not entirely charmless. "Thank you very much, Mr. Noseworthy," Blakely says to the stodgy butler, "and give my regards to the worthy Mrs. Nose." There are also some ordinary conversations. "Are you his missus?" the hitchhiker asks Liza Minnelli late at night in a roadside diner. "Well, not exactly," she says. "Ohh," he says slowly, "very nice." The conversation goes on. Other people arrive. And the direction—which is, after all, nearly always a matter of pacing—becomes very straight and real. The movie, in conversations, in gas stations, in elevators, always tends to stall exactly where life does. Very realistically, just long enough.

When Finney goes to visit his wife and son on the farm, the movie widens a little, into marriage too young, divorce, responsibility. In the quality of life it conveys, it is a becalmed *Blow-Up*. The young people understand each other, they are doing the best they can, nothing very dramatic is going on, yet they can't seem to help each other at all. The child, whom they mean so well by, has to survive almost independently. He is not really so much younger or more helpless than they. The ending, a low-key absurdist touch, is as quiet, beautifully made and carefully thought out as the rest.

. . . *The Fastest Guitar Alive*
at Exam Time

*2-15-68*

*The Fastest Guitar Alive* is an old-fashioned, good-natured bad movie—to be seen at exam time, or at a drive-in, or when you just feel like seeing a movie you won't have to discuss afterward. It is about a theft, and spies for the Confederate Army, and Indians, and romance; but the worst that happens to anybody in it is to be bound and gagged, and the love scenes are short, decorous and gallant.

Roy Orbison, a pop singer who sounds a lot like Elvis Presley and who has had some hit records ("It's Over") of his own, stars in his first movie. He has a nice, rather unlikely face—something midway between Presley and Liberace, which comes out friendly, goofy and square. His presence is not very forceful, but the movie does not require him to act much, and what singing he does is cooled-down Presley—not as great as the original, but better than most Country and Western.

The movie opened yesterday at neighborhood theaters, including Loew's at 125th Street and Seventh Avenue, which—being large, handsome, old-fashioned and serving popcorn, ice cream and candy—is as good a place as any to see it.

. . . . . . . . . .*Tell Me Lies*
Tells You How
to Go Mindless

*2-18-68*

One of the frightening things about our time is the number of people who think it is a form of intellectual audacity to be stupid. A whole generation seems to be taking on an easy distrust of thought. In everything from literary reviews and Pop journalistic publications, through radical political circles, chic art crowds and underground movie houses, it is as though information and reason itself were a form of pedantry. A symposium on a controversial subject almost anywhere is likely to be a nightmare. The excuse which is commonly given for the flight into mindlessness is a reluctance on the part of domestic problems to be resolved as fast as they should. And the war in Vietnam.

What brings this to mind is a British movie which opened last week—*Tell Me Lies*. It features a cast of young actors from the Royal Shakespeare Company, un-

69

der the direction of Peter Brook. They more or less improvise, for two hours, speak and act out their feelings about Vietnam and civil rights. A good part of the time they look agonized and face the camera. There can be no question of their sincerity. The only question is what sincerity uninformed by any sort of intelligence can mean. It is as though—confronted by an ambiguous and difficult world—instead of keeping their minds intact and struggling with complications, they have chosen to regard the world as simple, and go mindless.

"All one can do is to try to make Vietnam more present in everybody's lives," one of the characters reflects. To this end, they all look at photographs of the wounded, suggest to a lady pacifist distributing leaflets on a London street corner that she "use something with a bit more horror in it," sing cheerful songs about maimings and zapping the Cong, attend parties, re-enact the last day in the life of Norman Morrison (the American Quaker who burned himself to death), consult a Buddhist monk and a psychiatrist, and discuss things.

The discussions are the worst. They are of a really staggering triviality. Characters are forever hesitating, pausing on the brink of their inarticulateness as though about to deliver themselves of some truth too profound to be brought into the world without a struggle: "To us it was all somehow . . . unreal"; "The devastation would be . . . beyond understanding"; "There is something about mass movements that I find . . . terrifying." The self-indulgence here (the visit to a psychiatrist is key) is redolent of the worst of psychodrama and progressive education. Never an issue in the realm of ideas, only a personal problem to be worked through, therapeutically.

But *Tell Me Lies* is basically a piece of propaganda, with young testimonials and singing commercials; here, too, it shows what happens when an advertisement is sloppily made and conceived. Brand X makes inroads. Or, as in that terrible commercial with El Exigente, the Exacting One, and his happy natives waiting for him to test the coffee beans, something unexpected happens. (One begins to wish that he would just once make a disapproving face and be murdered, as he ought to be, in his sleep.) With this crowd, as their moral fervor makes them less and less willing to bother to think, one begins to wonder whether moral fervor is really underneath.

At a party, where the young actors challenge some Englishmen who do not share their beliefs, they are reduced to a kind of sigh—which passes for sufficient argument in their own circles but which is not likely to persuade. A guest speaks affectionately of America, less approvingly of Vietnam. An actor replies that women and children are being blown up. Another guest points out that napalm is a very ancient weapon and that in Asian terms Vietnam is not a very lethal war. The actor asks why nothing else is tried. He is asked what. "I don't know. You're the politicians," he replies. It is the classic maneuver of those who forget which minority is trying to persuade whom of what.

Sometimes the actors drop their look of fresh-faced, bewildered suffering and reveal something profoundly smug and patronizing. "Saigon is a brothel," one of them says, as scenes of Vietnam appear upon the screen. "Senator Fulbright said this, *but without quite knowing how true it was.*" Or, of a hypothetical Nebraskan soldier for whom they imagine the experience of sleeping, out of loneliness, with a homosexual, they say that he is "small-town, puritanical," and speak of his "Omaha upbringing which presents him with a conflict that his mind simply cannot cope with." This is the traditional snobbery of the far left, which seems determined to match dullness for dullness and inaccessibility to language with the far right—which, of course, it feeds. There is also a constant tendency to obliterate distinctions, as though it were an intellectual tour de force and an act of moral courage to call a club a spade. The references to genocide and a glad inclination to call Nazism in Germany and Western policy today "the same thing." Everything tragic or reprehensible is "the same thing." It makes it so much easier to discuss.

The only really moving moment in the picture—except for one brief sequence at the end, when a young man has a television screen with images of the war superimposed on his stomach—is a pseudo-documentary episode in which Stokely Carmichael appears. It is at the party, and Carmichael, who grew out of what was surely one of the greatest moral movements—most aware of the agonizing complexity of affairs—in this century, begins to speak the same inanities as everyone else. He talks, as though he believes it, of the third world's blowing the white world off the face of the earth and of black violence. His voice is theatrical. He looks like a cliché French perennial student talking the platitudes of revolution.

Then a Vietnamese girl appears, and after admiring him for a while and agreeing with him a bit, she asks him suddenly whether he is free. "Am I free?" he says, and laughs and says he is not. She asks if he is oppressed. He says he is. Then she asks innocently, "You're oppressed personally?" and the whole pretense crumbles. Of course, he is not oppressed personally. He is at a chic London cocktail party, diffusing celebrity on screen, absorbing adulation, safe. There is none of the risk of his days in Mississippi here. This is protest as a rhetorical idyll. He is acting. He is doing exactly what the whole cast of *Tell Me Lies* is doing, although a bit less emptily and boringly. He is taking refuge from real problems, from real necessities, and from his mind.

It is possible that the times are too serious now to leave room for all that. Hostility to our rational nature seems to be taking peculiar forms. Some of the young seem determined, by the use of drugs, to mutate. Others, of the radical extremes, seem prepared to become extinct. It seems not inconceivable that if the *Tell Me Lies* quality persists in the arts and in letters and in other spheres where the mind belongs, then all that will one day be left of us, as baby photos are the only traces of moments irreversibly lost, will be our own images on celluloid.

*2-20-68*

*The Two of Us*, which opened last night at the Beekman Theater, is a lovely, sentimental reminiscence of childhood in wartime. The child is an eight-year-old Jewish boy in Paris in 1944; and one of the unstated themes of the movie is the degree to which even the most catastrophic political developments can leave personal lives, particularly the private lives of children, virtually untouched—or touched in quite mysterious ways.

The child, played with a wonderful balance of gravity and mischief by Alain Cohen, keeps getting into trouble right along with the other boys, and thereby threatening to blow the cover of his Jewish parents, who are trying to represent themselves in Paris as Alsatians. A Catholic friend of the family makes a suggestion. The boy is taught the Lord's Prayer, a new surname and to call himself a Catholic. Then he is sent off to spend the remainder of the war with a lovable, but anti-Semitic old man in the country.

The old man is played by Michel Simon—who was already a great actor in 1934, when he starred in Jean Vigo's *L'Atalante,* and in whose honor a festival of six films opened yesterday at the Museum of Modern Art. Michel Simon has grown in size, his face has more crevasses. He is still great. He breathes in a slow, underwater sort of way—like an immense, thoughtful, warm-hearted, aquatic geological formation.

It is extraordinary to watch that live and serious child—with beautiful dark eyes and the marvelous dignity of children who are not trying to impress—playing against that enormous old genius. They grow to love each other. The boy shrewdly teases the old man about his anti-Semitism. The old man, in the context of his wife and provincial family, is an incarnation of everything French. He mutters. He listens to the B.B.C. He says, "In my house I decide who governs France." He listens to a German

73

propaganda station. He dotes on his bronchitic dog Kinou, who languishes as the Allies advance. (In fact, the whole movie is based on a kind of reverse eddy from the war: every Allied advance brings the relationship nearer an end.)

The movie, which is in French and black and white, is directed beautifully by Claude Berri, who also wrote the screenplay—and who directed the fine short film about a child and his rooster, *Le Poulet*. It is probably excellent for children who have seen more violent pictures about war. It has a splendid solemn little girl and geese.


......... *Half a Sixpence*


*2-21-68*


*Half a Sixpence* cost a fortune. Based on the novel *Kipps* by H. G. Wells and adapted from a show that ran in London and on Broadway for about four years, it should be visually fascinating to anyone in a state that I think is best described as stoned. The movie is flamboyantly colorful, full of mists and tints and prisms and filters of light. Under the direction of George Sidney (who directed *Pal Joey* and *Kiss Me, Kate*), it is wildly active; hardly anyone holds still for a single line, and the characters—in the ancient tradition of musicals—live on the verge of bursting into improbable song. The songs themselves, trite, gay, and thoroughly meaningless, make absolutely no concession to anything that has happened in popular music in the last ten years.

In fact, the movie (which lasts two and a half hours, with an intermission, and which opened last night at the Criterion) makes no concession to the outside world at all. It takes place in Edwardian England, where a draper's assistant, played by Tommy Steele (a former British rock'n roll singer and star of the original stage production), falls in love with a chambermaid. He comes into a fortune, nearly marries a rich girl, marries the chambermaid, loses the fortune and lives happily ever after. In the course of the story he encounters lovely sets of harlequins, carousels, balloons, chorus girls, Tunbridge Wells, landscapes, castles and Cyril Ritchard on a bicycle.

None of this makes any sense, but some of it is quite beautiful to watch. The camera has some annoying mannerisms, such as pointing to clouds for a cinema equivalent of chapter ends or using a filter to blur the image of the rich girl with whom Steele is supposed to be in love. Steele himself is an odd performer, smiling constantly, having moments of charm and an almost ferocious jauntiness. He looks like a soft, vaguely disquieting Mickey Rooney. Julia Foster, who does well as the chambermaid, looks like a girl who dreamed that she starred in a musical. Penelope Horner, as the rich girl, is required mainly to pose and be blurred. Among some of the largest, most elaborately choreographed dance routines in this bronze age of musicals, there is an excellent young actor and dancer, Grover Dale, who was in the Broadway production and whose first movie this is. I cannot imagine, though, that there will be many more musicals that are so lavishly, exuberantly out of touch with the world of rock and the music of our time.

. . Sidney Lumet, Groups and
*Bye Bye Braverman*

*2-22-68*

*Bye Bye Braverman,* which opened yesterday at the Fine Arts, is a movie about New York Jews, which—by some unlucky mixed perspective of affection and satire—turns into a pogrom. All the characters in it are unattractive and painful in a low-grade, humiliating way—like a backache or an allergy; there is not much the director, Sidney Lumet, or Herbert Sargent, who wrote the screenplay, can do for them. Not even the ironic kindness of hating them clearly. A literary style gives its own prejudices away, but

75

the camera seems to present these people straight—flat, petty, preoccupied with egg rolls, Volkswagens, literary scraps and the imminence of death and prostate trouble. It would redeem them to be funny, but they are too familiar—not in life but in stereotype—for that.

The movie is taken from a satirical novel, *To an Early Grave,* by Wallace Markfield, about second-growth Jewish intellectuals. Not the tall timber, the genuine poets and prophets and scholars; but the reviewers and contributors to periodicals. One of their number, Braverman the best ("Definitely. A second-rate talent of the highest order"), a man of integrity ("The way some people have B.O."), has died. His friends, Morroe Rieff, Felix Ottensteen, Barnet Weiner and Holly Levine, spend a day of their lives going to his funeral.

Morroe Rieff is reminded by news of his friend's death that Braverman owed him money. He is also stimulated to visualise the tragic possibility of his own death on a morning when his wife has refused to serve him orange juice. Barnet Weiner is interrupted by the news in his Sunday morning frolic and argument with his mistress, Myra Mandelbaum—played exactly right, in a smart, pert, horrible way by Phyllis Newman. Felix Ottensteen, a rigid old pedant of great viciousness and dignity (done very well by Joseph Wiseman), hears the news just after he and his aesthete son have been wishing each other dead. Holly Levine, a fat, materialistic specialist in pop culture, hears it as he is completing the first sentence of an attack on another man's book. The four friends set out to find the funeral. There are several contretemps along the way—including one pointless, tasteless encounter with Godfrey Cambridge as a Negro-Jewish cab driver. There are also some nice scenes, including a Chaplinesque one in which George Segal buries himself.

Sidney Lumet gets a chance to explore some Brooklyn neighborhoods and to show some Orthodox Jews in their relative Old Testament purity (the movie seems to be, in part, a lampoon of Reform Jewry, a bit intramural for a picture of this size). The photography, through some early shots of the city and some later shots of the rows of highwayside cemeteries on Long Island, certainly establishes the mortuary aspect of the New York skyline.

In the end, though, with *The Group*, and *Bye Bye Braverman*, Sidney Lumet has probably exhausted the cinema possibilities of drawing people together out of separate lives to attend funerals in semi-satirical circumstances. It hardly ever works in fiction, and it does not seem the best vehicle for his movies at all.

. . . . . . . The Imperialist
Scriptwriter and
*A Matter of Innocence*

2-22-68

*A Matter of Innocence*, which is based on a story by Noel Coward, is really a kind of remake of *Shakespeare Wallah*—with all the delicacy and background and nuance completely lost. Hayley Mills, who was so good as the little girl in *Tiger Bay*, plays a plain young Englishwoman on an Asian tour with her dowdy aunt (very much overacted by Brenda De Banzie). She meets an Indian gigolo in Singapore (Shashi Kapoor, who had a similar, better role in *Shakespeare Wallah*), has an affair with him, becomes much prettier, and goes away. Trevor Howard plays her uncle, the black sheep of the family, who oversees a plantation and also oversees his niece's progress to a shade of gray.

All three talents are wasted. Shashi Kapoor in particular is given lines in a kind of garbled English that no person of any nationality—even in the imagination of the most firmly imperialistic scriptwriter—ever spoke. But the movie, shot in color in Singapore, has some nice music by Michel Legrand and it is entertaining in a way bad movies are. It is always interesting to find any film that tries to depict in any way at all the lives of Westerners, no matter who, who are trying to live in and come to grips with the problems of the East.

*2-23-68*

*Windflowers,* which opened yesterday at the underground
New Cinema Playhouse, is a movie by Adolfas Mekas
(who directed *Hallelujah the Hills* and *The Brig*). It is
about a draft dodger who, having lived under a
pseudonym in a strange town for several years, is
discovered by the F.B.I. As he is trying to escape, the
police mistake a branch he has picked up in the woods for
a gun, and he is shot. The movie ends as it begins, with
the sequence of his flight and his death.

It is a very romantic and elegiacal little story—better
than most underground films, but not very strong. There
is some low-grade ideological discussion part way
through, which is static and out of place. And the movie
makes no pretense of engaging reality: the draft dodger in
the picture is chased at one point by a helicopter. But
Mekas is such a lyrical filmmaker that he seems more interested in cinema than in ideology; and scenes in which
the young man and his girl are photographed—by means
of a lens, the rim of which is coated with Vaseline—as
though they were at the end of a soft, fuzzed tunnel, are
lovely.

Also playing at the New Cinema is the first short production of Guerrilla Newsreel—a series of underground
documentaries for the New Left. There are interviews with
Establishment leaders of radical antiwar protest—notably
Professor Noam Chomsky of the Massachusetts Institute
of Technology and the Reverend William Sloane Coffin of
Yale. Guerrilla Newsreel intends to produce and distribute
regular short films of events from the New Left point of
view. A Guerrilla Newsreel of the recent Pentagon protest
rally—with participants marching to the citadel of the
military of a country involved in a war, to confront armed
soldiers there, without any persecution under the law or

any loss of life on either side—already exists. The theory behind the newsreels is that the media are misrepresenting the political truth of our time.

........ *The Fox,* and
*Charlie Bubbles* Again
on Sunday

*2-25-68*

*The Fox,* which has been playing to large but fairly jumpy audiences at both a conventional midtown theater (admission $3.00) and a smaller art theater (admission $2.50) eleven blocks farther uptown, is an interesting experiment. It takes a novella by D. H. Lawrence in which two young spinsters who run a farm together are disturbed first by the intrusion of a fox into their henhouse and later by the arrival of a young man, who ultimately marries one of them. It makes everything repressed in the book overt and explicit on the screen. Both girls are briefly attracted to the young man. One of them sleeps with him. The girls sleep together. And the anchor girl of the triangle has an auto-erotic episode of her own.

None of this happens in the book. And it would not be a suitable way to adapt, say, *Pride and Prejudice* or *Bartleby.* But for D. H. Lawrence, if only the movie were a bit more skillful, it would be a suitable modernization. What it does, in effect, is to turn *The Fox* into a story of two girls who are probably from some isolated New England girls' college. One is frilly, too feminine, lesbian, silly and rich; the other is intellectual, outdoorsy, less feminine and poor. They are, as the dean would say, too dependent on each other. When a man comes along, it is not clear at first who the left-out girl is; from there on it turns into a story of ganging up and leaving out. The end follows Lawrence.

The trouble with the movie is that Sandy Dennis' acting in the first half hour is terrible (later, the strain becomes

79

an asset), that the auto-erotic scenes are interminable, that the lovemaking is ambitiously but ludicrously cross-cut with a chase through the snow, and that some shouted plot-exposition conversations, particularly an endless one at the dinner table (I think eating scenes have really had their day), almost sink the movie entirely. What is good is the intelligence with which the ambiguities are kept, the straightening out of the meaning of the fox and his death, some experiments with simultaneity and interruption in dialogue, and a certain courage in following every exaggeration through. The audience, after each startling sequence—and prurient interest within decent social limits has always been one of the main legitimate attractions of film—begins talking animatedly of other things. There is one fine initial scene in which the camera swoops down on the henhouse with the fox himself.

Then there is *Charlie Bubbles,* at the Sutton, a wonderful movie in many ways. It starts out slowly, drawing the audience into the pace set by the director, Albert Finney (who also plays the lead). There is a bad food scene. After that, the movie turns into a beautifully directed record of a certain kind of person and a certain style of life, and the kind of person is probably us and the style of life, with certain modifications, is ours. Charlie Bubbles does not say or do very much. He drinks, he drives until late into the night, he smokes too much, he does not sleep enough, he loves his former wife (the first genuine woman, by the way, not exaggerated or in caricature, to appear in a movie in many months) and his eight-year-old son. He writes novels, but for now, he is at a loss.

People say the most awful things around him. Not that he says such wonderful things himself. It's just that other people are forever turning themselves into lifeless stereotypes through the use of a kind of cliché which they think establishes their credentials but which actually disqualifies them from all personal interest. I don't know how to describe this sort of cliché, except as the too self-revealing brag-formula. Liza Minnelli, who plays his shrill, child-woman American secretary and mistress, uses it when she describes the "contributions" she sends to her hometown newspaper, or when, in a marvelous sequence of scenes and conversations in a diner late at night, she becomes deviously proprietary about him. There is a malicious killing squareness about her. The same with a reporter who knew him at school, and who makes insinuations about Charlie's values in moving to London. Everything said this way grates on Charlie Bubbles; he lives in almost total irony.

The movie is beautiful and honest throughout, with perfect dialogue by Shelagh Delaney, genuine straight performances by Finney, Colin Blakely (who plays his only friend), Billie Whitelaw (who plays his former wife, who still troubles to warm the plates for breakfast), Miss Minnelli, Timothy Garland (as his son) and the players of smaller parts. It is about dehumanization through the dead use of words (in an unpretentious way), about the sadness of young aware adults at a particularly modern moment (but not in a self-pitying sense). It has humor, and visual beauty, and the rhythm of real life—with honest pauses and full stops. It can be seen as a movie, or as something more serious. It can accommodate any plane of attention at which you feel like watching it.


*The Treasure of San Gennaro:*
Breaking-and-Entering Addicts


*2-27-68*


*The Treasure of San Gennaro,* which opened yesterday at the Paris Theater, is another breaking-and-entering movie that looks as though it must have been more fun to make than it is to watch. The theft this time involves some jewels from the Church of San Gennaro in Naples, and the gang consists of Senta Berger, as the inevitable statuesque lady friend; Harry Guardino, as the nervy, mean-tempered young mastermind; Nino Manfredi, as a relatively sweet romantic lead, and Mario Adorf, as the inevitable stooge.

The movie clearly conceives of itself as a spoof. There are a lot of contretemps, incompetencies, hitchhikers, eavesdroppers, delays, and other crossings-up. Since very few gang, jewel-theft color films are done in deadly earnest, it is not quite clear to me where the genre ends and its spoof begins. Dino Risi, who directed such fine films as *The Easy Life* and *Love and Larceny,* directs this one at a rather sluggish pace. The late Toto has an extended walk-on as a wise crook too old to be bothered with anything but consultations. The dubbing of both Italian and English voices (there are also sub-titles) is terrible, and there are some rather doubtful jokes involving the robes and the speech of the Roman Catholic clergy. But the acting is not bad, and there are a few nearly funny seconds of chase on the way to an inevitable surprise ending. I find most of these *Topkapi* offshoots, with their casts and their plots and their ideas of humor, virtually interchangeable, but some people must be addicts, or *Grand Slam, The Biggest Bundle of Them All* and *The Treasure of San Gennaro* could not come out as from an assembly line.

.......... *We Still Kill*
*the Old Way*

2-29-68

*We Still Kill the Old Way* is a strange little Italian film, written and directed by Elio Petri, who also made *The Tenth Victim.* The movie is about the Mafia in a small town in Sicily, and it has the same air of brooding, genuine but not quite credible oppression as Haiti's *The Comedians.* It must be very difficult to convey, in color, the political terrors of radiantly sunny islands, whose people are not normally thought of in oppressors' roles.

The camera begins by scanning the landscape from the air, flies out of the sky into a street, and thereafter continually zooms, with great fanfare from the soundtrack, to almost irrelevant objects—a dish of melting ice cream, a car door handle, a mark in the molding above a door. The screenplay is equally peculiar: it starts with a threat and two murders, becomes a kind of thriller, and ends with the death of the main character, a young professor played by Gian Maria Volonte, which leads to the reunion of two lovers and therefore works as a happy ending.

Irene Pappas plays a nearly impossible role in further, indescribable complications of the plot. The music, composed by Luis Enrique Bakalov, is a kind of cheerful Calypso mixed with elegiac concerto and occasional ominous drumbeats. There are several allusions to the classic Italian novel of medieval banditry, *I Promessi Sposi,* and some reminders of *The Leopard.* The camera lingers on Sicilian mannerisms: fingers jabbed at sets of teeth and wardings off of the Evil Eye. The movie can't seem to commit itself to a tone or a form: a polemic against the Mafia, a stark portrayal of contemporary Sicily, a detective story, or an Italian marital comedy. There are some dark, interesting, and completely bizarre closing shots of a mass of people marching toward the camera—gradually converging in silhouette, like an immense, time-exposed amoeba.

.......Paul Newman in
*The Secret War of
Harry Frigg*

*3 - 1- 68*

*The Secret War of Harry Frigg,* which made its double-consonanted four-letter end run into Radio City Music Hall yesterday (and into the reviewing columns this morning), is a very familiar, old-fashioned comedy without any of the style or wit or conviction that made old-fashioned comedies of its particular genre funny. The plot involves four Allied generals (one English, one French, two Americans) who are taken prisoner in a Tunisian Turkish bath by an Italian colonel. They are installed in a villa in northern Italy, where—since they are all of equal rank in their respective armies—they cannot agree on the protocol of escape. Private Frigg, an American loser whose only demonstrable talent has been escaping from Allied stockades, is promoted by the Allies to major general and sent to command the escape of the other four.

From the opening credits, it is clear that the movie is going to be all wrong. Paul Newman plays Harry. The parts Newman has played in the past have all been essentially one role played in different contexts—in a pool hall, on a ranch, in detective work or in counterespionage. He has always been tough, quiet, not insensitive, with that mannerism originated by Brando of seeming constantly, casually aware of his mouth, as though he were speaking with tobacco or a Lifesaver in it. The part was often interesting, always hard and serious.

As Private Harry, Newman is supposed to be slope-shoulders, floppy and comic—and it is clear from his first appearance during the credits that he has no talents in this direction at all. He sits, in a ragdoll way, on a prison truck and fakes a yawn; and the part won't bend. The scene becomes a charade in which Paul Newman is trying to communicate that he is not playing Hud this time: and what we have here, as Cool Hand Luke would say, is a failure to communicate.

The screenplay, by Peter Stone and Frank Tarloff, is uneven and boring. It gets a lot of unearned modern mileage out of the hero's name. (Hollywood's secret war for frank speech in movies ought to be waged more nobly than in surnames.) It raises respectably modern questions by introducing Nazis who contend that they are only doing their duty to their country. It enlists on the side of enlightened attitudes by having Sylva Koscina (who plays the owner of the villa and the romantic lead) speak of sex in terms of there being "no more elegant or more civilized" way of saying good-by. It makes little contemporary in-jokes.

In fact, it seems to be bowing incessantly to the decade we are in. On the other hand, the plot machinery is ancient, and there are infinitely dated jokes about manners, about putting catchup on fine food or drinking from fingerbowls. It is as though no one could be bothered to straighten things out—the mechanics of the plot, the date and level of the humor, the degree of seriousness, or even the celluloid, which sometimes has double image "ghosts" as in poor TV reception.

There are two nice things: somehow the climax of the movie occurs in German, with somebody actually stuttering in German. It seems a rather far-out and daring device. And two characters, to express despair at various times, turn their heads away from the camera and lean headfirst against a wall. This seems rather endearing and far out as well.

........ The Negro That
Movies Overlook:
Stereotypes

*3-3-68*

It seems inevitable that somebody will soon start making some honest and important American movies with Negroes in them. Not false and worthy movies like *Guess Who's Coming to Dinner.* Or even, necessarily, films that come to grips with hard political realities. Just movies which draw upon some of the experience, the personal and social history, the drama and the look of Negro American life. You wouldn't know from current movies that there have been black men of great courage, intelligence and gentleness working in the South. You wouldn't know there has been a Watts, or ghetto life, or a Negro family, or a love affair, or a marriage, or a musical world, or an intellectual community, or dealings of most kinds between Negroes and whites. It is all a blank where the richest fiction and documentary material should be. And from the response to what little there is, it is clear that audiences are eager for anything that even pretends to be more.

Two of the most electric moments on film in the past

year—at any rate, two of the scenes which seemed to get the most obviously warm response from audiences—were the sequence in the greenhouse in *In the Heat of the Night* when Sidney Poitier slapped a white Southern gentleman, and the one in *The Dirty Dozen* when James Brown ran, dropping hand grenades into the ventilators of a German château. Both movies played to enthusiastic mixed audiences, lined up around the block all summer long. And at the end of both, a substantial part of the audience stayed on to applaud.

Applause in the movies normally means something quite different from what it means in live theater. It seems to have some belligerence in it, an assertion of will. Nobody simply wants to sit there applauding a blank screen or warming the heart of the projectionist. People applaud at movies, I think, because they want to insist on seeing more of something; and these movies they applauded had Negroes in them, involved with whites in some fairly credible way.

In both movies the involvement itself was essentially hostile, and the high point—the slap, the explosion—was violent; but that did not seem to be entirely the point. When I first saw *In the Heat of the Night,* I sat near two Southern Negro couples who, at the blow that released a perceptible tension in the rest of the audience, simply averted their eyes. It was only when the Uncle Tom Negro butler in the greenhouse did a perfectly timed double-take at what he had seen that the whole sequence was assimilated into a tradition of comedy, and the two Southern couples were as delighted as everyone else.

Neither film is remarkable for its realism: James Brown in *The Dirty Dozen* plays one of twelve American criminals recruited from death row to cross German lines in World War II and blow up the château. If they return safely to Allied lines, their reward will be a reprieve. What is extraordinary about Brown's grenade run, aside from the way it is timed in the film's own terms, is that it seems to work so well for audiences just because they know who James Brown really is. It is not as an actor that he makes his run with those grenades; it is as a great Negro football star and a man with a public career. (Of course, it is not

New Yorkers in the château he is blowing up; perhaps his run would arouse less enthusiasm in Düsseldorf.)

* * *

As for Sidney Poitier in *In the Heat of the Night*, the enthusiasm for his small act of violence also contains a strong awareness of his real situation. He is playing once again, patiently, angrily, that young Negro—better educated, more intelligent, finer grained, better mannered, than any of the white people around him—which he has managed to turn, over the years, into a kind of deliberate, type-cast, reverse racial stereotype. Parts for other Negro actors have already grown out of it: the black scholar in *Planet of the Apes*—pedantic, myopic and unathletic in the extreme—echoes the Poitier schoolteacher who danced, with so little sense of rhythm, in *To Sir, with Love* last year. Even the unfortunate roles that Godfrey Cambridge has been trying lately—beginning with the C.I.A. analysand in the virtually unwatchable *The President's Analyst* and continuing through his double caricatures as a Negro Jew in *Bye Bye Braverman*—are type departures after Poitier.

For an actor, of course, this can go on too long. Breaking racist stereotypes can become as confining as playing them out. But to have a personality at all, it is necessary to run away from one's own stereotype, not just in a racial sense, but in any sense—and then to pick it up again later if one likes, or choose another, or choose no stereotype at all. The important thing is to be free and unstereotyped enough to have a choice. Anyway, there is Poitier in one of these roles in *In the Heat of the Night*—brighter, and more attractive, and a better man than any white Southerner around. No one in the audience believes this quite to the extent of permitting his prejudices to be reversed, but the fact is that the *real life* Poitier is a very successful man. This reinforces the sense of outrage at the abuse which, until the point of the liberating slap, he has had to take in role after role. He is still more refined than any Southerner in the film but, for once, just for once, a New York audience can see a Negro clearly winning at something all

87

along the line. The reaction is shock and pure relief.

What Poitier has been doing worthily in roles for years is what *Guess Who's Coming to Dinner* tries to do as a film. The movie is completely silly, sentimental and false; but it is a kind of fantasy breakthrough from which some good can come. The story is that a famous young Negro doctor and the daughter of some white California liberals have met in Hawaii and fallen in love. The young couple return to her home and present her parents with a surprise and an ultimatum: either they give whole-hearted consent to their daughter's marriage by nightfall or the doctor will leave, out of pride and responsibility, and the girl will be irreversibly disappointed and estranged from her home. For the plot to work, the girl has to be tactless, shrill, insensitive and obtuse, which she is. The young man has to be sanctimonious but nonetheless far too good for his dreadful fiancée, which he is. The parents have to be worried and upset, and look at each other and their daughter with eyes brimming with tears of pride, disappointment and love, which is what they do. In fact, everyone in the movie is always looking at everyone else with eyes brimming with tears. The thing is, the years have passed these people by. It is a forties confrontation. In the sixties a black doctor's engagement to a white educated girl has turned out not to be the context where problems exist. And the ultimatum is only a spurious plotting device. None of it is true.

What is good about the movie is the real affection Katharine Houghton, Katharine Hepburn and Spencer Tracy obviously bear one another and the dedication of the actors to the treacly enterprise they are in. What is good by extension is something deeper, which grows out of the film's essential falseness: famous Negro doctors do not often carry off the daughters of rich white liberals, with or without ultimatums, and this is not really the problem to which the film is addressing itself. It is really a fantasy about miscegenation for ordinary people. What Hollywood has traditionally done with its fantasies—given a false picture, a romanticized precedent, an unreal model for people to measure their own lives by—this film does for miscegenation. It is Hollywood's imprimatur and a kind of first. As documentary or as a work of art about real Negroes involved with each other or with real whites—well, we simply haven't got any yet. Except the TV newsreels, where an interview that was held with Charles Evers of Mississippi last month probably had as much truth and interest, and real dramatic content, as any movie that was made all year.

........... Voices in
*Here We Go Round
the Mulberry Bush*

3-5-68

If sound in movies does not matter to you—or if only *Here We Go Round the Mulberry Bush,* which opened yesterday at the Baronet, were a silent film—it might be a good movie to see. Directed by Clive Donner, and adapted by Hunter Davies from a novel of his own, it has the worst script, bar none, I have ever heard. One wisecrack relentlessly follows another—neither funny nor true to the unfunny wisecracks people make in real life. There are countless strongly off-color remarks—all of them embarrassingly not quite humor, the way the off-color jokes of children are.

But if you can ignore lines on the order of "This is how the world ends, not with a bang but with a wimpy," and "What about the starving goats of China? Don't they matter?" (it is impossible to convey this sort of thing accurately—its awfulness is cumulative), and if you also don't mind voices pitched to a shrill unpleasantness, there is still the plot. It is a kind of cross between *Billy Liar* and *Closely Watched Trains.* That is, the hero (played by Barry Evans, whose first movie role this is) is always hoping to get a girl into bed and having daydreams. For the rest, he has a series of slapstick encounters with girls before he seduces any.

There are few plot devices more boring, in Czechoslovak films or in English, than having people talk about their sexual problems for the duration of a film; and the fact that most of the exposition in this movie takes place in the high, husky voice of Mr. Evans in interior monologue does not help matters much. But when all that is said and done—and it is hard to tell whether the uncertain acting of the entire cast is wholly the fault of the lines they have to speak—the movie is visually quite varied and rich.

There is an extraordinary tableau of Mr. Evans participating in a children's play—reminiscent of the child scenes in *Juliet of the Spirits* and the apple festival in *Privilege*. Some naked scenes of Mr. Evans and Judy Geeson (who co-stars as the girl he wants) have a lovely white-on-white quality. There is also a particularly effective, well-timed and well-grouped, fulldress orgy scene near the end—a bit naughtier than the puppy-play orgy in *Blow-Up*, a bit less earnest than the grim one in *Red Desert*.

. . . . . . . . Whole Cloth:
*30 Is a Dangerous Age,*
*Cynthia*

*3-5-68*

Another film, *30 Is a Dangerous Age, Cynthia*, which opened yesterday at the Cinema Rendezvous, has a number of similarities to *Here We Go Round the Mulberry Bush*. It is English, too. It also has a young man—Dudley Moore, the jazz pianist and star of *Beyond the Fringe* —looking for a girl and living through Billy Liar fantasies. There is, in fact, one virtually identical sequence in the two movies when both heroes imagine themselves on a bus filled with women, trying to decide in what order to take them. But *30 Is a Dangerous Age, Cynthia* has more than a nominal plot; it concerns a young musician who is trying to make a mark in the world and find a wife before his thirtieth birthday. It proceeds almost completely out of the sensibility of Dudley Moore—who, along with the director, Joseph McGrath, wrote the screenplay and who, sharing a lot of the comic sense of Peter Cook (another star of *Beyond the Fringe* and one of the funniest men alive) is a very funny man himself.

Moore does some brilliant musical parodies—Mozart, Beethoven, Bach, even some singing in countertenor. He also creates some fine cliché-mocking dialogue, ranging from "Would you mind putting your John Hancock on my swindle sheet?" to an elaborate sequence that—after the Irish have been repeatedly described as flocking to a particular theater—builds to the line, "Yes, this is a great day for the flocking Irish."

There are some quick comic shots and scenes: the composer's room, absurdly filled with coffee cups; a shot of people up through the surface of a glass coffee table. A lot of bits like that. The acting, particularly by Suzy Kendall, who plays the girl he loves, and by Patricia Routledge, who plays his landlady (Miss Kendall co-starred and Miss Routledge also appeared in *To Sir, with Love*), is superb. But the most interesting side of the film is how it works as an example of what it is about: talent, no longer that young, trying to do something in the world. It recognizes the pressure of great men (Beethoven, etc.); it acknowledges a need for romance and to found a family. Yet it works out strangely: success, when it comes—Mr. Moore writes a musical—is a travesty: someone has completely changed his script.

The problem with the movie itself is that, like almost all of contemporary comedy, it has something sophomoric about it—one foot always behind in the university. This seems to stem from a sense in the movie and elsewhere that this particular generation of satirists has to make itself up out of whole cloth, that there are no useful precedents. The movie views people at thirty as still young, still postcollegiate really, because they move into adulthood with no sense of a comic past to lean on.

*The Power*, which opened yesterday at neighborhood theaters, is a science-fiction movie about a mind, a mind so strong, in fact, that it can rotate a sheet of paper impaled on the point of a pencil whose eraser end is stuck between the pages of a book that is upended in the center of a conference table. It can rejuvenate its thinker, or age him, or change the color of his hair. It works household appliances. It can give people choking sensations of heart attacks. For some reason, this mind is out to choke George Hamilton.

George Hamilton plays the director of a clinic that tortures young volunteers to determine how much pain astronauts can take. Michael Rennie plays a Government inspector who comes to inspect the workings of the clinic. At a staff conference Mr. Hamilton calls, this strange paper-turning intellectual gift manifests itself. The question is, who has it? In the course of finding an answer, the mind stalks nearly all the members of the conference. Normally, it likes to accelerate hearts to do people in, but sometimes it exercises its penchant for twirling things by trying to spin them to death on space machines or carousels.

There are all sorts of Daliesque visual effects by Gene Warren, Wah Chang, J. MacMillan Johnson, and art director Merrill Pye: accelerating naked hearts, mechanical toys and, in one sequence, George Hamilton in his entirety spinning off into the firmament. The music that accompanies all appearances of The Power is played on an instrument that looks like a cross between a xylophone and a sitar and that is called the Gypsy cimbalon.

One of the first requirements of science fiction—that any supernatural phenomenon must have a limit, that it must be quite clear how much power is being ascribed to it—is violated very early: since The Power can do anything, it is not at all clear why it hasn't done everything it likes many years before it meets George Hamilton. At the end of the film, when Mr. Hamilton stands with his co-star Suzanne Pleshette and contemplates a model of the earth, he says, "They say that power corrupts and that absolute power corrupts absolutely." It gives one pause.

But the movie, though low grade, is a good neighborhood movie to go to because it has the grace to be completely serious. It never invites the audience to laugh at it in the hope of getting a little credit for camp. It is loyal to its own inspiration and to anyone who wants to take it seriously. In recent science-fiction films, which lapse in and out of the put-on decadence of the form, this is very rare. There is also a scene in which George Hamilton meets The Power's parents—Western American gothic, with flyswatter in hand—a bit like Bonnie Parker's family reunion. Yvonne De Carlo, Nehemiah Persoff, Gary Merrill, and Aldo Ray are also in the cast. It is not the sort of movie where acting matters much.

........Not Tuning in
to the Sound
of New Music

*3-10-68*

A few weeks short of twenty-five years after *Oklahoma!* opened on Broadway on March 31, 1943, the movie *Half a Sixpence*—inflated from an earlier Broadway production—opened last month at the Criterion. *Oklahoma!* marked a change. The American musical had broken free of the European princeling operetta on the one hand, and the vaudeville star revue on the other. *Oklahoma!* was about just folks, and so on. Twenty-five years is about a generation, and *Half a Sixpence* is what we've got. Before that, *Camelot, Mary Poppins, The Sound of Music*. It is not that these musicals in any way increase the sum of harm or boredom in the world. They have, instead, given great pleasure to an unprecedented number of people

—but conventional musicals, although they still generate money and sentiment, hardly generate anything else any more. They no longer affect fantasies or change the character of lives. They still satisfy an audience with a legitimate claim; but the claim of another, probably larger, audience for the music of its own time is being ignored.

The audiences are not entirely incompatible. A good tune still catches on and one of the few things people of every age still have in common is the repertory of show tunes their minds are programed with. Show tunes cut across ages and classes; everyone knows hundreds. A great old musical, if someone should happen to write one, would be lovely. A popular tune to be sung in the car or the shower is still a nice thing. (Look at Paul McCartney's (*Yesterday*.) But it hasn't happened lately and Hollywood—with forced, listless, overblown reworkings of dead tunes and ideas like *Half a Sixpence*—goes on as if it had. The inspiration is simply elsewhere.

The problem with movie musicals is that they are now anachronisms in every sense. They cost a fortune—although to a generation that is most characteristically post-Depression, raised in uninterrupted prosperity (with a dawning consciousness of poverty in its midst), a lavishly overpriced musical is at best unimpressive and, more normally, downright offensive. The musicals are boring, unrelated even to the fantasies of the young. One has only to look at faces in audiences. Ten years ago every European could say all young Americans looked alike, or wanted to: crew cut, fresh-faced, conformist, untenanted. Whatever one may think of the state of the young, they are not that way now. The old musical princes and princesses are not models for them. Artists and poets are. Not alone on the grounds of musicianship, the age follows Bob Dylan and Joan Baez.

And countless other performers in other styles. The curious thing is that just when popular music is flourishing—when it is varied enough to include many genres, when a whole generation has been virtually formed by it and when its technical problems are most closely related to those of film—the movies keep betting so heavily on decadent versions of precisely those shows which have

*3-14-68*

*Up the Junction* is the latest in the series of British
working-class color films that seem to come from British
directors with the regularity of episodes from "Our Gal
Sunday," and it is by far the best of them. A lot of things
are wrong with it, but a lot is going for it, too. It stars Suzy
Kendall (of *The Penthouse* and *To Sir, with Love*) fighting a part that requires her to be on screen nearly all the
time and that is almost impossible to play. She portrays a
rich young woman, who, tired of what she considers the
hypocrisy of upper-class life in Chelsea, decides to find
happiness among the genuine, lovable poor who live "up
the junction" in Battersea.

Such a person—who insists on wading into the lives of
other people and finding their deep social problems neg-
ligible or picturesque—is either a ninny (such as the
daughter in *Guess Who's Coming to Dinner*) or a hard
lady journalist. In either case, she has to be so insensitive
that it is difficult to make anyone care about her. Miss
Kendall opts for the journalist, which makes for an interesting performance of a part that has been suppressed
in the script. That is, *Up the Junction* is based on a series
of articles in *The New Statesman* by Nell Dunn (who also
wrote the screenplay for *Poor Cow*). In the articles, Miss
Dunn describes her experiences in moving to the
neighborhood of Clapham Junction, working in a candy-
packing factory there, and observing the people. In the
movie, there is no indication that Miss Kendall writes. But
for a good part of the film she plays it that way—quite
shallow and hard—not so much talking to people as lurk-
ing around interviewing them, with a certain mixture of
warmth, condescension and reserve.

When she falls in love, she has to lapse gradually into the ninny to behave as insufferably as the script requires her to. She keeps expressing her delight with everything squalid and poor. And when her young man reveals—in one of those instances of someone's most personal secret having been a matter of public knowledge from the beginning of time—that everyone always knew she was not really working-class, the characterization falls completely apart. Miss Kendall simply looks too intelligent and even too old (she is twenty-five) for the giddy young grotesque of tactlessness she then becomes. But it is a rare instance of a very talented actress trying to rescue a part.

There is a really beautiful piece of characterization by Dennis Waterman—whose first adult movie role this is —as the furniture-truck driver and leading man. He plays one of those solid, gentle young people, infinitely more sensitive and perceptive than they look, who are always being hurt by people who ought to know better. It is rare to find a portrayal of a gentle young man without any air of effeminacy or saintliness. Dennis Waterman does the whole difficult thing exactly right.

It seems that in British movies of this genre one always has either a birth or an abortion, and Adrienne Posta, in a part that consists mainly of being a rather leaden ball of fluff, has the abortion scene. Maureen Lipman plays Miss Posta's sister, a wise, mischievous young woman, who, but for her lack of education, would probably have become a considerably less charming intellectual. Michael Gothard plays a boy next door, who dies, twitching, in a motorcycle wreck. Other minor characters, including some real Battersea residents in a pub, are convincing, too.

The movie, which opened yesterday at the New Embassy and 68th Street Playhouse, was directed by Peter Collinson, who last directed *The Penthouse*—without any of the earlier film's brutality. There are well-shot scenes of Battersea and of the candy factory. Some of the ladies' dialogue at work is rather broad and forced, but it is rare to find working people characterized in terms of the place they work and the work they do. The music, by Mannfred Mann, consists of complete soft-rock songs done while some other bit of business is going on.

. . . . . . . . . . Nemec's
*Diamonds of the Night*
and Eisenstein's
*Strike*

*3-15-68*

*Diamonds of the Night,* which opened yesterday at the
Bleecker Street Cinema, is a realistic Czechoslovak film
about two escapees from a German concentration camp; it
makes one realize just how valid and necessary absurdism,
particularly the austere absurdism of great dramatists like
Beckett or even Pinter, is. The two young men (played by
Antonin Kumbera and Ladislav Jansky) run for a long
time, and the hand-held camera runs realistically with
them—becoming dizzy when they tire, taking on their
memories and hallucinations, ducking and hiding, and
resting when they do. With one of them, it keeps removing
a shapeless bandage to examine an injured foot. It shows
the condition of their mouths when, after starving for
many days, they try to eat a piece of bread. It shows them
hounded and caught and released. For long stretches of
the film there is no sound except their breathing, or
church bells, or the ticking of a clock. It is all quite depressing and real, and when one sits through it all one
feels one has accomplished something.

The problem is that it doesn't really work and that it
probably cannot be done this way. If you want to convey
monotony it has to be stylized; it cannot be lifted from life
intact and conveyed on the screen. And for characters on
the outer edge of existence, living an extreme of misery,
realism is somehow inappropriate. It looks unreal. One
loses interest. Two men running, one ceaselessly preoccupied with his foot, the other in a kind of trance, both
hounded by a band of toothless German-speaking Czechoslovaks—in Beckett it would be stark and stylized to the
point of ritual. The documentary spirit is too real to draw
one in.

Jan Nemec, who directs, seems aware that when an artist is being deliberately dreary he must know exactly what he is doing. The movie, in its own slow time, is very carefully made. It is only that one becomes accustomed to its desperation very quickly—as eyes adjust to the dark—and then one finds one's way about too comfortably.

*Strike*, which opened with *Diamonds of the Night* at the Bleecker Street, was made by Sergei Eisenstein in 1924. It was his first mass-uprising film (*Battleship Potemkin* and *Ten Days That Shook the World* were done in 1925 and 1926), and it is still strong and elegant. There are grand, swarming crowd scenes and shots of all things fascinating—from a flock of ducklings to heavy factory machinery. It is an industrial-age epic. There are all the dramatic sight ironies that one normally thinks of as "visual," although they are not really visual at all. When scenes of Cossacks on horseback surrounding seated strikers, for example, are cross-cut with shots of a capitalist squeezing juice from a lemon and brushing the fallen rind off his shoe, the irony, though the film is silent, is entirely verbal. It requires the intervention of the word "crush" to connect the two sequences at all.

*Strike* has certain resemblances to *A Corner in Wheat*, made by D. W. Griffith twenty-five years before. In both movies the sweep of consequences that are set in motion on the screen is so convincing and powerful that the only possible ending involves the defeat of whoever took the initiative. That is, when Griffith's tycoon corners the wheat market, the movie conveys a sense of escalating devastation so great that the tycoon has to die at the end—or the audience would be left with the feeling that he was taking over the entire world. When Eisenstein's strike gathers momentum, it has to be broken at the end or the uprising would go on into infinity.

3-16-68

"How will we feel the beauty of the sunrise if we don't feel the beauty of the sunset?" "What is destiny exactly?" "Can the eye resist the spear without being pierced?" These are some of the interesting questions posed by *The Broken Wings,* a movie based on the love story of Kahlil Gibran, author of *The Prophet. The Broken Wings* began flapping softly yesterday at the 34th Street East.

When he was eighteen, Kahlil Gibran (played in this movie by Pierre Bordey) fell in love, in his native Beirut, with Selma Karamy (played by Nidal Ash Kar), the nubile daughter of the wealthy Ferris Affandi Karamy (Philip Akiki). Ferris Affandi, however, had already been persuaded by an evil bishop to marry Selma to the bishop's profligate nephew, Mansour Bey Galib (Aaladin Nader). Selma was married to Mansour, and after five childless years during which—being very devout—she went to church a great deal, she gave birth to a son, who died at once. So did she.

Gibran himself went off in despair from Beirut to Greenwich Village, where he wrote his account of the matter, *Broken Wings,* and among other successful works, *The Prophet*—which still sells approximately four thousand copies a week. In 1931, at the age of forty-eight, not poor, he died. People who like *The Prophet* should like *The Broken Wings* a lot.

"Life is a feather," Mr. Bordey says. "Imagination is a feather in the wind. Hope is imagination. Dreams are imagination." ("Let us drop imagination," Ferris Affandi says.) "He who doesn't rebel against oppression," Mr. Bordey says later on, "does himself an injustice." "It is nature's power that drives the moon around the earth." "True love is the result of spiritual affinity, not of courtship." "What power love possesses!" Miss Ash Kar marvels. "To feel the beauty of life is wonderful."

But these are only the sub-titles (perhaps a great deal

has been lost in translation), and there is no need to read them. The movie itself, the first Lebanese film to be released in the United States, is in Arabic, which sounds quite soft and beautiful. It is done very simply in black and white, and whatever has to do with life in Beirut—the chanting call to mosque, the smoking of the nargileh, the landscape—is worthy and interesting. There is also a gentle moment when Mr. Bordey seems to be drawing something quite lovely and sinuous in the sand. If one did not already know, one realizes slowly that it is the word Selma in Arabic.

...... On Reviewing, I:
Turnstiles

*3-17-68*

There is probably no more unedifying and, in many ways, valueless kind of communication than everyone's always expressing opinions about everything. Not ideas, or feelings, or information—but opinions, which amount to little more than a long, unsubstantiated yes or no on every issue. People begin to identify themselves by opinion-clusters: on the basis of a few simple questions (Do you believe the Warren Report? Did you like *Bonnie and Clyde?*), you can project whole personalities and—better than on the basis of class or education—social groups. Since nothing more than endorsement or rejection is involved, arguments are reduced to a kind of *de facto* sarcasm, insult controversy, the unbacked scornful remark: "He *admires* McNamara," or "She *sobbed* during *Guess Who's Coming to Dinner*" might constitute a full description of you in some circles. Plain opinions are much over-rated.

The problem is that reviews are read almost completely for opinions, and with movies this can be especially inadequate. Most movies are not very good. Most people know it and like to see them anyway. Without too much fuss or

an inventory, of what one's own opinions will be. Whether they vulgarize. And more important, on the rare occasions when a beautifully made movie comes along, whether they call attention to it. *Charlie Bubbles*, I think, was such a film. Other reviewers thought *China Is Near* was. Both movies, naturally enough, are director's films, dominated by a single sensibility as most movies are not. It is a question of which sensibility one responds to. The question is important, a kind of critical watershed; it is the only place where critical opinion really matters. A reviewer's case rests on the things he deeply likes.

One of the interesting things about reviewing movies is finding a vocabulary for saying why. The question has been raised: What would happen if critics reviewed books as cinema buffs review films. X writes superb chapters, they might say; his use of the colon and comma is much imitated. Part of this is frivolous, of course; the main reason why book critics don't spend too much time on grammar is that everyone knows what writing style and grammar are.

In Truffaut's book of interviews with Hitchcock, the conversation dwells happily on the use of a champagne glass—bubbly in one shot, dead in the next—to denote the passage of time. It is a neat touch, but no one would make quite so much of a single well-turned phrase in a novel. There is so much more to say. In movies a lot remains to be worked out. In the meantime, a lot of the mystique of the "visual" seems to me silly and obscurantist. A movie works or it doesn't. Most people agree most of the time with the people they normally agree with about most other things about which movies work. It is only the vocabulary that is undeveloped still. I suspect one of the most productive areas for study is the television commercial. It is brief. It is often beautiful and extremely well made. It is an art that still has an evangelical message—as religious objects have. A perfect commercial is nearly an icon. A movie is still a mass project, on an architectural scale. The problem is how—beyond a simple yes or no or a complete *explication de texte*—the thing can be best discussed. Checking in with opinions is not really saying much.

*3-19-68*

*The Producers,* which opened yesterday at the Fine Arts
Theater, is a violently mixed bag. Some of it is shoddy and
gross and cruel; the rest is funny in an entirely unexpected
way. It has the episodic, revue quality of so much contemporary comedy—not building laughter, but stringing it
together skit after skit, some vile, some boffo. It is less
delicate than Lenny Bruce, less funny than *Doctor
Strangelove,* but much funnier than *The Loved One* or
*What's New, Pussycat.* It begins with Zero Mostel,
overacting grotesquely under the direction of Mel Brooks,
the famous 2,000-Year-Old Man and writer-narrator of
the Academy Award-winning cartoon *The Critic.* Mostel,
as a producer who gets investors by giving old ladies
"their last thrill on the way to the cemetery," is first
shown in silhouette through the glass door to his office, as
he nuzzles one of his elderly ladies. That is his last funny
time. We next see him rolling about with them, being
chased by them, making lewd conversation with them, and
generally being as gross and unfunny as only an enormous
comedian bearing down too hard on some frail, tasteless
routine can be.

Gene Wilder, who plays the young bookkeeper who inspires Mostel to oversubscribe with backers a show that
will close after a single night (leaving Mostel and Wilder
with the amount that has been oversubscribed) is wonderful. Last seen as the young man who was stolen—along
with his car and his fiancée—by Bonnie and Clyde, he
plays his present part as though he were Dustin Hoffman
being played by Danny Kaye. Going through long, infinitely variegated riffs and arpeggios of neuroticism, he

blushes and gasps, "I'm hysterical," and grins shyly and fondles his security blanket. He is forced to be as loud and as fast as Mostel (and as the crude and incredibly amateurish cutting). But he's fine.

There is a great scene when the deal between them is consummated at night in front of Lincoln Center, and all the fountains soar at once. They decide to produce "Springtime for Hitler," a play by a helmeted Nazi in Yorkville, a play true to "the Hitler you loved, the Hitler you knew, the Hitler with a song in his heart." They hire a transvestite director, whose plays have never lasted beyond the first rehearsal. There is a lovely conversation with the director's roommate, played by Andreas Voutsinas as a prancing young person in black slacks, black turtleneck, beads, and a beard curled up in front like the toe of a dancing slipper. As leading man, they hire a mind-blown hippie played by Dick Shawn. Mostel hires for himself a blond receptionist, who does not speak English and who, when told to go to work, begins to dance frenetically.

Strangely enough, the first act of "Springtime for Hitler: A Gay Romp with Adolf and Eva in Berchtesgaden" is the funniest part of this fantastically uneven movie. The Gestapo chorines, the opening number, "Look Out, Here Comes the Master Race"—well, it loses absolutely everything in transcription. But there is just enough talent and energy to keep this blackest of collegiate humors comic. Barely.

Then the movie makes a terrible and irreversible mistake. It allows the audience onscreen to find the play funny. This turned the real audience in the theater off as though a fuse had blown. Hardly anyone laughed again. Partly, it must be admitted, because "Springtime for Hitler" itself gets less funny at this point (even Shawn becomes quite weak). But mainly, because there is nothing like having your make-believe audience catch on to a joke—and a joke that absolutely capsizes the plans of your leading characters—to make your real audience really hostile to you. The ending, when all the comic props are supposed to be in motion—Mostel conning, Wilder hysterical, German fanatic, girl dancing, etc.—goes better than one might think. On the whole, though, *The Pro-*

*ducers* leaves one alternately picking up one's coat to leave and sitting back to laugh.

. . . . . . Awards, Feathers,
*I Even Met Happy Gypsies*

*3-21-68*

*I Even Met Happy Gypsies,* a Yugoslav movie, in color, which opened yesterday at the Regency Theatre, stars Bekim Fehmiu, a young actor who looks and behaves a lot like Jean-Paul Belmondo and who, in 1966, won the Silver Arena in Pula for his performance in *The Journey.* The movie was written and directed by Alexander Petrovic, who has made a number of documentaries, as well as *When Love Has Gone, The Days* and *Three. Three* was shown last year at the New York Film Festival and was awarded first prize at the Festival of Karlovy Vary. The leading lady, Gordana Jovanovic, is a sixteen-year-old girl whom Petrovic found gathering feathers in the gypsy suburb of Vrsac. The film also stars Olivera Vuco, one of Yugoslavia's most popular singers and actresses and a member of the National Theater of Belgrade; and Bata Zivojinovic, who won an award at Pula for his performance as Milos in *Three.* Mr. Zivojinovic plays Miss Jovanovic's stepfather.

The movie itself is a little hard to follow. It is about a lot of gypsies living in thatched Busiri-Vici white cream houses, in mud and color and squalor, north of Belgrade in the Panonian Plain, where they deal in goose feathers. There is some trouble over women, and feather-trading territories, and Fehmiu has a moment of existential refusal—like the halt in the run of the Long Distance Runner—when he releases feathers he has just bought, from the back of a truck all over the road. There is also a knifing, and a quotation from Scripture about the evil spirit passing into some swine, who subsequently do away with themselves. But aside from people getting drunk or

110

going back and forth from Belgrade to visit relatives, it is nearly impossible to understand the broad outline of the story without program notes.

What happens, then, is an almost pure case of being amused by some of the film without the slightest idea of what people are up to. There are some pleasant gypsy songs, Miss Vuco is a fine performer in a happy, feral way. Fehmiu narrows his eyes and scrunches his cigarettes, and one has beautiful shots of landscapes and gypsies with a kind of travelogue interest. There are all those feathers, the film is a little scratched in places, and the sound is (as it has been in a number of movies lately) quite out of synchronization with the lip movements. There is a slang word, "Jok!" pronounced sort of yock, that recurs a lot and is translated in the sub-titles as "by no means."

Some parts are shot with the foreground sharp and the background blurred; others with the background sharp and the foreground blurred. There are a lot of Bosch-like groupings and lovely scenes of gypsies and horses and plains. It is a movie for watching in idle incomprehension—like sitting by the window watching what goes on on one's block, in a foreign country, in a crowded neighborhood, on a passing day.


........ Bette Davis in
*The Anniversary*


*3-21-68*


Bette Davis's seventy-eighth movie, *The Anniversary*, which opened yesterday at the Selwyn and other neighborhood theaters, is a horror film for faint-hearted horror movie fans. It has no horror music. Or any serious crimes. It is not scary. In the serious bars of pure terror, it is the ginger ale. The cast seems to have a pleasant time. Miss Davis plays a one-eyed mother of three, who wears a lurid eyepatch. She leaves a glass eye under her pillow to

111

alarm the fiancée of her youngest son (who insists on spending the night with his girl in his mother's bed). Miss Davis is a widow. It is her anniversary.

Her middle son wants to emigrate with his wife and five children from England—where the movie is set—to Canada. Her youngest son wants to get married. Her oldest son likes to dress in ladies' underthings. Miss Davis opposes all these things but the last. There is a lot of caustic dialogue. Miss Davis gets a chance to sing "Rock of Ages" under her husband's portrait. Sheila Hancock and James Cossins of *How I Won the War*, and Elaine Taylor and Christian Roberts of *To Sir with Love* (Mr. Roberts played the boy who gave in last) get a chance to appear again. *The Anniversary* is not a distinguished example of the Terrifying Older Actress Filicidal Mummy genre, but it isn't too heavy. And the genre isn't that distinguished after all.

........ Disney Studios'
*The One and Only
Genuine Original
Family Band*

*3-22-68*

Tensions over the election between Grover Cleveland and Benjamin Harrison are not running too high this year, and *The One and Only Genuine Original Family Band,* which opened yesterday, with the Easter show, at Radio City Music Hall, is about as pepless and fizzled a musical as has ever come out of the Walt Disney Studios. It stars Walter Brennan, as a grandfather who supports Grover Cleveland in 1888; Buddy Ebsen and Janet Blair, as a father and mother who support Benjamin Harrison; and several assorted children, who are taught by grandfather to sing a dreary and interminable campaign song called "Let's Put It Over with Grover."

"Let's Put It Over with Grover," however, is practically

rousing when compared with "Oh, Benjamin Harrison," one of the movie's other enervating numbers. All the songs are out of synch. (One needn't be obsessive about this, but a convention that deals in illusions ought to *deal* in them and not leave its characters mouthing.) The movie's romantic leads, Lesley Ann Warren and John Davidson, are carried over from Disney's *The Happiest Millionaire*. Miss Warren has a certain friendly rabbit air, with an intensity about her large, close-set eyes that suggest the rabbit might turn carnivore. Mr. Davidson is not too memorable. There are lots of anachronistically ill-bred children.

Walter Brennan, with lines like "That's enough, grandpa," or "Get back in the house, Grandpa," is constantly being suppressed by his family, and the little children are incessantly being called upon to talk, or simper, or sing. (If movies at the Music Hall can be said to have a subconscious, this one is really about getting rid of the old and having a fear of children.) There are also several uneasy, convictionless patriotic numbers—with talk of unity after fights that divide a nation—which suggest that worry about national ideals is shaking even the values of musicals.

. . . . If You Need Anything,
Just Whistle: Sex

*3-24-68*

Some weeks ago, in trying to see all kinds of movies—in Puerto Rican theaters, college auditoriums, drive-ins—I went to a movie on Forty-second Street called *Censored*. The audience was seated singly, with as many seats as possible separating everybody from everybody else. People arrived and left throughout the movie. There was really not much plot development. When I came in, a thin man on the screen with a thin, threadlike moustache—surrounded at his desk by tiers of tins of celluloid—was discussing the

113

problems of art and censorship. "These next scenes that you will see," he said thoughtfully, "were very important to the continuity of the story." (He was evidently referring to the continuity of some earlier story.) "But they were cut," he said.

A slim teen-age boy in khakis appeared on screen, dragging an apparently unconscious teen-age girl into a furnace room, where, with a furtive look about and a distinctly preoccupied air, he sawed off her leg and threw it into the incinerator. She awakened once, looked down, saw him at work, screamed and passed out again. The narrator with the moustache reappeared, with more reflections upon art and censorship in a free society, and introduced a clip—without subtitles—which he said had been cut from a German film. A rather large, manly woman in Gestapo uniform was asking a younger woman, suspended by her wrists from the ceiling, the names of some American pilots; the older woman had a branding iron. The younger woman fainted. (Some deep strain of kindness in the audience for these films apparently requires that victims be allowed to faint.) At this point—about eight minutes after I had walked in—I left.

My conclusion was that, of the sex and sadism fans who evidently used to frequent the Forty-second Street theaters, the sadism fans still frequent the Forty-second Street theaters. The sex fans go to the same movies as everybody else. I couldn't really verify the first half of this idea (out of a reluctance to return to Forty-second Street) but I do know that of the more than thirty movies that have opened in regular theaters since the first of January, about half have been more frank sexually—verbally and photographically—than would have been possible five years ago; and about three have been as frank as any movies I have ever seen.

I don't really think there is much point in pretending that sex in the movies is a subject like any other—a routine development of the plot, like a shooting, or an element, like damask curtains, of the decor. It is still, fortunately, a fairly high-charged subject for most people and I think a review ought to let them know, just as it would in highly charged questions of religious belief, what sort of movie they are in for. So far this year, there has been one color British working-class movie (*Poor Cow*) with a real birth taking place through the credits. One color British working-class movie (*Up the Junction*) with an *Alfie*-type abortion (abortions in better class British working-class pictures seem to take the place of births with biting on a bullet in serious American westerns). One color British working-class movie (*Here We Go Round the Mulberry Bush*) with a naked love scene. One black-and-white Danish movie (*Venom*) with portions of a pornographic film-within-the-film blocked by great slashing white X's of the Danish censor. (The American censor simply cuts out additional portions inconspicuously.)

There were two movies (*Wild 90* and *Tell Me Lies*) which made use of the whole range of Anglo-Saxon expletives, and one (*The Secret War of Harry Frigg*) that slunk into the Music Hall using only one. There was one *The Fox*) that included heterosexual love, lesbianism and (debatably, no one seems to be quite sure what was going on) masturbation. At the Music Hall again, instead of those interminable seduction-innuendo comedies, there was a movie (*Sweet November*) about a girl who had a different affair each month. (True, she more or less died for it and the movie didn't run very long, but it certainly was an updated Pollyanna or Bobbsey Twins.) There was the (apparently now annual) shot of Elizabeth Taylor's alleged bottom in *Dr. Faustus*. There was an anthology of four Italian sex comedies (*The Queens*). And so on.

Sex has, of course, always been extremely important in movies. Letters protesting the increasing explicitness of it on screen usually express despair over two things, sex and violence, as though they were equally deplorable, or at least comparable. I do not think they are. I think being entertained by the spectacle of protracted physical suffering is, at best, brutalizing. I do not know what being absorbed by the physical contact of people on screen for joy or affection is. Educational, probably. It has always been one of the major functions of movies to arouse lust, and to educate young people in the manners and fantasies of romantic love. I doubt that any axiom is much falser than the one which claims no one has ever been seduced by a book. It seems more likely that everyone has—by a book, or a play or a movie.

But movies can go too far. Not in objective terms—a Victorianism dead is probably always a good thing—but in terms of their own interest. If films become much more explicit, half the reason everyone goes to see them will disappear. Sex is kind of the rabbit in the hat of the industry; once it's completely out, the magician might just as well leave. The great romantic lines and behaviors on screen have always been delicate and allusive. "If you want anything, just whistle," after all, was not a dirty line. And no one will ever build a dream on *The Chelsea Girls*.

Which reminds one about sex comedies. Off-color humor has to be one of the most stylized, formal, controlled kinds of humor there is. Almost completely unphysical. No one can effectively tell a dirty joke with his clothes in disarray. The rolling about in most of *The Queens*—even the sensual aspect of some of the heroines—makes comedy almost out of the question. So does the gross behavior between Zero Mostel and several old ladies in *The Producers*. It is too far removed from the verbal and it is out of control. It does not allow the audience the sense that everything in the world is in order but the last phrase of the comic machine. Joan Rivers will always be able to make an off-color joke funnier than Claudia Cardinale can; and Dustin Hoffman, extending one mechanical hand toward Anne Bancroft, will always be funnier than Zero Mostel rumbling distractingly through an old harem in search of a joke.

.......... *Benjamin*

*3-24-68*

*Benjamin*, which opened yesterday at the Paris Theater, is a sick, stylish libertine farce, in color, set in eighteenth-century France and directed by Michael Deville, whose earlier films were not released in this country. It stars

Pierre Clementi as a young man—somewhere between Tom Jones and Rousseau's Emile—who, at seventeen, rides with his mangy old tutor to the estate of his aunt, where he is to learn the ways of the world. The rest of the movie is a series of attempts to seduce him and Catherine Deneuve, who plays an orphan living with her chaperone on a neighboring estate.

The movie is entirely tongue-in-cheek, a parody on all kinds of seduction comedies. There is a sense of enameled decadence: teeth and jeweled rings and switches torn from trees are always doing minor damage to someone—as elegant tableaux vivants unfold in the French countryside. Miss Deneuve is in love with Michel Piccoli, the lover of Mr. Clementi's aunt, Michele Morgan, who has not been exactly estranged from her nephew, who loves Miss Deneuve, who is not indifferent to him either, or he to his aunt, who is really desperately in love with Michel Piccoli, who loves Miss Deneuve. Not *La Ronde* exactly, but a kind of current that could blow them all either way.

There is really no plot, just a succession of other characters, and flirtations, and falls into the bathtub, and surprises in the garden house, a rather redundant, elaborate tease. The denouement is very odd, quite different in style from the rest of the movie—less formal, in fact, more relenting and natural, and then more sharply satirical than anything that has gone before. The movie's humor is a kind of special taste, like cloves or pepper, or all things polite with a tinge of viciousness.

. . . . . . . . *Psych-Out* and
*Cobra*

3-28-68

*Psych-Out,* which opened yesterday morning at eight to a fairly full house at the Lyric and later at other neighborhood theaters, is a color movie released by American International Pictures, producers of *Beach*

*Blanket Bingo, I Was a Teen-Age Werewolf, The Mask of the Red Death, The Fall of the House of Usher, Wild Angels* and other movies wonderfully suitable for drive-ins.

It has about the most loaded climax imaginable: Susan Strasberg, as a deaf teenage runaway to the Haight-Ashbury, has just been freaked out on STP and nearly seduced by a guru friend of her hippie lover, when she rediscovers her long lost mind-blown brother, who, having been chased by a relentless gang, has barricaded himself in a burning house from which he refuses to come out. She is standing outside. He is standing inside. The drug really begins to take effect. The house is burning. And then, almost casually, the movie decides to forget the whole thing. Very frustrating. Her brother may be burning still.

Nonetheless, the film, directed by Richard Rush, has considerable élan. There is music, including the hit song "Incense, Peppermint," by the Strawberry Alarm Clock and the Seeds. There are a lot of beads and spangles and prisms and fabric and pads. The onturnage and the outfreaking leave room for a lot of surreal and science-fiction effects—although Miss Strasberg's STP delusions are not very imaginative.

What is most interesting, though, is that the demands of plot seem to make it necessary to superimpose the structure of a Western onto hippie life. These hippies take part in chases and fistfights. They are quite brave. One of them, described in the plot outline as "a Negro cynic," saves Miss Strasberg from the gang rape when he is high on pot and imagining himself Sir Galahad. There are some excellent scenes—always on the Western model. Someone breathless at one point announces to the hippie lover (wonderfully acted by Jack Nicholson), as one might announce to a marshal that outlaws are shooting up the saloon, "Warren is freaking out at the gallery." The rescue that follows is very convincingly done. There is an Orpheus-descending quality about it all—even about attending some of the theaters where *Psych-Out* is showing. Dean Stockwell plays the perfidious guru. "I hope," he says, as he lies dying on a highway on a bridge in the half-denouement, "this trip is a good one."

* * *

"Good to see you again," one man says in greeting another at a bar in *Cobra*—the American International Pictures release playing with *Psych-Out* at the Lyric. "Do you still know how to fake documents?"

"I wasn't like this once," a dissolute blonde recalls from the bed, in another piece of straightforward, flat-out exposition, "but little by little . . ."

"Oho," the hero says when he figures something out. "There's no time to waste with recriminations." Another character detects a piece of villainy. "Very clever, these Chinese," he says. "What's that?" a terrified brunette who won't talk asks when the hero lifts a glass bottle with a death's head on it. "Carbolic acid," he replies. "A few drops of this and you're not likely to win the Miss Universe contest." The whole movie is like that, very direct, familiar, self-explicating, poorly made, old fashioned and aimed with great sureness at an existing audience. It takes place in Lebanon. The plot is summed up by the hero in a single sentence. "How they manage to pass the drugs across the mountains and all the way to the sea," he says, "is a mystery."

What is pleasant about this incredibly shoddy, widescreen movie is not its familiar comic book dialogue, but its complete underside-of-the-system view of life. The hero is poor and unjustly suspected of crimes. The villain has a black stocking over his head, which makes him look like a Negro—*and* a German accent. He is rich. There is a lot of racial fear (those clever Chinese), and an awful lot of talk about food. "Let's have lots on the table," the hero says to his girl, "and on us nothing."

It seems really extraordinary that of all the recent movies that everyone who cares about movies is going to see, not one makes any serious effort to move people. I don't mean to engage them morally or politically, or to make them laugh, or to startle them. I mean, to make them care what happens to characters. I cannot think of a character in an important American movie of the past year with whom audiences are able—without irony—to identify. No one seems to cry at movies any more.

I think what has happened is that moviemakers are getting the sympathy that used to go to characters. Nobody seriously identifies with Bonnie and Clyde (in a film which, incidentally, I liked a lot). Nobody cries when they are killed. People care more about Arthur Penn and Warren Beatty and Faye Dunaway, and about the movie itself. Everyone is attuned to, or alienated by, what a movie is trying to do, not moved by what is going on in it. The style of movies has become, in the imagination of many people, what the hero used to be.

In certain cases, playing to this kind of awareness can be a good thing, but something is lost. It reverses the field. The artist's constant risk that his serious work will be laughed at turns into the audience's risk that its sincere involvement will be mocked. Artist and audience reach an understanding that shuts the emotional demands of the characters out. The audience's reward for not being moved any more is a sense of knowingness about what the artist is doing; the filmmaker's is not working too hard and feeling safe.

This complicity makes it possible to enjoy individual movies, even to be ardently in favor of them, but not for one moment to be taken in by their characters. Artist and audience simply agree to look at plot and characters with a certain ironic condescension. I am not sure what we are all laughing at or feeling superior to, but it certainly favors style at the expense of content; and I think all this knowing about style has its price. Style is not substance. The medium is not the message. The message, in point of fact, is the message. And the medium is the medium. Anyone who chooses to take the metaphor as anything more than an interesting light in which to look at things for one instant of time before going about his intellectual businesses (anyone, in fact, who is all McLuhan, and no Wittgenstein, Jakobson, Richards or Levi-Strauss on questions of style and content) is a kind of jerk and just now perhaps even a little dangerous. Since style-substance questions have become, precisely in the last weeks, peculiarly acute in politics, and a vote for substance over style is always the only moral option.

The lack of emotion generated from within movies must be a temporary thing, if only because audiences want so badly to be moved. Not just sentimentally. A film that is beautifully made and thought out—as for example Bergman's classic *Persona* was last year—involves people emotionally by the sheer sustained brilliance of its effort. There were, of course, good sentimental films like *La Guerre est Fini,* and *A Man and a Woman.* People want to lose their awareness of the movie for the characters just briefly, and it seems strange that in the past year or so they have been, in American films at least, by some strange suspension of feeling, unable to do so. Not deplorable. Just strange.

For some actors, used to working very warmly and creatively with theater audiences, something goes quite wrong in movies. For them, the response of a live theater audience is both warming and limiting; it defines a performance. Acting before a camera, on the other hand, is projecting into infinity. No soundings can be taken. There is no baffle. Zero Mostel seems to be that kind of performer. He swims through the celluloid like a great bat or fish without his sonar. The camera seems to affect him as the telephone affects men who do not really believe in it. He roars and overdoes.

This is particularly true in *The Producers.* Every joke, every throw-away line, every serious bit of characterization (and the script is treacherous in this respect, uneven in quality, full of high volume padding, and wavering in degree of seriousness) is played full tilt with stress by a performer who can be marvelous and subtle on the stage. (He can be awful there too, but so can anyone.) On screen, this creates an effect almost of electrical failure. As when a light switch begins to buzz.

The whole movie, from the first moment, is in serious danger of drowning anyway. But one comic routine after another keeps bailing it out until almost the end, when it sinks. It is very much like watching a rowboat in rough waters, with wonderful breaks and terrible accidents. Gene Wilder saves the ship early on, with a comic routine that is absolutely musical. He has been playing an accountant, who looks something like a tall blonde Graduate on the verge of a bip. His comic thing has already announced itself once, with a little paroxysm over "My blanket, my blanket, my blue blanket"—the remnant of a security blanket which he pulls from his pocket. Mostel has a padding line, "Oh, I want that money," and Wilder, who has just fallen on the floor, has a weak response, "Oh, I fell on my keys." Then, the comic routine sets in, like a "Minnie the Moocher" of paranoia. From "You're going to jump on me," through "Don't touch me, don't touch me," "I'm hysterical, I'm hysterical. I'm wet," the whole thing is musical, baroque, resolved. And Mostel playing into it is perfect too.

Later, there are all kinds of hazards. The concierge—pronounced like a relative of demiurge—of the place where the Nazi playwright lives is fine. The Nazi playwright himself, overacted and underwritten, threatens to sink the thing again. Andreas Voutsinas, as the director's slinking lover, in black turtleneck and slipper beard, is marvelous; the director himself is not so fully realized. Dick Shawn, as an enormous aging hippie in musketeer boots, earring, daisies and Campbell Soup Can saves the day again as he auditions for Hitler, with a perfectly done hippie's lament ("I gave flowers to the garbage man/He put my girl in the garbage can"). And so it goes, up and down. Bravura whimsy.

I never thought black comedy of this dilute order could

be made with the word or idea of Hitler in it anywhere. I would have thought the name was still too dark and heavy, and that anything short of an austere, perfectly worked through black comedy would seem poor taste. I was wrong. The musical number of "Springtime for Hitler'" itself, which culminates in a rotating swastika, is hilarious. (It is only something completely talentless, like "Hogan's Heroes" on television, that seems brute vulgarism.) I suppose we will have cancer, Hiroshima and malformity musicals next. This one is so very mixed.

The late Erwin Panofsky, in his famous essay "Style and Medium in the Motion Pictures," compared the movies—their permanence, the enormous amount of patronage and cooperation among participants they require —to the medieval cathedral. Lately, they have been more like the department store or the supermarket. Interesting, but enormously varied in what one finds in them. Only the greatest movies are of a piece.

. . . . . . *A Dandy in Aspic:*
Trying to Play Monotone

*4-3-68*

*A Dandy in Aspic* is a very wobbly spy movie that opened yesterday at Cinema I. Based on a novel by Derek Marlowe, who also wrote the screenplay, this color film begins with shots of a wooden puppet being jerked about through the credits; and Laurence Harvey, who stars as the Russian-British double agent Krasnevin, quite deliberately plays for the wooden effect—keeping his voice dead, his manner stilted and his face empty of any human expression.

Very few actors can play this sort of role, a man whose life has gone flat, without having the performance go monotone as well. It is like people who keep implying that something tragic has happened and, when one asks what is the matter, keep replying, "Oh, nothing." Sooner or later, one loses interest. On the screen such a part requires the support of a very strong, live story. Harvey's is an oh, nothing part in the middle of an oh, nothing movie.

The film itself is very mechanical, right down to the use of Harry Andrews as an official in British intelligence. Harvey is a Russian agent in British intelligence, who has had enough. Harry Andrews gives him the assignment of killing a certain Russian agent in West Berlin. Tom Courtenay, who suspects Harvey of being that agent and wishes him ill, is his partner in the assignment. So is Peter Cook, in a supporting role. Per Oscarsson and Lionel Stander are on the Russian side. Enter Mia Farrow.

She represents youth, mischief, innocence—everything that would draw Harvey into life again—and he falls in love with her. We know this only because it is the convention in movies of this kind. It is no fault of Harvey's or Miss Farrow's; their parts are props. Normally, in the James Bond sort of movie where all the characters are stock, the gadgetry at least is animate. Not here. It is all slow, blank, decorous and completely devoid of suspense.

Mr. Oscarsson (star of the prize-winning Danish movie *Hunger*), whose part includes being a drug addict, does very well in his high scene—pale, intense, perspiring. Tom Courtenay (of *Billy Liar*) is effective, as always, in a part that requires him to show a tense, continuous and somehow pitiable malice. One of the movie's misfortunes is that these two men look a bit alike and that, in their first few scenes, it is difficult to tell them apart. Lionel Stander is wonderfully fat, jovial and malevolent as Harvey's Russian superior. But it is no use. The aspic is bland. Anthony Mann, who produced and directed the movie, died in the course of production, and Laurence Harvey took over the direction for the last few days of shooting.

*4-4-68*

Even the M-G-M lion is stylized and abstracted in Stanley
Kubrick's *2001: A Space Odyssey,* a film in which infinite care, intelligence, patience, imagination and Cinerama have been devoted to what looks like the apotheosis
of the fantasy of a precocious, early nineteen-fifties city
boy. The movie, on which Kubrick collaborated with the
British science-fiction author Arthur C. Clarke, is nominally about the finding, in the year 2001, of a camera-shy
sentient slab on the moon and an expedition to the planet
Jupiter to find whatever sentient being the slab is beaming
its communications at.

There is evidence in the film of Clarke's belief that
men's minds will ultimately develop to the point where
they dissolve in a kind of world mind. There is sub-plot in
the old science-fiction nightmare of man at terminal odds
with his computer. There is one ultimate science-fiction
voyage of a man (Keir Dullea) through outer and inner
space, through the phases of his own life in time thrown
out of phase by some higher intelligence, to his death and
rebirth in what looked like an intergalactic embryo.

But all this is the weakest side of a very complicated,
languid movie—in which almost a half hour passes before
the first man appears and the first word is spoken, and an
entire hour goes by before the plot even begins to declare
itself. Its real energy seems to derive from that bespec-
tacled prodigy reading comic books around the block. The
whole sensibility is intellectual fifties child: chess games,
body-building exercises, beds on the spacecraft that look
like camp bunks, other beds that look like Egyptian mum-
mies, Richard Strauss music, time games, Strauss waltzes,
Howard Johnson's, birthday phone calls. In their space
uniforms, the voyagers look like Jiminy Cricket. When
they want to be let out of the craft they say, "Pod bay
doors open," as one might say "Bomb bay doors open" in
every movie out of World War II.

When the voyagers go off to plot against HAL, the computer, it might be HAL, the camper, they are ganging up on. When HAL is expiring, he sings "Daisy." Even the problem posed when identical twin computers, previously infallible, disagree is the kind of sentence-that-says-of-itself-I-lie paradox, which—along with the song and the nightmare of ganging up—belongs to another age. When the final slab, a combination Prime Mover slab and coffin lid, closes in, it begins to resemble a fifties candy bar.

The movie is so completely absorbed in its own problems, its use of color and space, its fanatical devotion to science-fiction detail, that it is somewhere between hypnotic and immensely boring. (With intermission, it is three hours long.) Kubrick seems as occupied with the best use of the outer edge of the screen as any painter, and he is particularly fond of simultaneous rotations, revolving, and straight-forward motions—the visual equivalent of rubbing the stomach and patting the head. All kinds of minor touches are perfectly done: there are carnivorous apes that look real; when they throw their first bone weapon into the air, Kubrick cuts to a spacecraft; the amiable HAL begins most of his sentences with "Well," and his answer to "How's everything?" is, naturally, "Everything's under control."

There is also a kind of fanaticism about other kinds of authenticity: space travelers look as sickly and exhausted as travelers usually do; they are exposed in space stations to depressing canned music; the viewer is often made to feel that the screen is the window of a spacecraft, and as Kubrick introduces one piece of unfamiliar apparatus after another—a craft that looks, from one angle, like a plumber's helper with a fist on the end of it, a pod that resembles a limbed washing machine—the viewer is always made aware of exactly how it is used and where he is in it.

The special effects in the movie—particularly a voyage, either through Dullea's eye or through the slab and over the surface of Jupiter-Earth and into a period bedroom —are the best I have ever seen; and the number of ways in which the movie conveys visual information (there is very little dialogue) drives it to an outer limit of the visual. And yet the uncompromising slowness of the movie makes it hard to sit through without talking—and people on all sides when I saw it were talking almost throughout the film. Very annoying. With all its attention to detail, a kind of reveling in its own I.Q., the movie acknowledged no obligation to validate its conclusion for those, me for example, who are not science-fiction buffs. By the end, three unreconciled plot lines—the slab, Dullea's aging, the period bedroom—are simply left there like a Rorschach, with murky implications of theology. This is a long step outside the convention. In all that knowingness, something else seems required.

..... .Jean-Luc Godard's
*La Chinoise*

*4-4-68*

*La Chinoise*, which opened yesterday at the Kips Bay Theater, is a kind of color sequel to *Masculine Feminine*, and one of Jean-Luc Godard's best films since *Breathless*. It is about a cell of four or five Maoist students in Paris, and Godard uses the technique of the off-camera, almost inaudible interviewer to produce some of the most sensitive and intelligent work on the new young and the New Left that has ever been done in any medium. The talk in the movie is almost entirely of ideas. (Among other things, it is the first instance I have ever seen of ideology used on screen for characterization.) It makes *Tell Me Lies* seem in retrospect a more false, pretentious and even derivative little talk idyll than it seemed at the time.

The question at the heart of the movie is the one at the center of the new radicalism: are things bad enough to make it worth dismantling everything and starting at zero? The young Maoists, more influenced by the idea of Götterdämmerung than perhaps they know, are for burning down and starting over. Anne Wiazemsky, who plays the young lady Maoist of the title, plans to begin by blowing up the Sorbonne and the Louvre. Jean-Pierre Léaud plays her boyfriend (whom Godard, without dwelling on it, calls

127

Guillaume Meister, after Goethe's hero). He also plays an actor—all the characters seem more or less on the verge of playing themselves—very much preoccupied with another problem at the heart of the new radicalism: the relation between politics and theater. In one of the most dramatically effective moments of the movie—which incorporates the printed word in some extraordinarily interesting ways—Léaud approaches a list of the names of several columns of distinguished writers and erases them one by one, leaving only Brecht. It comes with the shock one might get from the image of Miss Wiazemsky's projected bombing.

There are all sorts of conversations, conversations about making a revolution for the people in spite of themselves, love conversations, suicide conversations, lectures with pauses and repetitions for notetakers in the cell, readings from Mao, a Mao rock song, talks of sincerity and violence. Godard interrupts them with slides of comic strips, slides of engravings of Alice in Wonderland, and slides of commentary. (From several movies lately, it seems film titles, in new forms, are coming back.) There is one almost Socratic conversation between La Chinoise and the famous old French leftist, Francis Jeanson.

But what Godard has caught, in absolutely pure, flat beautiful photography, is the look of these young who are so caught up in the vocabulary of the class struggle of a class to which they do not belong—the look of hurt and intelligence and gentleness quite at odds with what they are saying. (When La Chinoise finally kills a man or two, it seems almost absent-minded.) Also—through something as banal in transcription as clasped hands, or three on a bed, or communal exercises in the morning—the special quality of intimacy between them.

In a way, La Chinoise is the perfect companion piece to Gillo Pontecorvo's The Battle of Algiers. In both films, the sensibility of director and cast is somehow completely gentle, completely fair, and completely engaged. It is as though the cell of children from La Chinoise convenes while The Battle of Algiers goes on. And both films, in a half-documentary, more than half-poetic spirit, permit people to be as complicated as they are.

128

*4-5-68*

Using nonprofessional actors on the screen is a bit like collecting found objects on a shelf—it is personal, it relies a lot on felicitous accident, and it puts a burden on people who are asked to admire them. Pier Paolo Pasolini directs a nonprofessional cast in *Accattone!* his first and, so far, best film, the story of a young Italian procurer. The result is uneven, but not without distinction. It opened yesterday at the Fifth Avenue Cinema.

The sensibility of the film is religious, effete, Italian Communist. Baroque music accompanies streetwalkers and street fights and, although the film is without any humor, or power, or bitterness—one does not really care about the characters, none of whom even has an interesting face—Pasolini's direction has a certain squalid lyricism. Accattone, played by Franco Citti, lives off the earnings of his mistress, Silvana Corsini. He is accorded all the sneaking respect that men of the really lowest classes in Latin countries can have for a man who does not need to work for a living.

When his mistress is arrested he becomes, as the publicity notes to the film so distinctively put it, "destitute without a prostitute." He starves for a while, falls in love (with Franca Pasut) and decides to work. The work lasts a day. He becomes a thief and comes to grief.

Scenes of streetwalkers waiting to be picked up in the night were done better in *Nights of Cabiria* and some other things were done better in *Rocco and His Brothers,* but what is interesting about *Accattone!* is the lightness of it. Lightness not in the sense of frivolity, but in the sense of a very curious absence of passion. Part of this seems to have been imposed on Pasolini by the frailness of his central character; when Accattone steals a religious medal

129

from around the neck of his own small son, the act has no moral overtones at all and a scene in which Accattone goes back to eat an entire meal, of which he has cheated his friends, apparently had to be cut. Citti simply will not support a sense of tragedy. But, after a very halting start and some well-done scenes of Roman street life, the movie somehow goes incandescent in an innocent, religious way.

What seems to happen is that the picture becomes softer as it goes along; the camera cannot help taking on Accattone's respect for idleness and it is made quite clear that his poverty is the result not of social injustice but of an extreme distaste for manual work. There is also a sentimentality about the innocence of women. It is a strangely mixed leftism that regards with fondness—not as exploited, or as parasitic, but as poetic and tender—thieves and prostitutes, the two most decidedly capitalist métiers in the world. The first prostitute in the film is called Maddalena.

. . . . . . . . . .Drive-Ins:
To Park and Get Protection

*4-7-68*

Of the approximately 18,000 movie theaters in the United States, nearly a third are drive-ins. No one can be certain exactly how many drive-ins there are, because the Texas Drive-In Theater Owners Association (which is, for some reason, the only drive-in association that exists) has 700 members from all over the country, with no clear record of how many drive-ins they own, or how many anyone else owns either. The fact is, though, that particularly in the spring (although drive-ins now stay open all winter long), almost every evening after dark one great American industry goes out to pay homage to another: automobiles assemble in the fields in the night before the screen at the drive-ins.

Every American city is surrounded along the outer edge

of its highways by thin radial wisps of drive-in theaters—there are thirty-seven, by my count, within an evening's drive of New York. As cities expand, property values force the screens further into the countryside; and one of the strangest sights of our time and place (very few other countries, except Australia and Canada, have many drive-ins) must be riding along a highway on a summer night and finding the enormous image of a movie star projected against the dark. With the great screens illuminating the landscape, the countryside seems to be taking part in some vast electronic druid ceremony.

The first drive-in was built in 1934, by R. H. Hollinshead, a machine parts manufacturer in Camden, New Jersey. He rooted up a parking lot behind his shop and originated what became known as the graded drive-over ramp—which enabled cars to park in tiers of semicircles facing a screen, with their front wheels up on a ramp that allowed the occupants to see over the cars in front of them. He patented his idea and rented franchises to local operators, mainly in the South and West. But, his grading patent was soon called into question, and the courts ruled that his ramp idea was as old as the Roman amphitheater—and that he could not, in any case, patent the formation of the earth.

The drive-in in its early years faced several problems: the speakers used to blast so loud that neighbors as far as two miles away were bringing suit; the film companies simply would not rent the drive-ins good pictures; and the clientele of drive-ins was such that, in the words of a former president of the Texas Drive-In group, "couples used to pay a fee just to park and get protection." The sound problem was eventually solved with in-car speakers. In 1938, MGM became the first film company to sell regular-run pictures to drive-in theaters. And by admitting children free (and thereby eliminating even a babysitting problem), the drive-ins ultimately gained something of a young family reputation.

There are many Spanish drive-ins near the Rio Grande and in El Paso and San Antonio. There are drive-ins that play first run or even art movies (*Blow-Up* was the greatest success in the history of some of the Texas drive-

131

ins) in summer, and sex and sadism movies in the winter, when business falls off. Owners are drawn together over zoning, access, censorship, taxes, film distribution, concessions (ranging from pizza to croquet, which now bring in most of the average drive-in's profits) and a relentless opposition to Daylight Saving Time. Sunlight and fog are still the special nightmares of the drive-in theater.

The experience of the drive-in seems to lie somewhat between those of the regular movie and the television set. Customers are as cut off from the audience at large as families isolated in their living rooms, and yet it is a conventional movie they are watching and they have to leave their houses to go to it. I suppose a drive-in is most unsuited to comedy (as television, with or without canned laughter, is) because the audience has none but the most surreal sense of community. It is difficult to laugh when everyone is motorized and encapsulated.

On the other hand, drive-in theaters are especially receptive to action movies. An action movie, according to James H. Nicholson, head of American International Pictures—which made such drive-in hits as *Wild Angels*, the beach party films, *I Was a Teen-age Werewolf* and so on—is a movie in which no more than twenty five minutes out of eighty are talking minutes. As the soap opera is suited to the housewife, who can leave her set for minutes or days on end and return to find the plot not incomprehensibly advanced, the action picture is suited to the people in the car. (The soap opera is the reverse of the action picture in this respect. The talk-action ratio is turned around.) Some of A.I.P.'s action pictures have been so popular at drive-ins that old releases are brought back to play as co-features with new ones two or three times. The western on motorcycles has become a special tradition of the drive-in crowd.

The fortunes of drive-ins have gone up and down quite a bit in their thirty years of respectability. During the war, naturally, hardly any were built. After the war, until 1951, many were. The television boom in the early fifties cut them down again, and thousands of little town drive-ins folded. In recent years, they have been doing better than the indoor theaters. In fact, it is largely the drive-ins which are responsible for the fact that, whereas in the old days, Christmas and early winter were the best time for releasing movies, there is now a summer boom. But indoor theaters in shopping centers are making inroads, and then there is always the possibility that drive-ins may one day be superseded by the—altogether inauthentic and isolating—experience of the inflight motion picture.

...... Ingmar Bergman's
*Hour of the Wolf*

*4-10-68*

The hour of the wolf is that hour of night when most phantoms are at large and fears of the unknown grow, and in *Hour of the Wolf*, which opened yesterday at the 34th Street East, Ingmar Bergman takes on again, as he did in *Persona*, the power of one person's insanity or silence over another. Silence, especially among beings (God, for example) who have populated worlds of their own without offering the key to them, has occupied Bergman for a long time. This time, he populates the screen with a few of his own apparitions, some of whom—notably a 216-year-old lady with a parasol—are quite charming. Others are disgusting or terrifying. And then he himself is silent, or at least only raises the question, whether these characters exist or not.

The movie begins with a black screen, and titles telling what it is about. (The written word becomes more and more important in films as it accustoms the eye incidentally to moving about the screen, instead of being passively receptive to it.) The story concerns an artist, Max von Sydow, who goes with his pregnant wife to a hut on an island—where he goes mad and vanishes, leaving his diary. The wife, played by Liv Ullmann, remains on the island and—in a very long monologue spoken directly to the audience—continues the story where the titles leave off. Then, the movie of their time together begins.

133

Von Sydow's sanity is disintegrated under the pressure of an old erotic obsession, a real or imaginary memory of the murder of a small boy, the limitless tactlessness of some real or imaginary characters at a neighboring château, and the demons who—when he is painting, or at the hour of the wolf—appear to him. His wife, out of love, grows to share a little of his madness; some of his apparitions appear to her, too, and at the end of the movie she wonders whether her failure to accept all of them was a failure of love. With the ambiguity about whether the apparitions can be said objectively to exist or not—the camera, after all, presents them as ontologically there—the implication is that a failure to accept them would be a failure to responsiveness to Bergman on the audience's part.

And it would. It takes great power for an artist to win through to the edge of madness, suicide, memory and guilt so continuously as Bergman does and come back with so much that seems familiar, out of an old dream or an old nightmare. Bergman works where people's nightmares converge. The acting, of course, by Von Sydow, Miss Ullmann and Ingrid Thulin, as the object of his former love, is too good to be apparent, and some of the images—the arrival by motorboat of Von Sydow and Miss Ullmann on the desolate shore of the island, Von Sydow running his hand over a naked body he believes to be a corpse, Miss Thulin's legs gradually appearing down from the upper left edge of the screen as she runs to meet him—are as memorable as anything from Bergman's earlier films. The circus performer's rescue of his naked wife in *The Naked Night* and the procession in *The Seventh Seal* come to mind.

There is also a very eccentric kind of humor. Von Sydow, on his way to Miss Thulin, sees another character walk across a floor and up a wall. "It's only my jealousy," the character says, "Please go away." One scene, in which a lady dismantles her face when she takes off her hat, is very strongly repellent, and it might be a good idea to look away for a few seconds when it begins. *Hour of the Wolf* is not one of Bergman's great films but it is unthinkable for anyone seriously interested in movies not to see it.

4-11-68

"You ain't fightin' proper," a minor character says to Charlton Heston as the hero of *Will Penny*, which opened yesterday at the R.K.O. Coliseum, on Broadway and 181st Street, and other neighborhood theaters. "You're the one that's down," Heston replies.

The movie, which is set in Montana in winter, shows cowboys as they probably were—mumbling, fairly foul-mouthed, warmly dressed, sleeping uncomfortably in their underwear, ready to fight over a killed elk, eager to go to Kansas City to see an elephant—and the frontier as it probably was, mean, bleak, sparsely populated with a few unattractive women, and a few ragged packs of dangerous religious fanatics—one of whom, who is out to kill Will Penny, is played with terrifying piety by Donald Pleasence.

But for one scene too cruel for the story to support, and one scene in which the hero is taught Christmas carols too maudlin to believe, *Will Penny* might have been the best cowboy movie in some time. But by some mistaken model of artistic integrity—taken, probably, from *Shane,* or some other movie better than *Will Penny* is—this movie has a realistically unhappy ending. It is simply not good enough to support that either.

The R.K.O. Coliseum is one of the most handsome movie theaters in New York. It is well kept, and it has a lovely oval opening, surrounded with a wooden railing, from which it is possible to look down from the balcony onto the first floor.

*4-12-68*

*The Young Girls of Rochefort,* a musical that opened yesterday at the Cinema Rendezvous, is another of those strange, off-beat movies produced by Mag Bodard in which a conventional, gay form is structured over what would be, in its terms, a catastrophe. In *Le Bonheur,* it was a happy young marriage in which the husband's happiness was immeasurably increased by his wife's suicide. In *Benjamin,* it was a seduction of innocents, in which the girl slept with the right man all right, but fell and stayed in love with an aging roué. In *The Young Girls of Rochefort,* directed by Jacques Demy, who directed *The Umbrellas of Cherbourg* (also produced by Miss Bodard), a musical takes place in a town where soldiers continuously march, where the headlines are bleaker every day, and where a sadistic killer is part of the happy cast. It has again that air of a fleecy inferno or a frosted concentration camp.

The movie has the sisters Catherine Deneuve and the late Françoise Dorleac playing twins who run a ballet school in Rochefort and who dream of meeting their ideal men; Gene Kelly and Jacques Perrin, as men in Rochefort who dream of meeting their ideal girls; Danielle Darrieux, as the girls' unmarried mother, who dreams of meeting again the love of her youth (whom she did not marry because his name was Monsieur Dame), and Michel Piccoli, who dreams of meeting the love of his youth (who did not marry him on account of his name). There are many strange songs, and dances and contretemps. Some of the best dancing, again, is by Grover Dale, in a minor part; even his hair joins in the general elegance with which he moves. There is a lot of witty, high elegant and absurdist dialogue and some terrible puns. The movie is in French (in which Kelly does admirably), but the sub-titles, in an attractive kind of lettering, are discreet and excellent. The music, by Michel Legrand, is sometimes funny, sometimes undistinguished, and sometimes just lovely. There are always those soldiers and that sadistic killer, of course, which give the whole movie a fine, eccentric, pastel, and dreamlike irony.

......... Horror Films,
Bergman and
*Belle de Jour*

*4-14-68*

An interesting problem in movies is to make some serious use of the almost automatic powers of the horror film. The fear aroused by horror movies is unrelated to fears of any practical kind. It is an uncanny, almost metaphysical dread—as different from ordinary fears as a toothache or a bruised nerve can be from other pains, no matter how intense. It is not a question of violence. *M* was a horror movie; *Point Blank* was not. (There have been no real gangster, war or western horror films.) It is rather a matter of easy access to metaphysical terrors—composed in part of the fear of insanity, in part of the fear of death. The quintessential horror situation is the imminence of death at the hands of someone—a person, a monster, a world of oneself—gone insane.

The mechanics of horror movies (lighting, timing, music) have been perfected over the years to a point where they startle irresistibly, not with brutality or gore, but with the sneaking sudden, portentous unknown. They are not unlike the mechanics of comedy: a spiral of attention, expectation, suspense, shock, then attention coiled at a higher pitch; the horror reflex is often a kind of laughter. Almost any filmmaker with an eye for shadows and a macabre soundtrack has access to that reflex now. The problem is what serious use, apart from the ordinary horror film's test of audience nerve, to make of it.

Movies of the last ten days have been so incomparably

better than all but one or two in the preceding months that they might have been made in a different medium—as in fact (if music can be said to be a different medium from homogenized droning in elevators, or novels from toy catalogues) they were. What the recent films, as varied in style, level, and content as Bergman's *Hour of the Wolf*, Buñuel's *Belle de Jour*, Godard's *La Chinoise*, Kubrick's *2001: A Space Odyssey* and even the musical *The Young Girls of Rochefort*, have in common is something that might be called the inward camera—the camera turned upon the mind of an author, or of characters, so that what reality there is is interior; the world on screen is personal, a fantasy or a convergence of fantasies. It is not the outside world.

It could be argued, of course, that this is true of every non-documentary film ever made, that even a film as "exterior" and panoramic as *Ben Hur* was just as interior to the mind of its director as, say, *Persona*—now playing again at several New York theaters—was to Ingmar Bergman and his characters. I think, though, that there is an obvious difference between the introspective and the panoramic camera; and that just now, in the hands of several directors, the inward camera is doing its most interesting work.

Ingmar Bergman's *Hour of the Wolf* is a horror film, but since he uses the power of the form so responsibly, it may not always affect people that way. The director has tapped around again in his mind, and whether the images of death and insanity, a personal world out of phase, strike home with the force of *déjà vu* depends on what your metaphysical fears are like. As in *Persona*, there is the story of a stronger soul losing its sanity—partly by choice—and drawing a weaker soul into its derangement. In this case the couple, played by Liv Ullmann and Max von Sydow, are husband and wife; and the husband's sanity is dissolving in an old erotic obsession, images of the real or imaginary murder of a child, and some private demons who—late at night or when he is painting on the cliffs by the sea—appear to him.

As in *Persona*, the weaker and essentially more loving character wants to enter another's private world, and is

138

rebuffed mainly with silence. "(I want to grow so old that we know each other's thoughts," Miss Illmann says. One of the demons warns, "Dreams can be made known"). But a difference between the films is the position the movie puts the viewer in.

In *Persona* the viewer begins on the side of a small boy reaching out his hand and then, as it were, follows the camera around the boy's hand and into the screen. Once there, he is asked only to believe in the boy's mother's insanity, not to enter it. In *Hour of the Wolf*, he begins as a listener being addressed by Miss Ullmann directly, in a long, straightforward monologue. If he accepts what follows, if the demons with which Bergman this time populates the screen have any power for him, then he is dominated by the movie's world as Miss Ullmann was by von Sydow's. It is an invitation and an expression of force: to take on an author's and a character's insanity.

Bergman's *Hour of the Wolf* is not as inventive as his *Persona* or as beautiful as his *The Seventh Seal*, but it has moments of beauty and humor and it simply depends whether it gets to you. Luis Buñuel's second color movie, *Belle de Jour*, is the most funny and complicated he has ever made. It is not simply a matter of people trying to enter each other's fantasies. It is nearly impossible to establish, after only one viewing, whose fantasy the entire cryptogram is in.

Buñuel's particular combination of religion, decay, and morbid eroticism has never been my absolutely favorite kind of cinema—although *Viridiana* was great, and people who say they have an interest in the arts, "if only the subject matter were not so depressing," are of a particularly philistine order of square. But with *Belle de Jour*, somehow, letting the color in—this is Buñuel's second color film—has changed the emotional quality of his obsessions in a completely unpredictable way. All these clean, lovely, well-dressed people preparing for the unspeakable practices are very attractive; and *Belle de Jour* is, among other things, Buñuel's first true comedy.

The story begins as though it were about a lovely but sexually unresponsive young woman, Catherine Deneuve, whose husband, Jean Sorel, takes her out in a horse-drawn coach to the woods, where he has her whipped and leaves her to his coachmen. But the lash leaves no mark at all, and when Miss Deneuve, from her bed in a Paris apartment, tells her husband she has been having her coach fantasy again, one assumes the rest of the film is either real or takes place in her mind.

After hearing from a middle-aged philanderer the address of a small brothel in Paris, she begins to go there secretly almost every afternoon until five. At the brothel—a wonderfully middle-class household, run by a very kind, sensitive madam, played to perfection by Geneviève Page—Miss Deneuve, who takes the name Belle de Jour, accommodates a series of gentlemen of eccentric tastes: a jolly, but obligingly sadistic spherical candy manufacturer, an amiable single-minded Japanese, who hopes to pay with his credit card. Just as one thinks the whole movie is about to become a dreary series of sex tableaux by Jean Genet, a customer—a gynecologist in bellboy uniform, with whip—whose tastes we think we already fully understand, demands an inkwell. The movie becomes comic again. One afternoon in the park, she meets a duke, who takes her home to lay her out in a coffin and cry over her. ("*Que voulez-vous,*" he says as though he were the most conventional man in the world, "*je suis un homme d'une autre époque.*")

Pierre Clementi, as a zoot-suited, cap-toothed young gangster with whom Miss Deneuve falls kind of in love, is marvelous; a grotesque parody of every young hero, Jean-Paul Belmondo in *Breathless* included, out of the "milieu." And since, in the cinema daydream convention, almost anything goes, Buñuel is able to put in any number of sequences—a thundering herd of bulls, one of which is named Expiation while all the rest are called Remorse, a child's refusing the sacrament—that have less of the ring of false profundity to them, since they appear in the minds of his characters this time, and not necessarily in Buñuel's own.

Near the end, the young gangster shoots her husband, out of jealousy. The movie takes two turns more, and suddenly nothing is clear, certainly not who has imagined what. But there have been clues all along—characters speaking with motionless lips or uttering nonsense syllables, a recurrence of the original coachmen at the house of the duke, countless references to and mewings of cats, and the fact that the duke's favorite cat's name is Belle de l'Ombre, bells, children subjected to lechery, references to pardon and remorse, chimes, an incessant ticking or viewing of clocks and an occasional retrogression in time, storms, unlikely doors in a hospital ward, and a premonitory view of a wheelchair. The gangster's bullets leave no mark. One is tempted to assume either that Belle has imagined the whole thing, or that she imagines her husband's recovery at the end, or that she has imagined at least some of it.

But the absolute end throws everything in doubt, and it becomes most likely that the whole thing has transpired in the mind of her sleeping husband. The conclusion is inescapable that it was all his fantasy. Or that it was her fantasy that it was his. Until bells, cats, the chiming of five and, finally, a window from their Paris balcony leading out—as it could not conceivably in fact—into the original woods, remind one that the mind is ultimately Buñuel's, and that he can use the inward camera—and restructure the narrative or metaphysical world on film—as he likes.

...... *The* Underground
*Illiac Passion*

*4-19-68*

*The Illiac Passion,* which opened yesterday at the Film-makers' Cinémathèque, 125 West 41st Street, is a film straight out of the most bloodless element of the New York underground. Starring Jack Smith as Orpheus, Andy Warhol as Poseidon, Gerard Malanga as Ganymede, Taylor Meade as Demon or Sprite, Richard Beauvais as Prometheus, and David Beauvais as His Conscience, the film (garbled from a translation of *Prometheus Bound*)

141

was directed by Gregory Markopoulos, who also narrates the unfortunate script.

"I, I, I, I," the narration begins, "contemplate far bounding earth"—and so forth. "Mist has come surcharged with tears looking upon. Mist has come surcharged with tears looking upon. Mist has come surcharged with tears looking upon," etc. "Mind piercing fear disturbs." "Knowing necessity is a resistless strength." "Not weeping in images but in simple speech." "This oracle is not easy to be guessed." Markopoulos reads all this, an hour and a half of it, in a completely loud, toneless, regionlessly accented voice—which makes words like "mortal," "endure," "soften" an agony of mispronunciation. It seems to be a case of being so alienated from language, not knowing how to use it or speak it, that there is a delusion of mastery to the point of poetry.

The visual work is not much either. The camera, which hardly ever moves from side to side, for the most part zooms in and out in a kind of sucking motion. Markopoulos edits mainly from single frames, a technique that has no demonstrable advantages. What is in the frames is people with boneless, uninteresting faces; naked bodies (mostly male) photographed with a remarkable infelicity of line; a few lovely Oriental landscapes; a number of superimpositions of one shot upon another, a kind of heaped, agglomerate photography. No style, not even the freshness of an amateur. There are a lot of shots of veined foreheads, however, and underground personalities filmed in their entirety. The movie is in color. Markopoulous himself, whose *Twice a Man* was awarded the Prix Lambert at the Third National Experimental Film Competition in 1964 in Knokke-le-Zoute, Belgium, appears several times.

*4-21-68*

There is probably something to be said for nearly every-thing boring except boring movies. Boring people, boring books (boring criticism, certainly), boring days—all of them are likely to have something decent, restful or even liberating about them. Boredom in politics on a global scale might be utopian. The problem with movies that are just plain boring is that—unlike other forms, which leave the attention free to wander elsewhere—movies impose upon our attention even when they have failed to gain it. There is no way to think of other things at a movie or to lay a movie aside for a moment and pause. The only way to disengage yourself from a movie you are bored by is to leave it.

The year 2001 is a year that most people alive in the United States today have a highly reasonable expectation of living through and yet it seems fairly clear that one of the things Stanley Kubrick was not trying to do in this space fantasy, *2001: A Space Odyssey,* was to make some sort of cautionary projection into the future on the model of *1984.* The only thing different about Kubrick's trav-elers thirty-three years from now—bored, haggard, sus-pended, completely estranged from all people stationed in one place—is that they travel farther and that their machines both serve them better and frighten them more. The only real story development—that is, the only one that Kubrick did not abandon, either out of lapse of in-terest or lack of time, to the extent of leaving it unin-telligible—is a secondary story about a conflict between two astronauts and their computer HAL. In expiring, HAL sings "Daisy"—which, I am told, is the song with which an original computer was programed in 1956. It is the "Daisy" sort of detail, an absolute mania for authenticity in small things, which—aside from the fact that the spe-cial effects, the tremendous sense of space and mystery,

143

are the finest I have ever seen—accounts for the very special sort of boring fascination in *2001*.

In the major plot, apparently (and the word "Odyssey" in the film's title would seem to confirm this), the astronaut, Keir Dullea, returns at the end to earth—which he saves from destruction and where he is born again. None of this is contradicted by the movie. On the other hand, none of it is clear in it either. Nor is anything about the exceedingly beautiful ending. Or about the slabs in general. It is as though Kubrick himself had become so rapt in the details of his fantasy that he lost track of, or interest in, the point of it all. It is the sort of thing that might happen to HAL. Or to Dullea, as he passed through the fantastically beautiful corridor of the slab. Perhaps it is what happened in the Creation of the universe we actually inhabit: someone got fascinated with the details of it and lost track of the central idea. It is a bit like three hours of Tolkien without the ring.

One of the authentic details that Kubrick has lavished attention on is boredom—the almost cosmic boredom of space travel. (There are so many shots of bored people exercising in the centrifuge that one rather suspects it was not just a question of authenticity here but a matter of having spent so much money building the centrifuge that the filmmakers felt they had to make some use of it.) But the fact that something is boring in reality is not a justification for making it so in art. It is a bit like the question of what we might call self-addressed polemics: self satirizing satires, cruel works that try to draw attention to the phenomenon of cruelty, mindless polemics against mindlessness, boring tracts about boredom. It will not do. One of the things that Kubrick has left out of his movie to a truly astonishing extent is people. It is about a half hour before anything but marvelous apes, tapirs, landscapes and machinery appears, and about an hour before the main human characters arrive. Perhaps it is this that makes it possible to watch the movie idly, with lapses of attention, as one might look at a painting or listen to music. It is one of the rare movies that ignores one, and therefore, when it is not fascinating, leaves one free as movies normally do not.

*La Chinoise*, Godard's color sequel to *Masculine Feminine* is a movie about the Maoist young, which manages to
enter so deeply and interestingly into their frame of mind
that the least dramatic moment in the movie is its most active—two murders—and the most dramatic moments are
claspings of hands, conversations, interviews, lectures,
written titles and pantomimes. If *Masculine Feminine* was
about the generation of Marx and Coca Cola, then *La
Chinoise* shows—through four or five completely lost, ar-
rogant, dangerous and gentle young people—the generation of Freud, Mao, Camus and Hemingway.

The private world here is a party cell of modern revolutionaries—who find the Club Méditerranée indistinguishable from concentration camps, who want to dynamite the
Sorbonne for some purpose which they think is not really
their concern, who believe rather poetically in the process
of revolution and upheaval as an end in itself. They are
people with whom the events of recent months all over the
world make it clear that their elders will have to deal.

Godard portrays them ambivalently, seriously and
humorously in pure, flat, beautiful photography. There is
something orphaned about this international fraternity of
the young—and something which does not distinguish too
clearly between art and reality, theater and politics. Some
of the techniques which Godard uses in this film—
parables, slides, ambivalences about what is script and
what is spontaneity—bridge these distinctions as imaginatively as film has ever done. It is one of Godard's best,
most subtle, difficult and lovely films.


*The Young Girls of Rochefort* doesn't belong in this piece
at all—except for its absolutely stubborn refusal to con-
cede anything to any reality but its own. It wants to be a
musical, even with Gene Kelly in it, and if the world
includes wars and sadists, it will simply include them too,
without losing anything of its gaiety on their behalf.
Everyone in the movie dreams of meeting everyone else in
it, and does. It is a matter of happily coinciding fantasies.

And punning phrases. And velvet suits and men who cut out paper dolls, and girls who compose very familiar-sounding concertos, and everyone at a dinner party speaks in Alexandrines (the movie is in French, with discreet and excellent sub-titles).

It is the world where everyone still danced and took piano lessons, superimposed on a world in which a killer hacks a lady apart and rearranges her parts (according to one lilting song in the score) "with discernment." Made by Jacques Demy, director of *Umbrellas of Cherbourg,* it has a quality of fey, dilute and candy-coated Brecht. It is really no more an escape from what exists than the party cell or the spacecraft or the daydream or the insanity or all the private, encapsulated worlds the films of the last two weeks have drawn us into. Or any less hellish, for all its color and gaiety, either.

....... Lucille Ball and
Henry Fonda in
*Yours, Mine and Ours:*
Don't Look at Me.
I Just Got Here

*4-25-68*

*Yours, Mine and Ours,* which opened yesterday at the Astor and the 86th Street East, is a leering, uncertain, embarrassing, protracted little comedy—neatly divided into television intercommercial periods, each terminated by an abysmal, inevitable joke—quite anti-sex and pro-compulsive procreation. It stars Lucille Ball, as a widowed mother of eight in San Francisco, Henry Fonda, as the widowed father of ten, Van Johnson as a bachelor friend of the family, and eighteen not altogether saccharine children. When Miss Ball is free to cut loose with voice and facial expression from the demands of the script—in a flirting or a drunk scene, for example—she is very funny; and when Mr. Fonda has pins in his

146

mouth—hemming the skirt of his five-year-old—he brings the calm of his presence to the infinite incompetence that keeps buffeting the entire movie. Van Johnson also does his best. But nothing can keep this old-fashioned comedy all right.

For one thing, although it is only an inflated *Cheaper by the Dozen* superimposed on a spoken *Sound of Music* and variations on a scene from *Divorce American Style*, it keeps peeking out from behind its fingers into modern times—drawn to the serious realities of the present in a schizoid, pretentious, and hypocritical way. Mr. Fonda, who is by profession a navy officer, goes on a merry little off-California cruise, for example, on, of all things, the nuclear-powered aircraft carrier *Enterprise*; his eighteen-year-old son is drafted; yet there is absolutely no indication in the film that the country is not at peace. There are serious little sermons—pro-virginity, anti-long hair—and a scene with a nun in a parochial school; and yet the film can't resist all sorts of sleazy dirty lines, and coy bedroom scenes and smily, hesitant conversations about puberty, which would (one hopes) alienate just that audience that might enjoy a good, old-fashioned comedy about the logistical problems of raising eighteen children in a middle-class, modern American family.

Strangely enough, though the film lingers with infinite patience on the things it ought to drop, although the pacing is slow and every punchline declares itself a mile away, there are one or two swift, absurdist touches: a scene in which a little boy shakes his sibling's ant farm, shouting "I hate ants," passes almost before one realizes what he is shaking. A piece of dialogue in a crowded bar in which Miss Ball keeps rehearsing the line "I have eight children," and an absolute stranger turns to her and says, "Don't look at me. I just got here," goes by very fast. Then the camera dwells drearily and forever on the fact that Miss ball is losing her slip.

*4-26-68*

*Les Carabiniers,* which opened yesterday at the New Yorker Theater and Bleecker Street Cinema, is a film of such extraordinary and understated brilliance that it advances the possibilities of film a step. It is an allegory of two men, two women and war, and since it is predictable what course such an allegory must take, one wonders what Jean-Luc Godard, who directs, and Roberto Rossellini and Jean Gruault, who collaborated with him on the script (based on a play by Benjamin Joppolo), can possibly bring to it. What they bring, finally, is a comment that works both at the allegorical level and at the real—on war, symbols, the quality of modern life and the meaning of photography.

The movie opens with titles scrawled, black on white, and a quotation from the great Argentine writer Jorge Luis Borges on "worn metaphors"—which, as it turns out, disarms any criticism one might subsequently wish to make of the film. Then, there are shots of a car advancing, with one headlight burning, across a bleak, flat landscape to a single, isolated hut. Two carabiniers get out and deliver to Michelangelo and Ulysses—two brothers who live with their wives, Cleopatra and Venus, in the hut—a "letter from the king," which asks them to go to war.

Michelangelo, the cigar-chomping, weathered older brother (played by Albert Juross on the order of a character from *Tobacco Road*) is impressed by the king's expression of friendship and the prospect of spoils—particularly a Maserati—which the carabiniers offer him. Ulysses, a subliterate spastic (played by Marino Mase, rather on the order of C. W. Moss in *Bonnie and Clyde*) looks forward to the "mozibilisation," for the opportunity to steal juke boxes, to break old men's glasses and children's arms, etc. Venus and Cleopatra (played by Geneviève Galéa and Catherine Ribéro), like characters nine tenths of the way between Gelsomina and the mad fat

lady on the beach in *8 1/2*, draw up battle shopping lists. (Godard's lists and inventories are always fantastically selective and intelligent.)

The men send postcards back from the front: "There is no victory, only flags and men falling," but what happens to them there is simultaneously so inventive and inevitable that one begins, by degrees, to trust Godard absolutely. There is a very daring and yet offhand scene in which the brothers, now carabiniers themselves, shoot a young blonde Marxist as she is coolly reciting a long, beautiful poem by Mayakovsky. And then there are scenes just as impressive purely pictorially—a Beckett-charged bleakness and austerity over all. The photography is by Raoul Coutard, who did *Breathless, Jules and Jim, Shoot the Piano Player* and *La Chinoise*.

The film gets better and better as it goes along, but a very few lapses into the banal (those "worn metaphors") keep the audience wondering whether Godard is going to bring off the turning point and how. The conclusion —what the men bring back from the war—is one of the most impressive sequences in any movie ever. There have been intimations all along—the relationships between the carabiniers and art objects of various kinds—but what they do bring home is no less than Godard's complete pictorial inventory of Western civilization. It is entirely casual, ironic, selective, deep and true. It is about man and film. Yet it holds at the level of bubble-gum wrappers and trading cards. Almost the entire movie is like that.

. . . . . . . On Short Films

*4-28-68*

One of the best and most popular kinds of film—and the only one in current danger of becoming as extinct as the silent and the non-propaganda newsreel—is the honest, non-advertising short. There is a highly perceptible murmur of enthusiasm whenever the titles for a film of less

than feature length appear on screen and yet, more and more in recent years, audiences are being disappointed with what turn out to be advertisements, concealed or overt, for oils, telephones, machinery, travel to South Africa, or something else. Or no short film at all. The reasons are simple and obtuse.

Independent firms make advertising shorts—or pay the major studios to make and put their imprimatur on them—and then lease them to distributors for nothing, or for far less than the makers of legitimate shorts could afford to lease them for. Sometimes, after a few days, theaters cut shorts out of their programs entirely, in order to get an extra showing of the feature in. Although quality short films do not cost that much ($100 a week is New York's highest going rate), the assumption is that no one cares or knows the difference. Of the two shorts that won this year's Academy Awards, one, *The Box,* has been playing only at the Sutton and only since the awards were announced; the other, *No Place to Stand,* is not playing anywhere. It is true, after all, that most movie goers go to see the feature, and that critics rarely get around to viewing anything but feature films.

Yet nearly every viewer—whether or not he spent the Saturday mornings of his childhood watching programs of cartoon shorts at some theater in his neighborhood—has seen a short film, though he may not remember its name exactly, which he would count among the best movies he has ever seen. The boy riding his wild horse bareback, and ultimately into the sea, in *White Mane;* the marvelous drawings and voices in the night nursery capture of *Moonbird;* the little old lady in her desolate flat, potting and nursing her stringbean, taking it out for walks and planting it in the Tuileries in *Le Haricot*—these are among the most moving, memorable sequences on film, and yet one sees the work of the Hubleys (who made *Moonbird*) and Edmond Sechan (who made the other two, and who was chief photographer for *The Red Balloon* and other films) only randomly or by luck.

Public interest in short films, however, is enormous and growing. Plans are always afoot for starting little theaters where only short films will be shown; and the Donnell

Branch of the New York Public Library—which has a collection of about 1,000 shorts, of which 600 can be borrowed gratis by anyone with access to a 16-mm. projector and a library card—simply cannot keep up with anything like the demand. Pathé-Contemporary—one of the few private companies to hold the line for quality shorts—sells and rents to individuals, libraries, and regular theaters a collection of about 1,000 shorts, including the above three and *The Chicken* (directed by Claude Berri, who made *The Two of Us), The Hunters,* an extraordinary documentary of giraffe hunting by John Marshall of Harvard, and any number of beautiful shorts by the Canadian Film Board (which takes account of the fact that the short film is not only an art form in its own right but a perfect form for young talent to get its start).

The Museum of Modern Art's well-attended Wednesdays at Noon program now consists of shorts; and if the trends for private collection of films and videotapes continues, everyone may one day have a collection of short films in his library. Janus Films, in despair of the conventional commercial outlets, has, since January 1967, been circulating two highly lucrative "concerts" of short films on college campuses throughout the country. The programs, which have sold out from Princeton to the University of Hawaii, include early works by Truffaut, Lester and Godard—as well as Bob Godfrey's *Do It Yourself Cartoon Kit;* Jean Herman France's superb pinball metaphor for the world, called *Actua-Tilt;* Mogubgub's cartoon *Enter Hamlet;* Valerian Borowcsyk's destruction allegory *Renaissance;* and Ballentine and Shepard's remarkable profile of Hugh Hefner, *The Most.*

Universal is trying to put together a similar package. Brandon has always collected distinguished shorts. United Artists made the Pink Panther series and has Noel Black's free and lovely *Skater-dater.* Cinema 16 is in the field. Columbia released *No Place to Stand.* There are independents and students, and, increasingly, N.E.T. and the sponsored, but not commercial television programs—like Xerox's documentary *China: Roots of Madness.* Television, with its time intervals, ought to be an ideal market for short films made for theaters, but so far, except

in Canada, it simply has not worked that way. That's about all there is: as the audience for theatrical short films grows, the sources become fewer. Pathé-Contemporary, recently acquired by McGraw-Hill but still under the direction of Leo Dratfield and Duncan Macgregor, is the most prolific buyer and source.

Somehow the short film must become remunerative again. So many fine ones—the works of Maclaren, Resnais, Renoir; *That's Me* (with Alan Arkin as a Puerto Rican on a park bench), *Night on Bald Mountain, The Critic, The Calypso Singer, Symmetry, Two Men and a Wardrobe, Space, A, The Hand, Toys, The Fatal Glass of Beer, Antonio Gaudi, The Egyptian Spoon* and countless others—eventually come to mind. The short film is ideally suited to profiles, short stories, fables, allegories, satires, jokes. It ranges from the most realistic world of documentary to the most arbitrary, reversible and anarchical world of the animated cartoon.

One reason why short films are often likely to be superior to the features they accompany is that shorts without the cumbersome apparatus of features—the sums of money and quantities of people involved, the many-leveled decisions, the compromise—can be made with a particular unity and coherence out of a single mind and imagination, or two. They are more likely to be of a piece.

One of the best recent films in Pathé-Contemporary's collection is *A Day With Timmy Page.* Timmy is a nine-year-old boy who makes movies, and *A Day* is made of interviews with the young director and excerpts from his films. It is a microcosm of the filmmaker's world. "I'm known to say to the gang," Timmy confesses, "Anyone got an idea for a scene?" Timmy shouts a great deal, evolves several techniques, is a self-conscious interview and directs quite closely. "You," he says to a member of his cast, "will be sneering cruelly." He refers to shooting film interchangeably sometimes with shooting violently; he is full of ideas and intelligence. Of an awkward, not overly star-quality boy who seems to be hurting himself as he falls down a lot, Timmy says casually, implying the expendable, "Don't worry. He's our stunt man."

Asked why a particular girl seems to appear quite fre-

quently in his movies, he explains that he "used to like Amy a lot." But his most inspired technique is in dealing with enemies at school who would like to have a part in his films. "I ask them to drop by and have a screen test sometime," Timmy says. "We don't have screen tests. But it gets them off my back." This marvelous little movie played with the feature *We Still Kill the Old Way*. Neither is playing any longer in New York.

........*War and Peace*

4-29-68

*War and Peace*, which opened yesterday at the DeMille, is a very large and important movie. It had to be made, in just this way on the basis of just this novel, perhaps with just this director—Sergei Bondarchuk, who also collaborated on the screenplay and who stars as Pierre Bezuhov—serious, grand, respectful, with five years of work, seven hours and fourteen minutes of playing time (in this country, the film has been cut to six hours and thirteen minutes) and unlimited funds (the report is $100 million) at his disposal.

In art it is as though money were meaningless. One cannot permit oneself to think what $100 million could buy (half a great tycoon, a few days of modern war, fifty Rembrandts, nine *Half a Sixpence*, a poverty program) or what it means that the Union of Soviet Socialist Republics (Lenin said, "Of all the arts, the cinema is the most important to us") should now be sponsoring a proud spectacular beyond old Hollywood. It is an elegant, almost dogged adaptation of Tolstoi's novel in which the Czarist aristocracy prattles in affected French while Napoleon and the modern age of total war advance through Austerlitz, Vitebsk, Smolensk, Borodino. And Pierre, the unlikely modern hero who seeks "to restrain the harm in himself," grows from an infatuation with Napoleon to a love of peace, and the beauty and immutability of Russia endure.

153

The point is that this film represents the outer limit of something—the outer limit of the panoramic film, the outer limit of the long film (if it succeeds and sets a trend, theaters will ultimately have to be redesigned, equipped perhaps with couches or with walking space) and the outer limit of an attempt on the part of filmmakers with talent but without genius to bring a great literary work to the screen. It is good that someone has done it. There are some classic scenes and sequences. Everyone with a serious interest in cinema is obliged to go and see it. But in a way it is ridiculous. It is the apotheosis of the audio-visual aid.

The titles, by Eleanor Bunin, begin with the name Leo Tolstoi in marvelous fire and blast, then the dark solid word, War, and a frail, almost stenciled, Peace. After that, for long periods, the film is almost muted and reverential, or treble and chirping—the drawing room scenes are often louder than the battles. The movie has none of the roll, sweep, subtlety and thunder of the novel, or of *Boris Godunov* or of spoken Russian. Although the dubbing, by Lee Kressel, is remarkable—an outer limit of what can be done with lip synchronization—it was a mistake to dub the film into English.

It is not just that it is a hopeless thing to separate an actor from his voice. It is that this particular movie, so quintessentially Russian, gains nothing by dubbing. It loses resonance and authenticity. And, if there were subtitles to read, the time would seem shorter and the audience could be more alert and less passive. (The movie in this country is shown in two major parts, separated by a two-and-a-half-hour intermission and interrupted by ten-minute breaks. It is advisable to see it all in one day, because somehow exhaustion contributes to the effectiveness of the second half.)

The acting—perhaps through loss of voice, perhaps in deference to Tolstoi's belief in historical forces over individuals—is, almost without exception, wooden. The characters—including Lyudmila Savelyeva, who, as Natasha, looks a little queasy and has perpetually brimming eyes and a kind of forced vitality, and Bondarchuk, who looks too heavy and too old to play the twenty-year-old

154

Pierre—are dowdy automata. It is a terrific relief, for the most part, when they are all off the screen.

The stars of this film are not the characters—one never cares about any of them and the movie itself is strangely cold—but the shots and the scenes and the sequences. The early parts are suffused with a kind of Dutch yellow light (at moments, this seems like a failure in the quality of the color, rather on the order of the musty shades of the drapes in an old ornate hotel.) Then there are shifts, almost animated canvases—from Vermeer to the posed and costumed soldiery of Delacroix. In the burning of Moscow by night, Goya. Later still, in the revelry and the horror, Bosch. And finally, in the executions on a hill against a dark sky, Mantegna. And, of course, throughout the immense defiling lines of men from Eisenstein.

The battle of Borodoin; a night sleighride by troika across flat snow; a wolf hunt with borzois; Dolohov (the young fop who sleeps with Pierre's wife) biting the snow as he falls in a duel; the brave Captain Tushin at his cannon; General Kutuzov galloping away from his troops to retirement after the victory; Pierre appearing in a light top hat, looking like the White Rabbit, at the front; in particular, a ball scene in which the camera sweeps incredibly up the stairs, through a door, back again, along an immense gallery, into the ballroom, to the grand promenade, to Pierre as he incites Andrei Bolkonsky (played by Vyacheslav Tihonov, like a young John Gilbert) to dance with Natasha (for a moment, they are both superb here) to the absolutely radiant dancing couple and over the chandeliers; other scenes of running hooves and feet, of mummers in the snow, of fires, and armies, and smoke and death, and bodies strewn and heaped—these are fantastically impressive pictorially. Bondarchuk strews the land so eloquently with the bodies of 120,000 extras that he seems a master of interior decoration—outdoors, with the human form.

The battle scenes are almost too pictorial. They are fascinating (and at least there is some genuine Russian bass choral singing before them); but they are merely cumulative, unemotional. One views the destruction coldly, with a kind of visual gourmandise. (An early scene of dancing while the war goes on and Pierre's dying father's hand is twisted by a stroke has more emotional content.) Countless scenes are worth the price of admission. After all, one often spends seven hours before a television set. The worthy experiment turns in the end, inevitably, through the lack of genius to match the novel, into a marathon vulgarism, a full-length animated classic comic. But it is a milestone in trying to draw great literature and cinema and their audiences together, and it has a strong right to be seen.

........ The Spy Film:
Yul Brynner in
*The Double Man*

*5-2-68*

Lately, the conventional spy movie has been curling back more and more tightly on itself, so that in *The Double Man,* which opened yesterday at the R.K.O. 86th Street and other neighborhood theaters, as in *A Dandy in Aspic,* it is some version of himself the hero has got to kill. The whole form may eventually dissolve, with a double agent chasing himself about in place, into stories of suicide from ambivalent paranoia.

*The Double Man* itself is a modest third-rate film, set in the Austrian Tyrol and starring Yul Brynner as an American agent whose son has been pushed off an Alp in a ski murder. The color of the movie is not good, some covering scenes that were shot on fake snow in England in summer look fake, and real ski scenes are done more effectively each year in television's sports coverage. There is also a sequence in which Britt Ekland, who plays some very mild love interest, gets knocked about a bit too brutally and Mr. Brynner is too viciously scratched in return.

But the plotting is tight and Mr. Brynner looks exotic and stony enough to keep one's mind off the title; when

the denouement comes it is a moderate surprise. The
movie was directed by Franklin Schaffner, and Clive Revill
appears as an intimidated spy.

...... *The Odd Couple,*
from the Stage

*5-3-68*

*The Odd Couple,* which opened yesterday at the Radio
City Music Hall, is a very funny, professional adaptation
of the Neil Simon comedy about two men, estranged from
their wives, who move in together and become estranged
from each other also. Walter Matthau plays, as he did on
Broadway, the messy, bleary-eyed, amiable, grumbling
one in the sweatshirt, and Jack Lemmon plays the weepy,
hypochondriacal one in the apron. Since the part is less
broadly comic than the sort he is used to—it teeters between being soulful and unendurable—Mr. Lemmon sometimes overacts. Mr. Matthau is completely low key and
lovable as the slob.

The camera's freedom to roam the streets, as the stage
could not, has advantages—particularly some convincing
shots of sleazy hotels on West Forty-seventh Street. But
these are nearly lost in an early scene, not in the play,
when Jack Lemmon, trying to open a hotel window to
defenestrate himself, inevitably hurts his back, and the
whole film threatens to go down the drain like the tritest
of television comedies. After that, it picks up. The Friday
night poker group—played by John Fiedler, David
Sheiner, Larry Haines and particularly, Herbert Edelman
as Murray, the cop—is very warm, in fact sweaty. Their
lines and behaviors are funny, like people one knows.
They are the sunny lower aspect of *Bye Bye Braverman.*

Monica Evans and Carole Shelley repeat their stage
roles as the English secretaries—with orders for double
vodkas and double Drambuies with crushed ice, and hopes
of romance. The direction, by Gene Saks, and the set, a

very convincing Riverside Drive apartment by Robert
Benton and Ray Moyer, cannot conceal the fact that this
is a play, filmed and ready to reach a wider audience. But
the funny bits, including a splendid scene in which Mr.
Lemmon's lighter snatches Miss Shelley's cigarette, are
still there, and the faces—particularly Mr. Matthau's
jowly, otherwise expressionless look, a wise double take in
his eyes—can be very effective close up. Mr. Lemmon has
some very funny moments barking to clear his head.


> . . . War, Foreign Languages
> and War Again
> on Sunday


*5-5-68*


It would be an act of great condescension to the makers of
*War and Peace* to say, as someone always does, that audiences should put the novel out of their minds and relax
and enjoy the film—rather as one might say to a chef who
has spent his entire life making an immense, exact pastry
replica of Chartres that, if one forgets the cathedral, the
frosting is nice. The Russian film is not a pastry but a
highly serious attempt to see whether perhaps the most
cinematic of great novels can be translated into another
medium. The film has a right to be measured seriously as
a translation—at great financial and human cost, spread
over five years and with a cast of more than 100,000—of
the original.

In several ways *War and Peace* marks a turning point in
the history of the movies. For one thing, it proves once
and for all, on the grandest possible scale, the futility of
dubbing. This is no longer a niggling point. It turns out
that one of the essential powers and beauties of the
cinema is that it is truly international, that it makes
language accessible in a highly special way. Only in movies can one hear foreign languages spoken and—by the
written word in sub-titles—participate as closely as one

ever will in a culture that is otherwise closed to one.

Quite apart from the pleasure of hearing the sounds of a foreign idiom, deducing meaning and discovering homophones, this approximates the experience of learning to speak. It is, moreover, the reverse of what one has to do with books in languages of which one has only partial command. In books, one has to infer the picture—a mental screening—on the basis of what may be insufficient verbal cues. In movies, one is freed to attend to language. It is an extraordinary thing. A mark of the moviegoer as the first real citizen of the world. *War and Peace,* impeccably dubbed, deprives one of this experience and, in effect, puts the mind to sleep. (One's belief that it is Moscow that is burning is also continually subverted by the fact that its inhabitants sound as though they might be from Albuquerque.) And of course, half the acting is lost.

But the main thing is this: that a great epic novel brought to the screen at great pains, integrity and expense has turned out to be only an interminable series of immensely impressive tableaux. And some not so impressive. (A scene in which Andrei, on his deathbed, envisions the globe and then a single living cell is, for example, awfully banal.) With no dramatic momentum at all. This does not mean that great novels are closed to film. Only that, to make a film worthy of a great book a great talent is required. And that the apparent "cinematic" value of a novel does not add much to its suitability for the screen. It is a matter of directorial genius only. And we have had no directors to match our great novelists yet. But a failure of genius is not reprehensible, and—out of respect for its integrity and ambition, and for the sake of the beauty of some of it—*War and Peace* ought, like some historic landmark, to be visited.


Meanwhile, *Les Carabiniers* has opened at the New Yorker Theater and the Bleecker Street. It is, in a poetic and understated way, a great movie. Directed by Jean-Luc Godard, the film is—in stark black and white—an antiwar allegory. Four characters (Ulysses, Cleopatra, Michelangelo and Venus), living in an isolated shack on a

159

desolate marsh, are approached by two carabiniers, in a car with a headlight smashed. The carabiniers are tremendously ominous. Their uniforms are shabby and black. Their only insignia are crosses, like truncated swastikas, at cap and lapel. They recruit Ulysses and Michelangelo —with professions of the King's friendship and promises of spoils—for war.

*"La guerre, c'est pas drôle,"* Ulysses says at first. *"Au contraire,"* a carabinier replies. The whole movie is like that, terse and comic with terror underneath. The characters are the generation of Samuel Beckett, of Everyman living in squalor and confronting the absurd. It is austere. (Only the idle and trivial these days are rococo.) Ulysses and Michelangelo go to war, with battle shopping lists drawn up by Venus and Cleopatra. Predictable things happen to them. They undress women, they kill. There are drums and the music of carnivals. It is all as it always is.

What is remarkable is the sheer beauty, intelligence and invention with which Godard has managed to freight this allegory, to play with symbols and to include simple things that have never been done on film before. From the moment the titles come on, scrawled like a postcard—the whole movie is a postcard—one recognizes the authority with which it is done. One is in good hands. There is a title card (more and more the written word is coming into film again) with a quotation from Borges about "worn metaphors." One becomes aware that all allegory is worn metaphor, and that Godard knows and has discounted any fears of the banal we might have on this account.

The film includes a moving, unpretentious recitation—by a blonde girl before a firing squad—of a poem by Mayakovsky, and it includes fashion photographs from magazines held before humans as though they were body parts. There are countless brilliant juxtapositions of people with words, and with works of art, and with objects symbolic of their dreams—and most of all with pictures. A lot of the film reflects the relation of people to film. The turning point—to all intents and purposes the ending—is quite simply a masterpiece of an idea. (It has been criticized, but then so has the ending of *Charlie Bubbles*, which I liked, and the ending of Sidney Lumet's *The Hill*, which was that intelligent picture's entire point.) The ending concerns what is inside the pitiful suitcase the men bring back from the war.

What is inside is postcards, picture postcards selected by Godard to represent nearly everything important—from the temples of Angkor Wat to a photo of Cleopatra, *Elizabeth Taylor* as Cleopatra—in contemporary western consciousness. It is dazzling. Ulysses and Michelangelo deal the postcards out—like playing cards, or bubblegum wrappers, or trading cards—before their women. It is pure art, ready to hold its own, even intellectually (rare in movies, after all) with art in any other medium.

There is a peculiar thing; the battle scenes, on the model of World War II (the only war that, on screen at least, still looks like a war in human terms) do not always look real. At first one thinks they are so thin because they are so stylized, and then one realizes that the opposite is true: they don't look real in this movie because they are the way war really looks, diffuse, meaningless, with great pockets of peace in it. Wars in conventional films are crowded and stylized—paradoxically, to make them look believable. They are glamorized. Godard's stark, symbolic war is curiously more real. And that is one of the remarkable things about his film: like all effective and living allegory, it is equally effective at the non-allegorical, real, plane, taken as a movie story. Straight.

...... Physical Courage,
*The Fifth Horseman
Is Fear*

5-7-68

*The Fifth Horseman Is Fear*, a Czechoslovak film that opened yesterday at the Baronet, is so beautifully and thoughtfully made—well written and acted, shot with perfect economy and care—that one is almost surprised at the end to be very much moved by the substance of it.

Written and directed by Zbynek Brynych, who become
with this movie quite simply one of the best director
around, the film is about courage and honor. Very muc
in the old style: physical courage, moral honor—th
sacrifice of one life for another and in the name of th:
historical optimism that is at the heart of all faith an
morality.

In a way, the film is about a house—a house full (
tenants in Prague, in the face of the Nazi apocalypse. Th
tenants are a Jewish doctor (Miroslav Machacek), forbic
den by the Nazis to practice but asked by another tenai
(Ilja Prachar) to perform an operation and find morphin
for a wounded member of the underground; a bespec
tacled informer (Josep Vinklar); a rich lawyer (Ji:
Adamira), who is tempted to inform, and his wif
(Zdenka Prochazkova), who ultimately wants him tc
their son; an old music teacher (Olga Scheinpflugova
going mad; an eccentric (Alexandra Myskova) alread
mad; a baby, a dachshund, some rabbits, Prachar's wif
Adamira's maid. All these, Jiri Vrstala, as a police inspec
tor, and several other characters in minor parts ar
absolutely right and natural. The search for morphin
virtually defines their times.

The movie opens with shots of violins and clocks an
pianos being tuned—in a warehouse for confiscate
Jewish property. There are also shots of Prague, of cob
bles, and streetcar wires, church ceilings, peeling wall:
crowds, houses and stairs, criss-crossing traffic, alleys
arches, posters, lightbulbs against the light. There ar
scenes of the Desperation Bar, a beautifully crowded wil
nightclub for the doomed. The Jewish doctor approaches
van, on whose panel one reads "er." The camera move
left: "berger," "chenberger," "Kirchenberger"; a plain
clothesman is leaning against it. The doctor runs in fear.

When his courage is tested, though, he is not presente
as one of those shambling, sentimental stereotypes con
mon in stories of this kind. He looks forward to doin
surgery again. He is proud. He regards his life as ende
anyway. He is glad to do his bit for a cause. And, c
course, he is appalled and afraid. There are moments c
great suspense about what will happen to him, and to hi

patient, as the degrees of fear represented by the other tenants of the house come into play. There is the informer, even the dachshund drawn to a spot of blood in the hall. Everything, every sound is a threat.

But what is most impressive about the film is certain ironic and moving events. The boy, seeing a man fall off his bicycle to the cobbled street, laughs. Seeing him fall a second time, he laughs again. The third time a look of horror comes over his face. In a forced brothel for soldiers where the doctor's sister works, there is a long scene of naked women under the shower heads, with baroque music playing and a sense of imminence of death. There is a Jewish insane asylum, with a kind of ballet and symphony of the voices of the mad. (The use of music and sound generally in this film is very effective and delicate.) Finally, there is a scene in which all the tenants but one file past a corpse, as the Fascist radio blares. Characterization throughout the film has been so sharp that the behavior of each one as he walks by seems exactly true. And the message of the film—although it is by no means a work of propaganda—seems so well taken and inspiring that it is odd it should work at all in these neurotically skeptical, morally inert times.

. . . Bob Hope, Phyllis Diller
and N.B.C. in
*The Private Navy
of Sgt. O'Farrell*

5-9-68

*The Private Navy of Sgt. O'Farrell*, which opened yesterday at the Trans-Lux East, Trans-Lux West and neighborhood theaters, sounds as though it had been done by some writers not quite refurbished from drydock in 1942. They sink at once. They lie there, rusting and creaking and emitting bubbles, in the sand. Actually, the movie was written and directed by Frank Tashlin (who wrote

163

*Paleface)* and produced, in part, by Bob Hope and television network. The movie is set in the South Pacific i World War II, and only Hope, who stars, could survive th endless progression of unfunny lines—each delivered in more hopeful, laugh-expectant voice than the last—whic succeed one another like snores from the next room, o hands over grubby hands in a child's game, or drops in water torture. "Rots of ruck," he cries to a Japanes fighter plane strafing overhead. He asks an enlisted ma why his father in a photo is wearing a funny hat. "That my mother," the soldier says. "Oh," Hope replies, "m apologies to both of them." It's like that.

Somehow Hope's comic dignity makes it through. So strangely enough, does Phyllis Diller, who saves herse from time to time with her personal bitter caw straigl from the heart of the fortyish nurse, private secretary, o receptionist. If this film were really a rerun, there migl even be a kind of humor from nostalgia. When Hop pointing his gun at a Japanese, shouts, "Hey, stop o you'll be leaking soy sauce"—well, it might have bee funny once. So might the now forever dated jokes abou drunkenness. And it's kind of fun to have a score that ac companies the voyage of a boat called *Sweet Adeline* wit an old-fashioned, resigned Wah, wah, wah, wah. But joke about marching into Tokyo to "leave those kids round eyed." No.

There are two genuinely funny touches: a parody of th scene on the beach in *From Here to Eternity,* and a scer in a Japanese submarine, spoken in English, wit Japanese sub-titles. But then—out of Hollywood's recu rent fear that an unannotated joke is a joke lost—bot scenes are repeated and explained, until the most arder war comedy fan would long to go out and have a beer.

Which raises another point: the movie features in numerable cans of beer, all of the same, very clearly ider tified brand. I suppose this might be all right but bran names have figured prominently and consistently in s many movies lately that the combination of a beer and television network in the production of a film amounts t the sponsored movie.

5-12-68

The radical conflict of generations results as much as anything from a failure of the arts. It is not just that large
numbers of the nominally educated young have no stake
in Western civilization that they know of, that the art of
the past has not been made live, and worth preserving, for
them. It is also a failure of the arts in our time. There is
simply not much joy or conviction, or power, or sense of
community in them. They seem anemic or kidding. Or
waiting around for a handsome political star to invite
them to dinner again in Camelot. Politics combined with
the media now—in terms of illusion and drama—has it all
over the arts.

The theater has not brought an audience really to its
feet in years. Nor has anything else, except political style.
Not even movies. We are accustomed to say that movies
are the live art of our time. Everyone wants to think so.
Especially the young. Movies are so contemporary. But it
is true only to a very limited extent. Though people care
deeply about the form, the product has lately not been
much. There are the ghastly, sub-pap movies for the
hardbitten elderly ladies, of all ages and sexes, of the
*Valley of the Dolls* set. There are the few solid, good
movies for everyone, like *In the Heat of the Night*. There
are the art frontier movies, like *Persona*, which not many
people see. There are the countless low-order movies for
drive-in crowds who don't care too much what's playing, as
long as it moves and leaves them alone. There are other
kinds.

But basically, there are not many lines or scenes or
behaviors on the screen just now that a generation would
want to imitate or even remember. And though people go
to the movies all the time, it could be argued that hardly
anyone's sensibility is affected by them—that the real

165

form for our time is politics. Style politics, glamour, i
substantial politics, politics as art. Of course, this
frivolous and dangerous, but it seems fairly clear. Fro
the politician-as-film-star days of the early New Fronti
through the film-star-as-politician days of Sacramento,
the star as engaged citizen (thank heaven for the sinceri
of Paul Newman in this regard) there has been a tren
Now we have the young, middle-class political demo
stration, still relatively free of physical risk or cons
quences—the demonstration as art. Before the cameras
the media. The demonstration as film.

Of course, one cannot use the movies to account for
middle-class protest phenomena, but they play their pa
For one thing, because the outlaw hero from great movi
of the past did form a sensibility. The football hero nev
really had it on film; now he hasn't on the campus eith
The big man is the loser, the outcast, the four-letter va
sity intransigent. For another, because protest can provi
an aesthetic élan that the movies, along with the other ar
have temporarily lost. For a third, because our socie
does not now offer any genuine moral outlet for physic
courage—think how many people are reduced to going
horror movies as a test of nerve. The demonstration, wi
what passes among American liberals for police brutali
looks dangerous in a precisely theatrical way. And
dangerous, of course, not to persons but to the democra
experiment; aesthetics as politics is always subject to t
totalitarian turn.

One of the reasons movies have lost some of th
power over imagination, I think, is that they are so oft
mindless and poorly written now. At precisely the mome
when the visual arts are falling back increasingly on verb
or conceptual elements, the movies have decided to go v
ual. Not visual in the sense that the great silents were—
terms of acting, good motion, the meaningful juxtapositi
of forms. Visual in technological, photo-optical sense, cu
and zooms. This is bound to pass. Every film that ev
mattered to anyone since the silents went out was a writt
film. A lot of the written films one gets just now are telev
sion gag writer marathons. That should pass, too. ●
perhaps the silents will come back again.

One reason one has to keep praising Bergman, Buñuel, Godard, Truffaut, Fellini, Antonioni, Finney, Chabrol, and (as of the opening of *The Fifth Horseman Is Fear* last week) Brynych, is that they are producing, among other things, written films—lines that risk sounding pretentious or empty, but that address themselves to some of the problems of the soul: sin, loneliness, crime, love, God, death, whatever. In terms that would be respectable in any of the arts. There is, of course, a school of buff that thinks one should put literary values out of one's mind and relax and enjoy a film as art. This is simply silly. A work of art always wants to be greeted by the sum of the tradition into which it was born.

Another querulous word on dubbing. Nowhere is it clearer than in foreign films on television that the process is hopeless, destroying any illusion of life, and leaving the actor somewhere between a mouthing fish and a blubbering grotesque. In Germany, where film is not exactly thriving, all films are dubbed. In France, no one with any sense goes when they are. On television, dubbed actors look, in a way, helpless and at home—mouthing, as it were, in a bowl.

....... Robbe-Grillet's
*Trans-Europe Express:*
The Notion That Things
Make Any Sense at All

*5-13-68*

*Trans-Europe Express,* which opened yesterday at the Plaza Theater, is the second movie to be directed by Alain Robbe-Grillet, who wrote *Last Year at Marienbad*. It is about three characters on a train from Paris to Antwerp making a gangster movie about the drug traffic on trains from Paris to Antwerp or from Antwerp to Paris. The screenwriter, played by Robbe-Grillet himself, is not quite sure which way the traffic runs. The hero, played by Jean-

Louis Trintignant (of *A Man and a Woman*), is not quite sure what the extremely incompetent filmmakers on the train or the elliptical members of the dope ring in Antwerp want him to do. He rushes about, deadpan and puzzled, looking for the drugs and the plot. He also devotes a great deal of time to chaining, to rape, and to discussing his predicament with Marie-France Pisier, whom he ultimately strangles from behind—in a boyish, puzzled and entirely solicitous way.

All kinds of wonderful minor characters bustle in and out with threads of the plot that the major characters have been trying to learn or conceal. Near the end of the film, there is a long, attentive sequence in which a plump naked girl in a nightclub is picturesquely chained to a turntable she is rotating on. The writer has put this in because it pleases him. Also, music from *La Traviata*. Minor inconsistencies of the plot—pointed out to him by a pedantic script girl, played by Catherine Robbe-Grillet, with a tape recorder on her lap—can be cut later on. The film is a little parody of the old New Wave crime eroticism movies, and the process, in general, by which films are thought out. Or not thought out. It was greeted in France as a statement about the confusion between appearance and reality, but it seems rather a parody of boring statements of this kind. The writer's powers of comic invention occasionally run down. ("Repeat where," a character says after giving complicated directions to the hero. "Where," the hero replies.) For comic dialogue, Robbe-Grillet is no Ivy Compton-Burnett.

But the incessant reshuffle of props—mirrors, posters, places, people and hardware in sado-masochistic juxtaposition—is often funny. There are some excellent sharp scenes, including an inevitable one among abandoned railroad cars. And there are all sorts of evocative, improbable objects included—a paperback by Sacha Guitry, a stack of crates of Royal Crown Cola—as clues that one neither wants nor expects to lead anywhere. The gangster genre in which everyone's role for good or evil is constantly in doubt begins to seem a bright, arbitrary relief from the serious artist's necessary but probably paranoid notion that things make any sense at all.

*5-15-68*

*Thérèse and Isabel* is a film about those failures of love and excesses of sensuality on the part of adults toward their children that seem to create severe sexual problems in the young. Based on a memoir by the French novelist Violette Léduc, of a lesbian affair in boarding school, the movie is so relentlessly explicit physically that it sometimes seems a sincere, misguided attempt to use the screen as a confessional. Sometimes—more often, in fact—it seems an attempt by the producer-director, Radley Metzger (whose previous successes include *Carmen, Baby*), to make a mint out of a growing audience of specializing sex watchers.

The movie stars Essy Persson (of *I, a Woman*) and Anna Gaël (of *Benjamin*) in an affair that is meant to convey, among other things, the loss of innocence. But since both women appear to be in their early thirties, and rather swaybacked and out of condition, there is a certain lack of poignancy and freshness in the long and frequent love scenes they play out together in the lavatory, open air, school chapel and so on. It all has the stale, gray, not-quite-right air of people one finds too late at night hanging about railroad stations and subway cars. The movie is, however, quite well photographed. It opened yesterday, in black and white, in French, with very straightforward subtitles, at the Rialto and the Trans Lux 85th Street theaters.

*5-19-68*

One of the things democracy may be the system least equipped to deal with is revolution as an aesthetic exercise. It is not really foreseen in any philosophy of history that a group of middle-class young people, against whom the system has done no injustice whatsoever—whom the system was actually educating for positions of power—should want to bring the system down for fun. The gratuitous personal act has long been famous in literature, but it took the age of the movies to bring us the gratuitous political movement. Reactionaries still look for simple evidence of international conspiracy. Old liberals look for simple idealism and lost youth. And both find what they are looking for: style-politics demonstrations do not occur all over the world at once by coincidence and they cannot enlist the sympathy they need without a germ of an ideal, and a nerveless or frozen institutional opponent.

The reason democracy is peculiarly vulnerable to style-revolution is that the new kind of rebellion accepts no concessions and makes no specific demands. It is committed to the process of destroying order. There is no way democratic institutions can accommodate that aim. (If they try to rival demonstrations as entertainment, they fail in their responsibilities. If they resort to repression they lose their democratic character.) The art revolution itself, on the other hand, is infinitely flexible. Committed to nothing substantial (the dangling radical use of the word "relevant" is key; no one asks relevant to what), it can take on the vocabulary of any true political movement with real and legitimate claims. The only people to lose by the art-revolution so far have been the genuinely poor and oppressed. Young joy-radicals take on their style, while undermining their substantive goals as selling out; and simply bring the system down upon their heads.

In Jean-Luc Godard's film *La Chinoise*—made, after

170

all, early last year—the aim dearest to the heart of the young Maoist student heroine is to blow up the Sorbonne. Francis Jeanson, an old Marxist and fighter for Algerian independence, asks her why. She is free not to attend the university if she likes. Very few students would welcome her plan. There is nothing she would wish to build in the Sorbonne's place. The Maoist girl played by Anne Wiazemsky, replies that none of this is her concern. It is really only theater—the drama and style of revolution—that interests her. She is not concerned with consequences.

One wonders how much of the radical casualness toward where things lead is derived from a world view created by movies—particularly cartoons, but movies in general. Where everything is reversible and can be undone. Where heroes are killed in one movie only to rise in the next. The same is true, of course, in theater but not to the same extent. You cannot, for example, run a theater reel backward. And, more important, the stage does not encapsulate an actor for all time in celluloid. Movie actors survive physically on film long after their deaths. So do real events, conserved in documentaries. It is hard to sustain a traditional logic—an awareness of any sort of rational consequences—when a movie sensibility blurs even the terminal fact of mortality.

It is not surprising—although it was probably not inevitable either—that the Red Guard movement at Chinese universities began (according to much of the European press) over a question of movies, a piece of movie criticism about which the students and Mao disagreed with Liu Shao-chi. But neither art nor politics can be sustained forever as an orgy; it becomes ultimately as joyless a form of play as blowing bubbles through a straw into a glass when one has been told not to. In this country, the ultimate response of the system to style radicalism will probably also be an aesthetic one: the law and a bored or laughing audience.

On Wednesday, at Lincoln Center, the American TV Commercials Festivals will hold its annual awards. The morning program, to be held from ten until noon in the

171

Library of Performing Arts, will show commercials from abroad. Between 2 and 5:30, there will be a showing of about 250 U.S. commercials. And at 8:30 in the evening, in Philharmonic Hall, there will be an Academy Award model ceremony—complete with Overture made up of commercial tunes.

The movies owe a lot—the helicopter shot, the fast pan, the zoom, Richard Lester—to commercials. The Museum of Modern Art owns reels of them. And the television ad, as Wallace Ross, director of the festival, points out, is becoming a director's medium. There are plans in the industry to have commercials not as frequent interruptions but, as they do in England, in clusters at the beginning and end of programs. This will put commercials not only into direct competition with each other for quality, but into competition with the programs as well. Presumably, there will be fewer of the unendurable ones. I particularly detest those which show somebody throwing out somebody's old dentifrice, or deodorant or whatever, and then smugly producing a new one, and those which show wives criticizing the detergent husbands have chosen to scrub the floor with.

I really look forward to the disgruntled Qantas koala bear, the Alka Seltzer altercation between a man and his stomach ("You never did like my mother")—the Blahs won last year—and the incomparable Stan Freberg ads for Sunsweet Prunes ("Today, the pits. Tomorrow, the wrinkles"). But many other excellent commercials—with fine, still photograph-influenced graphics, good performers, experiments with not tipping the product's hand until the end, and best uses of intervals of time—will be shown too.

5-24-68

*Prudence and the Pill,* which opened yesterday at the Victoria and Murray Hill theaters, is a nauseating little sex comedy in which somebody is always substituting a vitamin or an aspirin for somebody else's oral contraceptive until everyone gets confused and pregnant. Lovers and hypochondriacs will realize that such a substitution would be unlikely to confuse anyone. Other people will notice that one hundred repetitions of a bad old dreary joke do not make a comedy.

David Niven plays a rich husband, mixing pills so that his wife, Deborah Kerr, will conceive by her lover. Judy Geeson plays a ghastly girl, whom the script imagines to be modern, substituting pills so that her mother, Joyce Redman, conceives by her husband. In a bit of dated and witless snobbery that is a side order in the film, a weepy housemaid, through another chemical mixup, becomes pregnant by a silly chauffeur. Irina Demick, playing Niven's mistress, becomes pregnant for no discernible reason. All of them, presumably because their parts are unendurable, give the worst performances of their lives.

Dame Edith Evans—no, the screenwriter, Hugh Mills, has managed to leave her medicine cabinet alone—has one good scene in the entire 92-minute gross thing. She walks straight across a track on which an auto race is being run, and, when she arrives at the mechanic's pit, says, "Oh, so this is the pit." In context, it seems funny. It shows you, in movies of this sort, how little one is grateful for: Twentieth Century Fox and the Emetic. Hollywood and the Nembutal.

# Fracas at the Cannes Festival

5-26-68

*Cannes*

From the beginning of the Twenty-first International Film Festival at Cannes until the end last weekend, when Jean-Luc Godard, Francois Truffaut, Louis Malle, Claude Lelouch, Claude Berri and Alain Resnais called a strike and practically every filmmaker of any consequence took part in it, it was clear that the festival could not go on while there were general strikes in France, or even while the students occupied the universities.

For one thing, the filmmakers felt, and not without reason, that the entire political crisis had begun with them—in February, over L'Affaire Langlois. Henri Langlois was (and is again) the director of the most important, active film library in the world, the Paris Cinémathèque, which he helped to found in 1936. He not only saved any number of movies that the film companies, as strongly committed to artificial obsolescence as any other industry, would have destroyed, he was responsible for the recognition of countless films as worth saving. And his regular showing of old movies from all over the world had the greatest possible influence on a young generation of directors, including, of course, Godard, Truffaut and the rest of the Nouvelle Vague.

Early this year, on the basis of some never quite formulated accusation having to do with solvency, efficiency and politics, Langlois was dismissed from his job. Every serious filmmaker in France protested, and telegrams came in from Kurosawa, Chaplin, Welles, Hawks, Buñuel, Bergman, the Italians, and so on. A Comité de Défense de la Cinémathèque was formed, and L'Affaire Langlois was under way.

Truffaut in particular was tireless. An essentially private person, he had always kept aloof from politics. The Langlois affair occupied him to such a degree that he helped to organize strikes, boycotts and demonstrations in which actors, critics, directors and, of course, many stu-

174

dents—all *cinéastes* for whom film is, if anything, more important than it is for us—took part. At one point, Godard and Truffaut actually fought with the police. It became an issue of artistic freedom versus the national bureaucracy. Mendes-France supported the committee. Langlois was restored to his job in April, but the national subsidy to the Cinémathèque was withdrawn.

That was how matters stood when the festival began. On the third day, there was a strike in sympathy with the students and workers of Paris. Rather token. A meeting of the Comité de Défense de la Cinémathèque had, however, been scheduled for last Saturday morning. Langlois himself was supposed to attend a conference in memory of the late French critic Georges Sadoul that afternoon. All week, among the many booths in the lobby of the Carlton Hotel—advertising films and film companies and publications—there had been a booth for the Comité, occupied, as often as not, by Truffaut himself passing out leaflets and soliciting sponsorship for the Cinémathèque. It was clear, however, that if the festival survived beyond Saturday, the Comité would have lost its solidarity with the national movement of which it was a forerunner, and it would be something of a cinematic anticlimax.

Of course, that is not how it turned out. Godard and Truffaut announced Saturday morning, in the Salle Jean Cocteau of the Palais du Festival where they occupied a stage with Lelouch, Malle and Berri, that Lelouch and Resnais (he had gotten no further than Lyons because of the strike) were withdrawing their films from the festival, that Roman Polanski, Monica Vitti and Louis Malle had resigned from the jury (Terence Young later resigned as well) and that they recommended a strike, with occupation of the main and smaller auditoriums. Godard was for continuous projection of films, outside the framework of the festival, within new structures. "Films are for projecting," he said. Truffaut favored closing entirely.

Milos Forman, the Czech director, whose *Firemen's Ball* had generated serious political controversy in Czechoslovakia, announced that, even though he did not understand too deeply the issues of the strike, he would withdraw his film from the festival in solidarity. This represented a serious sacrifice for him since his movie was among the leading contenders for first prize. In fact, the strike presented so considerable a sacrifice for all the young French filmmakers who joined it, both in cash for films unbought and in trust among distributors, that some people began to refer to the strikers in some bewilderment as "*ces anarchistes millionaires.*" It seemed to some that the artists in power were fighting to depose themselves.

Christiane Rochefort, press director of the festival and a distinguished novelist *(Le Repos du Guerrier)* in her own right, arranged a meeting between Truffaut, Godard and Robert Favre Le Bret, the president of the festival. Favre Le Bret agreed that there should be no prizes this year, but asked that foreign filmmakers who still wanted to show their films should be allowed to do so. By this time, quite a number of the best films had been withdrawn from competition, and the jury, pronouncing itself unable to function, had resigned.

But the festival did try to go ahead with the projection, scheduled for that afternoon, of a Spanish film, *Peppermint Frappé*, directed by Carlos Saura and starring Geraldine Chaplin. Saura had, however, withdrawn his film, and citizens of Cannes, who had filled the auditorium to insist that the festival continue, were presented with the interesting spectacle of a stage full of strikers, including Godard, Truffaut, Jean-Pierre Léaud (star of Godard's film on the Maoist left, *La Chinoise*), Saura and Miss Chaplin herself, holding the curtain shut as the titles, including Miss Chaplin's name, appeared on the screen. Since this was the Spanish director's first appearance at Cannes, Saura's sacrifice in the name of the strike was perhaps the greatest of the festival. The young group holding the curtains shut, being very careful not to damage the screen, looked a little like the group planting the flag at Iwo Jima—only in the dark, as in a time exposure.

Several local residents had already attacked Truffaut and Godard, slightly scratching Truffaut's cheek, and since another scuffle was clearly about to begin, the house lights were turned on and the projection stopped. From that moment on, although there were days and nights of discussion, the festival was really at an end. It was rumored that students would be arriving at four o'clock from the already occupied university at Nice, and that the more radical of them might throw Truffaut and Berri, particularly Lelouch, and perhaps even Godard, out anyway—for being successful and for not making films that were politically engaged. But this never materialized.

It was clear to all the young directors, however, that if the present regime fell, and if there occurred that state of continuous revolution and uninterrupted self-criticism which the new radicals were striking for, the artist's predicament would become acutely difficult. Art does not function well in the service of politics, it does not work by majority rule, and in this kind of reverse Pirandello situation—where politics was crossing the line, to become art—the directors' position had to be ambiguous. They felt, though, that they had to support the revolution when it came to them and, not surprisingly in an age so much under movie influence, movie directors turned out to be the most effective political leaders imaginable.

...... How Their World
Might Ideally Be

*6-2-68*

*Paris*

In the strange week interval after the Cannes Film Festival, when responsible people whose sympathies lay with the striking students and workers took advantage of the air of incipient change to talk and to think, the filmmakers—like nearly everyone else—met in almost continuous session to discuss how their world might ideally be. It is a question people in large groups rarely have to pose themselves: how would they do things if they had the power to begin all over again? The question is usually academic and silly, but when the forms are breaking up it more or less poses itself in practical terms, and the French filmmakers were very serious about it. There were meetings all over Paris—screen actors, technicians, producers, two groups of thirty directors—with liaisons among the groups and to the students meeting in amphitheaters at the Sorbonne.

There was a continuous intergroup meeting, in a school on the Rue de Vaugirard, of the Etats-Généraux, a successor organization Truffaut and Godard had proclaimed at Cannes to the Centre National du Cinéma. Members of all the groups and of none would drop in at the Etats-Généraux, and discussions would overflow the meeting hall, out through the windows, and into the street. A red-bearded young man kept insisting that the revolution would have passed films by if it did not inspire *cinéma engagé,* films completely at the service of the revolution. Jean-Pierre Rassam, brother-in-law of Claude Berri (*The Two of Us*) and assistant to Jean-Luc Godard, accused the young man himself of never having made films about anything but vampires.

Claude Chabrol, whose *Le Beau Serge,* released in 1958, is regarded as the first movie of the Nouvelle Vague (although Truffaut's *400 Blows,* made later that year, is better known), shouted himself hoarse at the Etats-Généraux. Truffaut and Godard themselves, apparently appalled by the public personalities they had assumed at Cannes, did not take part in the Etats, and friends particularly mourned the nonappearance of "la Truffe" (the Truffle), who is probably the most liked and respected director in France. His friend, Czech director Milos Forman, did not appear either. Although he had withdrawn his *The Firemen's Ball* at Cannes—as Roman Polanski had withdrawn from the jury—the two young eastern European directors seemed less confident about where the revolution would lead. Polanski, who left Poland in 1963, had expressed doubts about quitting the jury. Forman became sick. At the festival he had been asked by a fan why his comic film had such an unhappy ending. "*A la fin, on est toujours triste,*" he said.

The critics were meeting, too. In France, the line between directors and critics is not as clear as it is here and critics, although they do not have much power (people being much too knowledgeable about films to take much advice about what films to see), sometimes make films and always consider themselves creative participants in the art of cinema. At Cannes, the critics, including Henri Chapier of *Combat*, Michel Aubriant of *Paris Presse*, Samuel Lachize of the Communist *l'Humanité*, Michel Delahaye of the respected *Cahiers du Cinéma*, an unidentified old gentleman representing a string of Catholic newspapers in Switzerland, and so on, had so monopolized a discussion of tactics and goals for the strike—in accordance with their various politics, and occasionally walking huffily out—that the directors thought it better, by the time they got to Paris, that the two groups meet separately. Or almost.

One directors' group met at the apartment of Jacques Doniol-Volcroze, a critic of *Cahiers du Cinéma* and director of two experimental films *Le Viol* and *L'Eau à la Bouche*. Alain Resnais (of *Hiroshima Mon Amour*) was in this group. So were Roger Vadim (*Les Liaisons Dangereuses*), and the actor Jean-Pierre Léaud, star, in his childhood, of *The 400 Blows* and now, ten years later, of *La Chinoise*. The second and more vocal group met at the apartment, on the Rue Rousselet, of Serge Roullet (director of Sartre's *Le Mur*). It included Claude Berri, Louis Malle (*The Fire Within*), Gabriel Albicocco (*The Wanderer*), Yves Robert (*The War of the Buttons*), Philippe De Broca (*That Man from Rio*), Marcel Carné (*Les Enfants du Paradis*) and occasionally Claude Lelouch (*A Man and a Woman*), who commuted between the two groups. There were also Michel Piccoli (*Benjamin, Belle de Jour*), representing the actors, Marcel Benayoul, former film critic of the *Nouvel Observateur*, representing critics, an unidentified student in khakis, representing students, and any number of others.

What they were doing was trying to work out a system for distributing "difficult" films, and, especially, a way to give new directors a chance to make films. With the help of Roger Errera, a former professor of Jean-Pierre Rassam's, whom Rassam suggested for the job ("But I don't know you at all," Albicocco had said after Rassam had made a particularly fiery speech proposing Errera. "My name is Rassam," Rassam had replied, "I am the brother-in-law of

179

Claude Berri. I have worked with Godard. And," he smiled, "I live with my mother"), they drew up a series of demands to present to the Etats for approval and then to the government on behalf of the filmmakers of France. "None of us wants to be rich any more," De Broca said. "We only want to make the films we want and to be surrounded by the films of those we love. Movies belong to those who make, and not to those who profit from them."

The demands included a say, on the part of young filmmakers, in the appointment of representatives to the organization that would replace the Centre. And a use of the Centre's tax on every movie ticket sold in France to help finance "difficult" films with revenues from the commercially successful ones. Claude Lelouch, the richest of the young directors, proposed the formation of a society of all young producer-directors to circumvent distributors altogether. The society would distribute films on behalf of the directors themselves. It would be cheaper and fairer. And they would levy a 5 per cent tax on every ticket sold to finance the work of directors who had never made a film before. Movies would continuously find new talent and renew themselves. Many other proposals were made. Everyone was exhausted (the sessions had lasted more than four days) and yet good-natured and argumentative. Everyone deplored again the *spectacle absurde et odieux* of rich distributors in evening dress at Cannes. In the end it was Errera's formulations and Lelouch's proposals that were adopted. It remains to be seen whether the French film industry will readily be changed in this way.

At around eleven o'clock on the night of the worst rioting last week, the meeting on the Rue Rousselet was interrupted by the arrival of a courier, in khakis and raincoat, who announced that violence was growing in the Latin Quarter and that many were hurt. De Broca, Berri and Carné and several others immediately adjourned to a smaller room to listen to the radio reports. When requests were broadcast for first aid and medical supplies, the entire meeting adjourned more or less spontaneously for the barricades. Some of the youngest film people joined the chains of students and others passing cobbles and rocks down the Boulevard St. Michel to pile up behind overturned cars. The rest wandered about, muttering to themselves, watching the trees fall, and red-eyed from the tear gas like everybody else.

.......... Bellocchio's
*Fist in His Pocket:*
People for Whom Happiness
Is Not at All Possible

*5-28-68*

*Fist in His Pocket* (for some reason someone has amputated a fist and a pocket from any likely translation of *I Pugni In Tasca*) is the first and stronger movie by the Italian director Marco Bellocchio (whose *China Is Near* was released earlier this year). It is sealed and stifling, gray and extremely powerful—about as attractive as somebody coughing wretchedly beside you on a subway. And as insistent. It is not for seeing on a day when you are celebrating something. On the other hand, on a day when you can face it, it is very much worth seeing.

The movie is about four people in an Italian provincial family, whose very existence drains the possibility for the happiness of a fifth, the oldest son. The mother of the family is a blind and whimpering widow, who collects dusty closets full of *Pro Familia* (a magazine she requires her sons to read to her) and who sits passively as the cat licks the food from her plate. Her youngest son is demented and misshapen, with an insectoid thorax and a moronic laugh; he steals spoonfuls of sugar from the sugar bowl. Her middle son is only an epileptic, and her daughter—but for her isolation in the oppressive villa in which they live—is almost normal. But the quality of their lives is illustrated by what the oldest, healthiest son does for entertainment: he shoots rats at night on the town garbage dump. This son wants to get married; with his familial responsibilities, he does not have the freedom or the money to.

181

The middle son, as an act of intelligence and courage, decides to do himself and all the defective others in, so that his healthy brother can be free. He fails when he tries it in one fell swoop, but he does better when he works by degrees. He pushes his mother off a cliff. He drowns his younger brother in the bath. There are shots of wakes and the depressing snows of Northern Italy. It is morbid, and convincing and written exactly right, yet everyone who has ever thought for an instant that his only hope lay in doing somebody in can't help indulging in a small, dark Rickety, Tickety Tin.

The movie is absolutely true to the writhing, sordid and incestuous predicament of the family and yet it leaves each person touching and even reasonable. The acting, on the part of Lou Castel, Paola Pitagora, Marino Masè, Liliana Gerace, Pier Luigi Troglio and Jennie MacNeil is so convincing, as a unit, that it seems the family has been lifted from life, in a jar, intact. Miss Pitagora is particularly fine as the sister—horrified, guilty and yet aroused and released by what her brother has done. And Mr. Castel, as the brother Alessandro, epileptic and also choking on his desire to live, is remarkable—through a daring final scene in which he is required to have a terminal epileptic fit in time with the "Sempre Libera" aria from *La Traviata*.

What is strong and original in the picture is that it shows people just poor enough and just handicapped enough to be unfit to join the community of people for whom happiness is at all possible. One sees such people everywhere, in the cities and in the towns; everyone occasionally teeters far enough out of life to be among them. And yet they are very seldom effectively portrayed on film. In this line Bellocchio's talent is altogether new and powerful.

Also playing at the Carnegie Hall Cinema is *Off-spring*, a five-minute antiwar short, set to a child's voice singing "Where Have All the Flowers Gone." It is not very well done, but the idea nearly works by itself.

*The Long Day's Dying* is one of those pictures that go on the assumption that if you avow your sensibility early enough as tough antiwar, and if you dismember your characters incessantly, an eye at a time, with mud, and gore and blood vomiting, you can make the same picture the prowar people have been making all along and find an audience warmed by the intensity of its humanism. The color of the picture is beautiful, misty cold, early-morning precise. The acting, by David Hemmings of *Blow-Up;* Tony Beckley of *The Penthouse* and *Up the Junction* directs. Things explode and people die at a distance beautifully, weightlessly, like kites in the park.

The plot is that three young English parachutists find themselves cut off from their unit in World War II. While they are waiting for their sergeant to return, one of them slaughters a chicken, another blasts a German soldier and—almost as an act of mercy—puts a needle through his heart. They are all skilled military men. A second enemy soldier, stalking them, is stalked and shot. A third enemy soldier, who has taken them prisoner in a farmhouse, is taken prisoner in turn. He is a conventional villain, a machine of efficiency with perfidy in his heart. The sergeant, it turns out, is dead. The others try to return to Allied lines.

The story, taken from a novel by Alan White, is all right. There are some excellent scenes, a meticulous laying of booby traps, the German prisoner's ominous entry on screen, a machine-gunned man's death dance, war at night, the careful killing of three men who turn out to have been dead already. But the screenplay—the writing by Charles Wood, who also wrote *How I Won the War*—is unendurable. Megaphone ironies with repetition for slow learners and a share in the insatiable, self-righteous blood lust of the camera. "I'm a pacifist, I'm a pacifist," Hemmings keeps saying as he kills. "I'm a pacifist, I'm a pacifist," he is screaming as he gets shelled by mortars and machine-gunned while trying to return to his own lines. Someone describes the sergeant as a man who would be late to his own funeral. "Maybe that's what kept him," someone else replies. "Who won?" Hemmings asks the German prisoner, as they both lie wounded and everyone around them is dead. "We won," the German says. "We exist." The movie opened yesterday at the Paris Theater and the Criterion.

...... *Wild in the Streets*

*5-30-68*

Events overtake fantasy so quickly now that any movie about the generation gap ought to be dated almost before the titles run, but *Wild in the Streets* is a kind of instant classic, a revved-up *La Chinoise* or *Privilege* for the drive-ins in summertime. Blunt, a little preachy, a product of American International Pictures (of beach party and teen-age werewolf fame), the movie is philosophy with dual exhausts and a very clear logic about where things lead. A boy of nineteen (played by Christopher Jones), alienated by his mama, poisons the family bulldog, blows up the car and goes out to seek his fortune. Within a short time he is a famous pop singer—"a multimillionaire," the script is careful to point out, "after taxes"—surrounded by sybaritic hippies, a Black Power drummer (author, the script says, of the best-selling *Aborigine Cookbook*), a fifteen-year-old Yale law grad, and other friends.

A liberal candidate for senator from California, inevitably, seeks their support. When he gets it, and wins by offering to lower the voting age to fifteen (a compromise figure they reach so the Yale grad can vote), the kids become aware of their power and decide to run a candidate of their own. She wins. In Washington, the youngsters don't bother with rhetoric about loss of faith in the electoral system. They riot until a dozen of them are killed, then put LSD in the water supply so that Congress amends the Constitution to lower the Presidential eligibility age to fourteen. The pop singer is elected President, sweeping "every state, with the single and remarkable exception of Hawaii." The liberal senator who started the whole thing tears up a Donald Duck poster in his rage. The administration establishes a mandatory retirement age at thirty. At thirty-five, citizens are escorted—by blackshirted young goons in baseball caps—to "rehabilitation camps," where, "in groovy surroundings," they are given compulsory LSD from a row of green water coolers.

The script is rather heavily weighted against the old. When the pop singer's mother, played with wonderful exaggeration by Shelley Winters, recognizes him on a television program—a recognition she manages only by consulting an old family photograph—she crows, "I'm a celebrity." When she drives to see him, she manages to run over a child and cripple her husband. The only dated thing in the picture is the treatment of the very young. The kid insurgents feel a certain amount of pressure from the three-year-olds ("That's right. They're better than we are," Diane Varsi, as Mr. Jones's freaked-out girlfriend, says) but they are very kind to them. One realizes that last year's flower children have also been overtaken by events; they seem as dated as the sweet vegetarian brontosauruses.

The writing (by Robert Thom, on the basis of his own short story) is often marvelous. There are some monotonous, ringing banalities spoken by the young, but there are other lines: when the liberal senator (played with power-corrupt cool by Hal Holbrook) visits Miss Winters to complain that her son is paralyzing the country, she answers with the dignity of any up against the wall mama. "Senator," she says, in what might be a slogan for our times, "I'm sure my son has a very good reason for paralyzing the country."

The movie, which opened yesterday at the New Embassy Theater and the 72nd Street Playhouse, also features Millie Perkins, Ed Begley, Richard Pryor, Walter Winchell, Kenneth Banghart, Louis Lomax and Melvin Belli. It was directed by the TV director Barry Shear. The music is quite live rock.

*6-6-68*

I don't think anyone really wants to read reviews today of
*Shatterhand,* a gory, Italian-made Western, and *The Name
of the Game Is Kill!* a horror movie which opened yesterday at Loew's Delancey Street and other neighborhood
theaters. Both films are designed for exactly the audiences
their titles would attract. There is nothing good in them.

Loew's Delancey is an interesting theater with purple
pink decor and tiers of seats steeply banked so that it is
easy to see. When I was there, two old men, one of whom
had apparently sat accidentally on the other in the dark,
were having a long, vicious argument that the rest of the
audience, rather sparse and lost in the large theater,
seemed to enjoy.

. . . . Very *Far from Vietnam*

*6-7-68*

The narration of *Far from Vietnam* is of such serene
banality and ugliness that it might have been written by a
misprogramed spokesman for the military-industrial complex. But if the narration were cut—and I seriously think
it is impossible for anyone concerned with facts, or words
or the war to sit through it—the result might be interesting,
a kind of rambling partisan newsreel collage. The film represents a collaboration by six directors (Alain Resnais,
Claude Lelouch, Jean-Luc Godard, William Klein, Joris
Ivens and Agnes Varda) who wanted to do a work of an-

186

tiwar (or more accurately, anti-U.S. involvement in the Vietnamese war) propaganda, without spending much thought or effort on it.

There is a fine short interview with Ho Chi Minh, in which he says Vietnam can wait as long as it takes, and an interview with Fidel Castro, in which he says that a guerrilla war that has the support of the people is the only force stronger than the new technology. There is a very moving conversation between a Vietnamese lady living in Paris and Mrs. Norman Morrison, widow of the American Quaker who burned himself to death to protest the war; it becomes clear why this strange gesture of most extreme nonviolence meant a great deal in many lives.

But there are so many easy ironies. A television commercial for Band-Aids juxtaposed with war scenes, with more television commercials in case anyone missed the point; a broken film from the defective camera of Michele Ray in Vietnam, with a suggestion that a broken film is what makes the best sort of statement about the war, "the cry that [Miss Ray] would have wanted to utter": a sneaking endorsement of violence in the name of peace, or race, or poverty, or powerlessness—or, in fact, anything that is not U.S. foreign policy.

Shots of demonstrations in New York, in Paris, even clips of *La Chinoise*. It is all too facile and slipshod and stereotyped—designed to enrage one cliché cast of mind against the Administration and another against the enragés. The movie has, in any case, been overtaken by events. The last thing we need now is political stereotypes in a rage. A broken film doesn't really make the best statement about anything. Or utter a cry.

*6-9-68*

It occurred to me as I watched *The Long Day's Dying*, an
over-easy war satire in the course of which every member
of the cast is slowly and hideously killed, what I think the
problem of violence in movies is. Violence in movies itself
is nothing. It presents no problems, no matter how much
blasting and crunching and shooting and dueling there is.
It is suffering on screen that presents problems. Wounds,
screams, pain, blood, agonies—these raise the aesthetic
and perhaps even the moral questions. At first, this seems
paradoxical and even inhuman. It is violence, after all,
that is ugly and suffering that should make an appeal to
our humanity.

And, of course, that is exactly the point. The camera
endorses action—fast, violent, transitive action. So do we.
It is one of the pleasures of the cinema. The victims of
screen violence, however—the maimed, the bleeding, and
twitching—are another matter. The camera dotes on
them, too, and we react to them. They are objects of
revulsion. Pure revulsion. That is where the problem lies.
Not that the same reaction does not occur in life, but it is
likely to be more mixed. The camera isolates a fastidious
absence of feeling for suffering and turns it into a reflex:
we see them lingering there in agony and we either turn
away or we want, out of courtesy, to do them in.

Makers of movies in which violence is the point ( and
these are the only ones I'm discussing here; films in which
violence simply occurs are individual matters, they are
good or bad movies on other grounds), particularly
makers of pious agony movies, view things another way.
See, they say, as Peter Collinson does in *The Long Day's
Dying*, here is the result of your war; this severed head,
this missing eye, this shriek, this blood from the lungs.
This is what your guns, grenades and mortars do. Quit or
live with a horrible responsibility. The argument is not

only bad pedagogy. It is also bad art, and especially bad cinema. The viewer is perfectly aware that it is not his war that he sees there on screen, that he has no responsibility for the action of the guns and grenades, that this responsibility extends only to the buying of a ticket—and to his subsequent complicity with the camera in cinema Guignolism. The machine, except in cases of gimmick photography, is never the receiver of action. It participates on behalf of whatever is going on. Of course, it can take on the perspective of the sufferer, but to do so it must be used in more subtle, limiting ways than in examining and collecting wounds. A simulated slaughter is simply never, of itself, an effective sermon; it is only an ambiguous, sensory occasion. There is something about physical suffering on screen that is too real, too literal, too easy anyway; *The Long Day's Dying* becomes an approved *The Good, the Bad and the Ugly* any pacifist can enjoy.

The question of suffering in art comes up in film in another way all the time. Not just shown suffering. The physical cost involved in producing films. It seems that all those stunt men, for example—particularly in a film like *War and Peace*—cannot be falling off their horses all the time and crashing around without quite a number of them getting hurt. One doesn't know what the human cost of making a screen epic might be. Of course, there was much death and pain involved in building the pyramids and a lot of money wrenched from the poor to build cathedrals, and we have them now as works of art. There is no way to tell.

Every cocktail party dilettante is aware that the value of a work of art is divorced from content, that literally anything can be included in a work of art, that moral considerations do not apply. It is a question, however, that does not arise in fact. The day may hypothetically come when someone will compose an immortal mobile out of four dead cats and an index finger, or a symphony for voices in a burning old-age home, and both will be masterpieces. But it is unlikely. And if such a day did come, art itself would have to be redefined so drastically that it would be something else and we would not want it.

189

....... Richard Lester's
*Petulia*

*6-11-68*

*Petulia* is a strange, lovely, nervous little film, very jaggedly cut (by Richard Lester, who also directed *Help!* and *How I Won the War*) so that the parts don't quite match and the plot is almost scattered through. It begins with a rich, married, kooky waif, played by Julie Christie, propositioning a tired divorced surgeon, played by George C. Scott, at a San Francisco charity ball. The waif kook-at-the-top type is becoming a little worn, and Petulia isn't as inventive a character as Morgan or Holly Golightly—she only arrives with a tuba and bruises at Scott's apartment quite early one morning—and yet there is something awfully nice about this film.

For one thing, George C. Scott and Miss Christie are such human and inhabited actors. Early in the movie, when it seems the whole thing is going to expire in flat, heavy whimsy, Petulia says to the surgeon, "I'm going to marry you, Archie." Very soon after that one begins to care about them, hopes they will marry, fights the story as, with its own peculiar pace, it keeps turning up odd little plot fragments. Archie's friends, Barney and Wilma (played by Arthur Hill and Kathleen Widdoes), understanding nothing, show him films of himself and his former wife, in hopes of a reconciliation. Then, in a single line it turns out their own marriage is a nightmare.

A few moments, and the whole life and atmosphere of a hospital are there intact; another fragment and one knows just what Archie's life was like with his wife Polo (Shirley Knight); what it is like with his mistress (Pippa Scott); a short scene on a boat and the quality of Petulia's marriage is clear (her husband, played by Richard Chamberlain, simply throws her an orange and one jumps a mile); her father-in-law (Joseph Cotten) visits her bedside and a whole kind of Californian, a surface-calm nightmare of the far Right is on screen; Polo's relic of a new lover; Ar-

190

chie's relationship with his sons—everything is illuminated very fast, economically but separately, as though someone had deliberately shattered a perfectly formed and crafted film.

The story of Archie and Petulia is there, too, although the movie itself seems to forget it from time to time: whether a bored man will risk the relative order of his life for this violent and poetic idyll; whether she will take on the risks of the normal. Like that. Very odd. There is some very good music by The Grateful Dead, Big Brother and the Holding Company and other groups. There is just too much talent in Lester's use of his own skittish comic techniques for serious purposes to miss. The movie opened yesterday at the Plaza Theater.

. . . . . . . . *Survival 1967*

*6-12-68*

*Survival 1967* got to Israel on the seventh day of the six-day war and looks it. Like some veteran who arrived at the front when the guns were still and who feels compelled for life to boast about what a brave war he spent, the movie keeps climbing truculently onto your barstool and being obnoxious. Missing the action seems to have broken the spirit of the really distinguished writer, Irwin Shaw, and the director, Jules Dassin, entirely.

The narration, delivered by a series of persons who manage to sound simultaneously insincere, patronizing and indignant, consists of whole volleys of dud sarcasms. "Do you expect peace here," the narrator demands to know early on, as he enumerates the wars that have taken place in the Middle East through history, "just because it is the second half of the Twentieth century?" One feels that just by buying a ticket one has offended him in some way. "Forgive us, ladies and gentlemen," he says at another point—in fact, at many other points; he seems fascinated by the irony of variants of this line. "We did not want to be exterminated." Or, "They came for less romantic reasons [than to die here]. They came to live here." Or, "Thou shalt not kill. They observe a new commandment: thou shalt not perish." It keeps breathing these heady parallelisms in one's face like an overstimulated presidential speechwriter.

The movie, which describes itself as "a paean to Israel," opened yesterday at the Cinema Rendezvous. What gets lost is the brave, tragic war itself. (There is hardly any documentary war footage at all.) And the film, which keeps crossing what little moving footage it has—wounded men, monuments to Babi Yar and Buchenwald—by an inability to shut up, is poor and ineffective propaganda. It is also poor reporting. It simply does not tell us anything that we did not already know, and what it does tell—in fuzzy interviews about, for example, the Arab refugee problem—it tells unclearly. Everything about it is off.

. . . . . . Roman Polanski's
*Rosemary's Baby*

*6-13-68*

If a person exhibits paranoid symptoms these days it would seem common decency not to report him, at least, to the persons he claims to be persecuted by, and when Mia Farrow tells what is, after all, a highly plausible story to her obstetrician in *Rosemary's Baby,* it seems wrong of him to deliver her straight to a coven that has designs on her baby. Lord knows how many cases of extremely accurate reporting are cured each day by psychiatrists.

The story, based on a novel by Ira Levin, and written and directed by Roman Polanski (*Repulsion, Knife in the Water*), makes absolute sense in several ways. It is a horror film, not very scary. There are several false frights—a closet door opening ominously to reveal a vacuum cleaner, a letter in a dead woman's hand that reads "I can no longer

192

associate myself," dropped objects in a dark cellar at the Dakota on West Seventy-second Street. But the only really jumpy second occurs when Miss Farrow speaks suddenly and startles a reading witch.

It is a fantasy of the What could have happened to me while I was asleep sort, What did I do when I was drunk, How do I know I'm awake now, What if everyone is lying to me, What am I really pregnant with—not as effective as it might be, because it is a little hard to imagine more than two or three people conspiring in a single pregnancy. And it is a highly serious lapsed-Catholic fable, going on the assumption that God is dead to imagine a Nativity for the dark powers.

The story concerns a young couple, Miss Farrow and John Cassavetes, who move to the Dakota—as likely a place for horrors as any—where Miss Farrow ultimately has reason to believe that her husband, in return for success in his career as an actor, has arranged something with the people next door for her forthcoming child. Ruth Gordon overplays one rouged, elderly witch, with clear joy and overlapping, mutually interrupting sentences. Sidney Blackmer plays her smooth old husband. In the conception scene, there is a whole crew of aging, naked others. Maurice Evans has a small part as a friend who tries to warn her and is put into a coma.

Miss Farrow is quite marvelous, pale, suffering, almost constantly on screen in a difficult role that requires her to be learning for almost two hours what the audience has guessed from the start. One begins to think it is the kind of thing that might really have happened to her, that a rough beast did slouch toward West Seventy-second Street to be born. Everyone else is fine, but the movie—although it is pleasant—doesn't quite work on any of its dark or powerful terms.

I think this is because it is almost too extremely plausible. The quality of the young people's lives seems the quality of lives that one knows, even to the point of finding old people next door to avoid and lean on. One gets very annoyed that they don't catch on sooner. One's friends would have understood the situation at once. So for most of its length the film has nothing to be excited about. It has Miss Gordon bringing herbs and cookies and Miss Farrow eating or not eating them—nothing cumulative—to fill that time with suspense. But the good side of that is that you can see the movie, and like it, without risking terrors or nightmares; it opened yesterday at the Criterion and the Tower East.

.. Elvis Presley in *Speedway*, and *Sol Madrid*

*6-14-68*

*Speedway*, which opened yesterday at the Lyric and other neighborhood theaters, is the latest Elvis Presley picture. It stars Nancy Sinatra, as a blonde, and Mr. Presley with hair dyed black, and it has to do with stock-car racing at the Charlotte, N.C., Speedway. The movie has some high lunatic moments—as when a man being investigated by the Internal Revenue Service assures Mr. Presley that he has wothing to nurry about, or when a waitress at a drive-in hamburger stand, a profoundly depressed person, who is always terrifically moved by everything, begins to sob over a side order of tomatoes and becomes almost uncontrollable over the rest of the order. "Hold the onions," she repeats weeping. "How thoughtful."

Miss Sinatra, however, is far better singing than dancing or acting; the "These Boots Were Made for Walking" spirit is just too formidable in a dancer. And this is after all, just another Presley movie—which makes no great use at all of one of the most talented, important and durable performers of our time. Music, youth and customs were much changed by Elvis Presley twelve years ago; from the twenty-six movies he has made since he sang "Heartbreak Hotel" you would never guess.

*Sol Madrid*, which opened with *Speedway* at neighborhood theaters, stars David McCallum (of "The Man From U.N.C.L.E."), Stella Stevens, Telly Savalas (of

194

*The Dirty Dozen*), Rip Torn, Ricardo Montalban and Pat Hingle. It is a strong cast. Telly Savalas and Rip Torn, in particular, act fine, consistent villains—Mr. Savalas heavy, comic, and civilized, Mr. Torn, callow and lip curling.

The plot is old fashioned and solid, about the police and the Mafia and running heroin from Mexico. The tricks are mean—like getting Miss Stevens hooked on drugs for punishment—and the ending might have been happier, i.e., no Muse would have been seriously betrayed if Mr. McCallum and Miss Stevens had been allowed to stay together. But they were good, and so was Mr. Montalban as a cool Latin. The audience at the Lyric, which was sold out all day yesterday, cheered a lot and it was like a great episode in a first-class TV serial.

. . . Children and Metaphors

*6-16-68*

The best American film of the year so far—and this has been the worst year in a long time for, among other things, movies—is *Wild in the Streets*. It is a very blunt, bitter, head-on but live and funny attack on the problem of the generations. And it is more straight and thorough about the times than any science-fiction or horror movie in a while. What it sees with gay clarity is the absolute tyranny at the hands of the young to which adults in this country seem determined, for fairly odd reasons, to subject themselves. What it knows is what every Brownie troop leader and new kid on the block used to know—that there is no more violent, demagogic, elitist, vicious and totalitarian society than a group of children. All the adults and children in *Wild in the Streets* are thoroughly nerveless and disgusting. The adults, like Shelley Winters, can't even drive out in their cars without running over someone, and the kids, with a kind of nursery Marcusian doubt of the wisdom of the adult majority and faith in the will of a dedicated and violent few, keep presenting totalitarianism as though it were a new discovery, and regarding the information that democracy is frail and flawed as a reason to take the system over by force.

The thing that is surprising about a movie of *Wild in the Street*'s élan and energy, (and although it is quite botched together in many ways, it runs right along) is the number of philosophical bases it manages to touch. It is a brutally witty and intelligent film. Along with publicity as a value, any number of casts of mind are satirized. The idealization of youth, with an aging liberal the most fervent youth cultist of them all. Of course, any society that adores only youth, that does not love and revere the old, must generate violence; when the idea of obsolescence is applied to persons, when the value of lives is not considered partially in terms of the accumulation of years, there is a terrible social logic in cutting lives short. The adolescents in *Wild in the Streets* are already feeling pressure from the under tens.

The adults in the movie, the generational Uncle Toms, have the same reasons for abdicating their responsibility for the world as it is—with murmurs about the mess they have made of things—as their contemporary counterparts who leave things to be run by the lawless among their children: they *must* have a good reason for paralyzing the country, and anyway they couldn't do as badly as we have done. Ignoring the likelihood that the reason the young have not scorched the earth just yet is not infant pacifism but a lack of access, so far at least, to the new technology. (Meanwhile, they do pretty well at their respective age levels with hands, thrown objects, bricks, cars, guns, and rhetoric, adopting, in the name of revolution, the violence of adult society pure; it is the books, order, frail democratic processes and sense of the best in the past that the radical young reject.)

The young in the movie have the contemporary habit of treating metaphors as though they were equivalences and being outraged by them: violence in the streets, institutionalized violence in the system; dying of hunger, dying of boredom. The violence and dying seem to the youngsters in both cases literal—generating revolution equally. This inability to distinguish between metaphorical and literal levels is related to the no doubt television- and movie-conditioned idea of reality, the news as entertainment. Which presents the generation war, the revolution of the young, in what may be its most salutary aspect: a metaphoric war, with ideals, and minor risks, and camaraderie and sense of right, which real war no longer offers. The activity of war without the consequences.

The problem with adults though, is that in being entertained by their young, in using reality as theater to overcome their own boredom, they may be losing hold of the world. It may be that the responsibility of the individual for peaceful reform of a democratic society is just too great, that totalitarianism as spectacle outdraws individual responsibility in fact. In which case we can all gather round in our robes at the water coolers.

. . . . . . . . . . *The Queen*
of the Camp Pageant

*6-18-68*

*The Queen* is an extraordinary documentary about the Miss All-America Camp Beauty Pageant held at Town Hall in 1967. The contestants were transvestites from all over the country—some of them winners in regional contests—judged for walking, talking, bathing suit, make-up, hairdo, and, of course, beauty. The star and the winner was Harlow, a frail, blond, pouting young man, formerly Miss Philadelphia. The director was Frank Simon (his first feature film), and the movie itself is funny—not tactless—and inspired the way *The Endless Summer*, of surfing, was inspired. It shows us another America.

It is good to watch for about an hour these colorful human beings whose entire self-image is a put-on, in their Atlantic City of Genet, in their Forest Hills of drag. The drag queens are, of course, perfectly aware that they are not women, and even their mannerisms—the flatted
197

vowels, the relaxed wrist, the gait of the homosexual who wants it known—are not female imitations at all, but parodies. Very witty, detailed parodies at that. The question of invasion of privacy does not arise; one is watching actors, very conscious actors, at work. They may be absolutely miserable (like others) in their private lives, but in their costumed appearances they enrich the landscape enormously.

At times, Miss Sabrina, Miss Crystal and Miss Harlow and the rest seem to have taken Hollywood's old message very much to heart: Both the two-fisted gunfighter and the sex queen could find stardom, but the sex queen really had all the lines. The cosmetic idea was bound to spill over a bit. So here are all these gentlemen in bras, diaphanous gowns, lipstick, hairfalls and huffs—discussing their husbands in the military in Japan, or describing their own problems with the draft. One grows fond of all of them. They are much more entertaining than the conventional Miss This or Miss That.

Two shorts opened at the Kips Bay Theater yesterday with *The Queen*. One, French, about a factory where plaster mannequins are molded, filed, hammered and repaired, is about the most extreme, laconic anti-female movie since Dean Martin last starred in anything, and the other, called *2* and spoken in American-accented Italian, is hilarious. Written by Renée Taylor, it is about a couple of people about to make love on the beach, who start confessing to each other. He tells the most outrageous things. She pardons him. She tells the most outrageous things. He pardons her. ("I have been with all your friends, Irving, Lewis . . ." she begins. "So have I," he says.) It is a fine program altogether.

*The Green Berets* is a film so unspeakable, so stupid, so rotten and false in every detail that it passes through being fun, through being funny, through being camp, through everything and becomes an invitation to grieve, not for our soldiers or for Vietnam (the film could not be more false or do a greater disservice to either of them) but for what has happened to the fantasy-making apparatus in this country. Simplicities of the right, simplicities of the left, but this one is beyond the possible. It is vile and insane. On top of that, it is dull.

The film, directed by John Wayne and nominally based on a novel by Robin Moore, has no hero. It is vaguely about some Green Berets, led by John Wayne, trying to persuade Wayne's idea of a liberal journalist (David Janssen) that this war is a fine thing for Vietnam and for America. The movie has human props taken from every war film ever made: a parachute jump; an idea of Vietcong soldiers, in luxury, uniform, champagne, and caviar, apparently based on the German high command; a little Asian orphan named Hamchunk, pronounced Hamchuck but more like Upchuck than anything; battle scenes somewhere between *The Red Badge of Courage* and *The Dirty Dozen;* a pathetically dying dog.

There is inadvertent humor: "He's dying," a Negro medic says, thoughtfully spooning Jim Beam bourbon down the throat of an elderly Oriental. "Poor old thing can't even keep his rice down any more." What is clearly an Indian extra in a loincloth somehow straggles in among the montagnards. A Vietcong general is dragged from a bed of sin (which, through an indescribable inanity of the plot, the Green Berets have contrived for him) with his trousers on. He is subsequently drugged and yanked off into the sky on a string dangling from a plane. A Green Beret points out to the journalist some American-made punji sticks (the movie is obsessed with punji sticks): "Yup," the Green Beret says, "it's a little trick we learned from Charlie. But we don't dip them in the same stuff he does."

What the movie is into is another thing entirely. What is sick, what is an outrage and a travesty, is that while it is meant to be an argument against war opposition—while it keeps reiterating its own line at every step, much as soap operas keep recapitulating their plots—it seems so totally impervious to any of the questions that it raises. It is so full of its own caricature of patriotism that it cannot even find the right things to falsify. No acting, no direction, no writing, no authenticity, of course. But it is worse. It is completely incommunicado, out of touch. It trips something that would outrage any human sensibility, like mines, at every step and staggers on.

The first Green Beret comes on speaking German, to show his versatility in languages. When the VC have just been sprayed with flames, a Green Beret is asked about his apparent affinity for this kind of thing. "When I was a kid," he says modestly, "my dad gave me a chemistry set. And it got bigger than both of us." When the VC, nonetheless, win the Special Forces camp in hand-to-hand combat, a soldier calls in air support. "It'll only take a minute," he says, like a dentist, as the VC are mowed down from the air. The journalist, "the former skeptic about the war," the press kit synopsis chooses to say at this point, "leaves to write about the heroic exploits of the American and South Vietnamese forces."

The point is that Wayne is using spoken German, lunatic chemistry sets, machine killing of men who have won fairly hand-to-hand, without apparently noticing that this is not exactly the stuff of which heroic fantasies are made. This is crazy. If the left-wing extremist's nightmare of what we already are has become the right-wing extremist's ideal of what we ought to be we are in steeper trouble than anyone could have imagined.

6-21-68

*Nazarin* is the most relentlessly pessimistic of Luis
Buñuel's films, less brutal than *Viridiana,* more Buñuel
than *Belle de Jour.* It is so grim that it lacks even the
energy to present itself dramatically. The sense of misery
is so profound that everything, except the pure, etched
photography of Gabriel Figueroa, comes out mediocre.
The French newspaper *La Croix* thought the film carried
an evangelical message, very fierce; the Communist paper
*l'Humanité* found blasphemy and rabid anticlericalism.
The film is so bitter, with just a ghostly, uncontagious
smile, as to be almost bored with itself. Any ideologue
who could take heart from it must have gone to see it on a
very sunny day.

Francisco Rabal plays a vapid young priest in Mexico,
under the dictator Porfirio Díaz—plays him without
vitality, without purity, without even a lovable, bumbling
goodness. The priest lives in a slum house, teeming with
thieves, whores and entrepreneurs of various kinds. As
the movie begins the poor man has been robbed. The architecture of the house makes it easier for people to step
into his room through an arched window from the corridor than to go around and enter by the door and, in a
kind of dim, recurrent joke, people keep climbing through
his window. He takes alms and gives them away; he
preaches.

He says a few pious banalities to a ruined young
woman (Marga López), who is supposed to be wildly in
love with a gross, ridiculous horse trader who has abandoned her and for whom she tries ineffectually (the smile
again) to hang herself. He harbors a prostitute who has
killed somebody. He is forced to flee on a pilgrimage and
he manages to bring complete unhappiness to nearly
everyone with whom he comes in contact. Except for cur-
ing one superstitious hysteric, he manages everywhere to
leave the world just a little worse than he found it.

There are plagues, brutalities, uglinesses throughout the film, and Buñuel smiles just about twice more. Once, when the priest is boring an already dying young woman to death, she keeps murmuring quite distinctly that she wants her lover. "Not heaven. Juan," she says repeatedly. Again, when Miss López faints and has convulsions at the merest suggestion she might be in love with the priest—and she goes off, in despair, with her horse trader. Finally, and this is the closest the film actually gets to a kind of bubonic mirth, the priest is offered a pineapple by a sympathetic woman as he walks in chains across Mexico along a long hot road to jail. He rejects the pineapple. Then, in an agony of spirit, he accepts it after all. The soundtrack is rising drumbeats. Faith, his anyway, renewed.

The acting, by Mr. Rabal, Miss López, Rita Macedo as the prostitute, and the rest of the cast, is quite equal to what Buñuel is trying to do. In other films, quite notably *Viridiana,* Buñuel's recurring themes—poverty, meanness, religion, sexual pathology—were there in force. You might share them or be moved or repelled or even bored by them; but they assaulted you. This one is milder, passive, deadlier. It is so tired, that—aside from its photography and one fascinating dwarf—it hardly exists at all. You have to be determined to like it in order to be affected by it.

The screenplay by Buñuel and Julio Alejandro is based on the novel by Benito Perez Galdos. *Nazarin,* which won a Grand Prix at the Cannes Film Festival in 1958, opened yesterday at the Carnegie Hall Cinema.


. . . Claiming Responsibility,
Asserting Control


*6-23-68*


Just as they were beginning to look almost hopeless, things have gotten a lot better with American movies since last week. *Petulia, The Queen, Rosemary's Baby,* even *Sol Madrid* and *Speedway* are all worth seeing in their way—the last two maybe on the spur of the moment if they happen to be nearby. *Speedway* and *Sol Madrid* opened at the Lyric Theater on Forty-second Street, which is kind of a movie experience in its own right—nearly every seat filled from 8:30 in the morning until 4 A.M., with a kind of restless, roving day and night audience, some sleeping, a few sampling the air conditioning, some creaking with what sound like the world's driest teeth on popcorn. Lyric audiences respond very discriminatingly to a program like this one: laughter at good lines, hoots and comment for bedroom scenes, complete sympathy for every embattled underdog, dead silence for bad comedy. The ushers are very alert in case anyone gets carried away.

*The Queen* is a funny, tactful movie about the Miss All-America Camp Beauty Pageant, held for transvestites from all over the country, in 1967, at Town Hall. Drag queens present all sorts of questions about what parody is, since every queen is, in a sense, a living put-on, a denial of very convincing evidence. Teasing their hair, sulking over the failure of their falls to arrive, discussing their dresses, and backgrounds and experiences with the draft, they seem really a cross-section of America, integrated racially and regionally, and even personally. There is a tendency to regard these colorful, perhaps not too well adjusted people as a product of modern life, as a community that by some parental or societal failure we are all responsible for—as people seem determined to claim guilt for violent political events. (Claiming responsibility for the acts most remote from one seems a way of trying to assert control over things, of denying that events can be random, pointless and chaotically horrible.)

But the drag queens, flatting their vowels, mincing—parodying, not even women, but themselves parodying women—seem all right as they are, part of the American dream as defined by the narcissistic sex goddesses of old Hollywood. It is as though Hollywood made the star queen so alluring that everybody has since wanted to be one. From the brisk, spinsterly mistresses of ceremonies to the huffy but generous runners up, Sabrina,

Crystal, Harlow and the rest are all personalities new to the screen and very welcome there. The choice of subject for this film was inspired; the treatment, by director Frank Simon and the cast, is almost as good.

*Speedway* is only the latest Elvis Presley film but it has some unexpectedly comic scenes in it—a chronically depressed carhop waitress profoundly moved by an order of hamburger without onions, and so on. Presley is, of course, one of the most successful, talented and durable performers in history. Since the fifties, when he became the first important white singer of Negro music, when he shifted pop from crooned saccharine to rhythm and blues and rock, he has set a lot of forces going in this country. In a way, apathy's end, sex, even youth activism and civil rights began again with Elvis. But he has never made an ambitious film. Perhaps he will.

Richard Lester's *Petulia* is a fine, troubling movie, very strangely cut and dense with detail, every fragment perfect but—unlike Mike Nichols' detail in *The Graduate*—not always relevant to the main line of attention, so that the impression is that of an intricate, lovely thing deliberately shattered out of some odd sense of time. It stars George C. Scott as a doctor and Julie Christie as a hurt kook, and with every supporting actor from Kathleen Widdoes and Shirley Knight to a young man with a walk-on as an intern, it is probably the best-acted film in many months.

The beginning is bad; Miss Christie's early whimsy is poorly written and flat. Then, there is one beautifully conceived scene after another; Scott waking up with a smoker's cough; Scott walked in on by his ex-wife, Miss Knight, drawn to her and then put off by her icky triteness, her use of words like icky, her determination to turn any unfamiliar object into a lamp; Scott with his sons on a Sunday; Miss Christie in scenes of just checked violence with Joseph Cotten, as her father-in-law, and Richard Chamberlain as her husband.

The story is shot through with allusions to violence—the war in Vietnam always on television, beating, car accidents, fights at the Roller Derby, even visits to a military reservation and Alcatraz, as elements of the plot—and also to the horror of marriages. The seals at Marineland are
204

described as recently divorced. The story is mainly about Miss Christie and Scott—through failures of courage and through the violence life does to them—passing each other in the night. But where it is almost uncanny is in its evocation of the quality of life in California, hippies, motels, Mexican-American housing, all-night supermarkets, gift indoor greenhouses, sunshine, and all. When Miss Christie, having been beaten almost to death, is carried awkwardly downstairs out of a house on a stretcher, one neighbor remarks that he had the same trouble moving his piano; another says "She'll have a heck of a time washing all that blood out of her hair."

There is also an extraordinary evocation of the mood of hospitals, a kind of surgical comedy of malice, absurdism, pain, and healing hands. (Miss Christie is fond of Scott's hands, which are, in fact, beautiful). The pace of the cutting runs counter to the viewer's tuning in, but *Petulia* is very much worth seeing, brilliant for short turns, like trills.

. . . . . .François Truffaut's
*The Bride Wore Black*

*6-26-68*

Even working lightly, on a film not his best in a genre not his own, François Truffaut is such a rare talent that one knows instantly, as soon as the credits for *The Bride Wore Black* appear on screen, that this is what movies are about, this is how they can be done, this is why so few people do them beautifully. The movie is technically a suspense and horror film—a tribute to Alfred Hitchcock, with whom Truffaut did a fascinating book of interviews last year—in which Jeanne Moreau murders a number of gentlemen. But Truffaut is such a poetic filmmaker that the film turns around and becomes a gentle comedy and one of the few plausible and strange love stories in a long time.

Miss Moreau murders five men in all—Claude Rich,

Michel Bouquet, Michael Lonsdale, Daniel Boulanger an Charles Denner—and every one of them is a gem c characterization, lines witty and right, acting subtle an thought out, the decor of their lives and even the manne of their deaths inventive and expressive of personality Miss Moreau herself, who is always dressed in black or i white (this is a color film), has to maintain a kind c Mademoiselle and Kriemhild deadpan in an uncharac teristically young unsensual role and does it fine. Alexar dra Stewart as a schoolteacher, Jean-Claude Brialy as friend, even Frédérique and Renaud Fontanarosa playin musicians (which they are)—every member of the cas gives a performance that makes other people's movie seem keyed loose and out of tune.

There are all kinds of little things: the look of fear tha crosses the expression of Claude Rich when he thinks h is going to be pushed off a balcony, then the look of en barrassment over this silly fear, then his look as he fall Michael Lonsdale's minute, self-satisfied nod toward h Legion d'Honneur lapel; a small, perfectly timed clappin of the hands, in a game of hide and seek by Christoph Brunot, a little boy from whom Truffaut gets the be child performance since Alain Cohen's in *The Two of U* The boy knows an adult is being misled; his behavic towards adults, suspicious, canny, stubborn, terrifie amused, is one of the most remarkable evocations c certain moments in certain childhoods on screen.

The photography is by Raoul Coutard—who also di Truffaut's *400 Blows, Jules and Jim* and *Shoot the Pian Player!*—and it, too, is beautifully and carefully worke out. A sign of the absolute confidence one has in ever moment of the film is that, although one of the killings i done by high-powered rifle, from a window to the stree the movie recovers from real associations to that act a most at once. Everything is so clearly the result of thougl and wit; this is, for a change, a film in which it is pur pleasure to be alert. One does not want to review th refinements of the plot away. It is not a great, great pic ture but it is touching and fun at a level so much highe than other films that it is just a great relief to have it t see. The film opened yesterday at the Festival Theater.

*6-27-68*

*The Thomas Crown Affair,* starring Steve McQueen and Faye Dunaway and directed by Norman Jewison (of *In the Heat of the Night*), is just the movie to see if you want to see an ordinary, not wonderful, but enjoyable movie —of which there have been so few this year. In a way it is the last word in a girl's career versus love story; Miss Dunaway plays a single-minded insurance investigator determined to arrest McQueen, a millionaire who robs a Boston bank to express his alienation from the System. It is not quite clear why she pursues him in a mono-maniacally professional way, but the ending is just right and it is very important not to walk in late and see it before the beginning, which is the lovely robbery itself.

The movie has many problems. For one thing, the love story itself doesn't work very well. Both McQueen and Miss Dunaway are required to smile a lot, in fact almost incessantly, with savvy, quizzical, sizing each other up, sad smiles that become distracting presences, like lights on the ceilings, in themselves. One begins to wait for them. Then, there is a kind of an oral chess scene, modeled after Tom Jones at table, which is just about as subtle and ef-fective as its predecessor. For all the finger in mouths and stroking of chess pieces, it is just impossible to castle in-sinuatingly. Finally, there is a long, soon-to-be-famous kissing scene that is so mis-directed that one thinks of Ed-sels on a summer night.

But there are a lot of good things; McQueen is always special, and although this role is too indoors and formal for him, he does get a chance to race across the desert, or fly a glider or lounge on the beach, in the casual-intense work he is best at. Miss Dunaway has some nice scenes in which she struggles tearfully with her monomania. Alan R. Trustman, who wrote the screenplay, has tried for some flat, straight ersatz Bogey lines, "I know who I am. Don't you pin your labels on me, Eddy," or "It's my funeral. You're just along for the ride." Sometimes this gets to be like the smiles. But the robberies themselves are graceful and funny. Peggy Shirley has a pale, screaming walk-on as a nagging wife, and there are a couple of songs, written and sung by Noel Harrison (who recorded Leonard Cohen's "Suzanne"), just put in, almost irrelevantly, as they were in *Up the Junction,* to cover the action. They work out very well. The movie opened yesterday at the Astor, the 34th Street, and the 86th Street East.

.....*Have You Heard of*
*the San Francisco*
*Mime Troupe?*

6-28-68

*Have You Heard of the San Francisco Mime Troupe?* which opened yesterday at the New Cinema Playhouse, is a kind of American *La Chinoise*—minus Godard. Since the movie is technically quite primitive, this is a fairly important lack. The dialogue, even for those who already know and admire the troupe, is very hard to understand, and the group is such an essentially living enterprise that its best routines—six minstrels, three white, three black, in blackface, inviting white girls in the audience to dance, or leading the audience in a sing-along version of the now embarrassing "Ol' Black Joe"—are lost at the extra remove celluloid.

But there are some moments in the life of this radical left, vibrant, hate-free band of troubadours that are worth the price of admission if you can pass through a little incomprehension and ennui to get to them. A young lady San Francisco Chinoise, arguing with Ronnie Davis, the director, that his theater is not making revolution, gives a short disquisition on Brecht, "Brecht was hooked up, he was hooked up in such a way . . ."; or, when Davis asks her for solutions instead of revolutionary questions, she insists in a not at all dreary voice, that solutions are "irrelevant, irrelevant" or, with a shrug, "What am I? Am I Karl Marx?" The minstrels, minus blackface, in rehearsal are also very good.

At worst, the film is a long, quite ideology-ridden commercial for the troupe, which really does need and deserve money and which is often closed, in its travels, for what officials consider obscenity. At best, it is a kind of bulletin—like *The Queen*—from another colorful world. In the middle, it is a view of an awake and spirited, troubled but sense-of-humor left. "They don't have any purpose in life," a citizen of San Francisco says, after one of their free performances in the park. They clearly do.

The players themselves are talented, admirable and kind, whether joking with some difficult children ("Go play in the traffic for a while"), or gently summing up something everyone has thought ("I'm just hoping something's gonna happen soon," one of the minstrels in rehearsal says to the camera. "Something good, for everybody").

Also playing at the Cinema Rendezvous is a not very fascinating short, *Split Decisions*, starring José Torres, the prizefighter; Pete Hamill, Norman Mailer and Caine Young.

∴ . . . The Absolute End of
the Romance of War

*6-30-68*

It is often the people who are most comfortable insisting that movies are, without question, the only serious art form of our time who are also the first to say, when someone actually takes a movie seriously enough to listen to and be appalled by it, Oh, what the hell, it's only a movie. Well, the realities of filmmaking are such that films rarely have anything at all to do with art, but that quite fre-

quently a film is more than just a movie. *The Green Bere*
is a pivotal event. The antiwar people have had a string
films all along which add a new dimension to the e
ecrable; the pro-Vietnam war people were entitled to ju
one. The point about *The Green Berets* is not what i
worth but what it means, and it means a lot of things.

To begin with, it marks the end of the traditional w
picture and a tremendous breakdown of the fantasy-ma
ing apparatus in this country. It had not occurred to *
until I saw *The Green Berets* that I had not seen a film
many months which unequivocally, unironically endors
violence—not even war—just violence. There have be
cruel, vicious, messy films all over the place but the a
titude toward and within them has changed. Everyone is
pretends to be laughing or tongue-in-cheek (laughing wi
Clyde, or Lee Marvin, or Sinatra, or Perry and Dick)
moralistic (as in the bleeding antiwars). In both cas
violence is used ironically, often to endorse its opposite.
course, this sort of irony has its ugly side. It gets so o
tries not to polemicize against a thing too thoroughly f
fear people will go to see it just to laugh. And camp iro
always conceals a moral failure and a lie—a sec
idealization of what one claims to be laughing at or, in t
case of an ideological opponent, a refusal to come to gri
with an argument. But the fact is that the romance
violence on screen is dead. So is the romance of war. A
*The Green Berets*—as compared to any war film of t
past—marks the absolute end.

It is not just that anyone who has ever been in Vi
nam, or heard of Vietnam, or read the news, or watched
television set knows that the film is false—that the Vi
cong do not wear full dress uniform, drink wine, eat cavi
drive about in flag-flying, breathing new Citroens and
motorcycles, attack in crowds, spend countless manho
inter-weaving punji sticks so elaborate they amount to
national handicraft; the Green Berets are not of an avera
sixty years of age, do not parachute about as in World W
II, spend hours at nightclubs à la Fontainebleau, set v
tuous Vietnamese ladies to seductions, abduct V.C. of
cials in the night with the help of montagnard crossbo
drugs, and a most ridiculous balloon and string, so t

210

passing aircraft can yank them off into the sky; Vietnam is not full of artificial foliage and white birch. No.

And it is not simply that the war is resistant to romance, that its public relations viability seems zero and that (in spite of what revolutionaries like to say about the media) nothing has contributed so much to national distaste for the war as television screen coverage. It is not just that for all the movie's striving slang the quality of slang in the real war shows almost perfectly what it thinks of itself. A war in which the enemy's first name in our own slang is "Victor" has got to be the worst slang war in history.

It is not even the fantastic, incredibly jarring, inadvertently comic tastelessnesses. When the virtuous Vietnamese lady has seduced and delivered a V.C. official, who has only one line in the entire transaction and in the entire film ("Wine?" he says to the lady. "Later," she replies. His only subsequent sound is a faint mewing when he is dragged out of bed), Wayne has an avuncular chat with a South Vietnamese colonel, her brother-in-law. "Colonel," Wayne says, "her whole future, her self-respect, everything is in your hands." The colonel gets the point. Overcoming his native Vietnamese puritanism in matters of sex, he approaches his sister-in-law.

"Lin," he says, "you're a brave woman."

"Not a brave woman," she says, "just a woman praying that her family will forgive her." Laying her head against his shoulder, she weeps.

But the piece of dialogue that is beyond belief occurs at the end of the movie. A thoroughly unconvincing little Vietnamese boy, an orphan of the Japanese-Korean movie genre, has lost his only friend, his dog, and has been more or less adopted by an American, who has just been impaled on the crossweave of punji sticks. The little boy searches every helicopter returning to base, and figures it out. John Wayne walks him to the sea.

"What will happen to me now?" the little boy asks. Wayne has put Peterson's beret on the orphan's head.

"You let me worry about that, Green Beret," he says. "You're what this is all about."

I don't want to create the impression this is a funny

211

film. But there is clearly a certain out-of-touchness here. Never mind who really orphaned that child; just point to it reproachfully. Of course, the Left has been doing this sort of thing for years, but nobody sees their films. And that is what is pivotal about *The Green Berets:* whether people will pay admission to it. If so, the fantasy-making machine will be losing its grip and everyone will begin to condescend to films. If not, it will also have marked a turning point. Films can devote themselves to the immense and serious problem of finding an imaginative substitute for war, the heroes, the risk, the bond, the conviction of being in the right. Violence and war simply do not have it any more, except in the nostalgic black-and-whites. The war-fantasy substitute problem is arising on every domestic barricade. For the movies, though, as terminally represented in *The Green Berets,* I think the war is over.

. . . . . . . *Dark of the Sun*
and *Custer of the West:*
Hostels

7-4-68

*Dark of the Sun* is a kind of cross between *The Dirty Dozen* and *The Comedians,* which stars Jim Brown and Rod Taylor in a kind of "I Spy" duet. The movie, which was filmed in Jamaica, is about mercenaries in the Congo who go by train to rescue some diamonds, refugees and Yvette Mimieux from the rebel Simba. It did not seem to me very plausible. There is a lot of carnage on every side, in contexts that will probably infuriate anyone who scrutinizes movies for their politics. There is none of the liberal idealization of people who, through lack of technology, kill more personally and less efficiently than we do; on the other hand, there were signs of sympathy with colonial aspirations and pacifistic longings for nonviolence. The end of the film is a little stroke of plotting

212

lunacy, which seems to reflect the movie's standoff ambiguity about what it thinks.

But the direction by Jack Cardiff, who did *Sons and Lovers,* is sporadically interesting. These are scenes—of a black, cigar-chomping engineer starting a train at dawn, of warfare, of the refugees at the mercy of the rebels—that don't look like anybody else's scenes. They might be at some point of comedy and menace where *Heart of Darkness* and *Scoop* converge. Jim Brown is quite good in short speeches, but when he has long lines that are silly or hard to take—as when he has to explain that for him being a mercenary in the Congo is like Bunker Hill—he begins to sound embarrassed and artificial.

Rod Taylor clearly has a fine time as a tough, no-nonsense guy who finally reveals his gentle heart by running amok, slaughtering a German murderer to avenge Brown, and then, and this is the plot stroke, turning himself in for court-martial. Yvette Mimieux, who mostly pines about for him, is O.K. and Calvin Lockhart has a serene and deadly walk-on as the Congolese president. The film is basically low grade. It seems to have more than its quota of violence about the head (heads held under advancing engine wheels and so on) and yet, at moments, it rises far above itself and becomes worth seeing and almost fine. It opened yesterday at Loew's 83rd Street and other neighborhood theaters.


"Did you see any hostels?" was, I thought, an odd line to address to a frontier scout in *Custer of the West,* but it turned out to be "hostiles" that were under discussion. The hostiles were Indians and *Custer of the West* is clearly a film that too many people have meddled with. Shot in Cinerama but released in ordinary wide screen, the quality of the print is abysmal. There are signs that the movie was never marvelous—even Robert Shaw and Mary Ure, who star, seem to have only one expression, and there is a lot of anachronistic slang; but there are also signs that somebody meant to try something fairly ambitious, to show the Indian wars through a contemporary sensibility,

Custer as a thoroughly modern man who would have li
Camus.

But there is no point in going on about it. So m
strange cutting and botching went into the job that i
nearly impossible to follow the story and the momen
Custer's great crisis of some sort is completely imposs
to understand. Robert Siodmak, who directed Hemingw
*The Killers,* directs. The film opened yesterday at the 8
Street Coliseum and other neighborhood theaters.

．．．．． Anyone for a Laugh:
Exemptions

7-7

For so long in the fifties, when the young wore crew
and ponytails, varsity sweaters and circle pins, kha
kneesocks, kilts, loafers with pennies in them and, ins
as possible, identical expressions, humor was d
Laughter, irony and scorn were the prerogatives of
investigating committee, the small-town school,
system, the bully in every form. They were directed alw
at weakness and diversity, never at sameness and po
Not humor, but persecuting laughter. It was the era of
mocking tyranny of the same. We had just not won a
people demanded to know whose fault it was. All but
best lay low; the young got the message and standardi
their plaids and metals and jokes. Talent and differer
were persecuted hard and a whole generation has
emerged from its separate crannies and accommodati
yet—except for the thirtyish leaders of the very you
who do not count. (It is always self-defeating to pret
to the style of a generation younger than your own
simply erases your own experience in history.)

I think humor now is just about as dead as it
was—the isolated talents that grew up when laughter
authoritarian, unfunny and at their expense are
remarkable now for their wit—but a curious thing

214

happened. People are determined to regard something as funny if somebody says it is. There are laughers now in almost every movie theater in town. Unhappy laughers, at some level they consider suitable. Thus, there is *Prudence and the Pill*. There are people who consider it necessary, in their particular bracket of sophistication, to show that they can laugh publicly at contraception. There is not a single funny moment in the film, not one line, not one plot situation, not one character (with the possible exception of Dame Edith Evans' crossing a track where an auto race is in progress and saying, "So this is the pit"). The whole plot bogs interminably in the proposition that there exists some pharmacological, chromatic, spatial and tactile idiot who could mistake an oral contraceptive for an aspirin or a vitamin pill. Yet people laugh; nobody wants to miss the joke if there is one.

And *The Producers*. The audience laughs with apparent misery at all the lewd, hideous tumble of old ladies at the start. The film has been described everywhere as hilarious, after all. It is like a test. One can feel the relief when the much more comic, much less cruel, Hitler scenes occur later on. But it is not merely intentional comedies that keep laughers alert. They are on the qui vive for anything that might have a faintly satiric, mocking or just plain unserious sound. This leads them to laugh at jokes within films, which are meant to reveal character by being unfunny, at violence, sweetness, anything. As long as it is at a level they want to be on. (*Pill* laughers say, think themselves at a higher level than *Family Band* laughers.)

But this is unimportant. What seems really strange is that at this time, in the mind of almost everyone, anything that claims to be funny or, better yet, claims to be *satire* immediately enjoys a series of critical exemptions. We look at it more kindly. We approach it with a special vocabulary. Something that says it is humor faces the unsmiling viewer almost like an accusation. I recently saw Robert Downey's *No More Excuses*, which followed *Chafed Elbows* as an underground comedy success. The film had clearly been spliced together from several movies in progress, each of which seemed to me so devoid of humor, of wit, of form, of even silliness of an inventive

kind that it brought on a whole new order of depressi
There was one sequence in which a preoccupied sol
stands with his back to the audience, which reminded
of the highly comic new interpretation the San Franci
Mime Troupe once gave, with the same scene, to the "
a'coming" line from "Old Black Joe." And there w
several long cuts of a speaker for the society to clo
naked animals—which was a confessed joke in its o
time. That was all. But one wants to give it credit for
context of comedy.

But sex is not funny, race is not funny, and certai
nothing is *satire* simply by virtue of being included in
context of somebody's work that is not serious. You h
to do something, say something, take pains. (Of cou
there are whole keyboard sensibilities now where j
referring deadpan to President Johnson or Congressio
Medal of Honor Winner will sound satirical.) For the r
I simply don't know what it is we think we are all laugh
at, how we arrived at these exemptions, why we h
agreed to accept so much as humor that is simply
measuring up to the standards we set for seriousness.

*The Bride Wore Black* is funny. There are six killings
the film and four reruns of someone being gunned do
from a window on the street, and yet the film is so ge
and poetic that it is hardly affected by the associati
guns now arouse and it is a kind of romantic and plausi
love story besides. Jeanne Moreau, who plays the br
seems a bit older than she might (it is a color film)
she has to keep the same deadpan she had in *M
emoiselle*, but she acts so well and Truffaut is so c
pletely in control that Miss Moreau gets a chance to
mate that expression in some marvelous comic-threat
ing scenes.

In frame after frame Truffaut's details are per
—even carrots still on a murder knife—down to any de
one wants to watch or listen to the movie at. There
superb performance by a child (Christophe Brunot) wh
helpless in the face of a semantic problem in which h
being deceived, who claps briefly, with exact timing i
game of hide and seek, who turns the semantic trick, f
fully, cannily himself later on. Ever since Jean-Pie

216

Léaud in *The 400 Blows*, Truffaut has always called forth fine performances from children (and, interestingly enough, there are important, grave child performers in the films by Brynych, Finney and of course, Berri, too). But Truffaut is special and one of the few directors who makes simple, personal, great films.

........ Alan Arkin in
*Inspector Clouseau*

7-25-68

*Inspector Clouseau* is a comedy so uninspired, so relentlessly awful that one occasionally laughs for it—more like a moo or a snort or a gagging noise—just to interrupt it a little or help it out of the room. The absence of humor is particularly glaring because the writers, Tom and Frank Waldman, and the director, Bud Yorkin (*Never Too Late*), were clearly free to let their imagination run—without plot or structure or limit. The result is one of those episodic, all-purpose arbitrary comedies often described as zany or a spoof, in which anything goes and nothing works.

From the first appearance of Alan Arkin, as an inspector called in from Sureté to solve a British bank robbery, it is clear that it is all a mistake. He has to do a lot of absent-minded running about with a hole in his sock, which it would take a clown, or a mime, or a precise silent comedian to bring off. Then, he has a lot of stupid lines, which, surprisingly, he delivers in an accent that is not French. He has got it wrong somehow so that the bumbling Gallic inspector sounds like a Hispano-Slavic customer's man. He has a funny line or two (the only one I can remember is a distrustful "Are you pushing my leg?") and he has a couple of funny, modified Gene Wilder verbal tantrums. And that's it.

But Arkin off his stride is the least of the films' problems as it flails about to a prison barbershop, a highland

217

fair, a clubroom, a bomb in a plum pudding, a Swiss chocolate factory, and so on, in search of a joke. The direction has turned the whole movie blurred and imprecise. The timing of many of the lines is off and the film lingers longest over every anecdotal mistake—particularly Beryl Reid, as the aging, kilted lassie wife of a British inspector, as she tumbles all over Arkin in one of those menopausal female assaults that Hollywood finds so amusing these days. Everything is done too long, too slowly and too often—which would be more of a shame if it had been funny to begin with. The movie opened yesterday at the Trans-Lux East and West.

. . . Marcello Mastroianni in
*Kiss the Other Sheik*

7-30-68

*Kiss the Other Sheik* is one of those sodden, gross off-color comedies that the Italians do so badly and export to us. The plot, in partial narration (in dubbed Italian) by Pamela Tiffin, concerns a Roman husband who tries to sell his demanding wife to a succession of Bedouin chiefs, the first of whom tries to pay him in IOU's and the last of whom turns out to be homosexual and buys the husband instead. A recurrent joke consists of an earring torn off an earlobe, which, covered with blood and tissue paper, appears repeatedly on screen.

If that absolutely cracks you up, there is another visual joke, in which an entire hotel lobby is filled with girls dressed in Pucci prints. The dubbing of the film is almost completely divorced from the lip motions of the actors and from the sub-titles, which brings on a kind of Excedrin fraying of the mind. But since Italian directors are often less than fanatic about synchronization (some actors have been known, in the past, to recite poetry or the Twenty-third Psalm on camera, leaving dubbing for later on), it doesn't matter much. Miss Tiffin has been mis-

218

photographed, or mis-directed (by Luciano Falce) or mis-made-up, so that she looks simultaneously inflated and floury, like some kind of Betty Crocker water toy. Virna Lisi is featured in a minor part.

The real problem, however, is Marcello Mastroianni in the starring role. Whenever an actor of distinction manages to create a whole range of character that sums up something special about the sensibility of his time—in Mr. Mastroianni's case it has been intelligent, moderate decency, physical health and utter spiritual exhaustion—there seems to be a temptation to use his name, surround him with incompetents and cast him as a tap dancer or den father to a household of koala bears. If Garbo were acting now, someone would probably cast her in this sort of merry part. Mr. Mastroianni keeps appearing in bad sex farces.

Loew's Cine, Third Avenue at Eighty-sixth Street, where the film opened yesterday, opened as well. It has rather dark labyrinthine entrances, but the seats themselves are steeply banked so that you can see very clearly even if tall people are sitting in front of you.

........ *The Heart is
a Lonely Hunter:*
Place Resonance

8-1-68

*The Heart is a Lonely Hunter,* which opened yesterday at the Warner Brothers new Penthouse Theater and the Murray Hill, is an interesting example of how very difficult it must be for the arts when there is an immense political awareness in the air. So much in Carson McCuller's early novel about Singer, the deaf-mute whose silence became an expression and a magnet for all the lonely, life-impaired whites and Negroes in a Southern town, had to be updated and changed. And still one keeps scrutinizing the movie, almost hostilely, for where it politically stands.

219

It is not just that we know that no Southern Negroes speak quite the way Miss McCullers's Portia, the Beulah-Aunt Jemima talking daughter of a proud Negro doctor, spoke, with all her "I weres" and "They haves," and other exaggerated, unpoetic failures of speech—by which Miss McCullers signaled in every line just what kind of character Portia was meant to be. (The movie solves this problem by casting Portia, played by Cicely Tyson as a kind of articulate Negro militant, who expresses her rebellion by becoming a maid. Not very likely.) It is that the required changes—like who cuts up whom, and under what circumstances—in sidestepping or accommodating modern sensibilities, cause the plot and motivations to fall apart. At almost every dramatic moment, the story becomes frail in its sense.

But there are a lot of lovely things. Alan Arkin, as Singer, is extraordinary, deep and sound. Walking, with his hat jammed flat on his head, among the obese, the mad, the infirm, characters with one leg, broken hip, scarred mouth, failing life, he somehow manages to convey every dimension of his character, especially intelligence. There is nothing opaque in his silences or in the moment's delay with which he reacts to other people's lines. His use of his hands seems quite normal and personal, and when he walks in the night, talking, with his hands, to himself, it seems a perfect dramatic expression of what thinking is. This is his best performance since he played a Puerto Rican on a bench in *That's Me* and it becomes more and more apparent that his talent is not clownish, but serious.

Sondra Locke, in her first movie part, as the young girl who lives in Singer's boarding house, is as fine as she can be within the limits of a lot of rather mawkish business and corny lines. (The sappiness of life does not always transfer well, intact, to the screen; it also seems there have been enough scenes of girls' checking their bodies in mirrors to last awhile.) Percy Rodriguez, as the doctor, is very strong, and Chuck McCann (once the star of a TV kiddie show) does all right as Singer's mute, sick friend —although he plays him as a babyish imbecile instead of as the rather more interesting, brooding Greek gone to pieces he is meant to be. Since he is the first character to appear on screen (and since he appears, ill-advisedly, rolling a hoop), he sets a comic note that jars through the rest of the film. Wayne Smith, in a minor part as a boy Miss Locke sleeps with, is excellent; their love scene is done in a sentimental way, as teenagers often go to the movies to see them done.

Most of the movie was shot in Selma. There seems to be a trend in films—with the coven in the Dakota in *Rosemary's Baby* and Steve McQueen's polo scenes at Myopia in *The Thomas Crown Affair*—to shoot scenes in places with resonance in special orders of experience. Maybe marchers, jealous of their memories, will welcome seeing Arkin having supper at the Selma-Del.

...... Time, Old Movies
and Exhausting Life

*8-4-68*

Watching old movies day and night for a period of time—at the Bleecker Street Cinema, Cinema Village, the Fifth Avenue Cinema, the Pocket, the Elgin, the New Yorker, the Thalia and the Lyceum, all of which have fine summer repertory programs, or at the Museum of Modern Art, beside students silently running old films in small rooms for a book or a doctoral thesis—oddly affects one's sense of time and film. Total movie immersion is something I had done in the past, like other people, to learn a language (as students come out of consecutive hours of Paris films, bleary-eyed and speaking a kind of French), or out of depression or love or interest, or to study, or to avoid studying, or for the air-conditioning, or on the little vicarious film-life binges one has from time to time. But it occurred to me this time that while there are countless moments on film (the scream or the graveyard instant in *Great Expectations,* Miss Froy's "May I speak to you for a moment?" in mid-gun battle in *The Lady Vanishes*) which are part of the imaginative memory of a generation,

221

and while film lends itself to many rewarding pendantries, there is really no such thing as cinema literacy.

What I mean is that if someone with a normal intelligence and reasonably broad modern experience turned, without having read the classics, to books, he would not have the same claim to know what he is talking about as someone who, not having clocked fifteen Chaplins, five Griffiths, ten Hawks, would have in discussing films. This partly because there has been no distinguished tradition of film criticism yet. And partly why. It is essential for word literacy that people who read, write—and even film criticism is a written thing. It would be part of cinema literacy to have made films and, although many people make them now, not nearly enough do to put the pressure of everyone's free access to the form, on closing it, on limiting it to the natural selection of skill. Everyone dances, and sings and draws and acts, or knows to a degree what these involve. It is precisely because so few people make films that they belong more or less equally to everyone—are put arbitrarily before people for equal comment, within limitations of taste and experience, like a passing day.

But sitting through a lot of great films in succession makes it clear that time is key and that if there were a cinema literacy it would be easily acquired in segments of hours. One could sit clocking Garbos and racking up Flahertys, each occupying a fixed interval, measuring one's own life like a tape or a metronome. No other form clocks periods of one's life as films do. One enters a novel's time and leaves it at will and assimilates it gradually into one's own time. A play or a musical exists apart from its fixed performance in time and can be left or returned to freely in the abstract. A live performance locks players and audience in an equal commitment of time. They pass equal parts of their lives together—except that the actor is locked day after day in the play's time. But a movie involves the actor's time only once—and thereafter the audience's alone, and in fixed spans. Except to the degree that he can regulate the intensity of his attention, the viewer virtually obliterates his own time for the film's time. And that is one reason for going day after day.

One sits there reverentially among buffs of various levels and persuasions, cold—the air-conditioning at summer old film festivals is key—in the dark, watching lives frozen in celluloid (which is why making films in color can be a mistake; it is difficult to convey interior states, states of mind, except in grays) and one's personal time, in a sense, does not pass—as long as one does not go out, stays in films, below. The older the film the more of a film it becomes; it acquires distance in time and its errors are remote, forgivable, unembarrassing, not what errors in films made in one's personal time would be. It is way back there, in a temporal cocoon, a smooth gray mood. The whole experience is related to all arrests of time, entombments, tape cartridges, freezers, capsules, libraries, even heart transplants. The essential film-inspired film would be one in which time was arrested plausibly, in which adults became immortal, stopped their personal time by raising children conspiratorially, secretly, only for transplants, for body parts. No new characters, the old ones would live forever, as they do on film.

But it is not all like that. One becomes aware that films may have, in a way, exhausted the melodrama of life, by picking it up, mirroring it, exaggerating it so in the early films. Life may have mirrored it in return, imitating films, and then become drained of its crises. We seem to have fewer private pivotal acts, villains, irrevocable partings and decisions than there used to be. The importance of acts and finales on a personal scale has gone way down. One also notices, almost incidentally, that the crowds that go to summer movie repertory festivals are among the nicest in New York, very quiet, very pale in their addiction, the unaggressive film-buff somnambulist. So many people claim a unique, violent passion for film, not films, *film*—as free-floating libidos like to claim their love of *women*, or certain kinds of ladies traveling to the seashore assert a fierce intention to surround themselves with a first love, books, *books*—without regard to love's particularity. The summer film buff seems a more gentle soul—who likes to go to movies and who has certain films he loves.

There are so many American scenes—S.N.C.C. and
Haight-Ashbury, in particular—that have gone ov
reported and under-recorded, to vanish without any i
trace in the novel or on film, of how they were. Day
day coverage in the press or on television could not do
and now these scenes are gone, dispersed, or so m
changed they do not matter anymore. *Revolution,* wh
opened yesterday at the Trans-Lux West and the Gre
wich Theater, is a documentary about the drug scene
summer on the Haight, and already its hippie star, To
Malone, might as well be Last Year, or the Day before
Day before Yesterday. The community is over—scatte
by hepatitis, mental illness, crime, the horrors, so
pressure—and *Revolution,* although it is for the most
very dull and on one note, may be the best documen
record we shall have of it.

The main problem is the method of reporting in
views with hippies and squares on what they think.
knew what squares thought. What hippies thought
never the point—some inarticulate banalites about lc
colors, hassles, grooves. It was the way they soun
—overheard—and looked, a certain gentleness
poetry, which seemed to show a way the country co
use and cherish them, almost like aphids, for its leis
time. Instead, young people took what they could use,
music, pot and style of dress; and it is now an open q
tion where have all the flower children gone. The f
simply shows them talking to the camera or dancing na
or giggling or turning on. And there is nothing much
distinguish them from a left, Bohemian, fingerpainting,
terpretive dancing, New Deal and psychoanalysis-orier
adult community of thirty years ago. There are he
scenes of the Summer Solstice Human Be-In in San Fr
cisco last year and some undistinguished music by Cou

Joe & the Fish, the Quicksilver Messenger Service, the Steve Miller Band and Mother Earth. But for our notions of the colorful and bizarre we are stuck again with housewives in pedal-pushers and curlers at the supermarket and middle-aged tourists learning the hula on the sands of Waikiki.

#### . . . . Wholesomeness When
#### the Lights Went Out

*8-9-68*

Doris Day's honor, from movie to movie, was becoming a kind of drag as she tumbled from euphemism to innuendo. The beginning of each movie asked the question whether Anything was going to happen, the middle raised the desperate possibility that Something had happened, and then, just in time for the lapsed-consciousness-in-the-motel kind of family comedy, she was married. The formula has become a piece of folklore now, like Hiawatha or Evangeline; it seems to reflect a national worry or conviction that wholesomeness is a matter of being had in your sleep.

In *Where Were You When the Lights Went Out?*, which opened yesterday at the Music Hall, Miss Day is cast as a married star who plays virgins. During the blackout of 1965, she finds her husband with another woman, to whom he is bringing martinis and hard boiled eggs on a tray. She goes at once to Connecticut where, under the influence of a sleeping potion, she spends the night in her pajamas with a young man in a moustache who has embezzled corporation funds. He is also under the influence of the sleeping potion. Nothing happens. But only a small portion of the movie is devoted to this important question. Terry-Thomas has one of his long, bad ham villain appearances as a treacherous theatrical agent in psychoanalysis, Patrick O'Neal plays the husband, and Robert Morse is the reverse-Tristan in the moustache. Pat

225

Paulsen has a funny walk-on as a subway conductor.

But a good part of the movie permits Miss Day to pl
an actress something like herself, and this might be fre
and almost poignant. She is clearly an actress who nee
to be let out, and yet she seems doomed to exclaim
every movie some version of the "Oh, Peter, I'm ta
nished" line she has in this one—a perennial, uncertai
comic inspiration, by virtue of what doesn't happen to he
to somebody's idea of the teen-age daughters of Americ

. . . . . . . . . . Chance and
a Personal Signature

8-11-6

Nothing appears more square or less suited to the kind
style and rhetoric that generate fame than working har
This is not a very puritan moment and all the dreary, lit
impoverishing associations of pointless work—lesso
learned by rote, overtime hours on the way up, loggi
time, pedantries, bureaucratic snarl—have cut the r
mance out of taking pains. In a way, it is part of t
switch from money to publicity as a value. Fame is n
something you amass. It goes by blitz or felicitous ac
dent or—in a grotesque version of the theory that po
notices are better than none—by an act of extreme pub
violence. The media are almost necessarily impatient a
radical; the way names become known these days, f
what it's worth, is fast. (This is one of the arguments f
quiz programs, local coverage telephone directories, ev
that wave of the hand by the studio audience; people see
to want to be known, to be registered somewhere, insta
taneously. It is a more benign way of checking briefly in
history than guns.) It has been a long time since anyo
was much criticized for being a show-off, and that's pro
ably good—along with becoming "overtired" and "tl
will end in tears," showing off used to be one of the me
energy and laughter-killing ideas on earth. On the otl

hand, it's a long time since anyone has been much mentioned as the strong, silent, hard-working type either.

Not only have films virtually generated the idea of fame as pure, fast, preferably groundless celebrity, but the arts in general have contributed as much as anything to the idea of felicitous accident. Everyone knows that you can work for years alone without producing a masterpiece; a lot clearly rides on the stroke, the line, the knack, the instant breakthrough. And as a result of confusion between creative and promotional breaks—particularly in the visual arts where people, put off by modernisms, are often ready to admit they don't know what's going on—there seem to be an awful lot of lazy, no-talent celebrities around. But felicitous accident in the arts is rarely unearned. There is a lot of unavailing work, a continuous play of energy that yields nothing much, and then, with luck, something goes right. From old movies it seems that unearned felicitous accident becomes increasingly unlikely as a form develops. There is no telling how much in the early films happened by luck; a great deal was invention, after all. But in recent films it seems clear that you cannot just shoot all over the place and lean on your luck too heavily.

Of the best serious films, at their levels, we have had this year—*The Bride Wore Black, Charlie Bubbles, The Fifth Horseman Is Fear, La Chinoise* or *Les Carabiniers, The Two of Us, Hour of the Wolf, Belle de Jour,* perhaps *Fist in His Pocket* and, although it is a special case, *Petulia*—all have been made with intense and evident care, without covering each scene from everywhere and hoping for a miracle in the cutting room. The same with the dialogue. The moral of them all, if there is one, and of *Persona, Battle of Algiers, The Graduate* and *Bonnie and Clyde* last year, would seem to be not to think too large. There is nothing, intrinsically, about a grand, enormously expensive movie which makes it unlikely to be great just now. But there is such huge room for waste, all that money gambling that, if you just keep turning film, faith will prevail, which seems to give us *Half A Sixpence*'s.

There is also something about large sums that seems to keep a film from having a signature. It is not enough to take film, or prose, or canvas and perform with a skill equal to anyone's; the personal signature has to be in it all, and money seems to draw in too many hands. (It is akin, in a way, to the problem of poor taste. There are no subjects or treatments which, of themselves, are in poor taste, but there are subjects that generate terrific energy and power and if the artist's energies are not equal to the forces he liberates, then you have, not just a bad work, but an unsigned work and a work in poor taste.) And finally, there is so much political consciousness in the air. In radical times, the arts struggle just to maintain their right to exist independent of social concerns. The high-finance spectacular has strong odds just now against its understanding of its time. Not insurmountable odds, but strong.

In *Variety,* and in Jacob Brackman's essay about *The Graduate* in *The New Yorker* last week, it is mentioned that *The Graduate* is about to pull ahead of *The Sound of Music* as the most successful movie of all time. While there may be overlap, it is clear that these immense audiences are not identical. A modernistic composer I know once mentioned that a pure piece of theater might be one in which an audience found itself, when the curtain went up, face to face with another audience. With some blurring at the edges one can imagine *The Sound of Music* and *The Graduate* audiences in that kind of confrontation. But if two such immense, separate movie audiences can exist for films, there seems no limit to the number of audiences so far untapped and unmobilized. There are still five months to go this year, maybe some film will find or generate yet another new audience in the fall.

. . . . . . . . True *Hunger*

*8-13-68*

*Hunger,* based on a famous nineteenth-century novel by Knut Hamsun, which I should have read but have not, is a movie about hunger, not a violent pure Gothic hunger in the face of nature, or an unendurable contemporary Southern hunger in the face of human cruelty, or even a romantic, sentimentalized hunger of any sort, but the demeaning old hunger of a writer in the city, who thinks of his starvation not as a claim against things, but as something to be concealed, and lied about and dispelled with generosities that he cannot possibly afford. When the movie opens, Per Oscarsson, who plays the young writer, is eating paper and throwing delicately up (rather in the manner of Elvira Madigan), and thinking of drowning himself in a river in Oslo.

The movie is shot mainly from two perspectives, that of its period, around 1890, and the perspective of the edible. Both are completely convincing, so that when the writer looks down at his shoes one thinks at once whether it would be practical to chew on them; when two plates of soup are brought into a room one imagines briefly, against all given information, that one of them is meant for his. He goes along, courtly, feverish with a sense of his own talent, becoming progessively more dotty, both from hunger and from a need to distract himself with pointless fictions, lies, hysteria. A woman, played by Gunnel Lindblom, teases him and leads him on until he is aroused—almost out of weakness and as a gentleman. Then she becomes frightened and decides that he is drunk or mad. On a park bench after a rain he says, "Send me a sign, Oh Lord," and looks down to find a particularly repellent looking earthworm.

Yet the movie does not indulge itself or him. He is not saintly or really anybody's fault. The director, Hennig Carlsen, just seems to follow Oscarsson quite carefully about and let him act. And Oscarsson himself is extraordinary, ranging from a vertiginous, disgusting, almost verminous decay, with bad, stained teeth, to a completely incandescent, waif-poetic charm. Miss Lindblom too is fine, as the overripe and dallying, fairly obnoxious lady who is drawn to him. The supporting characters, pawn-brokers, beggars, tenants of boarding houses, editors of periodicals, are also excellent. It is a movie to see when you are in the mood for reading a short story that is almost entirely descriptive, hardly narrative, when you are in the mood for reading prose firmly grounded in a time and state of mind, prose by Rilke, say, or for all I know, by Hamsun.

The film, which is in Swedish and which was shown two years ago at the New York Film Festival, opened yesterday at the Trans-Lux East. In 1966, Per Oscarsson won a best-actor award at Cannes for his performance in the film.

. . . . *The Conqueror Worm*
and Other Horrors

*8-15-68*

*The Conqueror Worm,* which opened yesterday at the New Amsterdam and other neighborhood theaters, stars Vincent Price and features any number of attractive young aspiring stars who seem to have been cast mainly for their ability to scream. Scream as though they were being slowly burned to death, or kicked, or poked, or stabbed —mainly about the eyes—with sticks, or shot through, or otherwise tortured, which, in fact, they are. Vincent Price has a good time as a materialistic witch-hunter and woman-disfigurer and dismemberer, and the audience at the dark, ornate New Amsterdam seemed to have a good time as well. There are lines like, "Take three good men and ride into East Anglia," through which a man behind me snored and a middle-aged couple next to him quarreled viciously, but people woke up for the action and particularly cheered when Price was hacked to death.

*The Young, the Evil and the Savage* opened with *The Conqueror Worm* (both produced by AIP). It is set in a French boarding school and there is a strangling of a naked girl before the credits start. In the course of the movie, a thin streak of something soapy (which had also been apparent across the screen during *The Conqueror Worm*)

230

persisted. It must have been a watermark across the lens in the projection booth.

*8-18-68*

There was a long time in the fifties when things seemed fairly anti-issue and pro-personality. Young people were described as having "a nice personality" or being "leader-ship material"—in what, as it happened, was the blandest, samest, most unindividual time in recent memory. The vocabulary lied, or did not fit. People were "joiners" with no real issue, except the issue of unspecified belonging, at-tached to what they joined. Now, in a real age of joining, part of the vocabulary has come true; issues are almost everything. There is tremendous moral pressure and a so-cial obligation to take sides, so that every cocktail party can become a symphony of positions (or, more likely, a many-voiced duet) and almost every personality is a punchcard or a player piano of them. Writers aspire to be spokesmen for their time, and race and generation. Works of art are scrutinized as though they were position papers. It seems almost frivolous to do art when the politics of everything is so much present to the mind. And almost im-possible to have art received when audiences ask it to sum up where they stand.

One option is to take an occupied trench and widen it a little, to check in with just enough credentials to admit you to a side, and just enough idiosyncrasy—in phrase-making, in personal behavior—to set you off and make you recognizable. This is the most common option on which intellectual careers are made; it is a very small margin, outside factional cliché, for individuality and art. But Sidney Poitier, in recent years, has somehow taken on the whole thing, shouldered as much of the entire

231

ideological equipment of his time as he could reach, and tried to move it forward. It is a heroic option and one, for anyone short of a genius of synthesis (which we have not got), and particularly for an actor, nearly impossible. To grab the consensus around the middle and try to lug it, like some great cow, to a vanguard outpost. It turns both extremes against you—both those who think that just because someone doesn't want you to sit in the front of the bus is no reason why you should want to sit there, and those who are determined to prevent you from sitting in the front of the bus because that is where you want to sit.

The problem is what it does to talent and what kind of movies it produces. What it *can* do to talent seems clear from the case of Marlon Brando, who has made good, moral movies—movies that subordinate his talent to the will to improve the world a little—and cost his talent, in what another age would have called selflessness, a great deal. Now he seems to devote himself to social causes exclusively. But Poitier's case is different. He began by establishing an indisputable talent base in art films. Then came the series of helping white nuns to build what they wanted to build, or white blind girls and white English students to find a way or, in *In the Heat of the Night,* white audiences (and Negro audiences, too, perhaps preeminently; the kind of vanguard, after which no rearguard or middle trails, likes to say Poitier makes films for white men only, but any audience at a recent Poitier film anywhere in town shows this is not the case) to accept a semblance of a Negro triumph of intelligence over a white antagonist. In each film the skill that Poitier possessed, and which the white characters lacked, was at a higher intellectual level than the last; carpentry, sight, induction. By *Guess Who's Coming to Dinner,* he was nearing the Nobel prize—and by 1967, too, he was the strongest male boxoffice draw; Elizabeth Taylor was his female counterpart.

It can be argued that, regardless of aesthetic considerations, the fact that a movie in which Poitier married a white girl could become a box-office success, justified—by sole virtue of the fact that so many people would not want such a film to succeed—the making of *Guess Who's Coming to Dinner*. Perhaps not. But a preference for the back of the bus cannot be freely exercised when someone still denies you access to the front; and the radical line, *Guess Who's Not Coming to Dinner, Baby*, sounds a little hollow until you have been to dinner once or twice. I suppose it is a question of priorities. Of course, from an aesthetic point of view the movie was a colossal waste of talent and energy. Now, we have *For Love of Ivy*. It takes the *Guess Who's Coming to Dinner* family almost intact, and sends Poitier to woo the maid. It is a step forward all the same.

To begin with, there is a little intrusion of honesty. The white girl is sadly overweight; her brother is a mess. All is not well with the family. Then, there is an unreality so extreme—the plot—that one begins to wonder whether sacrificing personal talent for social causes does not cause the participants to lose some of their minds. In order to prevent Ivy, played by Abbey Lincoln, from giving up her job as a maid to go to secretarial school, the white kids conspire by blackmail to have a Negro truck owner (Poitier), who runs an illegal gambling operation in a moving van by night, take Ivy out. Well. Moreover, without clever, beautiful, elegant, efficient, feral, naive, pacifying Ivy, the entire white family falls apart. Perhaps. The situation is no more false, inept, and silly than any standard situation comedy of thirty years ago but, in a social enterprise, the silliness rather compromises everything. The movie is absurd.

On the worthy side, Abbey Lincoln, with acting of intelligence, beauty and absolutely radiant mischief, so far outclasses anyone else in the film that it is Sidney Poitier's being too good for the charactor played by Katharine Houghton made completely credible. When the white kid brother mess, in beads, proposes to Ivy it is entirely real. Moreover, with Sidney Poitier getting Abbey Lincoln for a change, we have the first popular love scene between Negroes on the screen. This is a major thing. When we think of fantasies movies endorse, they are not going to be just white romances any more. In fact, if the whole white framework had been peeled away from *For Love of Ivy*,

233

and if the Negro story had been better written, it would have been an infinitely better film. But these things seem to go one step at a time.

Sidney Poitier's talent in this film is nowhere in evidence. That is a loss. But a curious thing is that Negro culture is nowhere in evidence either. I don't mean that Poitier and Miss Lincoln don't have rhythm, or aren't athletes, or are in no sense racial stereotypes. I mean, that they bring none of their cultural baggage with them. It is as though Negroes in these tentative beginning ventures have to travel light, as though they had to leave a vital, important idiom and heritage completely aside and enter as Negroes by virtue of color alone. There are a few in-side, unilluminating references to Poitier's West Indian background, but that's it. The characters are almost uninhabited. That is a problem in the film of *The Heart Is a Lonely Hunter,* too. Carson McCullers' Negroes do not exist any more, even allowing for the exaggerations she had to use to make them sound real to an audience in their time. The movie has simply replaced the novel's characters, filling the Negro shells with characters that do exist but do not fit the plot, and the story falls apart.

But in the enterprise of carrying things forward—and while the arts are beleaguered in a politicized world that seems as worthy a thing as any to do—the Negro positions are bound to be inhabited by real persons soon. And *For Love of Ivy,* in a kind of blundering struggle toward what amounts to an almost entirely new grip on reality, seems an odd worthy step in Sidney Poitier's journey on the way.


. . . . . . *Hugs and Kisses,*
Beetles


*8-19-68*

*Hugs and Kisses* is a gentle, moderately lustful Swedish picture about friendship, which makes allowances for the new French tradition (*The Joker, The Cousins, The Five-*

*Day Lover*, especially *Jules and Jim*) in which love affairs are not quite symmetrical. The story is no longer boy meets girl, boy loses girl, boy gets girl, and the triangle is no longer a situation in which someone gets left out. With a little warmth, sadness and whimsy, everyone gets a little of everybody.

In *Hugs and Kisses*, which opened yesterday at the Beekman Theater, a young middle-class Bohemian couple (Agneta Ekmanner and Sven Bertil-Taube) take in an eccentric young writer (Hakan Serner) whose hairline is beginning to recede, who has a sad, awkward, comic air, and who can't sleep at night without being read to and without holding an old piece of cat's fur against his cheek. One night, the writer brings a frowzy type instructor (Lena Granhagen) home to sleep, and to get rid of her the young married pair decide, quite drunkenly, that the wife ought to sleep with him. In the morning, the wife holds this against her husband and, just to straighten things out emotionally, she sleeps with the writer once again. Her husband, feeling disconsolate, goes to the guest room and draws the writer's old undershirt on over his business suit.

There are a lot of nice things: A lady pianist playing Chopin in one scene, her music forming the accompaniment for the scene that follows (the background music throughout the film, by Bengt Ernryd, is fine); a kind of dreamy white, almost overexposed light over everything; a lot of well-written conversation that implies things not actually going on on screen, which adds a kind of resonance to the plot; the tight but imaginative husband, self-consciously proud of showing a little emotion, saying half humorously, "Look at this tear. You saw it, didn't you?"; the little fond, despairing convention among the friends of repeating something one of them has just said directly after him. There is a scene when the writer brings the couple their breakfast in bed and jumps on the bed to eat it with them—a genuine eating scene, with a lot of scrunching and sipping and touching of hands in trying to reach the marmalade.

In the end, the film (directed by Jonas Cornell) suffers from the same uncertainty and lassitude the characters have, its whimsies not always inventive, its charm not as clear and new as some of its predecessors. But it is a nice movie all the same. And there is a friendly little orthographic modernism in the sub-titles (which, like subtitles in so many black-and-white films, are often white on white and a little hard to read): "Don't be scared. That's not a beatle," the writer says to the husband about an insect crawling toward him. And there are two more references to "beatles" crawling toward their picnic on the grass.

. . *The Legend of Lylah Clare*

*8-23-68*

*The Legend of Lylah Clare,* which opened yesterday at the Loew's State and Loew's Orpheum, is a take-off on some of the highly serious tragic movies Hollywood has made about itself—a take-off so faithful in spirit that it is almost indistinguishable from its model, and the generation of ladies who used to swarm, weep, trample, and ask for autographs can bring out their handkerchiefs again as they did for *The Oscar.* Kim Novak plays a young actress whom Peter Finch, as a romatic has-been director, has cast as Lylah Clare—a legendary screenstar who died tragically in the course of making the director's film. The innocent starlet is soon so caught up in the role of the star that she begins to laugh hoarsely in German and to make deep-throated nasty remarks. All the dyed, Eastern European lesbians on the set fall in love with her as they did with Miss Clare. So do the gardener, the public and Mr. Finch. It has to end badly.

The movie features Ernest Borgnine as a crass producer-distributor, Rossella Falk (of *Modesty Blaise*) as a pining lesbian and Sidney Skolsky as Sidney Skolsky. It is directed by Robert Aldrich, who did *The Dirty Dozen.* Something went wrong with all the scenes in which Milton Selzer, as a dying theatrical agent, figures—so that

236

his voice is dubbed and seems to come, mumbled, from areas of the screen where he is not. This detracts nothing from the resonant, high kitsch effect. *Lylah Clare* is not funny, exactly—the old Hollywood responses are still enough in effect to bring one to the verge, once or twice, of choking up—but it is kind of fun to watch. And the emotional-fossil put-on is done with sufficient care to make the little heel marks at Graumann's Chinese seem as dead and long ago as the tracks of a dinosaur.

..... Traversing Distances
to Strangers

*8-25-68*

Near the beginning of Frank Conroy's novel *Stop-Time*, there is a scene in which a group of boys, about ten years old, at a progressive boarding school vote—very fairly, in a child's version of due process—to beat up a disliked fat boy named Ligget. There is a trial, in which he is found guilty, on some child's pretext, of what amounts to being insufferable. The boys line up, each one entitled to land one good clean punch on Ligget's jaw. The author makes it clear that the idea of the sound, perfect "dreams-of-glory" punch is movie-inspired. But although the boys line up wordlessly to try again, and although Ligget is ultimately taken, jaw broken in four places, to the hospital, the punch itself is quite unsatisfactory; "the whole complex of movements was too fast, somehow missing the exaggerated movie-punch finality."

Of course, children were beating up other children before movies came along. I remember nine-year-olds, in a similar school, voting to stone a fat, disagreeable girl. It was all decided democratically. Someone had the good sense to vote giving her a head start of a count to twenty-five; no fourth-grader, it turned out, could throw a stone that far. But the girl, waddling across the athletic field, losing a loafer on the way, must have had an awful time. Movies were in no way responsible. None of us had ever seen stonings on film.

Yet, even though there is no real way to establish it in surveys, people are *of course* inspired to acts—some of them violent—by what they see and read. After the publication of *The Sorrows of Young Werther*, young men all over the world put on yellow vests and romantically shot themselves. There is simply nothing that can or should be done about it. Violence would find its inspiration anyway, and censorship would be too costly an admission of what we think we are, and too severe a limitation on what art can be. There is something, though, about punches, stonings, contact mayhem, even throwing snowballs or spitting cherry pits from balconies on passers-by, that is quite personal. Movies might show these forms of activity; they might be widely imitated. But they would serve as examples only. One sees them but one does not participate viscerally in them. Everyone senses, physically, that a punching, or stabbing, or throttling on screen is not what it is in reality. Seeing it is not like feeling it. And when children try to overcome this physical intuition, when they try to land that good clean punch, it only takes one try to show them that it doesn't work, the experience is not the same. The film doesn't survive the reality.

Shootings, it turns out, are another matter, and this is extremely clear in a movie that opened last week. The movie began with a long printed sermon about gun control. I think it is almost always a mistake to present audiences with a message or a piece of information that is not part of the actual film (the disclaimer to any documentary footage at the beginning of *The Battle of Algiers* seemed to me almost a kind of boasting, and its weakest part), but *Targets'* little bit of moralizing seemed ultimately necessary and even timid—as though the filmmakers, appalled at what the impact of their movie actually was, tried sincerely to run counter to it by telling what it meant. The distinguished, beautiful part of the movie, by some cinematic quirk, is a rhapsody to shooting people.

The first part of *Targets*—an independent, low-budget

work—is talky, amateurish, hard to sit through. The script is poor, the acting shaky. Neither adds anything to the basic, incredibly powerful conception on which the film is based. Boris Karloff, uncertainly playing an actor like Boris Karloff, is about to retire from making horror films. A clean-cut young man (Tim O'Kelly) is an innocent, upstanding gun enthusiast. It is clear that these two are going to converge in some way, and how they do is nothing short of brilliant, completely unpredictable and right.

It is when the talking stops and the shooting starts—when the long, thin, unrewarding characterization is done—that the talent of the producer and director, Peter Bogdanovich, takes over. I am not a believer in the mystique of the visual; I think it is one of the easier outs for a film without a brain in its head. I don't normally believe in seeing parts of films either; it seems a kind of snobbery. But in the second half of *Targets* it is clear that Bogdanovich is an expert on the silent film, that he could easily have disposed of the first part of his film with a title or two, and that the moments when O'Kelly sees a man closing in on him—on film and in reality—and does not know which one to shoot; when a little boy sees his father lying dead at the wheel in a drive-in and, not being able to drive away, is both bereaved and trapped; when a couple making love at the drive-in refuse to open a window and be warned of sniping, in the belief that the man who is knocking at their window must be some kind of nut; when a projectionist is shot in the drive-in projection room—that these are some of the most effective moments of visual storytelling on recent film. And the encounter between Karloff and O'Kelly, only as ambiguous as it must be on the basis of what we do not know, is one of the most effective statements on the relation between violence and film that film can make.

And what is it? The content of this part of the film is not even acting, but shooting—shooting almost exclusively. People are picked off one after the other, as impersonally—and this is the point—as *satisfyingly* as cans were shot down in a row, earlier in the film, at a shooting range. That is the extraordinary thing: the perspective of

239

the film is almost entirely the perspective of the gun, things are seen through the crosshairs on the gunsight, and one does not want O'Kelly to miss. It turns out that the convergence between guns and film is ideal. There is a perfect affinity. The unreality, the distance, the lack of contact or intimacy with a target, imposes on the sniper almost precisely the condition of a film audience with the actors on the screen. Knifing, or choking, or even throwing bombs at strangers is relatively intimate; one becomes aware of them physically. But with a gun or a camera you cannot even see the trajectory; the victim is a perfect stranger even after you have shot him dead. The audience at *Targets* becomes the sniper, except for the impulse and infinitesimal action of pulling the trigger—and these exceptions are felt as a definite lack.

A rifle, after all, is to many people an attractive thing, of nice texture, and look and weight. One shares the experience of shooting on film, except for the actual feel, and one knows actually, intuitively, from film, what that feeling would be. A stranger far away or a photograph—it takes a whole range of social, moral and intellectual values to bear in mind that shooting one or the other makes all the difference. The media, so adept at traversing distances to strangers, without any awareness of physical effort that might constitute warmth, are terrifically suited to the sniping psychology—must in fact have contributed in just this sense, even without showing violence of any kind—to forming it. Cars, as murderous as they have been, are less dangerous: one steers, one dreads impact as a physical thing.

This makes cameras and rifles particularly apt for a certain form of lunacy. A failure to perceive things, physically, as alive, a separation from the real consequences of acts, these are insane. Seeing people, as it were, as photographs. Even all the bloody, vicious movies—and there have been a lot of them this summer, proudly advertising with quotes about their brutality on their marquees—are not like this. People who like seeing torture close-ups are a special breed, perhaps sometimes violent, but though the camera invites them to enjoy suffering, it does not, it *cannot*—since the camera cannot punch or throw or hang—offer them the sensation of taking part in inflicting it. The camera can only aim; that is what rifles do. And gun control or not, it would seem that there is an immense population of lunatics—certainly greater than any existent violent political force—which is being conditioned, necessarily—whether or not violence is what the media actually show—to a psychology of zeroing in. Bogdanovich's film (although by the nature of film, it cannot help endorsing what it deplores) shows—in perhaps the most film-critical film ever made—just what we might be in for unless we arrive at some unprecedented thought to fit the unprecedented frame of mind which guns and films (and other things, too, of course) are creating for us.

..... Joanne Woodward in
*Rachel, Rachel*

*8-27-68*

*Rachel, Rachel,* which opened yesterday at the Plaza and Trans-Lux West theaters, is a little sappy at moments, but it is the best written, most seriously acted American movie in a long time. The screenplay by Stewart Stern (based on a novel by Margaret Laurence) has a fantastic ear for cliché: the cliché of the classroom ("Have all my Walter Raleighs died?" Estelle Parsons, as a marvelous schoolteacher, asks, when none of her pack of children open the door for her); the cliché of manners ("I hope you are not coming down with something," as a kind of reflex of solicitude), and the dreadful formula witticisms ("Can't you do something about the humidity, Hector? If you were a real friend you would") that are the social interchange in a certain milieu in a town of a certain size.

Joanne Woodward plays Rachel, a spinster schoolteacher of thirty-five, who is going out of her mind with boredom, frustration and the care of a prying ailing mother (Kate Harrington) in their apartment over a funeral home.

"Thank you," she shouts when Donald Moffatt, who subsequently becomes her lover, asks her for a date and then, when he has not heard her, she tones it down. "I said O.K.," she says. The movie is full of little touches, phrases, gestures, even props (the apartment where Miss Parsons lives is a perfect piece of characterization, and so is Miss Woodward's first gross dirty joke after her love affair) that let you know just what kind of spinster, what kind of town, what kind of emotional quality this is.

The movie, directed by Paul Newman (his first work of direction), has countless flashbacks and flashes of fantasy, which sometimes (as in recollection of the affair, which goes a bit like Dottie Renfrew's in *The Group*) work extremely well, and sometimes (as in *Juliet of the Spirits* or *Elvira Madigan*-like nostalgic slowtime rompings through the grass) do not work at all. The direction is mainly sensitive and discreet, but now and then the whole thing goes awash in excess of sentimentality or even ambition. You cannot convey the quality of life in this sort of town, through Rachel's perspective, without losing proportion in melodrama and glop. Petty tragedies, faithfully portrayed, are a little embarrassing.

Miss Woodward, playing almost the entire movie on the verge of tears, is nonetheless extraordinarily good, as are Miss Parsons—kind, funny, submerged—and other members of the cast. Nearly everyone in the movie is likely to remind you of someone you know. (In fact, I do know Izzy Singer, a storekeeper, who appears in a minor role, in Danbury, Connecticut, where most of the film was shot.) Among many carefully thought-out scenes, including one brief, quasi-lesbian encounter between Miss Woodward and Miss Parsons that is a little too heavy for what the film prepares one to accept, there is a scene in which Miss Parsons delivers a note of apology to her friend by night. The scene is deft, sentimental and funny. So is most of the film. If this were a less ironic age, it might work seriously and completely—like a kind of American cinema Balzac.

9-11-68

*"Pronto!" "Silenzio," "Motore," "Sonore," "Azione."*

A cast of 120 extras, dressed in togas, sandals, pink and white chalky cosmetics and various costumes of first-century Rome, began rushing through the streets of the old port of Rome, Ostia Antica, where, among ancient ruins, Roberto Rossellini was filming his latest movie, *The Acts of the Apostles*. The cast was supposed to be running, laughing, applauding and dancing, to a circus. The Apostle Paul, bearded, balding, wearing only curly earlocks, sat under a parasol nearby, holding a thin chain, fastened at his wrist, with which he was supposed to be arrested in a later scene. He was Eduardo Toricella, a young actor Mr. Rossellini had found at Rome's absurdist Teatro del Nonsenso.

The young man shouting directions through a megaphone was Mr. Rossellini's twenty-five-year-old son, Renzo, who is producing the film. The script girl and general aide was Mr. Rossellini's sister, Marcella. The set painter and architect was Marcella's son Giuseppe. A frequent visitor to the set was Mr. Rossellini's nephew Franco. The cameraman, Mario Fioretti, worked with the help of his own son, Gianni. Since Mr. Rossellini has the gift of assimilating nearly everyone who comes onto the set into what seems like an immediate family, the set of *The Acts of the Apostles* seemed a benignly tribal affair.

Mr. Rossellini himself, dressed in a sport shirt, slacks, and a dark blue cap with a visor and a little blue bow at the back, sat on a platform next to his cameraman and worked a little on a dial on a tripod, which is one of two major innovations in his filming style. It is a kind of slow, coordinated zoom that works in tandem with the camera and makes it unnecessary to move the camera forward and back. The other innovation was a jagged mirror, affixed to the top of a picture window between the camera and the set.

The mirror reflected a painting by Giuseppe, Mr. Rossellini's nephew, which, when viewed through the camera, served to complete the old ruins that time had worn down. In the resulting processing shot, the line between the tops of the ruins and the bottom of the paintings is imperceptible. Two little holes in the mirror made two actors, who were really on the roof of a ruin far away on the street, appear to be at windows overlooking the street. "You have to spend as little money as possible on technical details," Mr. Rossellini said, making careful, fractional shifts at his slow-zoom dial, "or you never get a chance to say what you want to say.'

*The Acts of the Apostles* is a kind of return to his last work, *The Struggle to Survive,* a twelve-hour documentary for television, financed by an American foundation called Horizons 2000, in which Mr. Rossellini treats the history of Western man. "I am a maniac for education," Mr. Rossellini said. "I have wanted to make didactic films for years. Now, I want to return to the fresco of the twelve-hour film, not just do any film I want, but to return to a grand, single subject and make it more profound."

The scene of the circus run was not going well. One actor's toga had slipped, revealing the strap of an undershirt. Several members of the cast were chewing gum. An actor, with one of those long, distinguished, intelligent faces that look so old and spiritual on screen, kept forgetting to take off his sunglassees. A large lady from wardrobe wandered, with the impersonality of a doctor, among the cast, adjusting a tunic here, a part of the body there. All the heat-generating objects and the waiting and preparations on a set were fraying nerves. People ran too slow or too fast. The scene had to be reshot several times. Whenever Mr. Rossellini objected to something, he would call out "Renzo," and amplifications of "Renzo," through other voices, would travel down the set until Renzo appeared.

A young, graceful Negro woman had walked very slowly near the end of the running crowd. Mr. Fioretti wanted to get a good shot of her. But when the crowd ran again, at the crucial moment, another member of the cast obscured her face. By the final shooting, the young actress apparently thought the scene was being reshot because she

had made herself too conspicuous, so she ran in the middle of the crowd with the rest. Mr. Rossellini and Mr. Fioretti gave it up.

"In this film I want to treat the great impact that the Christian revolution had on the ideas of the world," Mr. Rossellini said. "First, the idea of the nobility of work. In Rome, work was degrading. It was the province of the slave. Then, the idea that the body is resurrected along with the soul. In the *Phaedo* of Plato, Socrates speaks so eloquently of the song of the swan as a song of joy for the separation of his soul from his body in death. In Christianity, resurrection is physical. And the idea of the humiliation of Christ. After that, there could be no community of the chosen. Religion could belong to the most humble, to everyone."

Several other scenes were shot, one in which Paul was arrested, with his chain leading now to a Roman legionnaire, in front of a marketplace, and another in which Peter looked so beautiful that Mario Fioretti, normally not a sentimental man, turned away from his camera and wept a bit. Some tourists had gathered and, overcome with interest, surged onto the set. The couple at their windows in the mirror were in animated conversation whenever the camera was off, but managed to freeze and look utterly lifeless whenever the camera was on, so that they seemed the only painted and artificial part of the scene. There was a break for a picnic lunch.

By late afternoon, Mr. Fioretti was shooting a long conversational scene involving four major characters, but the rest of the cast was becoming positively bestial. Make-up was running, from the waiting and the heat. Extras were scratching themselves, or spitting, or getting in the way. Renzo would no sooner shout "*Silenzio!*" than the extras, who had been sitting off camera in a kind of stupor, would become highly animated. Romances and arguments would begin. Some people would hum to themselves, or whistle, or fall thunderously over a drop.

Since the shooting presented no technical problems, always the same four faces in the same frame, talking, Mr. Rossellini lapsed into a long silence. Then he began, in a low but amused voice, a long anecdote to a French visitor about the lovemaking of captured elephants in India. Mussels and other fish, gathered since early morning as props in the market place, began to smell. "Ancient Rome, you see, was a luxurious but very sordid place," Mr. Rossellini said, pointing to the public lavatories of the Ostia Antica—where, on toilets arranged like chairs in a drawing room, the Romans used to gather for morning conversations. "Very sordid. Of an incredible sordidness."

"Without looking at the camera, especially you three over there," Renzo was shouting to a group outside a quiet, well-preserved, ancient tavern. Mr. Rossellini began to dismiss some of the cast. On the way out of the Ostia Antica, after collecting his salary for the day, one of the extras fainted from the heat. About ten people shouted for the company doctor, then realized that there was none, and Renzo solicitously drove the man to Rome.

"Perform us a miracle, Paul," Mr. Rossellini said to Mr. Toricella on the way out. "I will not show any real miracle in the film. On the screen, they are banal." He drove home with the fanatical speed and the extreme shifting ease of the perfectly natural driver. But the next morning, in a studio room in Rome, the rushes of the day's shooting were almost uncannily good.

. . . . . . The Insane World:
Where Will They Work?

*9-22-68*

*Paris*
On the day after the Russian invasion of Czechoslovakia, Claude Berri (*The Two of Us*) and his brother-in-law Jean-Pierre Rassam (who plays a part in Berri's latest fine film, *Marry Me, Marry Me*) set off from Paris in the car of François Truffaut (whose fine *Stolen Kisses* has just opened in Paris) to pick up the wife and twin sons of Milos Forman (*Love of a Blonde*) in Prague. A few days later, they set off again, to pick up relatives of another

246

Czech director, Ivan Passer. News of the invasion had reached the Czech filmmakers already in Paris quite late at night. They had been out with some French filmmakers in Pigalle. At three in the morning, they dispersed. A few minutes later, Rassam's date for the evening put on some light music, at her apartment, on the radio. The news came through. Rassam called his friends and the plans for driving to Czechoslovakia were made. Jan Nemec (*A Report on the Party and the Guests*) was in Prague, as were Jiri Menzel (*Closely Watched Trains*) and Jean-Louis Richard, who is making a film there with his former wife, Jeanne Moreau.

Since then, the young Paris film community has virtually absorbed the Czechs, with projects, collaboration and support. Temporary apartments were found. Renn Productions, a company founded by Berri, Truffaut and others to give filmmakers control over their films—Renn bought Forman's *The Firemen's Ball* and thereby saved it from changes the director did not want to make, financed *Naked Childhood,* a first film by Maurice Pialat, and produced, among other movies, *Marry Me*, permitting Berri to make an expensive post-last minute change of cast days after shooting had begun—was trying to arrange contracts for the Czechs' future work.

Where this work would be done was a problem. For a time it had seemed that the only good thing happening in the world was happening in Czechoslovakia. With the invasion, and that strange inversion of things whereby when Communism becomes repressive, left becomes right—that is, repressive government, no matter how far left in principle, becomes, in effect, right wing and a measure of free enterprise is left or liberal—the filmmakers were determined that their exile should be temporary, that Czechoslovakia would not, like East Germany, be gradually drained of its liberal element. Nemec, having been assured by the Czech film office that films on all but the most sensitive subjects could still be freely made in Prague, was going to continue filming there. So was Richard. All were planning eventually to return. In the meantime, the Czechs were faced with making movies in a country and a language not their own, without government financing for films distributors might consider less than commercial. One result was that for these filmmakers—and in the view of what happened at the other festivals—the New York Film Festival acquired enormous importance. Another was that, for the time being, some of the best and most responsible young talent in film is together most constantly and creatively in Paris.

At one point in an evening last week, twenty-two French and Czech film people were gathered in Milos Forman's apartment in Paris's XVI<sup>e</sup>. In the living room, the hall, the kitchen, the bathroom and on the terrace, conferences about various movies were going on. A transistor radio was communicating static and news from Prague. The telephone rang constantly, often with people who would begin conversations in French, to which Forman would reply in French, and only after a few amenities had been exchanged did it become clear that both speakers were Czech and could revert most comfortably to another language. Forman's four-year-old twin boys had come into the kitchen early, weeping silently. After a while it turned out that they had set a little fire in their bedroom and were disturbed by it. It did no damage and, as they did often in the evening, everybody laughed.

"The world is insane," Forman (who had grown a beard for a part in a film by Buñuel) would say from time to time and someone would tell an anecdote about the occupation. Nemec, who had just returned from Prague with some films of events there—including shots of a Russian soldier's painstakingly putting the pieces of a torn Czech liberal tract together again so that he could read it; the film will be shown at the New York Festival—was telling about a Czech director who had left Prague in an Italian car, with Italian license and Italian identity papers. He had been stopped by the Russians before the border and, in an inspired moment, had used the only Italian he knew. "*La Strada*," he said indignantly. "*Il Bidone*. Fellini. Bellocchio." It had gotten him through.

Richard told of having been stopped once in Greece and held up until the village's only French-speaking citizen—who had longed for years to speak French again—could be brought to him. When the Francophile

arrived, he beamed and murmured courteously, *"A droit,
En avant. Marche,"* and other useful phrases he had
learned in a World War I campaign in the Dardanelles. It
was clear that the new community of film is one of the
most international, linguistically, in the world. Forman
spoke of the news—300 Russians, stationed in the forests
around Prague and, tired of canned food, eating cham-
pignons and an occasional lethal mushroom by mistake;
twelve Czech criminals, two of them notorious, placing an
ad in the press, announcing their concern for the national
police and their intention, for the duration of the occupation, to withdraw from crime; a pro-Novotny former
defense minister, cooking for a protest meeting of the National Assembly and becoming a resistance hero; especially
the Albanian radio, announcing its support of the Czechs
(denounced by the Russians as revisionist) against the
revisionist Russian policy. "Paradox upon paradox," Forman said.

Several of those present—Forman, Nemec, Truffaut,
Rassam, Berri, Passer, perhaps Pavel Juracek (*Joseph
Kilian*)—and Menzel, still in Prague, were going to New
York for the festival, and Jiri Janousek, a twenty-five
year-old Czech critic who has published in France the
most thorough and intelligent study of Czech cinema,
mentioned the hazards of press conferences. "The press
always asks you what you really wanted to say in your
film," Forman said. "They treat films from the socialist
countries as though they had been made on the moon." A
Czech-French dictionary lay on the table, but no one had
recourse to it. There was a lot of fairly serious drinking
though, and when Nemec accidentally pushed a cork
down into the wine, a Czech girl said, "That is the Russian way."

That evening, as part of a Czech retrospective, there
was to be a showing of *Loves of a Blonde* in the Palais de
Chaillot Theater of the Paris Cinémathèque, and the entire
party took off for an early supper in order to be in time
for it. An elderly gentleman, who turned out to be a Czech
producer, said he had sold for a thousand dollars, to an
eccentric French lady aristocrat, the rights to a bio-
graphical film about the defenestrated Czech statesman

Masaryk. This story was much appreciated. Since the producer had no rights to the biography at all, it was a bit like selling a tourist a bridge.

Janousek explained what he thought had generated the present strength of Czech filmmaking. The Prague school has a five-year program, for directors, actors, technicians, producers, and one opening a year for a student in film history. "How many film critics and historians do you need after all?" he said. The program includes making films, many of them, short ones at first, then long ones in the later years. There are five film-producing committees, composed of filmmakers and experts, under the Czech government. If a filmmaker is turned down by one, he can always try the rest. The money comes from the state. In the last year it had been particularly liberal, not just for commercially obvious directors like Menzel, but for Nemec and the rest. The result was about thirty-five Czech films a year. Janousek had been enrolled as last year's film history student; he was not sure when he would be going back.

At the Cinémathèque, which was jammed to the aisles and the doors, although the entire audience had clearly seen *Loves of a Blonde* at least once before, Henri Langlois—director of the Cinémathèque, and once, even still, an embattled man himself—made a speech of tribute to Forman, and to Passer, who had collaborated on the film. In his reply, Forman said thanks in French, that while he was concerned for his country, politics passes while Langlois will remain. Nobody thought he had said exactly what he meant. *Loves of a Blonde* looked infinitely better than it had a year ago.

8-30-68

*Venice*

The Venice Film Festival, under the direction of Luigi Chiarini, has always been one of the purest—artistically and ideologically—of all the summer festivals. Most directors of movies entered in this year's competition, which started in 1930, are in their early thirties and several of them are entering their first work of feature length. The film producers associations of several Western countries have boycotted the festival this year as being too arty and not sufficiently in favor of commercial films. (The official British boycott was so complete that it prevented a retrospective showing of Alfred Hitchcock's films. Retrospectives have however, always been a serious program of the festival. This year's will consist of films by Jean Renoir.)

The festival is so shy of the corruptions of publicity that arrangements for journalists are downright primitive. Although they are granted free admission to the casino adjoining the Palazzo del Cinema, and to a special Mass for film critics, they are not invited to the main performances each night. Many movies are shown in their original linguistic purity, without sub-titles—which is all right in Western European films but creates a problem with those of the Yugoslavs and Czechs. Although the price of tickets to the late evening performance is high (about $9.00), there is an early evening showing of each movie out of doors at a price (about $1.80) the Venetian public can afford.

Last weekend, though, when the festival was scheduled to begin, a group of dissident artists and directors, led by Pier Paolo Pasolini (*Accattone!*), Gillo Pontecorvo (*The Battle of Algiers*) and Cesate Zavattini (writer of most of Vittorio De Sica's films), attacked the festival as not being sufficiently democratic—as failing in *autogestazione*.

251

*Autogestazione* was defined as the quality of giving birth to oneself. The festival should be allowed to give birth to itself, under the direction of filmmakers, at a time and place with a content of its own choosing. Since the mystical concept was a bit hard to implement, the dissidents suggested an interim "counter-festival," which would elect Mr. Chiarini, if and when he resigned from the regular festival, as its own director. Mr. Chiarini refused.

Pietro Germi (*Divorce, Italian Style*) subsequently sent a wire supporting Mr. Chiarini and passionately deploring the "pseudo-dissidence" of the counter-festival. Roberto Rossellini supported Mr. Germi. In the middle of a press conference on the Sunday the festival was to begin, however, a small group of protesters stormed in upon Mr. Chiarini and announced that the demonstrators outside the Palazzo del Cinema were being "massacrando" by the police and that Mr. Pasolini and Mr. Pontecorvo had been gravely hurt. The report turned out to be only a bit of radical stagemanship, but Mr. Chiarini, having been warned by Pasolini that there might be violent deaths in any case, promptly postponed the opening of the festival until Tuesday. On Sunday and Monday, there were demonstrations outside the Palazzo and conferences of journalists and dissidents inside. Mr. Pasolini sent a letter to Mr. Chiarini signed "Your Mad Buffoon," in which he withdrew his film *Teorema* from the festival and entered it in the counter-festival, which at that point consisted of one film with no place to show it.

The meeting of dissidents joined the meeting of journalists and asked for support. The Czechoslovaks made a brief and moving appeal to journalists and dissidents alike, saying they did not know what the festival situation was exactly but that they would appreciate political support for their country. On Tuesday night, Giovanni Favaretto Fisca, Mayor of Venice and ex officio president of the Biennale (since radicals and officials could not agree on an acceptable permanent president), called for a demonstration on the part of Venetians who supported the regular festival. The pro-festival demonstration drew a crowd of more than a thousand, and the counter-festival people grew alarmed and refused to come out of their meeting without police support. The police escorted them one by one—right into the middle of the pro-festival demonstration, where several were beaten quite a bit until the police came back to rescue them.

Maurice Pialat, director of the first film to be shown at the festival—*l'Enfance Nue*, a reminiscence of childhood much under the influence of François Truffaut —demanded meanwhile that all policemen be withdrawn from intimidating the dissidents. By the time the festival actually opened there was only an honor guard, consisting of pairs of policemen armed with swords and wearing caps pushed down over their eyes in the festival hall. The festival opened without further incident—except that a demonstrator, shouting "Viva Mao!" rushed, with arm and fist extended in salute, up to Mayor Favaretto Fisca and then back into the crowd again. The crowd shouted "Praga si, Mosca no!"

The interpretation of the "black tie" specified in the program was loose. Slacks, beaded Mao jackets and miniskirts were seen. There were few celebrities, except one squat, partriarchal-looking gentleman with a gray beard, print jacket, cane, a fan that resembled a ping-pong paddle painted by a child, and a bow and a radiant smile for everyone. It turned out that he was a Sicilian baron, Agostino La Lomia. As reported in the Italian press next day, the only star "of the greatest magnitude" in the audience was the feminine lead in a little Italian film about the life of Che Guevara.

Meanwhile Mr. Pasolini himself, in a passionate three-column, full-page article in the Italian magazine *Oggi*, sought to make his revolutionary position clear. The phrase that had been attributed to him, "Ci' scappa un morto" (literally, "if there should escape a death"; idiomatically, "if a death should result"), was, he said —as though the future of the world hung upon it—a phrase he would never use, a petit bourgeois phrase, an atrocity. What he had actually said—and to emphasize the tremendous difference, he rather fuzzily invoked the distinguished linguist Roman Jakobson—was that the demonstrations in Venice might end as did those in Rome,

253

where a student, Paolo Rossi, was killed. Having set this vital issue straight, Mr. Pasolini devoted himself to protesting the projection of *Teorema* at the festival.

The result of the screening of *Teorema* was that, at a preview of *Carnivorous Flowers*, a film about the Paris demonstrations in May shown at a meeting of Venice students and Paris revolutionaries (of the March 22 movement) in a building at the Venice University, Mr. Pasolini was forcibly expelled from the discussions, and spat upon by his co-demonstrators. The March 22 contingent, followers of the student leader Daniel Cohn-Bendit at Nanterre, had arrived in Venice on their way back from a Carrara meeting of anarchists. Among them was a French professor, La Passade, nicknamed "la Patate" (the potato) on account of his having thrown potatoes at the Avignon Film Festival to dramatize the relationship between cinema revolution and agriculture. Nobody at Venice, however, was paying too much attention to the protesters by the end.

. . . More Festival in Venice

*9-1-68*

*Venice*
The summer film festival trail begins at Cannes, passes through Berlin, Karlovy Vary and other places and ends, more or less, in September in New York. From the moment Cannes fell it shook the whole trail and it was particularly unlikely that Venice would make it through to a safe and comfortable end. There had been bombs in August outside the Palazzo del Cinema. The Biennale, of which the film festival is a part, had been disrupted earlier this summer by demonstrations of various kinds. When officials and radicals had been unable to agree on a new president of the Biennale, Giovanni Favaretto Fisca, Mayor of Venice, had temporarily taken on the job himself. (Favaretto Fisca was referred to among the demonstrators as L'affaretto Bisca, or the unsavory little affair-

254

let of the gambling den. This was partly because the Palazzo del Cinema adjoins the casino on Venice's Lido and partly because the mayor is a politician with holdings in real estate, but even the mayor's most ardent supporters would not describe him as an important creative force in the arts.)

Luigi Chiarini, director of the festival itself, tried hard to avoid a radical closing down. At one point, he invited the revolutionaries Danny Cohn-Bendit from Paris and Rudi Dutschke from Berlin to participate in discussions at the festival. He scheduled days of open debate on the question of *cinema e politica,* based on films of the events of Paris and Cannes. The official producers associations of various Western countries were already boycotting the festival (although individual producers did take part) as tending to favor art over commercial films. Jonas Mekas, in a letter to Chiarini explaining that he could not, on revolutionary and artistic grounds, serve on the jury of the festival, conceded that Venice was more "puritan and spartan" than the other festivals. Henri Langlois, of the Paris Cinémathèque, was also invited to serve on the jury. At the last moment, without mentioning it to anyone, Chiarini switched the opening program from *l'Enfance Nue,* by Maurice Pialat, to a Czech film, in the belief that even extremists would not block the opening of a movie made in liberal Czechoslovakia.

But by opening night last Sunday, the Palazo del Cinema—which the Italian press describes as Babylonian, although it looks rather like an American war memorial auditorium—was closed. Inside, there were negotiations which the local newspapers described, quite accurately, as Byzantine, while outside, two swarms of people —separated by a low iron barricade over which there was considerable climbing back and forth—were shouting *"Buffone!"* and *"Burfardi!" "Communisti!"* and *"Fascisti!"* at each other, while waving fists in each other's faces. "China Lovers!" "Servants of the Bosses!" *"Mostra* (Festival) *Livera!"* "Go back to Rome!" It was not much of a political dialogue; it seemed rather like those tribal wars Peter Mathiessen reported from New Guinea, in which each side does battle by hurling invective in turn,

255

much anticipated and appreciated by the other side, and then finally throws a few spears to end the day.

The French-inspired rhythms, "*Mostra Libera!*" ("*De Gaulle Assassin!*" "*Algérie Française!*" "*A Bas Jeune Nation!*") or "*Mostra del Popolo!*" ("*La Paix en Algérie!*") and so on, were clearly most suited to chanting in unison; the cadences come out right as long as you hit the syllables hard enough. A thick and disconsolate line of soldiers, meanwhile, only one of whom held a rifle, stood with their backs to the festival hall and occasionally marched about. Whenever television lights were turned on a particular area, people surged forward and grew intensely animated there. Never too near the soldiers. The lights seemed to try to nudge the crowd toward the guards now and then, but without much success. The main rhetorical problem seemed to be to define what the issues were. The operative word, apart from *contestazione*, on the Maoist model of continuous contestation, dialectic and struggle, was *autogestazione*. It was a little hard to see what the practical applications of such a concept were to the students, a good many of whom were not Italian and who looked more like tourists than revolutionaries—although revolutionary tourism may become a successor to other kinds, a nine-demonstration tour, say, of the Scandinavian countries or the Middle East.

Another question was why film festivals have become centers of radical protest all along the trail. Of course, there are serious artistic problems involved—the art-industry-popular-voice conflict, and the fact that large transactions inevitably generate and support an industry. But what is really extraordinary is how much *political* energy is being spent at festivals. At Cannes, the protesters condescended to the hesitant Czechs for being too conservative, liberal and unradical, and for their evident awareness that gestures have consequences and that carefree radicalism invites forces that submerge radicals and liberals alike. Perhaps it is a feeling of helplessness about the world that turns it all into a kind of charade, rather useless and angry, like flinging a teddy bear against the wall. But I think not. I think it has to do with questions of physical courage. There is not much risk in shout-

256

ing *"Buffone!"* *"Bufardi!"* at each other in the Lido—and yet it generates a feeling that political action is going on. On the other hand, good or bad, the festivals are the small film's best hope of finding an audience, and not too much has been accomplished just yet by shutting them down.

.... Our *Faces*, Laughter, Narrative

9-15-68

## Venice

John Cassavetes' *Faces*, which did not quite win first prize in Venice, is a movie so good that one can hardly believe it, on the basis of Cassavetes' earlier film *Shadows,* or on the basis of what is going on at festivals, or even in terms of the work being done just now in any other medium. To begin with, while most important work for the moment is quiet and shy and difficult, *Faces* is an extremely loud, aggressive film. It does not require a finely calibrated mood or sensibility. It is by no stretch, or shrink, of the imagination boring or thin. It is sometimes so blunt and relentless that one is virtually clubbed to the floor. And yet it does something that nobody else is doing and does it brilliantly.

The film, shot in black and white in Los Angeles, concerns a middle-aged, middle-class couple who laugh a lot. In fact, they laugh incessantly, pointlessly, at some of the most boring public and private jokes in memory. At first, this is unbearable; one thinks Cassavetes does not know what he is doing, or that he is overdoing it. Then, in the midst of all this laughter, which simultaneously fakes and precludes intimacy, the husband asks his wife for a divorce. He goes off and sleeps with a young prostitute, who had begun the evening as part of another double date; and his wife goes to bed with a thirtyish hippie whom she meets in the course of an evening spent with three other wives in similar predicaments. And through it all, there is this terrible, nervous laughter, which cracks open now and then to tell more about America than any other movie in a long time.

The relationships between the young and the middle-aged are the best drawn, least stereotyped, I have seen in years. In spite of the hammering bluntness of the film, no one—not the good-hearted prostitute, not a drunken, sex-and-dance-starved bridge-club woman, not the hippie singing off key and preaching love—is in caricature. The hippie and the whore are genuinely touched, trying to make contact of some kind; their middle-aged bed partners are ironic and self-absorbed, suddenly flashing their seriousness like a switchblade in the middle of the contract of facetiousness they have established from the start. The husband abruptly asks the whore to be herself, which, after the joking tone he has insisted upon, is an act of cruelty. The wife, feeling degraded, tries to commit suicide in the morning, without regard for the fact that the hippie might mind a bit. The young are in their own sad thing, singing lewd or dreadful songs to keep their spirits up. But throughout, there are these cruel flashes of the come-off-it signal, which have a terrific dramatic effect. "What do you mean?" one of the drunken ladies suddenly asks the hippie, "I just want to know what you *mean*." It is the conversational equivalent of a slap. "Where are you from?" another lady asks (not the New York question, "What do you do?" but "Where are you from?") and, hurt, he begins to laugh. The country's terrible secret, which the picture keeps breaking open to reveal, is what that laughter conceals—that people are aging, aging badly and alone. Background, family, continuity, the accumulation of years are regarded as a depletion of youth, and being serious without a jocular edge of hostility looks like a form of letting down the side.

The picture is superbly funny at times. The scene where the husband intrudes on the prostitute's double date ends with a business connection and a determination to have lunch. There is a beautiful, wittily shot scene in which the camera follows the husband up the stairs, confronts his wife, who backs against a wall, and then follows her line of sight after the hippie as he goes out the window, over the roof to the ground and down a hill. It works like a perfect run on skis. The audience applauded and cheered. The acting, by John Marley, Gena Rowlands, Lynn Carlin, Fred Draper, Seymour Cassel, Val Avery, Dorothy Gulliver, Joanne Jordan and Darlene Conley, is absolutely true—with a lot of what is clearly improvisation, extremely skillfully cut. The ear for dialogue is so acute that when one misses a few badly mumbled lines there is a real sense of loss. English-speaking members of the audience —since *Faces* is, in large part, a talked picture, foreign audiences must have a hard time with it—were constantly asking each other "What did he say?" not with annoyance but with the most lively interest.

The movie that did win first prize was a German film, *Artists Under the Big Top: Perplexed* by Alexander Kluge. It was a good, difficult film and the award was quite daring in that it clearly left commercial considerations aside. Kluge, who is thirty-six, was a writer before he became a filmmaker, and the movie—which is a surreal, didactic story of a girl circus-owner who tries to turn a circus into something deeper than a circus and then decides she is wrong—seems to have something to do with Kluge's own will to, and then decision not to, turn movies into literature. The film is beautifully written and dreamily shot, and very worthy of its Lion.

It is difficult just now to distinguish what is and what is not a plotted film. I suppose a plotted film is one in which the audience develops a sympathy with certain characters and wishes that certain things would—and certain other things would not— happen to them. In this sense, there were very few plotted films at Venice, and this general plotlessness seemed related to the farce which the cinema revolution ultimately became. It occurred to me at the Palazzo del Cinema just what I think the difference between style revolution and content revolution is. An act of content revolution—in all but tight totalitarian societies, where it is conceivable that any act of provocation is revolutionary—is one which expresses what it wants to accomplish. It need not always be so close a correlation, but the cause must always generate the act. At Venice it was the other way around. The talk was revolution, the act was revolution, but the cause was never there.

Defining a revolutionary not by what he wants but by what he says and does, is very much in favor now and it sounds superficially right. (Debray's oddly Wittgensteinian idea of a revolutionary as a man who bears arms against the system and then worries about causes afterwards—if ever—amounts to this.) But the end result is trying to bomb or occupy or plain shout down the Palazzo del Cinema—or, for that matter, trying to pinch the fannies of troopers under orders at the Pentagon. (I remember a lady shouting "I have seen the face of fascism," when a little tear gas came her way.) The reason seems to be related to the absence of plot in the cinema sense: nothing is desired, nothing is dreaded, but the action proceeds.

I think this is part of a distinctly contemporary sensibility which extends far beyond cinema or revolution. It is very clear, both in films and out of them, that there are people who no longer think of things as desirable or undesirable, no longer think of their lives as plotted in the sense that they wish for good things to happen to them and dread that bad things will. This is a very serious break; the idea of happening itself as a value discontinuous from the value of what actually takes place. I think it yields a certain kind of movie, a certain kind of art and certain kind of life. Perhaps even the collapse of a will to survive. But one of its aspects—and in some ways a sound one—is a belief in the meaninglessness of competition. Nearly everyone at Venice and at Cannes, from rhetoric radical to content reformer, believed that the time for prizes and competitions at art festivals is over. Competition is too closely tied to values that are alien to the arts. It no longer serves the arts. It does not suit the times.

*9-13-68*

*Rome*

Filming of a docile, amateur sort seems to be going on all over Italy these sunny days and one is constantly turning corners to find a hand-held camera filming sailors in Olbia, hippies in the Piazza Navona or Piazza di Spagna, tourists over their postcards at the Lido Excelsior, or Romans over their lunch almost anywhere. But the studios seem largely occupied with some phase of the production of Italian Westerns—those peculiar marathons of cowboys, gore, dubbing, sadism and trompe l'oeil, which young filmmakers call "spaghetti Westerns," but speak of, nonetheless, with affection, since they are one place in the industry where young people can get their start.

The spaghetti Western got its start in 1964, when a virtually unknown director, Sergio Leone, using the American pseudonym Bob Robertson, imported Clint Eastwood, who had been on American television, to star in *A Fistful of Dollars*, probably one of the nastiest, most brutalizing and emetic films ever made. It was a great success in Italy and elsewhere and Mr. Leone, using his own name, followed it up with *A Few Dollars More*. There were, almost immediately, a lot of imitations, with *Dollars*—in Italy at least—the operative word: *$100,000 for Lassiter, $5,000 on the Ace, A Few Dollars for Django*, etc. Then there was a swarm of Italian *Ringo* Films: *A Pistol for Ringo, Ringo the Face of Revenge, Ringo of Nebraska, A Woman for Ringo*. There were also the more sensibly titled slaughters: *Gringo, Throw the Gun Away, Three Crosses Not to Die, Shatterhand* (a clear case of synecdoche), *His Name Screamed Vendetta, If You Meet Sartana, Pray for Your Death, Run, Man, Run, Kill Them All and Come Back Alone*. Mr. Leone went on to make *The Good, the Bad and the Ugly*. He is now filming a Western with Henry Fonda, Claudia Cardinale, and Jason Robards, in Almería, Spain. (Almería has become an ideal set for films of this sort, with local gypsies, unemployed for generations, now serving as Mexicans or Indians of the plains.) The age of the paella Western may be upon us.

Intellectuals with a taste for dismemberment like to justify their interest in these films with grand allusions to the mythic field of the American West, into which modern political ideas can be introduced. But perhaps the most interesting product, and the best movie to come out of the genre, will be a documentary, *Westerns—Italian Style*, produced by an American, Frank Wolff (who has acted in several villainous Westerns), and directed by a Frenchman, Patrick Morin, who has done mainly short documentaries for television. The film, which is currently being completed in Rome, is really in the tradition of cinema short story reporting (*The Endless Summer, The Queen*) but it concerns itself with the way in which Italian Westerns are made and with the people who make them. The other morning, one of the stars of *Westerns—Italian Style*, Enzo G. Castellari, twenty-nine years old and the director of several Italian Westerns himself ("Only four. But very, very good," he said) was cutting and editing his most recent film, *I Come, I See, I Shoot,* in a studio called Safa Palatino, on Rome's Palatine Hill. "It's the only studio inside Rome where you can easily get a cow if you need one," he said.

Wearing an orange shirt, turquoise pants, and an enormous ring with his name inscribed on it, Mr. Castellari, who is one of the few directors of spaghetti Westerns whose first name does not happen to be Sergio (Sergio Leone, Sergio Corbucci, Sergio Solima), was leaning over the movieola with great cries of "Paff!" "Pah!" "Ecco paff paff! Bellino!" The footage was being edited partly in color, partly in black and white, although the entire film was shot in color. For reasons of economy, Mr. Castellari has scenes that seem to him least promising made up for cutting in black and white. But sometimes, the black and white ones turn out to be best, so he keeps them and has them printed in color. (The whole movie will ultimately be a color film.) Mr. Castellari likes to use stunt men as the stars of his films. In *Westerns—Italian Style*, there are interviews with heroines being violated on the set, who express tremendous annoyance with the last-minute changes in the gestures they are required to make. There are solemn analyses of how the degree of stardom in an Italian Western can be determined by the time and suffering it takes a given character to die. (Bit players expire almost instantaneously.) There is an interview with Jean-Louis Trintignant, who stars as a mute in a spaghetti Western called *The Great Silence*. He describes the intellectual relief of acting wordlessly as great, but the physical work as difficult. "Because I am clumsy, I hurt myself all the time," he says, "like when I draw my revolver." He tells how he practiced removing his glove and drawing his gun, by pulling a sock off his hand and drawing from his pocket a long stemmed artichoke. The movie's music, appropriately enough, is mixed bluegrass, by John and Wayne.

. . . . . Jean Renoir's *Toni*

*9-18-68*

Jean Renoir's *Toni*, which was shown last night at the New York Film Fesitval, is such a little classic that film descendants of Renoir—Rossellini, for example, and through him Truffaut and Godard, who worked with him —sometimes refer to themselves as the Children of Toni. François Truffaut, in reviewing a movie by Claude Berri, once wrote, *"Tous les enfants de Toni s'y reconnaitront"* (All Toni's children will recognize themselves in it).

The movie, which is, naturally enough, in black and white, is about Basque, southern French and immigrant miners in the Midi, and it has a curious, muted, infinitely poetic way of treating human passion. Although it was made in 1934, it is particularly moving now, adjusting moods down from a glare and a shout to a still, fine, quiet tone. It is virtually engulfed in the space of Philharmonic Hall, where one has the impression of focusing on a television screen at the distance of a drive-in; but it seems almost the distance of time.

........ Orson Welles's
*The Immortal Story*

*9-19-68*

Orson Welles's *Immortal Story* is ineffective in a surprisingly feeble way. The screenplay, based on a story by Isak Dinesen, seems just right for Welles. An old man in Macao, played by Welles himself, tired of being diverted with scripture and prophecies, longs to hear true things. He tells a story he once heard at sea, of a sailor who was paid five guineas by an old man to sleep with the old man's young wife and produce an heir. Welles's factotum, a young Polish Jew, tells him the story is apocryphal, that sailors tell it everywhere. Welles decides to make the legend come true.

What goes wrong, I think, is that the acting and post-synchronization are so portentous and terrible. The voices, particularly that of the factotum, are slow and uncertain and flat—as of non-actors self-consciously reading a script for the first time. Jeanne Moreau alone, as an aging prostitute chosen to play the young wife, escapes the dead off-key and is excellent, but the acting of Roger Coggio, who plays the young Jew, seems to throw even her off her stride now and then.

The film, which is in color and quite lovely to watch, if the sound didn't capsize it all the time, was originally shot for television and lengthened afterward. That may be the main problem. There is a moment when, as Miss Moreau's lover approaches her, she recalls an earthquake that happened during her first affair; it is dear, and funny and

dated now—like the moments when the earth moved in
*The Bridge of San Luis Rey.**

. . . . . . . . . . *Funny Girl*

*9-20-68*

It is a great credit to the talent of Barbra Streisand that
one keeps hoping, for three long solid hours with intermission, that *Funny Girl* will turn out to be something—an
old-fashioned musical, a successful adaptation of the
Broadway show, anything with just that breath of the
genuine that makes you have a good time, or want to cry
at moments or respond as one does to musicals with excellent scores and great entertainers in them. Instead, the
movie is an elaborate, painstaking launching pad, with important talents of Hollywood, from the director, William
Wyler, on down, treating Barbra rather fondly, improbably
and even patronizingly, as though they were firing off a
gilded broccoli. Miss Streisand's talent is very poignant
and strong, but the movie almost does her in.

Almost every shot is held too long, every pointless
scene is interminable, sometimes shots are held just to let
you know the scene has come to an end. Fanny Brice isn't
there, Nicky Arnstein isn't there, the live garish period of
the Ziegfeld Follies isn't there. Arnstein, in particular, in-
tead of being the special, smalltime gangster that the story
requires, has been cast—presumably for an audience in a
small-town typing pool—as an exotic seducer (Omar
Sharif). Everyone around Miss Streisand, in fact, has been
cast in stereotype, so that one's attention is continuously

* Here it is: "The earth moved," of course, is from Hemingway's
*For Whom the Bell Tolls,* also about bridges, not Thornton
Wilder's *Bridge of San Luis Rey,* as implied in Thursday's review
of Orson Welles's *Immortal Story* at the Film Festival.
                                        —Retraction, 9/23/68

drawn to a subdrama, whether Miss Streisand is making good, whether she is going to be a movie star in the great old tradition of stars. This kind of scrutiny puts the audience in a calculating frame of mind, and even Miss Streisand turns off at moments and becomes mannered or absent-minded.

The film has something a little condescending about it—as though there were some special virtue in making a movie star out of someone who is not likely to be whistled at on Main Street or featured in cold-cream commercials. I thought if one more joke or whimsical, self-deprecating reference was made to Miss Streisand's looks—and for most of the movie she looks great—some European filmmaker, accustomed to people with faces, moods, and expressions of their own, ought to liberate the Criterion, where *Funny Girl* opened yesterday, from these apologetic, brouhaha incarnations of "I Can Get It For You Wholesale" 's Miss Marmelstein.

Miss Streisand doesn't need any of this. When she is singing—in a marvelous scene on roller skates—when she throws a line away, or shrugs, or looks funny or sad, she has a power, gentleness, and intensity that rather knocks all the props and sets and camera angles on their ear. There is something, too, about the poignance of a particular kind of ambition that is dated and almost nostalgic now.

.... *A Report on the Party and the Guests*

9-20-68

Jan Nemec's *A Report on the Party and the Guests*, which was shown yesterday at the New York Film Festival and which will open next week at the 34th Street East, was delayed for two years before it was released some months ago in Czechoslovakia. It is certainly one of the best Czechoslovak films ever made.

It begins with a picnic that has an air of menace, which

266

one can't quite place. The picnic is interrupted by a guest with cronies, clearly mad; yet all the characters on the picnic except one insist on falling in with the pretense that the insults, humiliations and tortures that ensue are part of an uneasy but jolly game. They all go on to join a larger garden party; superbly photographed and done, where events are funny—but with that unplaced air of menace—until it is realized that the picnic guest who would not play the game has gone. Ultimately, he is pursued with dogs and guns.

One of the extraordinary things about the movie, which is in beautfully lighted black and white, is its delicate, restrained and sophisticated treatment of fear. Fear in dreams, in insanity, in every kind of persecution, from the metaphysical to the political, down to the hostile Brownie troop. Complicity and fear and the pretense that things are harmless after all. There is the merest touch of actual physical violence. The violence is in the air. The acting, dialogue and photography are so good one doesn't want to do them in with overpraise. Jan Nemec is clearly one of the most powerful and universal young directors now at work.

. . . . . . . . . Film Time:
*La Religieuse*

*9-22-68*

Jacques Rivette's *La Religieuse*, based on a novel by Diderot, is a long, slow, gradual film that was banned in France in 1965 on the grounds of its thoroughly persuasive anticlericalism. It was shown Saturday at the New York Film Festival. Anna Karina plays a girl forced by her family in eighteenth-century France to enter a nunnery, where she is gradually extinguished by the damp, the draft, the lack of vocation, and the pressure of being constantly surrounded by gray, robed presences who share a base of life in which she has no part. She asks for a legal

267

release from her vows, is tortured and ostracized for hours of film time, and is finally denied her suit and transferred to a more gilded, happy convent full of frilly lesbians. She gets the emotional and spiritual bends—so does the audience; the atmosphere of oppression, made worse by a few sympathetic souls, is suffocatingly convincing even in a secular world—and when she finally does escape into life, it is such a parody of what she vaguely senses that she wants that it kills her after all.

Rivette is a believer in keeping cinema time as close to real time as possible (his *l'Amour Fou* was four and a half hours long), and *La Religieuse* seems slower, more stylized and repetitive, than it needs to be. About midway through the film, when Miss Karina is being mad and reasonable, tortured and cajoled by turns, the tableaux go so dead that one thinks the director may be prolonging the thing because he is rather enjoying it.

But the movie is made with high artifice, and there are enough kind, thoughtful characters portrayed within the church and enough cynical idiots outside it so that the message is not as much anti-clerical as anti-repressive-social-contract. And the state of the true rebel, enclosed by worlds within worlds from which only the greatest suffering, trepidation and sacrifice can offer him even the mildest hope of escape, takes hold so solidly that one feels trapped hours after one has gone out into the street. The film also features Francisco Rabal.

. . . . *You Are What You Eat*

*9-25-68*

Peter Yarrow (of Peter, Paul and Mary) and Barry Feinstein (director/cameraman) have caught, in *You Are What You Eat*, which opened yesterday at the Carnegie Hall Cinema, the youth and Sunset Strip scene at its apogee. It is the *8½* of the younger set. The film is incredibly inept and ugly at times. It is too long—a movie to be seen when you are turned on in some way, and certainly not at all if you are a child or are worried about your children. But it is all there, the clothes, the flowers, the grace and sordidness, dirty feet, police helmets, thumb-sucking, surfing, miscegenation, whitecoated tongues, pot, bubblegum, humor; Father Malcolm Boyd (*Are You Running with Me, Jesus?*), signs, distortions, willies, chaos and moments of sheer joy.

There are wonderful lines, overheard and never quite pursued: "And you remember the situation there, when our little friend was in the laundry wagon . . . ?") "Two and two are four. Four and four are eight. . . . It becomes astronomical!"; "I knew that it would come to pass that I could create"; "Well, the day is extremely overcast, but my heart is light." For fans of the old WOR-FM, there is Rosko's voice, advertising plastic Nazi helmets, "like the ones your father wore. This item will never become obsolete."

None of the musicians, including Tiny Tim, who makes some complicated but winning appearances, are at their best in the movie, but a song by Peter Yarrow, "Don't Remind Me Now of Time," is nice, and rather sums it up. There are also remarkable scenes of dogs on motorcycles, sheep in the meadow, a towheaded boy crawling off into the high grass, integrated couples on the street, and wonderful special-effect sequences of hippies dancing.

An awful lot of it is gross and grossly done, but there are moments when one laughs and thinks. Yes, this was the answer (in the words of one of the songs, Go to sleep and dream another way); and the movie includes so much that even if one can take it only in short drags, it is just about the best document of that style and era, when it was thought you could freak out to love, that we have.

9-25-68

Based on a novel by Stefan Zweig, *24 Hours in a Woman's Life,* which was shown yesterday at the New York Film Festival, is what they call a period piece. The film, which is in color and set in the Italian lake region during World War I, was directed by Dominique Delouche (his first feature film) in a style that might be described as dilute Baroque. The story concerns an aging French woman (Danielle Darrieux) who spends the night with a young German gambler and draft dodger (Robert Hoffman) and fails to reform him.

The thing has a specialized, dated aura of romance, but there is something disturbingly unresolved about its sensuality—like an orchid pressed under a pile of undershorts or a riding crop in marzipan. The atmosphere of a certain kind of resort hotel, with depressing decor and music in the halls, is clear enough, but the acting is embarrassingly false, and the painted decay of it all—Miss Darrieux and the camera keep lingering over the gambler's Adonis reclinings and long, feminine hands—does not seem a particularly live or interesting decay.

. . . . . . . Intense Whisper:
*Two or Three Things
I Know About Her*

9-26-68

Jean-Luc Godard's *Two or Three Things I know About Her,* which was shown yesterday at the New York Film Festival, is not one of his better films, although the title, I think, is one of his best. The movie is a kind of treatise on a section of Paris, the 20th Arrondissement, where new lower-middle-class buildings are going up, and on a girl (Marina Vlady) who lives there. Godard's voice supplies a partial narration, in a tense whisper, about problems that preocupy him now: language, politics, comic-strip imagery, appearance and reality. The characters more or less interview one another, or are interviewed by an interlocutor off camera, mainly about questions of identity and sex. The photography, in color, by Raoul Coutard, is beautiful, clear comic-book precise; and the locations—a dress shop, a beauty parlor, the interior of a coffee cup—are informed by Godard's signature.

There is an almost intolerable, conscious tension in Godard's work now between word and picture; one's attention is so riveted to the work on screen that Godard seems to think he can afford to freight it—at one point he speaks of himself as a painter and a writer—with a verbal text that takes off at right angles and includes almost anything that he would care to say.

The trouble is that, except for a few funny pieces of dialogue, the offscreen interview doesn't work too well in this one, and that Godard, as a philosopher and something of a political dogmatist, treats questions of philosophy —How do I know that I exist? Can there be a private language? and so on—as though works from Berkeley to Wittgenstein had not gone before. There are a few interesting reflections about the limits of language and the first principles of the universe, but most of it seems affected and rather tedious. Also, a whisper is not very well suited, over the long haul, to discussions of philosophy.

There is certainly enough of wit and beauty, though, to keep the film afloat, and for people who are interested in what interests Godard, there is a particularly patent, conscious (Godard seems always conscious) ambiguity now in what he feels about America. The text is almost detestingly anti, and yet American shoes, and cigarettes, and styles and Cokes are treated by the camera with the feeling that nature lovers reserve for rocks and trees. It is this nailing of attention with something you cannot help wanting to see burdened by a text of words you may not care to hear, that does not work too well this time, seems even superficial, but is a direction worth exploring all the same.

. . . . . . Claude Chabrol's
*Les Biches*

*9-27-68*

*Les Biches,* which was shown yesterday at the New York Film Festival (and which will open commercially tomorrow at the 68th Street Playhouse), is Claude Chabrol's best movie since *The Cousins. Les Biches,* which means "the does," concerns a rich lesbian (Stephane Audran) who picks up an aging, unformed waif (Jacqueline Sassard), who earns her living chalking does on the sidewalks of Paris. The two go off to Miss Audran's house in Saint Tropez, which already contains two vicious far-out, free-loading homosexuals—one of whom looks very like Jean Genet. When Jean-Louis Trintignant, as a young architect, sleeps, first with the waif and then, on a more permanent basis, with the lesbian, he remarks that the ménage seems to him a little strange.

The movie is very funny in parts—Miss Audran has a fine, drawing-room-comedy sarcastic way with a line. What is extraordinary is the portrayal of a kind of deviate Dolce Vita, in which the waif comes to regard her former lovers, male and female, as parental figures, to whom she becomes quite filially attached. She suffers a Freudian Finnegans Wake kind of trauma when she observes them in bed together, and subsequently goes on an Electra kind of mad. It is post Freud, for those waifs who have no emotional past in the conventional sense. I have never seen this sort of waif portrayed before.

The colors at the beginning of the movie are muted and washed, like scrolls, for the odd feminine milieu that is introduced. The ending seemed to me loosely done—it does

272

not quite take, dramatically—but the music, by Pierre Jansen, is painstakingly appropriate. And for the lesbian-watchers—who, on the basis of the reception of *Thérèse and Isabel,* seem to be a substantial and growing public—this is a movie that they can see with people who just like Chabrol and films.

.... A Terminal Smashup:
*Weekend*

*9-28-68*

Jean-Luc Godard's *Weekend,* which was shown last night at the New York Film Festival, is a fantastic film, in which all of life becomes a weekend, and the weekend is a cataclysmic, seismic traffic jam—with cars running pedestrians and cyclists off the road, only to collide and leave blood and corpses everywhere.

In one tremendously long take, the camera passes along a highway where traffic is stopped by a long line of dead, smashed, burned and stalling vehicles—oil trucks, Renaults, sports cars, Mercedeses, a zoo truck with two llamas in it, recumbent tigers, people playing ball through the tops of their stalled Deux Chevaux, people playing chess, honking horns, making gestures, quarreling, crying and ignoring the fact that there is mayhem everywhere. The conception of the movie is very grand. It is as though the violent quality of life had driven Godard into and through insanity, and he had caught it and turned it into one of the most important and difficult films he has ever made.

There are plot fragments at the beginning, betrayals, dire conspiracies to murder, detailed, intimate (and highly comic) sexual anecdotes. They lead nowhere. There are a couple (Mireille Darc and Jean Yanne), who, like refugees from the world of Samuel Beckett, are always looking for a gas station, and later for a town. A lot of the movie is like Beckett, the despair (if this can be imagined)

273

not as it is on stage, simplified and austere, but rich, overloaded, really epic. At one point, as the couple sit by the side of the road, the woman is casually raped in a ditch. No one even bothers to mention it. This would not work in the theater or in prose. It works on film.

The movie is interspersed with little essays, idylls, jokes, a Mozart sonata, a frantic love song sung by Jean-Pierre Léaud in a telephone booth, noise, rituals, battles with paint sprayers and tennis balls. It ends in slaughter and cannibalism. There are a lot of infantile pretentious touches, punning flashcards (*Anal . . . lyse, Faux . . . tographie*) and the subtitles seem to have caught a bit of this. *La Paresse* (laziness) is regularly translated as press.

There is a moment near the end when the movie cracks up—long, dogmatic, motionless diatribes on behalf of Africa and the Arab countries with a peroration against black nonviolence, which keeps one thinking Biafra, Biafra, and wanting to walk out. (In fact, it might be advisable to walk out when the speeches begin for a cup of coffee and a cigarette). It's unprofessional, like a musician stopping a concert to deliver a bit of invective to a captive audience. But perhaps, like any serious artist, Godard cannot help including all his preoccupations raw right now, even if they bring his movie down.

But the film must be seen, for its power, ambition, humor, and scenes of really astonishing beauty. There are absurdist characters from Lewis Carroll, from Fellini, from *La Chinoise*, from Buñuel. At many moments the movie, which is in color, captures the precise sense one has about the world when one is in a city or in a rush, when one reads the headlines or obituary columns, when one drives, when one sets out, for that matter, on a weekend. It is as though the apocalypse had somehow registered on a sensibility calibrated very fine. It is an appalling comedy. It is hard to take. There is nothing like it at all.

*9-28-68*

*L'Enfance Nue* ("Naked Childhood"), by Maurice Pialat, is one of the few beautiful films I have seen this year that are moving in a human and sentimental way. It is the story of a little boy, with problems on the order of *The 400 Blows,* who meets a number of obtuse but charming old adults (rather on the order of *The Two of Us*) as he is shuttled about among foster homes. The boy drops a cat down a long stairwell to prove that the animal always lands on its feet, and then tries to nurse it back to health. He throws iron bars from a bridge and causes a severe accident.

He is, in short, troubled in not altogether endearing ways, and this is a departure into honesty for childhood films. The boy (played by Michel Tarrazon) causes physical pain. But the movie is so full of humor and a kind of anecdotal truth (I think a whole area is opening up for the autobiographical film) that one begins to care very much for the boy—and for all the other characters, especially the old. All the members of the cast are nonprofessionals. Marie Marc, who plays the ancient mother of an already old couple of foster parents (René and Marie-Louise Thierry), is alone worth seeing—as she sings a folksong off-key, or speaks of her past, or just conveys a sense of wisdom and love of life that weakens across the generation gap.

Another character in the movie sings a splendid song—a bride, at her own wedding reception, who clearly thinks she is in good voice. And there is a fine performance by Henri Puff, who plays Tarrazon's foster brother—awkward, ungrown and diffident. When homesickness and a death—the separation for which all the partings of childhood are a metaphor—bring on a crisis that begins to resolve the boy's delinquency, one becomes aware that Pialat is doing something that movies rarely do any more: tell a simple, touching story warmly, straight.

*9-29-68*

There has been such attendance, interest and sense of life and controversy at the sixth annual New York Film Festival that it seems more than ever extraordinary not to have in the United States anything comparable—in size, distinction or service for a clearly existing audience—to the Paris Cinémathèque. The Cinémathèque shows four films a day throughout the year in its 400-seat center at the Palais de Chaillot and three films a day in its 200-odd-seat room on the Rue d'Ulm. Admission is technically one centime (although the museum charges two 'francs more for passage through its doors) and students are constantly rummaging through their pockets for change so small that there is hardly anything else it will buy in contemporary France. (Lincoln Center originally had plans for a year-round, distinguished film center, but they fell through.)

Nearly all the postwar French directors educated themselves at the Cinémathèque. Truffaut in particular, who used to arrive with his trousers suspended by a belt of rope, attended so often that he was secretly admitted by Madame Marie Meerson—a formidable lady who is known as one of the Cinémathèque's three sustaining caryatids —free of charge. In this country we have the Museum of Modern Art, a better but less accessible archive at the Eastman House in Rochester, a fine ethnographic center at Harvard, and some collections at other universities, but nothing that compares to the working library in Paris, founded in 1935, initially for the protection of silent films, by Henri Langlois.

Henri Langlois was here last week to introduce an old silent film, *L'Argent,* and a new Yugoslav film, *Kaya* (He does not recognize a distinction between old, new and

276

future films, he said: unlike theater, which ends in time, all cinema seems to him contemporary), to the New York Film Festival, and to discuss cinémathèques in general. Asked why his collection was by far the finest in the world, Langlois explained that three organizations had been founded at approximately the same time: the film department of the Museum of Modern Art, the Film Institute in London and the Paris Cinémathèque. "The problem was, you see, that the other two societies had money," Langlois said, "whereas I had to work."

Langlois, a large, round, imperial-looking man whose hair hangs like curtains on the sides of his large, handsome face, was walking, without shoes, around his rooms in a hotel on Fifty-seventh Street. He explained that, by preserving, hiding, camouflaging, and collecting films throughout the occupation, the Cinémathèque had, by 1946, a collection of 50,000 films—many of them American classics which, from a psychology of obsolescence, the film industry had been trying to destroy. After the war he had to return many movies to their original owners for commercial distribution, but ten years ago Langlois established good relations with American studios ("They have, after all, their professional honor in the films they have made," he said), and now the collection contains 50,000 films again.

He said that the Cinémathèque is run like the old Republic of Venice: there is the council of the people; above that, an inner council of ten, and above that the Doge, Langlois. He compared the Cinémathèque to a bank, with filmmakers and directors as depositors. "You could never completely nationalize it," he said. "The bank belongs to those who make deposits there." In 1946 the French Government began to subsidize the Cinémathèque, and by 1963 the Cinémathèque's statutes were changed so that, in return for a larger subsidy, it was no longer a completely private enterprise but had, alongside its director, a functionary of the state, a poet and close friend of a government minister, who had many disagreements with Langlois. This precipitated the crisis of intrigue earlier this year when Langlois was fired and then—after expressions of outrage from filmmakers all over the world and violent street demonstrations in France—reinstated by André Malraux.

Langlois is one of the rare, eccentric and inspiring spirits of film history, and among the many not quite apocryphal stories of him in the crisis time is one that concerns a meeting of the council—to which, as usual, the directors were late. Langlois' supporters were outnumbered by functionaries. A vote against Langlois would have precipitated his resignation, had he not eaten the ballots and thereby postponed a validated count until a more representative quorum had arrived. There are legends about Madame Meerson, too. At the low point of the crisis (according to Rossellini) Truffaut and other concerned filmmakers were gathered, at 3 A.M., in a Paris apartment, when Langlois arrived, distraught. "It is over," he said. "Marie saw it. They have taken all the films from the Cinémathèque tonight." After much anxious discussion, Rossellini called Madame Meerson to confirm. "Yes, it is over," she said in lugubrious tones. "I saw them taking the films away." Very long and precise questioning on Rossellini's part revealed that Madame Meerson had seen this catastrophe in a dream. She was inconsolable. The difference did not seem to her significant.

Since the crisis and Langlois' reinstatement the Cinémathèque has reverted to its private status, with a considerable reduction in government funds. "It is far better than before," he said. "I have made economies, a less heavy administrative structure. And then, I have reduced my salary. There you have an economy!" One-third of the Cinémathèque's funds now come from tickets, and memberships, one-third from the state and one-third, Langlois hopes, from private contributors.

I asked Langlois about the argument, often made in this country to explain the absence of a cinémathèque, that original prints of old films are inflammable, do in fact explode. "If you want to sell something," Langlois said, "you say that your competitor's product is an explosive one." He said that although Flaherty had burned *Nanook of the North* by smoking in the laboratory, and that although he does not hire people who smoke (he stopped chain-smoking himself a week ago), he had never heard of an exploding film, except perhaps in Egypt or the equatorial zone. He said that although, for safety and insurance reasons, it would be unwise to smoke around old films in the projection booth or in the laboratory, the explosive quality of films was an American legend.

"The British believe old prints exude a poison. It has become a degree of psychosis," he said. "Once the chauffeur of a car in which I was transporting film trembled with fear. It is true that films that are not uninflammable are flammable. It is like saying cars burn when there has been an accident. Films have been handled and transported on trains since 1895 without explosions. If the Mona Lisa were painted on flammable canvas, would that be a reason to keep her in a vault?" Some years ago Langlois traded a fire-resistant copy of a Griffith film to a fearful collector for an original print. Original prints are invaluable for film study, since copies become progressively less true.

Langlois, who has just appointed Charlie Chaplin, Abel Gance and Marcel L'Herbier, among other honorary chairmen of the Cinémathèque, and Fritz Lang, Buñuel, Ray and King Vidor, among other honorary vice-presidents, will presumably become the catalyst for one of the plans for an American cinémathèque which are now being intensively pursued— probably not in New York, where tensions, prides and jurisdictions are too clear; perhaps in Illinois or Texas or farther west. Langlois was recently appointed jet professor at a college in Montreal, to which he commutes from Paris once every fifteen days. It would be natural for him to serve as a kind of bridge for all the isolated collections that there are. He claims that American organizations, like the American Film Institute, which have an interest in saving films, turn first to existing cinémathèques for copies of their copies—in other words, to films that are already saved. "The drama is to discover films to save. It takes work," he said. "The old employee of studios who knew where things could be found are gone, and the young ones often do not know." Marcel L'Herbier's *L'Argent* was one of the films Langlois himself has recently discovered.

I asked Langlois how he explained his close relationship with young directors, in France and everywhere. "I do not have a museum over me which considers paintings high culture and regards film as low," he said. "We run films without the explanatory notices that the museums have, almost always even without subtitles." (It is a standing joke that among prints which Langlois has gathered over the years there are bizarrely titled ones, Swedish films with Bulgarian titles, Spanish with Armenian.) "Films with sub-titles are for the ladies from the Sixteenth Arrondissement. But when you see a Japanese film twenty times, without sub-titles, you begin to understand, to watch. When you know what it is to watch in that way, then you are a filmmaker."

It would be logical, in view of the interest generated at universities and by the festival—and since movies are the only art in which we have antiques as old as anyone's —for Americans to have a place, besides museums, commercial theaters, television, in which to watch.

. . . . . . *The Firemen's Ball*
and *Oratorio for Prague*

9-30-68

The sixth annual New York Film Festival closed Saturday night, fittingly enough, with two small, brilliant films by Czechoslovak directors. *Oratorio for Prague* by Jan Nemec (who directed *Report on the Party and the Guests*) and *The Firemen's Ball* by Milos Forman. Although neither movie was shown under ideal conditions (the subtitles of the Forman film were hard to see in the vastness of Philharmonic Hall; the Nemec film lost a little of its impact by being shown there before people had a chance to settle down), both brought the audience to their feet. It was by far the finest movie program showing at that moment anywhere in New York.

*The Firemen's Ball*, which is in color and which will

280

open Tuesday at Cinema II, is a hilarious shaggy-dog story, with the pessimism of the exquisite logic that leads nowhere. The firemen's ball has been convened for the purpose of awarding an honorary hatchet to a retiring fire chief (Joseph Svet), who is eighty-six. (It would have been better to award it to him when he was eighty-five, before he got cancer, but procrastination is important to any functioning bureaucracy.) The poor man keeps tottering forth to receive his hatchet, but every time the firemen's band plays it is for some other part of the ceremony, a beauty contest, a raffle or a real fire, which burns down another old man's house nearby. (The old man whose house is burning is seated in a chair in the snow to watch. Then, out of concern for his feelings, his neighbors turn his chair around. When they think he might be cold, they back him closer to the flames.)

The movie is full of humor, dense in every detail, which works only on screen and not in prose. Forman's comedy is special—muted Rabelaisian in its view of human character. (A couple make love under a table from the top of which the trembling raffle prizes are being stolen one by one. When the lights are turned off so that everyone may secretly return what he has stolen, the only man who actually returns a prize, a headcheese, faints with mortification when he is seen by the crowd.) There is verbal satire, too—the retiring chief's deadpan acceptance speech is a comic gem, even in subtitles. But the timing and involutions of the humor are such that there is escalating laughter, while an awareness of the sadness of things —real fire, monumental pettiness—deepens as well. That a director who sees things so bitterly and clearly can be this funny now may mean that we are in for a comic renaissance after all.

*The Firemen's Ball* is universal in a way entirely different from Jan Nemec's *Report of the Party and the Guests*. *Report* is pure and universal, as a fable is. *The Firemen's Ball* is universal in the sense that it is rich in characters (perfectly cast and played) and situations that are everywhere. Forty thousand firemen resigned in a huff when the Czechoslovak Government, still under Antonin Novotny, released *The Firemen's Ball*. Then Forman, in characteristic fashion, parodied a critical interpretation of the film as allegory, and the firemen were consoled. The movie is about mortal stupidity as much as anything—all these people, whose life work is preserving life, failing each other through insensitivity and selfishness. It was bought by two French directors, Truffaut and Berri, when the original producer, Carlo Ponti, wanted changes that the director could not accept. It is just right as it is.


When seen in a small theater, under conditions that make it personal, Jan Nemec's *Oratorio for Prague* is a film so moving that one is near tears from the first moment after the credits appear. The movie was begun as a documentary about the liberalization of Czechoslovakia, and then simply continued when the Russian tanks moved in. "But we are beginning at the end," the narration, very low key, put together in four days with the voice of *Variety's* foreign correspondent Gene Moskowitz, explains. The movie is shot in a style so poetic and gentle that the humanism and generosity of spirit, which seemed about to radiate from Alexander Dubcek and Czechoslovakia into the world, is there intact.

There are shots of churches, where masses are being said; of the synagogue, where "Shema Yisrael" is being sung; of a monument inscribed with 70,000 Jewish victims' names; of a monument to the U.S Army in 1945; of weekend hippies, of dancing students who took so much of the responsibility of liberation; of President Ludvik Svoboda, who threatened suicide if Dubcek were not reinstated; of Dubcek arriving alone at the airport, and of students and old ladies facing tanks. (A passing student, protesting the invasion, ducks, so that the camera can catch the Russian infantry. One cannot imagine an American revolutionary ducking, under any circumstances, when a camera is around.) There are interviews with people, asking them their fondest wish under liberalization. "That we may all be successful in our work," Dubcek replies.

Nothing sensational, no scoops of extreme violence, only a bloodstain on the pavement, burning tanks, two corpses, young faces mouthing "Facist," a gesture to block the camera, a Russian soldier, in a private moment, reassembling a torn Czechoslovak tract. Nemec himself driving toward the invading forces, quiet Czechoslovak humor, a few verses of "We Shall Overcome," which, far from seeming trite or jaded, give one chills. The music is alternately rock, folk and liturgical. The whole film is marked with the restraint and beauty of Jan Nemec's style. Now that the newsreel is no longer with us, artists may turn increasingly to documentaries, and *Oratorio for Prague*—immersed in a sense of unradical continuity, full of solemn memories of World War II—has set the level of taste and humanity extremely high.

Nemec himself brought the film to New York from Paris, where it was put together quickly, after arriving secretly by way of Vienna, from Prague. Excerpts of it were among the first shots of the invasion shown on television. Part of the film's financing came from Truffaut and Berri, too. Nemec, who will be returning to Prague in two weeks to begin another film, was greeted with a prolonged ovation by the festival audience, which was as obviously and profoundly moved as any audience I have ever seen.

. . Patience for the Transition
to Little Films

*10-6-68*

With all the splits and churnings that there are in movies now—with *Funny Girl* opening commercially during the first days of the New York Film Festival—one thing seems fairly clear: the days of the single, grand film for everyone are nearly gone. Television has become the kind of mass entertainment that movies used to be—and any single appearance of Barbra Streisand on television or, for that matter, in person or on stage, shows her talent to better effect than the encrusted, underinspired star vehicle that *Funny Girl* became on screen.

283

Millions of people will probably see the movie, and presumably be disappointed by it, but the everybody-audience has clearly moved to "Bonanza" and Johnny Carson, and the apparatus for making everybody-films is grinding down. As the industry fragments and regenerates in more varied terms—smaller movies, more idiosyncratic talents, smaller, not necessarily overlapping but still, in sum, huge audiences—we will have lost the good old movies that everybody likes. But we have lost them anyway, the gift for making them and the habit of responding to them. All that remains is big budgets and nostalgia. Every special success, from *Bonnie and Clyde* to *Rosemary's Baby*, shows that the answer lies outside the rusty apparatus of the movie factory.

In the meantime, the question is what to do with the old impulse just to go to the movies, not to make a big thing of it, just to go out. I think most movies, particularly those that are highly praised in reviews (and television commercials have encroached on movie reviewing much as television has upon cinema, so that the way to help a movie is not so much to discuss it as to write advertising copy for it) are disappointing now. Expectations and possibilities are unclear. A movie. A film. I think the difference between the words (like Negro and black) is useful for sentence rhythm mainly, but there is also the matter of levels of expectation: entertainment, art. For the moment, one has to be patient if the impulse just to go to the movies is not to bring on a kind of depression between the two.

The question is which movies to be patient with. The big, star-factory flick will always find its audience—although there is nothing to match the high aesthetic indignation of people who have made a $15,000,000 extravaganza which they feel has not been received with sufficient critical warmth. (Makers of genuine, uninflated movies, who have been virtually ruined by unfavorable reviews, rarely complain.) On the basis of this years' New York festival—nearly all of whose performances were sold out, and nearly all of whose movies, *L'Argent, Mouchette, The Red and the White, Faces, Oratorio for Prague, Report on the Party and the Guests, Partner, Signs of Life, Naked Childhood. Les Biches, Weekend,*

*The Firemen's Ball*, many shorts and particularly *Kaya*, had access to more laughter, more tears, more rage in some cases, but nearly always more genuine, old-fashioned entertainment response than most films outside the festival—I think we have to decide, for the churning movie interim, what sort of audience to be, which movies to make allowances for, which way to lean.

And it almost has to be toward little films—not for moralistic reasons, or condescendingly, but because they are the way the form is developing and, mainly, because they are more fun. Even Jean-Pierre Léaud singing into the telephone in *Weekend* (a movie which is great, though in some respects almost intolerable) or an ancient grandmother and a bride singing proudly and off-key at the bride's wedding reception in *Naked Childhood* (a thoroughly endearing film) are more fresh musically than most genuine musicians in recent musicals. (So were *Bonnie and Clyde* and *The Graduate*.) At least there is some surprise to them.

*Report on the Party and the Guests* had a new air of violence; *Faces, Les Biches*, and *Weekend* had sex; *The Firemen's Ball* had comedy; *Naked Childhood* had sentiment; *Oratorio for Prague* had a political and emotional reality intact. Music, violence, sex, comedy, sentiment, humanity—the old movie responses have quietly slipped into the individual film and left most monster-budget movies with a shell. Of course, allowances have to be made (and films of the American underground do not so far fit into this discussion at all). But just now the balance seems to have tipped. With exceptions, far fewer allowances need to be made for signed films now than for large boring circuses running toward yesterday. Of course, one can go to both.

*Kaya*, which was shown toward the middle of the New York Film Festival, is the story of a small town in Yugoslavia, where, one night in World War II, a soldier of the Italian occupation suddenly and for no reason appeared at the door of a friend, a peaceful citizen, said, "Kaya, I'll kill you," and shot him dead. The whole town, the air itself, somehow conspired in this event, and the director, Vatroslav Mimica, has somehow succeeded,

285

where so many have tried, in taking a contemporary story and turning it into an extremely delicate and powerful parable of the life of Jesus Christ.

The movie lays its cards upon the table very slowly—beautiful color shots of the Dalmatian town and the sea, the village idiot, children gathering shells, bachelors hunting birds, tales told at night, music that carefully builds its mood. The town is very carefully established, geographically, and yet it clearly could be anywhere. There is a very odd and brooding personification of objects, waves, gargoyles, shutters, that seem to confer with a particular moral blindness.

Then there are Fascists, saluting each other at the window behind a balcony, as they always do in movies about World War II. Someone is forced to drink two enormous glasses of castor oil for violating a curfew, the Roman soldiers go on a mad, object-destroying rampage, burning books, sawing the head off an ancient wooden carving of a saint, saying "Kill his soul." All the characters seem simultaneously ashamed and yet submissive to the inevitable; and then it comes: a violence without courage or honor, the terrible determination of a dying man to stand.

The movie makes only one mistake, and that is very brief. At one point, when the major characters are having supper, there is a shot of a kitchen calendar with the Last Supper on it. It takes a few moments for the audience to recover from having the film declare itself so bluntly (and by this point, redundantly). But the rest is marvelous. At a time when all glory and honor have passed from acts of violence, there seem to be characters, from De Sade to now, who are willing to take on the responsibility for violence, plain, in almost a reverse Christ gesture, somehow do it and stare it down, exorcise. I do not think this is a very promising line, but seeing the soldier and his victim in the movie is almost like watching Christ split in two. One does not know which one to care for. At the end of the movie, the village idiot casts one short, frightened and devastating look upon the audience and walks off screaming. It is done so well. It is one of the few contemporary works about sin, in a religious context, that rings absolutely sound.

*10-9-68*

Franco Zeffirelli's *Romeo and Juliet* is a lovely, sensitive, friendly popularization of the play—the lovers, Leonard Whiting and Olivia Hussey, as young and full of life as they ought to be, Italy of its time there intact, a lot made of the relationship between Romeo and Mercutio, beautifully played by John McEnery. The prose suffers a bit, sounding more like *West Side Story* than perhaps it ought to. In the classic speeches, one begins to worry about diction and wish the modern would recede and let Shakespeare play through.

But the scenes, the ball, the duels, are so beautifully thought out and staged that things I had not noticed—the puppy-play character of the duels at first—become extraordinary, temporally present and remote. But for the poetry, and the fine archaic dignity of Romeo and Juliet, the story could be taking place next door. It is the sweetest, the most contemporary romance on film this year. There are fine, unanachronistic songs by Nino Rota and Eugene Walter, and scenes so human, social and derived from Dutch and Italian painting schools that it is a joy to watch, if not quite to listen to.

Romeo and Juliet, when racked with sobs, go on too long, particularly since the crying does seem forced. Pat Heywood, as the nurse, seems too bawdy, cold and almost terrifying—in the way that characters in Disney movies suddenly become uncanny, and haunt children's dreams. But these were clearly Zeffirelli's conscious choices and there is so much else that leads one to agree with what he does that he may be right in these uncomfortable choices, too.

There is a softly homosexual cast over the film—not

just with Romeo and Mercutio, but with Juliet's bodice being much too tight, or a kind of Greek attention lavished on Romeo in the bedroom scene. And yet Romeo, his face not quite yet integrated, and Juliet, with a special lady quality of lust, work absolutely right—as do Natasha Parry, as the classic beauty, Lady Capulet, or Robert Stephens, as the wise, liberal Prince of Verona. Milo O'Shea plays Father Laurence, rather as a modern, radical-understanding Dean.

It wouldn't be surprising if this film, with all its youth-adult misses of contact, and its failure of the bureaucratic post, should become the thing for young people to see. The business of locating Shakespeare so firmly in a place, some scenes and bodies, in opera, but not in language quite, is worrying. But the movie, which opened yesterday at the Paris Theater, is done with full awareness of the way it works, and it works touchingly.

### ... *Finian*'s Listless *Rainbow*

*10-10-68*

There is something awfully depressing about seeing *Finian's Rainbow* this year this way—with Fred Astaire looking ancient, far beyond his years, collapsed and red-eyed; with film work so shoddy that the camera hardly ever includes his feet when he dances and that people who have been sopping wet in one cut are absent-mindedly dry in the next; with nobody even bothering to put the whole cheesy, joyless thing, which is in execrable color—Technicolor, widescreen Panavision—into synch. Voices, Petula Clark's, Astaire's, Tommy Steele's, come from everywhere and nowhere, sometimes catching up with lips, sometimes floating in the general parallax that sitting near the sides of the Penthouse Theater (where the movie opened yesterday) brings on.

"How Are Things in Glocca Morra?", "If This Isn't Love," "Old Devil Moon," "Look to the Rainbow"—the magic, even the last bit of charm has gone out of them. It is not just that the musical is dated. Something lovely and nostalgic could have been made out of old Missitucky for the generation that grew up on *Finian's Rainbow* and *Brigadoon*. It is that it has been done listlessly and even tastelessly, with quick updatings of Negro personalities to match what people who have lived in Beverly Hills too long must imagine modern black sensibilities are. The cast is full of children who act as artificially and insincerely as the whole enterprise, directed by Francis Ford Coppola, would suggest.

There is a nice appearance by Don Francks, as a romantic lead with a good smile around his mouth and nose; and Petula Clark, we know from a record or two, can sing. But the whole story of the Irishman who buries his gold and the white Southern senator who turns black has just gone dim, as though nobody had troubled with it—hoping only to sell it to television as a family musical and get it over with.

. . . . . . . . . *Barbarella*

*10-12-68*

*Barbarella,* which opened yesterday at the Forum 47th Street, Loew's new Cine and the Murray Hill theaters, starts out as though it were going to be funny, or at least familiar. Jane Fonda, breathing credits, looking pretty and comical (it has been a long way from *Cat Ballou* and *Sunday in New York*), strips off some ant-like armor in a spacecraft. Roger Vadim, the director, reveals her, as usual, slowly, like some proud and solemn chef, until she stands naked before an elderly gentleman in a kind of mirror. "Barbarella," the old man says gravely. "Mr. President," she replies. It turns out she has an interplanetary mission.

Then, the movie, written by Terry Southern and seven other writers and based upon a comic strip, rapidly

289

becomes a special kind of mess. All the gadgetry of science fiction—which is not really science fiction, since it has no poetry or logic—is turned to all kinds of jokes, which are not jokes, but hard-breathing, sadistic thrashings, mainly at the expense of Barbarella. Throughout the movie, there is the assumption that just mentioning a thing (sex, politics, religion) makes it funny and that mentioning it in some offensive context makes it funnier. It is a humorist-advertiser's kind of experiment: Let's slab this through the midriff and see if anyone salutes it; let's throw in an allusion to faggotry and impotence and see if the cat laps it up. For a while, the audience, catching all the pointless, witless modernist allusions, feels in on something chic and laughs. Then it is clear that there is nothing whatever to be in on—except another uninspired anti-Mummy reflex omnispoof.

.... Temper, Misogyny and
Couples in Theaters


*10-13-68*


I don't know quite what to make of this, and perhaps it is only a reaction to the days when stars were blown up as love goddesses, but it is really startling what cinema, particularly American cinema, has done in the past year or so to women. With few exceptions (Virginia Maskell in *Interlude,* Maggie Smith in *Hot Millions,* Estelle Parsons and Joanne Woodward in *Rachel, Rachel,* and even these were actresses whose personal humanity overcame their roles), they have been grotesques—kooks, vampires, murderesses, spies, careerists, lesbians, objects of torture, torturers, nymphomaniacs or warmhearted, one-dimensional vulgarisms that pass for somebody's idea of what a Jewish mother is. What makes me think about it now, although it has been in the air these many months, is *Barbarella*—a movie so humorless and silly that it would not quite have made the grade as a fifties college musical, a movie that includes, among other overrated writers of our time, the author of *Candy*, and which suggests, almost incidentally, that some of the least imaginative minds of our generation are going farthest out.

*Barbarella* begins quite promisingly, with Jane Fonda in an insectoid carapace, shedding it gradually but with a trace of humor, as Roger Vadim does his mocking thing of revealing her to the world several inches at a time. There are some nice lines and touches—a lisping computer that mentions the pothibility of thtormy prethipitation. Then, the whole thing turns into a kind of ghastly spatial Krafft-Ebing; a flying vehicle that looks like a Revlon lipstick display case, a planetary landscape like an afterthought Christmas card, more thoraxes and carapaces, a kind of dogsled that is pulled along by what looks like a piece of calf's liver, a thinned mélange of James Bond, Dean Martin, *Planet of the Apes*, Strangelove, Orwell, *2001*, *Vivá Maria*, *Modesty Blaise*, Dante, Mordor (one longs for somebody like Tolkien, with the conviction of his own fantasy life). I have never cared for science fiction of the gadgetry rather than conceptual sort—science itself seems to have made this kind of fiction out of date—but I didn't expect such a violent turn toward sadism and misogyny.

There are jokes, at the level (in the noncommunicative, bad rock score) of rhymes between Barbarella, Psychedella, Cockleshella; an Exaltation Transference Pellet in place of sex; a translating machine called a Tonguebox; plastic antennae that wilt after people make love in the dogsled; an angel who is referred to as "your fine feathered friend" and who is crucified to prepare for lines like "Decrucify the angel. Decrucify him or I'll melt your face"; a death Chamber of Ultimate Solutions; women addressing women with "Hello, pretty, pretty"; men addressing women, "Vade in retro, Earthgirl"; and that oldest conceit of collegiate writers, a deathdealing nonstop sexual pleasure machine. There is an evil-devouring, power-generating fluid called the Mathmos, for lines like "You are so good you made the Mathmos vomit."

But what really got me about this one, what made it different from all the other booted, chained and leering art

291

nouveau extravaganzas with a blood idea of chic (and I ought to mention that Jane Fonda does show some talent as a comedienne and that David Hemmings does a good bit as an absent-minded revolutionary), was a scene in which Barbarella is captured by two little girls who set upon her a little army of advancing dolls with razor teeth. They go clacking and biting along until Barbarella is bitten decoratively, pretty well torn up. It suddenly seemed as though a whole genre of moviemakers were becoming that hideous little army, mechanical, full of wealth, cruelty and lurid, meaningless color for decorative uglinesses. It is not exactly camp or homosexual. It is not a comment on or a reflection of the way things are. It doesn't even look like an expression of a special taste in fun. It is an appraisal of a market, with all the hateful little sensibilities involved, a joke so in that nobody but moviemakers is getting it.

With the casting of women as instruments or victims of pain, something very odd is happening in the movies. Though films become more daring sexually, they are probably less sexy than they ever were. There haven't been any convincing love scenes or romances in the movies in a while. (Nobody even seems to neck in theaters any more.) There is something about the screen that seems to make it as severe with moralisms about sex without love, or the good uses of a little gentleness and passion as any embarrassed high-school hygiene teacher. When the mechanics and sadism quotients go up, the movie love interest goes dead, and the film just lies there, giving a certain amount of offense. I don't know where the movie dehumanization of women into menaced or menacing props comes from—as opposed to the old human story line of recognizable personalities who just wanted a man, and a child or two or six, and perhaps an interest. Maybe it represents a new idealization, and we are going to have love goddesses in the Buck Rogers line. But I doubt it. It does not even have access to the responses of melodrama. Audiences just seem jumpy or turned right off, with parodies of nothing and no one and all this cold suffering in fifty random directions for laughs.

292

*10-18-68*

*Bullitt,* which opened yesterday at the Music Hall, is a terrific movie, just right for Steve McQueen—fast, well
acted, written the way people talk. The plot is dense with
detail about the way things work: hospitals, police, young
politicians with futures, gangsters, airports, love affairs,
traffic, dingy hotels. There are a lot of Negroes cast, for a
change, in plausible roles. The setting, in San Francisco, is
solidly there, and the ending should satisfy fans from
"Dragnet" to Camus.

There are excellent chases, one around and under jet
aircraft taking off by night, the other, by car, over the San
Francisco hills. The car chase in particular is comic and
straight. (Nobody drives better than Steve McQueen.)
McQueen, quietly stealing a newspaper because he hasn't
got the dime or exchanging just the right look with a Negro
surgeon who understands, or even delivering a line that
consoles and sums up the situation with his girl, played by
Jacqueline Bisset, embodies his special kind of aware, existential cool—less taut and hardshell than Bogart, less
lost and adrift than Mastroianni, a little of both.

The movie, which is in color (rather dark and yellow),
was directed by Peter Yates and also features Don Gordon,
Robert Duval, Simon Oakland, Robert Vaughan (from
U.N.C.L.E.), and Norman Fell (of the "87th Precinct").
They and the minor characters are all fine, dry, and
natural, as this particular detective form requires. Television has almost stolen the genre, or made it unserious, but
*Bullitt* tightens and reclaims it for the movies. McQueen
simply gets better all the time.

293

*10-19-68*

*The Boston Strangler* represents an incredible collapse of taste, judgment, decency, prose, insight, journalism and movie technique, and yet—through certain prurient options that it does not take—it is not quite the popular exploitation film that one might think. It is as though someone had gone out to do a serious piece of reporting and come up with four thousand clippings from the *National Inquirer*. It has no depth, no timing, no facts of any interest and yet, without any hesitation, it uses the name and pretends to report the story of a living man, who was neither convicted nor indicted for the crimes it ascribes to him. Tony Curtis "stars"—the program credits' word—as what the movie takes to be the Boston strangler.

The film, which is based on a book by Gerold Frank, directed by Richard Fleischer, and which also features Henry Fonda and George Kennedy, begins as a split-screen collage (the effect is like flipping continuously among TV commercials), then goes on to enumerate the aberrations of a few people who did or did not confess to the crime, portrays the poor victims with a few intrusive lines and scenes, and finally attempts a long dimestore analysis with Tony Curtis ultimately, ludicrously but with evident sincerity, re-enacting a strangling in pantomime.

One indication of the accuracy, the fidelity to anything human or real in this film is that Senator Edward W. Brooke of Massachusetts (at that time Massachusetts Attorney General, and surely an important and familiar figure in American political life) is portrayed, by William Marshall, with a sinister intonation and a pronounced West Indian accent, as though he were the head of some world narcotics conspiracy out of James Bond.

The exposition, the dialogue throughout the film contribute what is almost a kind of comedy: After a strangling, "Was she raped?" The detective answers with a line that might have come from *Sanctuary*. "Then we've

294

got a fullblown maniac on our hands."

In an interview, "Lots of apprehension on your part, is there?"

"I think it's a very sad situation."

In a political conversation, "You want the stranglings to go on?"

"That's not fair. I just don't want to throw out the baby with the bath." The movie, which opened yesterday at the Astor, the Loew's Orpheum and the 34th Street theaters, is to be avoided as surely as a stranger who appears at your door and identifies himself as a plumber whom you have not called.


. . . Thoughts for 1,001 Nights,
and *Warrendale*


*10-20-68*

Going to the movies is getting to be a little like *The Thousand and One Nights,* with an odd audience that cuts across classes and generations huddled together in theaters, longing to be told something true (movies are still, after all, with rare exceptions a storyteller's form), something human, something that happened or occurred to someone, stories that pass the time and seem to ward off disasters in the world outside. There are people who find it important for the moment to sit very still, personally and in every sense, through a period of time until events declare themselves and it becomes clear what to do. Middle people—not indifferent, but concerned, isolated, anxious not to do anything loud or ungenuine, which might increase the sum of suffering in the world. Movies and tranquilizers pass the time one does not want to risk until the 1,001 or however many nights have passed.

Some of the most human films just now are documentaries, or documentary in style. Almost all are in black and white. I am more and more convinced that, unless you happen to have Raoul Coutard at the camera, or unless you have a story in which color itself plays a part, movie color is a useless extravagance, a television-haunted ploy that turns a serious film into a comic strip. It is more garish than the world or television, distracting, ugly and completely alien to the mood in which one enters movie theaters. The pure, infinitely varied and carefully controlled blacks and whites in *The Fifth Horseman Is Fear*, or *Report on the Party and the Guests,* or even the difficult Brazilian films just shown at the Museum of Modern Art, make most color films look over-rouged and powdered, and ungenuine.

There is a scene in *Warrendale*, a documentary by Allan King about disturbed children in a special kind of home, of the purest grief—tears, convulsions, silence, keening, a whole little room in an agony of mourning. Sane people no longer grieve like that, no longer have access to the same intensity. There are a lot of worrying problems about *Warrendale*. For one thing, through no fault of the filmmakers, they missed the story that they had. Dorothy, the Negro cook at Warrendale, suddenly died. Since most of the making of this sort of documentary consists in standing around and photographing ordinary daily things, and since the filmmakers, like the children, could have no premonition that Dorothy would die, the cook plays no great part before her death. Another problem is that although the film claims neutrality, it naturally endorses the therapy it shows, and one has doubts.

The therapy consists of "holding"—of physically restraining and engulfing any child in any kind of throes. The children, whom one never gets to know in any depth, although one is forcibly drawn to them, object to this, often in the strongest possible terms. (One of the special strengths of this movie, and the reason it was banned from Canadian television although Canadian television had commissioned it, is the extraordinary apt, spare, barracks language that the children use; it gives them an extremely touching directness and solidarity.) At one point, a marvelous small boy who is screaming, and being held and screamed at to find out why he is screaming, screams, "You have bad breath!" The therapists, including a young woman who has bruises all over her arms from holding a young man, the head of the clinic, who is simply beautiful in the softness and emotional energy he seems constantly able to impart, do not find bad breath sufficient explanation for not wanting to be held. They induce the little boy to say that he fears bad breath makes him inhale fire. It does not sound convincing. One wonders why he should be called upon to explain an aversion that has been an obsession of sane Americans for years.

Something else about the holding: at times it seems intrusive and about to bring a crisis on. Another lovely boy in the grief scene keeps insisting that he need not mourn since the cook was no relative of his. This seems quite reasonable. They start to hold him anyway. One thinks, Not me, officer, I was only watching. But the holding is not really the point of *Warrendale*. The point is the humane camera work and the fact that something genuine is being shown. What is interesting, too, even in movies, are the strange revisions we must make in our ideas of what it is to be disturbed. The sane have no assurances to give the insane now. These children, told so often and so confidently that no vibrations of theirs caused the cook to die, or that in a year or two they will get well—who can be so sure of either thing, or anything?

The children have a special reasonableness of their own. The full strength of four adults was required to contain their emotional response to death. (I was reminded of a piece in last month's *Esquire* in which a doctor, going on the analogy of teaching pigeons behavioristically to bowl, recommended giving electrical shocks to autistic children until they embraced the nearest adult, and sending unbearable noises into the earphones of a lady who thought she was persecuted, until she stopped mentioning what she feared—as though, long after the Gestapo came along, achieving behavioral change through cruelty were a new and exciting medical discovery.) Perhaps *Warrendale* does just what every local world should do, create a community in which people with special needs can be loved.

*The Diary of David Holzman*, a movie shown in a special category at the New York Film Festival, is the story of a young man who loses his job, is declared 1A by the draft and decides to make a film diary of a few days in his life. He loses his girl, who wants her privacy, he interviews a friend who considers the enterprise specious, he meets a remarkable lady in the street who challenges him to put aside his camera and come to bed. Finally, his camera and tape recorder are stolen and he completes the film in a station photo and record booth. It is remarkable to learn that all but a few parts of the movie were written and directed. It seems so real.

NOTE: As for the "Cinémathèque" letters of last week, yes, I have seen the film catalogue of the Museum of Modern Art, and yes, I have spent more than a year in Paris seeing a lot of what the Cinémathèque offers. I do not think there is a filmmaker in the world who would say there is any comparison between the two collections and the amount and quality of films they schedule. The Eastman House in Rochester is more respected than any other in the country, but is rather, as I mentioned, inaccessible. As for the relatively new American Film Institute, I have seen only its stationery and the salaries of some of its personnel.* I wish we did and could have a cinémathèque of the Langlois sort in New York, but only reported that, because of local cinema politics, it does not seem likely to happen.

....... Julie Andrews in
*Star!*

*10-23-68*

*Star!*, starring Julie Andrews, started yesterday at the Rivoli Theater. Miss Andrews, who plays Gertrude Lawrence, is not at her best in this one. There is some sort of clash between her special niceness and innocence and

---

* In the course of the year the American Film Institute began to seem to me a terrific boondoggle, but I never got around to doing an entire piece about it.

the attitude that the film, directed by Robert Wise (of *The Sound of Music*), has toward the star of *Private Lives* and *The King and I*. Miss Lawrence is portrayed as a kind of monster, with none of the crispness or glamour or wit that would give her ambition style. She says "cripes" an enormous amount, and lives with a lot of men for their money, but even the songs—from Noel Coward to Cole Porter to Kurt Weill—sound mechanical and cold, without any sophisticated, sentimental ring.

The movie, with intermission (by some convention that makes it possible to charge theater prices for mammoth musicals), is three hours long and it has the rickety structure of a movie within a movie. A lot of the sets are lovely, Daniel Massey acts beautifully as a kind of warmed Noel Coward, and the film, which gets richer and better as it goes along, has a nice scene from *Private Lives*. People who like old-style musicals should get their money's worth. So should people who like Julie Andrews. But people who liked Gertrude Lawrence had better stick with their record collections and memories.

........*Weekend,* and
Antagonizing Audiences

*10-27-68*

The question of why people do not go to see Jean-Luc Godard movies in commercial theaters has a lot to do with where movies are, who the audience is and what movies have to do with the other arts. It is clear that in every film since *Breathless*, Godard has either ignored or done his best to antagonize an audience, and that parts of his movies are nearly always insufferable. But in other forms —painting, sculpture, music, mixed media—there exists an audience that thrives upon indifference and antagonism. For movies, except at the Film-Makers Cinémathèque and on some college campuses, there is no avant garde audience in this sense—that is, willing to take just about anything, as long as it has an aura of novelty and satisfies their sense of themselves as being on the side of Art. The economics of movies are such that the Cinémathèque-style audience cannot support a film on any popular scale.

With Godard movies, though, there are other factors too. One is the *Cahiers du Cinéma* reflex, whereby movie buffs want to be alone, either engulfed in a popular audience that does not know (according to them) the value of the film it is seeing, or in some isolated, beleaguered space where a film is necessarily doomed to obscurity. At festivals, there are so many buffs for Godard films that it is almost impossible to find a place to sit. But commercial openings, and also enthusiastic reviews—particularly enthusiastic reviews; I suspect if *Weekend* had been panned almost everywhere, the loyal buffs would have kept it running for a long time—turn buffs right off, and dislodge them from their position of knowingness.

In a way, this is good. There are few things more disgusting aesthetically than an audience avant garde on principle. Beautiful people, pop innovators, style revolutionaries—they find each other almost naturally, on the territory of specious newness, the conspiracy of knowing where it's at. (Also at dinner and in the gossip columns.) It is always the façade, the chic, the crowd, the promise without the delivery, the soap box without the soap in it. This doesn't happen with film. There are no patrons of cinema in the pop fashion sense, no one to donate the $1,000 even that it takes to save an old print. (Among the studios Twentieth Century-Fox, ostensibly for lack of such a donor, has announced its intention of letting its original nitrate films decay; MGM, on the other hand, has taken the responsibility of preserving what there is.) Ironically, the thing about film art just now is that there is no glamour in it.

So Godard, or even such a film as *Faces,* which marks the end of *cinéma vérité* by being scripted, directed *cinéma vérité,* faces either an audience (small) that will sit through countless hours of the Empire State Building or some other lethally boring piece of idiocy, or an audience (smaller still) that jealously guards important films as a private thing, to be abandoned as soon as there is any chance of surviving at all. Or a film must make it on its own, in the true avant garde sense, from the bottom, on substantial grounds, into popular consciousness. It is a genuine, literary sensibility that a Godard film must win, and some personal quirk of the director's—as sensitive and literary, among other things, an intelligence as there is in any of the arts—causes him to laugh in the audience's face.

I ought to admit here that I had never liked Godard. I did not care for *Breathless* and it was only with such films as *The Married Woman, Bande à Part* and *Masculine Feminine* (there are a lot that I have not seen) that I began to think what a lot he knows. And then, there was *La Chinoise*, not just the scoop—the aspect of art as prophecy—of casting students from Nanterre as revolutionaries long before the world thought of Nanterre in revolutionary terms, but also the uncanny thing of politics as characterization. One knew so clearly what these young people personally were from what they thought.

There was also *Les Carabiniers*, on which Godard collaborated with Rossellini—the restrained, gray allegory of war, which no one else could have done so simply and movingly. Now there is *Weekend*, with parts and an ending so brutal, obtuse and ghastly that one can scarcely bear it in its entirety and need not bear it, unless one is an avant gardist or unless one cares for moments of total power and mastery in an art, in which case one owes it to him. The question is what to do. Not to sit through the intellectually insulting didactic parts, certainly, where either Godard's unworked and unenlightening political obsessions have simply forced themselves upon everything he does, or some personal inverse mania of sensitivity causes him to alienate an audience when he has it in thrall.

Certainly, to see the movie at least—if one cares to see a great young man at work, or if one wants to count for anything as the audience of one's time for history. The conception of life as a weekend, and a weekend as an unending slaughter on the highways, which encompasses sex, money, power, intelligence, the animal kingdom, is grand. Perhaps to see it and walk out. The money at the box office still means a lot in turning movies toward the talented, signed, live way they are going to have to go

301

anyway. And the walking out might be a kind of protest, that the cinema avant garde audience is still too grass-roots-general to sit there while anything goes. Or one might sit through the entire thing—we sit through so much else that turns stupefying, offensive or downright reprehensible just to go to a movie after all. Might as well go where the people who stumble, but know what they are doing are making films, and draw the festival and commercial audiences together there.

.......*The* Hard Ticket
*Lion in Winter*

*10-31-68*

It is a lovely idea to cast Katharine Hepburn as Eleanor of Aquitaine, with and against a very heavy and robust Peter O'Toole as Henry II, in a contest of will. Not a contest for the psychological upper hand, or whether the baby shall have a pacifier and which restaurant to go to tonight, but a contest transposed into twelfth-century terms—which son shall inherit the kingdom, who will marry the king's mistress and what will become of the provinces of Vexin and Aquitaine.

The dialogue of *The Lion in Winter,* taken from James Goldman's Broadway play, is witty and dated in a twenties way—as all wit from drawing-room and insult comedy seems dated now. At moments, the parents, sons and visiting royalty at Chinon in 1183 talk so nastily that they seem like a whole household full of men who came to dinner. But the movie, which opened last night at the Lincoln Art Theater is, for the most part, outdoorsy and fun, full of the kind of plotting and action people used to go to just plain movies for.

The film is far too faithful to the play. It divides neatly into acts, has a long sag in the middle, is weakest in its climaxes—Henry becoming violently upset about the $n$th time he hears that Eleanor may have slept with his father; Eleanor and her husband's mistress, played by Jane Merrow, falling into each other's arms. It has all sorts of intrigue and arguments on questionable grounds—baseless one-up-manship and pointless conspiracy.

But the acting—Anthony Hopkins, as a queer, manly Richard the Lionhearted; Nigel Terry, as a caricatured, spastic adolescent Prince John; John Castle, as an almost too attractive, scheming Prince Geoffrey; and Timothy Dalton, as a sensitive, regal, embittered Philip of France —is joyful and solid. The relationships between people, though ambivalent, are ambivalent with a certain satisfying ferocity. The only person who directly and unambiguously loves anybody is Henry's mistress and she seems rather beyond her speed with the fierce rest.

Katharine Hepburn, from her first scene when she is briefly taken out of her ten-year imprisonment, shows a fine relish for even the most unimpressive sarcastic line. "Well, what family doesn't have its ups and downs," she says, when sodomy, patricide, treason and incest are running their daily course. There is something about an actress with this degree of presence that gets her through even misplaced weepy or extravagant scenes.

A lot of the screenplay is in a kind of anachronistic near-verse—"I'm vilifying you, mother. For God's sake, pay attention"; "Hush, dear, mother's fighting"; "I'll have you by me and I'll use you as I like"; "I stole the candles from the chapel. Jesus won't begrudge them and the chaplain works for me"—that Mr. O'Toole, Miss Hepburn and the rest of the cast are somehow able to carry off. The movie is directed with evident pleasure by Anthony Harvey. Its high point—a long scene in which scurrilous revelations are made while characters lurk behind curtains in the bedroom of the king of France—has enough comic and dramatic energy to make the hard ticket prices worthwhile for a change.

*11-5-68*

For the first hour, *The Split,* which opened yesterday at
the New Amsterdam and other neighborhood theaters,
runs like any fast, conventional mob holdup picture, except
(and this is no small exception) that it stars Jim Brown
(of the Cleveland Browns) and Diahann Carroll (of
"Julia"), who are black. That first hour, although it is not
too well or tightly written, is extremely well directed, by
Gordon Flemyng, with fine chases and good uses of the
split screen when the credits are on. The acting by supporting characters—Gene Hackman, Julie Harris, Ernest
Borgnine, Jack Klugman, Warren Oates, James Whitmore
and particularly Donald Sutherland—is solid and lean;
and when Mr. Sutherland delivers one of a few perfect
lines ("The last man I killed for $5,000. For $85,000 I'd
kill you 17 times"), the audience at the New Amsterdam,
which limits its enthusiasm in other parts of the picture
(which is in color) to appreciative cries of "Punch him in
the mouth," goes respectfully wild.

The plot concerns a group, organized and led by Mr.
Brown, who steal the receipts at a professional football
game while the game is going on. This leads to a kind of
time-tension while sport is in progress, as in *The Killing* or
*Strangers on a Train.* There are many witty and excellent
scenes: a pickup in a bar while two gentlemen are in conversation, the look of lecherous, flattered astonishment on
the picked up gentleman's face; a man trapped in a safe,
who does not dare take his foot off the button that keeps
the door opened and who, standing on one foot, strips off
his clothes to fling them over a photoelectric cell; an
asthma attack in midrobbery) the shooting out, with a high-
powered rifle, of the tires of a car to cause a grand and
useful traffic jam. Mr. Brown's part is not written with
much characterization (his job is mainly to humiliate a
series of whites until they are sufficiently impressed to ac-

cept his leadership); neither is Miss Carroll's (she has to be insipidly used and nice).

But in its last half hour the picture (based on a novel by Richard Stark) makes a sudden and extremely ambitious leap outside its genre: a white neighbor, originally almost irrelevant to the story, tries to rape Miss Carroll and existentially spoils the crime. It is hard to adjust one's mood from pleasant, color-transposed genre thriller to something racially serious, yet the movie is tactful about it, and the film is almost completely successful in its two unmatched parts.

Although his role is not major, Donald Sutherland is remarkable. As the babyfaced soldier who impersonates a colonel in *The Dirty Dozen,* as the troubled friend of the family in *Interlude,* and particularly as an aristocrat dying of leukemia in *Joanna* (which was shown before the strike at Cannes and which will shortly open here), Mr. Sutherland has shown a range of comic-sentimental talent that is absolutely star quality. In *The Split,* speaking as usual slowly and thickly nearly to the point of speech impediment, menacing as a soft, funny maniac for guns, aiming his pistol at the trousers of a man he is guarding, he has both a specific personality of his own and the ability to vary it to the precise demands of divergent roles.

. . . . . . . . . . *Shalako,*
Cinerama, Sean Connery,
Brigitte Bardot

*11-6-68*

*Shalako,* which opened yesterday at the Lyric and neighborhood theaters, is a good, long, old-fashioned, wide-screen Western, with lots of horses, love and Apaches and Sean Connery and Brigitte Bardot. I saw it from a seat in the front row of the otherwise full Lyric Theater. Sitting very close up to the screen is something that film buffs like to do. (The need to keep turning your head from side to side to see all of the screen makes watching movies so different from watching television.) Strong action on a very wide screen from midfront row turns out to be quite wonderful.

Miss Bardot clearly has a lovely time speaking inflected English in an American Western, and Sean Connery is obviouly relieved to be, and very strong, outside James Bond. The plot concerns a lot of European aristocrats who insist on shooting wild sheep on a safari in Indian territory. The American Westerners keep putting them down in every way, except in rock climbing (the Europeans have practiced in the Alps), and when the Apache come they are no more villainous (or saintly either) than they ought to be. The movie, directed by Edward Dmytryk, is unpretentiously not so much antiwar as pro-peace ("There has been enough bloodshed," an Apache chief says near the end, and there has).

What makes it different from watching a good night of "Bonanza" or "High Chaparral" is not only the wide screen and the absence of commercials, but also the sheer joy and humor with which Mr. Connery, Miss Bardot and other members of the cast (particularly Peter Van Eyck, as Miss Bardot's class-conscious fiancé, and Stephen Boyd, as the sort of bumbling, supportive cowboy Andy Devine used to play) work out their well-written refinements on stock Western parts. Lots of shooting, galloping, terse dialogue—it is the perfect movie to see in a two-theater town on a Saturday night.


. . . . The Monkees in *Head*


*11-7-68*

*Head*, which opened yesterday at the Studio Cinema and Greenwich theaters, might be a film to see if you have been smoking grass or if you like to scream at the

Monkees, or if you are interested in what interests drifting heads and hysteric high-school girls. Dreadfully written, and directed by Bob Rafelson, who, with Bert Schneider, created the Monkees (on the basis of interviews) as a singing group, the movie is, nonetheless, of a certain fascination in its joining of two styles: pot and advertising. The special effects—playing with perspective, focus, dimension, logic, pace—and the use of prepackaged stars give the movie a kind of brand-name respectability, like putting Jim Dooley, of the "Come on down" commercial, on display in a hashish crowd.

The Monkees, who are among the least-talented contemporary music groups and know it, are most interesting for their lack of similarity to the Beatles. Going through ersatz Beatle songs, and jokes and motions, their complete lack of distinction of any kind—the fact that fame was stamped on them by hucksters as it might have been on any nice four random, utterly undistinguished boys—makes their performance modest and almost brave. They work very hard and they aren't any good. This keeps them less distant from their own special fans than the Beatles or, say, Bob Dylan and the Beach Boys are. They do not have to bridge the distance of talent or style.

There are some funny moments—an old joke about a regiment of Italian soldiers surrendering to a single man, a policeman posing girlishly before a mirror, a scene in which the boys are cast as dandruff in the hair of a giant Victor Mature, a war scene in which Ray Nitschke of the Green Bay Packers keeps senselessly tackling a G.I., an attack on a Coke machine, a breaking up of the film set, a nice transposition of the Columbia Pictures logo. There are some ugly scenes too—mock fights in which Sonny Liston badly beats one of the Monkees about the face.

But it will be interesting to see if the underlying fusion works, if taking essentially subversive styles and covering them with famous mediocrities assures their success. The aesthetic marijuana world is bound to come out importantly in films one way or another. This sort of movie may be testing the ground.

*11-10-68*

There is an oddly daring and subtle moment in *The Split*, a movie that stars Jim Brown as the head of a gang who rob a football stadium, and Diahann Carroll as his mistress and former wife. Until that moment the film has been content with a fairly conventional genre heist, remarkable only because its leading characters are black. The parts of the stars themselves are not written very well. The football hero, with ferocity under the cool of sheer athleticism, has been miscast as an underworld intellectual, and Miss Carroll has not much to do except pine and disapprove. The story has been good, the supporting characters are strong, there have been chases, suspense and humor, and it seems right and daring enough just to have had, for once, an unapologetic, unmoralistic, unsociological straight Negro hero and heroine. Then the moment comes.

Brown has just stolen more than $85,000. Miss Carroll looks at him, as usual, suspiciously and reproachfully. He spreads the money out on the bed, packets of it, sorted and counted and hard, in all denominations. Her face undergoes a change—humor and a recognition of how much money it is. As the scene ends, they are making love on a bed of $85,000. The scene is done so briefly and well, almost thrown away, that it seems almost unfair to make much of it (although the audience, mixed, clearly does). It seems so much more contemporary and local a conceit than leopard skin rugs, or taking baths in asses' milk.

In the line of opulent, strange unlocalized decadence, Joseph Losey's *Secret Ceremony* is the best film he has done in some time—although the screenplay, by George Tabori, is dreadful, full of false depths, meaningless

308

cadences, and savored by all of the characters, slowly and with infinite pauses, as though it were fine iambic pentameter. Elizabeth Taylor is kind of in love with a mad, orphaned Mia Farrow, who thinks Miss Taylor is her mother. Robert Mitchum plays Miss Farrow's stepfather and there are weird, quasi-incestuous relationships among them.

But there is something not at all arbitrary and far-out at the heart this time, with people—essentially confidence men—drawn into the frank needs of the insane, until their confidence roles become a personal truth about them. Miss Farrow takes a lot of sleeping pills with a glass of milk. (I wish a presence as delicate as hers were allowed to play somebody normal for a change; from Rosemary, the lapsed Catholic neurotic, to this doomed, loony child must be a harrowing professional route.) But there is something about people who have become addicted to other people, standing by them beyond some outer limit of rejection and yet abandoning them just one minute too soon—well, in all the elaborate fetishism and dragging prose, there is a touching story of people not helping enough. There is also a ceremonial quality—coffins like cribs, parallelisms, people reunited in death. Miss Taylor, as the role requires, is far more rotund in *Secret Ceremony* than she has ever been. Robert Mitchum is thinner than usual.


On the night before election, I went to City College, at 135th Street and Convent Avenue, for a showing of *Columbia Revolt* and *The Black Panthers* by the revolutionary propaganda film organization, Newsreel. That afternoon, some marshals had come (and gone away again) to arrest a G.I. who had left the army and taken refuge at the college. A vigil was in progress in the ballroom of Finley Hall and on the chance that a revolutionary crisis might be brought on that evening, some campus radicals had borrowed the films—which Newsreel lends to all interested organizations free of charge. At the gate of the campus some extremely kind and somehow touching-looking students eating pizza asked young people heading for Finley whether they were going "to vigilate." Some of them were and some were going, not to the ballroom, but to the Aranow auditorium, where an Election Eve rally, with comic skits from all the houses, was going on. The atmosphere at Finley seemed one of celebration and of dread.

Outside the ballroom, there were posters—for a ski club, for a two-day national student strike that S.D.S. was trying to call on November 4 and 5, for a showing of *Wild Strawberries*. One poster, showing dice, read "Elections are crap. The people always lose"; another said, "No vote is a vote for Wallace." Inside the ballroom, which has peeling, once off-gold colored walls, and chandeliers of the sort one associates with Elks auditoriums (although other facilities on the same floor of Finley Hall were clean, modern and not depressing at all), students sat or lay about in clusters, read, played guitar or double solitaire, or talked. *Columbia Revolt*, on the eve of the election, looked sad, simultaneously ceremonial and frivolous, a Before to which Leni Riefenstahl's *Triumph of the Will*, which I saw about a month ago at the Museum of Modern Art, might constitute the After. (*Triumph of the Will*, a classic, terrifying Nazi documentary made by a close friend of Hitler's, is still hardly ever shown publicly. With *Columbia Revolt*—the similarities, the crucial differences—it would make a fantastic double bill.)

What is clear from *Columbia Revolt* is that the students really thought they were at war—that their cause was grand and perilous, that they faced great risk and underwent physical suffering, that the songs of the South and what was probably the greatest moral and intellectual political movement of our time were theirs. "Keep your eyes on the prize, Oh Lord," sounds awfully strange amid all those Cokes and Seven-Ups, all those solid, healthy American teeth, the orange juice, the limbo dancing, the general impression that Northern radicals have more fun. There are funny lines (a respectful, "There were people who did nothing during the strike but relate to the mimeograph machine"), ugly ones (the constant reference

310

to fellow human beings in police uniforms as pigs) and the downright ominous, totalitarian ones ("Until we get those rights we have to act in a coercive way").

And yet, in the context of the night before an election, the film had a kind of dignity and importance of its own—like something that had already drifted way into the past. True the police, though brutal, were not anything like, say, the Paris police. True, student revolutions in Japan and India have caused some universities to lose their character as teaching and learning institutions. True, university professors in Copenhagen can be prevented by student committees from pursuing independent scholarship which the committees do not consider immediately "relevant" to their own immediate lives. But there is something about all this longing for decency and fraternity, these nostalgic barricades, this proud exhibition of pathetic little welts and scars—the wish to have a clear and definable evil to be brave before, the longing to be taking part in "Battleground."

The worst of it was the night crowds, the chants, the hands raised in salute and (this particularly in *The Black Panthers,* which contained, in effect, nothing else) the sad little quasi-military maneuvers (and that little "we have to act in a coercive way"). Because it is always clear which side marches best, in the most orderly fashion and in the largest numbers, and how it ends. But Columbia made its point and subsided and the audience at City College (several hundred) took the film enthusiastically but not adoringly, as a document out of its own ideological and imaginative history. It was a gentle crowd. Cookies were passed, money was collected. There were even traces of humor; a student raised his hands to make shadow rabbits, and turkeys and waterfowl on the screen and was much appreciated. The ballroom, for the duration of the vigil, had after all been renamed the Sanctuary—not the Fort or the Trench, but the Sanctuary—and a sanctuary is what our universities might, in crisis, become.

In the Aranow auditorium, where the regular Election Eve Rally had been called, another film was shown after the skits were done. It was a kind, despairing, almost

311

inaudible anti-war movie, narrated by a girl and containing a not altogether ironically applauded rendition of "God Bless America." A student came in and said quietly, "If anybody's into it, Allen Ginsberg is going to read some poetry in the Sanctuary." Very few people left. Most spent the evening consoling themselves with films.

...... *Yellow Submarine*

*11-14-68*

*Yellow Submarine*, which opened yesterday at the Forum and Tower East, is the Beatles' first feature-length cartoon, designed, for the most part beautifully, by Heinz Edelmann, in styles ranging through Steinberg, Arshile Gorky, Bob Godfrey (of the short film *The Do It Yourself Cartoon Kit*), the Sergeant Pepper album cover, and—mainly, really—the spirit and conventions of the Sunday comic strip. The Phantom appears. So do many other pop art and comics characters. (Dick Tracy's inspired Moon Maid would not have been out of place.)

The story concerns the kingdom of Pepperland, invaded by the Blue Meanies, the only antidote to whom is music. There are twelve songs, most of them from "Sergeant Pepper's Lonely Hearts Club Band," and it becomes clear throughout the film not only that the rhythms of music are meant for each other, but also that any human occasion demands—before pictures, before prose even—something in music.

"Do you ever get the feeling . . .?"

"Yeah."

"That things are not as rosy as they appear to be underneath the surface. . . ."

"There's a cyclops!" "But he's got two eyes?" "A bicyclops"; "Black, White, Red. Can I take my friend to bed" ("Can I bring my friend to tea" is another refrain); "Tell us where we're at," the Socratic question. The whole

312

movie, alternately washed and hard edge, art nouveau and full of flowering shrubs and thistles, is full of enfolded meanings, jokes, puns—some of them Lennon-infantile, none of them aggressive, pretentious or self-indulgent —that would delight a child, or a head or anybody who loves and admires the Beatles, even though this is a film in which they either redo old songs or appear once, in person, briefly, in one of their worst-acted appearances ever. "Come on. The whole world is being attacked"; "Hook up, and otherwise commingle"; "All together now"—these are the lines in which the Beatles, with their special talent, life and energy, launch their unfrenetic, unhardsell upbeat message to the world.

There are completely lovely visual ideas; a fish with hands, which swims breaststroke; a consumer creature with a trumpet snout, who ingests the whole world; decanting people out of a glass ball, by means of a hole that has been picked up from an op polka-dot field of right-side up and upside-down holes; a submarine that is convertible into a bravely smiling fish; a fort that disgorges a cavalry charge against Indians, and a cigarette lighter. The Dante-esque landscape of other-worldly types, the Alice in Wonderland snails, mushrooms, trains emerging from under sinks, bleachings of color from hyperactive corridors, teeny-weeny Meanies, and particularly the thistles are drawn with such care and amiability by Heinz Edelmann. (He is not so good on people or anthropomorphic types: they tend to Popeye distortions below the waist, and undistinguished faces above.) Not a great film, after all, but truly nice.

*Yellow Submarine* is a family movie in the truest sense—something for the little kids who watch the same sort of punning stories, infinitely less nonviolent and refined, on television; something for the older kids, whose musical contribution to the arts and longings for love and gentleness and color could hardly present a better case; something for parents, who can see the best of what being newly young is all about. *Hard Day's Night* and *Help!* were more serious, and more truly Beatle saturated. But *Yellow Submarine*, with its memories of Saturday morning at the movies, and its lovely Oswald the Rabbit in Candyland graphics, makes the hooking up and otherwise commingling very possible. When invited to, the whole audience picks up the "All together now" refrain and sings.

...... Anthony Quinn in
*The Shoes of
the Fisherman*

*11-15-68*

One of the early problems of *The Shoes of the Fisherman*, which opened yesterday (on a hard-ticket basis) at the DeMille Theater, is the plot. Unless you have read the novel by Morris West on which the film is based, the first two hours are unintelligible. The Russians seem to be planning something. A young Chinese leader, who looks like Marshal Ky, wants war. David Janssen, who plays the sort of journalist (flat, uncharacterized, belonging to no conceivable métier) he played in *The Green Berets*, seems to be having an affair, which he either wants or does not want to terminate. These strands and fronds of plot are almost completely forgotten after the intermission, which comes, oddly enough, where the book begins.

Another problem is the technique. The film, directed by Michael Anderson (who has done better work, like *The Quiller Memorandum* and *Operation Crossbow*), goes incessantly, almost pulsatingly in and out of synchronization and focus, so that when one of the characters actually has a fainting fit the world is only slightly more blurred than it has been before. Almost every cut or motion is a blur. There are tremendous crowd scenes in St. Peter's Square, but by some miracle of technological incompetence, the weather is rarely the same over any two members of the crowd at a single time. Sunshine, shadowy, overcast—the footage is completely bewildered in terms of light.

"Why have you brought me here to tell me this?" "I took you to pieces like a grape on a dying vine" (grapes on a living vine apparently wither in some less human way); an artifact "a thousand years young"—the prose also is not great as the narrative proceeds, with infinite slowness, to declare itself. Anthony Quinn is cast as a Russian Pope—an inspiration comparable to casting Yogi Berra as an Irish Faust—and his accents, like those of many other characters, keep casting doubt on what his national origin is. Laurence Olivier, John Gielgud and Vittorio De Sica appear in little parts, but Quinn plays his role with a lack of warmth, soul and intellectuality which characterizes the whole production.

There are two good moments: one, when the Pope is elected and the purple awnings over all the other cardinals are shut down; the other, when Oskar Werner, who does very well as a young Jesuit suspected of heresy, does a double take to find Quinn Pope. The music, by Alex North, is dreary beyond belief. There is not a sight or a sound with the impressiveness of even the shortest documentary on Vatican ritual. But the screenwriters, John Patrick and James Kennaway, take one curious daring and almost anticlerical option at the end: to avert war and alleviate starvation (this turns out to be the only glimmer of story there is), the Pope cedes all the church holdings to the poor and resumes the church's mission in poverty. This is not in the novel and its effect on screen seems intended, almost inevitably, to make you think, why not?

*11-17-68*

*Yellow Submarine* is full of so many allusions to the non-literary education of people under forty that it is open to a special kind of unbookish, pop pedantry. It is a delicate, friendly, unpretentious film which if it did not have the imprimatur of the Beatles, with their special talent, power and grace, would be of no great importance. As animation, it is not nearly as beautiful as the Hubley's *Moonbird*. (Of all the animated films I've seen, beginning with *Gertie the Dinosaur,* none is nearly so beautiful as *Moonbird*.) Heinz Edelmann, who drew the otherwise lovely landscapes and objects, is weakest in drawing people or anthropomorphic types—especially the Beatles themselves. All his characters tend to be wide and oblong below, like Thurber characters, and pinheaded above, with no particular distinction in the face. Also, some of his ideas—clowns like water toys, for example, whose noses when pressed set off mines in the fields—are downright banal.

But the film is beautiful, soft and rich, drawing its inspiration from almost every cultural source outside of literature: Art Nouveau, Steinberg, Mandrake; Arshile Gorky; stencils; breakfast cereal boxtops; Warhol and Rauschenberg screens; Christmas wrapping paper; traffic signs; Advent calendars; beach toys; Mad Comics; Big Little Books (where one used to be able, by flipping the corners of the pages, to stage a little movie of one's own); cutouts; playing cards; Alice; miniature golf courses; medical textbook diagrams; Op polka dots; penny arcades (particularly pinball machines); King Kong; Flash Gordon; Prince Valiant; decal transfers; poster buttons; Pooh; kites; the Little King; the Golden Books; radar screens; Little Orphan Annie; crossword puzzles; alphabet soups; particularly the rebus (the kind of puzzle in which a com-

316

bination of word, pun, and lettering yields a meaning).

In fact, if the movie is under any special influence, it would appear to be the Sunday supplements. There are comic-strip conventions to indicate motion (the arrow trajectories, the thin whisking lines, the splattered radiating graphic explosions) and the comic-strip relations between words and objects (an object eating the letters that denote another object, and so on). The convention of absolute reversibility, that any action is possible and any can be undone, is in the tradition of movie cartoons, but the balance between hard, plastic edges and gentle wash is pure comic strip. Also, a lot of Steinberg. The Sergeant Pepper album cover. Mad Comics. Lewis Carroll. Even *Ramparts* and Dr. Seuss. A character called Jeremy the Boob, for example, is drawn like a caricature out of Ed Sorel's Bestiary, says things like a rather underinspired White Queen—in rhythms that are unmistakably those of Horton the Elephant.

Everything is incredibly mixed. A hand that points directions is like the one in the Sunday supplements that directs you to the next page or panel. The line, "Go, glove, go, and, having pointed pounce" is like the Shakespeare parody in "Beyond the Fringe." ("A thing of beauty. Destroy it forever" is a little cruder Lennon-Keats.) A cigarette that burns off the G in GLOVE, leaving LOVE and an ash, is simultaneously a pot reminder and a grim bounce off that smugly cretinous cigarette commercial in which "not" is knocked out of "It's not how long you make it" and the words are rearranged. ("I'm surprised, really, that there does not seem to exist an organization to boycott products whose ads are completely awful.)

There are so many delightful moments, figures and drawings in the picture: the couple that consists of a puncher and a punching bag; the superconsumer, who simply vacuums everything into his snout and is finally left in an empty world, leaving only himself to consume; the corridor which, when a door is slammed, opens countless other doors from which a variety of marvelous creatures appear, to scurry across the hall behind other doors; a lot

317

of Sergeant Pepper songs; Purcell trumpets; schizophrenic images, like an eyed, toothed hand fighting the letter O; lindy hops; forefathers and foremothers; superbly drawn thistles and flowering shrubs; nice lines ("Here, Your Blueness, have some nasty medicine"); shoes that stomp, disembodied, on each other's toes; a butterfly-stomper in a sweatshirt; real photography amid the animation; little Beatle self-ironies . . . villains who bomb helpless characters with apples, while the Beatle production firm is called the Apple company.

It is the perfect film, I think, for children, never terrifying, often funny, sometimes inspired and yet (or maybe, and so), there is the matter of pot. There is no question that *Yellow Submarine* (and a lot of totally undistinguished movies, like the Monkees' recent *Head*) are to a certain extent informed by marijuana, and that regardless of what its legal implications are, its aesthetic importance is becoming more than marginal. That sense of perception washed clean—the delight in color transpositions, camouflage, code, correspondences, eidetic imagery, synesthesia, musical counterpoint, detail, even the sense of the affectionate cabal—is certainly accessible to people who are not high, but in an overstimulated urban environment, probably rarely. There is certainly no point in seeing *Yellow Submarine*, or anything else that is good, drunk. But the best music has been most accessible to an occasional high for a long time, and movies, as it turns out more and more, are such an intensely musical form—well, the audiences at *Yellow Submarine* so far have been, largely, not stupid and blunted like three-martini audiences, but fresh and open and precise in their response.

There is also the matter of animated films. *Yellow Submarine* presents the strongest case for animated feature-length films since *Fantasia*. All the imaginative animated shorts of every kind—from *Moonbird* through *The Pink Panther* through Bob Godfrey's *Do It Yourself Cartoon Kit* (on which *Yellow Submarine* also draws), the work of Saul Bass, the Alexeieffs, Disney, Pintoff, even splendid, non-anthropomorphic, nonrepresentational work like that of the great Norman McLaren—seem to make it remarkable that films have not gone the way paintings have gone, that they are still so strongly and pre-eminently realistic. The fact that the Beatles have chosen to make one—even though they are not very much in it—and that Heinz Edelmann has drawn it, for the most part, so beautifully ought to help animation along. I doubt that great possibilities for movies lie in that direction (except in that badly neglected field, children's films), but animation was, after all, once important in film. And there are borderline realism-animation cases, like Valerian Borowczyk's room which destroys and reconstructs itself in *Renaissance*. Perhaps animation will recur strongly, not just in titles, but in short films on non-television Saturday mornings at the movies again.

........ Godard Stalks
the Real Through Movies:
Report

*12-6-68*

At 5 A.M. one recent Friday, Jean-Luc Godard, the most difficult and by temperament the most radical of French filmmakers, was picked up by station wagon at the Muffin-Burger, on Sixth Avenue and Forty-fifth Street, and driven to Newark, to film an interview with the writer, LeRoi Jones. With Mr. Godard were his wife, Anne Wiazemsky (star of *La Chinoise*); the American actor Rip Torn (who will play the main part in Mr. Godard's new film, *One American Movie* or "One A.M."); Richard Leacock and D. A. Pennebaker, who are also working on the movie for the Public Broadcasting Laboratory; a writer; a sound technician for the Leacock-Pennebaker studio; and a young French producer, Jean-Claude Nedjar, who had met Mr. Godard on the street the night

319

before. The morning was foggy, the ride had been quite silent, and the New Jersey Turnpike was choked with trucks.

"It is like this that Western society will end," Mr. Nedjar said, "The roads full of trucks. The cities will suffocate."

"You do politics this early in the morning?" Mr. Godard, quite gently, inquired.

Even when he is directing, Mr. Godard does not talk much. It may be in reaction to his personal silence that his movies are full of so much direct, political and of late aesthetically disastrous address. Dark, intense, courtly, not very tall, wearing glasses tinted slightly green against the glare, Mr. Godard, who is thirty-eight, creates an impression of intellectuality under enormous stress. He spoke of a little girl from Ocean Hill-Brownsville, whom he is casting in his film. The idea of being in a movie did not impress her much. But the idea that the film would be shown on television delighted her. "The moment she sees herself on television," Mr. Godard said, "it will, in a sense, desanctify the television set for her. She does not go to the movies, but it is important that television should be desanctified."

When the car arrived at the house on a back street in Newark where the rendezvous had been arranged, Mr. Jones, who had also just arrived, after driving all night from a lecture at Brown University, was still upstairs. Mr. Godard and his crew waited patiently, smoking, in a room painted black from floor to ceiling, below. No one knew what sort of interview or performance to expect, or even whether it would be used in "One A.M.," but the light was changing fast and Mr. Godard wanted to film LeRoi Jones in the street at dawn.

At seven, the crew was waiting outside the building and Mr. Jones emerged, in an orange parka and maroon and pale blue turban, singing and playing a kind of xylophone, accompanied by a chanting group of five. Cars stopped for a while, in deference to the group being filmed in the street, then passed between performers and cameras. Some middle-aged women got into a taxi in front of a

Father Divine hostel across the street, and drove off to their jobs. Two children, a boy and a girl, appeared, dressed for school, in a doorway, and watched. "Get the children, please," Mr. Godard said to Mr. Pennebaker, who filmed the boy and girl.

"We are your nightmare," one of the performers chanted. "Some are raped, some are burned, some are decapacitated."

"I praise the black man," Mr. Jones sang, then corrected himself. "I praises the black man." The performance had the air of incantation, an American intellectual effort to endow the streets of Newark with something of Africa. Or the sadder air of a cargo cult. When the chanting was over, Mr. Godard thanked Mr. Jones and the performers and stopped filming for the day.

*One American Movie* will consist of ten sequences: five "real" (two interviews with radicals, Tom Hayden and Eldridge Cleaver, one with a girl from the stock market; shots of the girl from Ocean Hill-Brownsville, carrying a phonograph playing soul music through the streets of Harlem; a performance by the Jefferson Airplane on a hotel roof); five "cinema" (movie actors doing the same sequences, in cinema voices and cinema contexts). It is an effort, foreshadowed in Mr. Godard's use of direct address, or his use of the off-camera interlocutor, or, more particularly, his real slaughter of a real pig in *Weekend,* to establish the point where movies become real, where theater breaks into documentary.

On another morning, very foggy, Mr. Godard, Mr. Leacock, and Mr. Torn ascended, in an elevator, the forty-five floors of a building under construction—the new Random House building, at Third Avenue and Fiftieth Street. The elevator was a very flimsy cage, clearly labeled "No Passengers." Mr. Torn, with a tape recorder playing Tom Hayden's voice, was declaiming after Mr. Hayden, "Disrupt the supply line. The supply line . . . Magic, Magic, MAGIC," as the elevator went up and down. (Paula Matter, a model, will do the cinema delivery of Eldridge Cleaver's lines.) It turned out that as soon as an actor speaks a "real" line, it acquires a degree of irony—whereas the real line, unadorned, has always an implication of politics.

When the speeches were finished, with lavish gestures and changes of inflection, Mr. Godard was asked whether he did not have height fright. It turned out that he and everyone but the elevator operator and Mr. Leacock did. "But I do not feel it when I am working," Mr. Godard said. Mr. Torn agreed.

The construction workers were all intensely interested in the film and the prospect of being on television, and exchanged several jokes about celebrity.

The filming of the Ocean Hill-Brownsville girl, on Lenox Avenue in Harlem, turned out quite beautifully. Once, in the puddles, and the trash, and the flying bits of newspapers, the record was blown off its turntable. But the music set men to smiling, little boys to asking, "Hey, what you doing?" a dog to barking, and, as it worked out in the rushes, a siren to screaming and several pigeons to syncopated nods.

"Tell her you have to hold it very flat, very level, as if she were offering a song to the people in the streets," Mr. Godard said. Then, with an expression of great gentleness, he showed her how to hold the turntable himself—like a waiter bringing a tray to a room.

On the way back by taxi from another shooting sequence, a truck ran into a car on West Fifty-first Street. The car's driver, a frail man, was inarticulate with rage. The truck's driver, very large, got out of his truck, inarticulate with cool. Mr. Godard will be filming the remainder of *One American Movie* in January.

. . When Color Adds Nothing

*11-24-68*

"The Late Show," which, having started in 1951, is one of the oldest shows in television, has made a terrific contribution in its time to the American insomniac and movie buff. From the early fifties, when the studios, still in mortal and justified fear of television, refused to lease their film backlogs (although it is unclear what else they were planning to do with them), until December 1, 1956, when (with *Command Decision*) television began to work through the great studio archives, stations thrashed about in British and independently made movies, and some Charlie Chan. Then the distinguished era of films on several channels began, with all its complicated deals—700 films leased at a time, MCA buying Paramount's backlog, Screen Gems leasing Universal's, General Tele-radio buying RKO's from Howard Hughes, special movies, like *It Happened One Night* and *Indiscreet* going to the Schaefer Award Theater—and everything from the early thirties to 1948 began to run, from *A Night at the Opera* to *30 Seconds Over Tokyo*. What Europeans saw at museums and film libraries Americans saw in their bed or living room.

Of course, there were problems. Actors on TV seemed, not framed as they are on the screen, but impermanent and swimming through a bowl. There was cutting for time, and commercials and prudery. No actors or directors in pre-1948 films received royalties for their appearances on TV. Reception could be poor. There were no festivals for the work of a single director, or actor of genre running through several nights (although a series of Academy Award winning films was run in a row. The spirit was more that of what program directors like to call "anthologies," varying as much as possible from night to night in order to keep an audience. But cuts are restored after the TV leasing time is up and the film reverts to the owner or studio; actors and directors in films after 1948 now get their royalties; and TV has done a lot, not only in preserving and showing films that might otherwise have been destroyed or lost, but also in keeping the movie industry alive. (At $150,000 for an old film these days, a package of 700 films is a rewarding thing.)

But there is that other problem now. At 9 P.M.—in prime television time—on Monday, Tuesday and Satur-

323

day at N.B.C., on Wednesday and Sunday at A.B.C., on Thursday and Friday at C.B.S., relatively recent movies are shown, first TV run, across the country on network television. As more people have color television sets, the networks increasingly demand that Hollywood (and hardly anything outside Hollywood is in question here) make color movies. Non-Hollywood directors are required by producers to make color films to compete with television. C.B.S.'s "Late Show," the "Late Late Show" (and when the "Late Late Show" is short, the "Late Late Late Show"), N.B.C.'s "Great, Great Show," A.B.C.'s "Best of Broadway" and other movie programs, although they are not network-wide, and although they still show older films, have reached, upon occasion, as far as 1967. The prime time, first run movies are frequently released, and then rerun on the late night movie shows. Here too, the demand is increasingly for color films.

For movies, this is a mess. Just when the epic, panoramic movie is running down (and these do seem to require color unless you are Eisenstein), just when the personal dream or state of mind is working through, directors have to work in color when they don't want to, or as soon as they are successful enough to raise studio money for their films. Of course, a lot of distinguished pictures are color films. But a lot of these would have been more distinguished in black and white. Color is not, like sound, a movie breakthrough. For one thing, at best, it is never natural. Beautiful sometimes, but never real. Flesh tones, grains, textures, gradations of light—there is something about the colored strip of celluloid that can make them hard and cold.

Because of TV's alarming movie appetite, because of the sums involved, and because of some industry tradition that if a thing has worked in one place it is necessary and desirable to try it in another (successful plots and casting are immediately tried many times again with the slightest variation, out of this cinema reduplication drive), television is beginning not just to use movies but to determine what they will be like. Watching movies on television, though, is inevitably different from watching them in theaters. For one thing, there is that ineluctably liquid bowl. For another, the quality of TV's black and white was never very good. One watches TV alone, or among friends or family, and the smallness of the object requires a narrowing of focus, a confinement that can be color-eased or liberated. But there is a special large, gray night quality of movies. It would be a mistake if films, to feed or compete with television, lost some of the qualities that TV cannot transmit. (It seems possible that the relationship between the media will, in any case, soon become reciprocal. Distinguished TV programs, documentaries, commercials, might be shown in theaters, on screens where they can be precisely seen.)

. . . . . . *Joanna* (and *Faces*)

11-25-68

At the Cannes Film Festival, at the end of *Joanna* (which opened yesterday at the Cinema I), when Joanna cried, "This ain't the end, you know. I'm coming back," part of the audience shouted, "No! No!" but some of the rest were in tears, and others had simply had a good time at the movies. There is a lot in the film, which is about the mod scene that never quite was, to support all three responses. By the time Joanna kisses the director, Michael Sarne, good-by and the cameras become visible, it is clear that, rather like a late meal by somebody confident who doesn't really cook, this has been a peculiar and highly mixed event, with moments of technical brilliance.

A lot depends on whether you can stand Genevieve Waite, who plays Joanna (a promiscuous London art student waif, daughter of a magistrate) with Walter-Keane-wide eyes, vacant face and a baby monotone that several of the other actors catch. As she wanders about, being surprised in beds where she doesn't belong, being lectured by

325

her grandmother when she oversleeps at home, searching for commitment, falling in love with a Negro nightclub owner (ably played by Calvin Lockhart), she verges (although it may be the part) on being unbearable. I didn't mind acutely, but the charm of it rather passed me by. Also, Glenna Forster-Jones, who plays the nightclub owner's sister, might have been very good if she hadn't been dressed constantly in spangly eye make-up that made it difficult to see her face.

But Donald Sutherland—lisping, handsome, warm, a bit gopher-like—gives a plausible interpretation of what a contemporary, slowly dying saint might be. He plays an aristocrat with something like leukemia, and it is astonishing how moving a plain old sentimental, nonviolent, natural death can still be on the screen. One sees so few of them. Christian Doermer also gives a fine performance, as an art-school instructor who—with Mr. Lockhart and Mr. Sutherland—gathers Joanna into something like a serious, conventional life again.

The trouble is that the movie keeps going true and false by turns. There are genuine, well-struck scenes on free-loading jaunts and in classrooms and nursing homes, good fantasy sequences out of Joanna's nightmares—and then hours of one-note, hard-edge, baby-voice hipness that is about as alive as polyethylene. Nobody stands at this vinyl distance from his own life, and it is the shallowness of the mod convention to pretend that they do. Rachel, of *Rachel, Rachel,* after all, has nightmares too. If you see the two movies in sequence, *Joanna* has an air of carnival distortion, the flatness, lacquer and voice track of a plastic doll. Rachel seems somebody real, but stranded from other conventions and other years. They are light years apart, but in Rachel's case the world has frozen flat, while in Joanna's it is the main character who has.

The beginning of John Cassavetes' *Faces*, which opened yesterday at the Little Carnegie, is at so much lower a level than the rest that it is like stumbling over something, which it takes a half hour to recover your composure from. But as soon as the husband, John Marley, goes home to his wife, Lynn Carlin, and they begin laughing falsely and uncontrollably together, the film hits its stride and becomes far and away the strongest, bluntest, most important American movie of the year. It is about a middleclass version of love, aging and being mortified. Even a young hippie and a prostitute, played by Seymour Cassel and Gena Rowlands, are already over the hill and fighting the drain.

Miss Carlin and Mr. Marley play a suburban couple who drink, horse around and talk to each other in formulas. None of the understandings between them, the moronic jokes, the ritual behaviors, work any more. They separate. Mr. Marley joins two men and their dates for the night, Miss Carlin goes with three women, in comparable predicaments, to a hippie bar. These scenes are long, funny and horrible. "You son of a gun," a young customer's man type on the double date keeps saying to his boss, Val Avery, who keeps talking compulsively about a son who walks around in tennis shoes. "So what if he wants to nance around?" Avery says. The awful virility conventions between the men keep ironically shutting the women out.

When Miss Carlin and the three matrons take the hippie home, she goes into a kind of lady freeze, restrained and condescending, with lapses. The other ladies simply fall apart. Later, when they have thrown him back on his own desperation, he says quietly, "I think we're all making fools of ourselves." (I have never seen a movie that throws its characters and audiences so relentlessly and brutally back upon themselves.) At another point, summing up their lives and the generation gap, for what it's worth to either generation, he throws away a simple line: "Well, I don't want it."

Miss Carlin sleeps with the hippie, Mr. Marley sleeps with the prostitute. The young people sing stupid songs to keep their spirits up, and the older people have no real levels of contact left. On the way to the empty end, the acting has been superb, the camera work (in black and white) and the script (apparently written, improvised, and written again) have been comic, dead right, almost too relentless (no point is dropped until it lies exhausted there) and very rough.

The picture was shown this year at the Venice and New York film festivals.

...... On Reviewing, II:
A Wayne Sympathetic
Frame of Mind

*12-1-68*

I don't normally believe in metawriting—journalistic pieces about the great obstacles a reporter encountered on his way to an interview, fiction about the intense struggle it has been to write. Writing about writing is a bit like talking about a conversation you are having; it tends to obscure desperation about where the next word is coming from. But the past two weeks in movies have been, except for *Faces,* part of the pre-December lull before the year-end rush and the year-beginning calm. It seems all right to mention a few thoughts about what daily film reviewing is or, I think, should be.

First, the context. In this country, where film is regarded simultaneously as high art and something pleasant and frivolous, like a candy bar, nearly everyone is a film critic—with a double focus and a plane of discussion that constantly shifts. Thus, the same highly serious film buffs who regard film as the most important art form of our time are absolutely outraged when some reviewer reveals a late development of the plot. (No seriously literate person gets upset when critics mention the ending of *Coriolanus* or *Anna Karenina.*) People, including filmmakers, tend to be both oversaturated with films and —owing to the absence of any really vital and sensitive collecting institution—undereducated in them. The most serious film buff is often most determined that, outside his own discussions, films shall be allowed to remain unserious.

The situation is complicated by the fact that, with exceptions, the film industry is one of the most unresponsive, antiquated, and disingenuous that we have. Movie advertising, with its distortions, cuts, misrepresentations and downright camp reversals, seems to go on the assumption that the public would rather be misled, time and time again, by a few ineffective superlatives lifted from a critical context than read what the person the comment is ascribed to actually said. Distribution is odd and elephantine, from metropolitan theaters reserved for the work of particular studios through a nationwide system that virtually precludes wide viewing of anything unexpected, small, and original. The technology of filmmaking itself is often still as cumbersome as if the idea of miniaturization did not exist.

There are problems with even the smallest professional details—the little sexy stills outside theaters, which are often not included in the film they have lured an audience to see, or even the plot summaries that are helpfully handed to reviewers at screenings, to refresh memories at reviewing time ("Refusing to accept this fact, she does two things: she arranges for piano lessons, which she will pay for with the money meant for her lunch; and she loses her virginity to her first date"). Some of them, particularly on foreign films, are just plain wrong—which gives monolingual reporters from trade papers a chance for some misguided pedantry when the reviews come out. But there are beautiful films, and moving or just entertaining films, although (naturally enough in any medium) not many great ones—and the question is what the daily review has to do with them.

To begin with, there is the ordinary audience service part: giving some idea, in the course of the review, whether or not the reader is going to want to see the film that opened yesterday. This is important, but it works almost inevitably, regardless of what the critic's actual judgment is. Reviewing movies is, in a lot of cases, like reviewing candy bars. Candy is important, a valid creative and social expression, but once you have described what the ingredients are and what the genre is, you have pretty well let the consumer know—even if you adore or detest a particular order of candy bar—whether he is going to like it or not. If a movie stars Doris Day, or if it is directed by John Wayne, the reviewer tries to put himself in a Day or Wayne sympathetic frame of mind and argue, on other grounds, that the film is better Day or lesser Wayne, but once the ingredients are fairly named, the reader knows and is freed to his taste. The same with Luis Buñuel. Of course, if you have a film that stars Doris Day *and* is directed by Luis Buñuel—and comparable situations with great directors do arise—the critical inventory part gets complicated.

I think it is absolutely essential in a review to establish the level of ambition that a film is at, to match it, if possible, with the level of your own, and then to adjust your tone of voice. There is no point in admiring an Elvis Presley film in the same tone of voice as a George C. Scott —or in treating simple lapses of competence with the same indignation one has for what seem to be failures of taste and integrity. The tone of voice question is difficult, because I also believe in the high attack. Not attack in the aggressive sense. I mean that the level of a regular review should go as high as the subject will permit, set the fastest possible pace for the later appraisals, which come to the film not under the pressure of deadlines, but out of pure interest. Ideally, a review should draw on the widest possible field, a whole range of vocabularies, moods, personal and cultural experience, for what is appropriate to a given film.

The trouble is that the high attack can lead to colossal blunders; you can go wronger the deeper you try to go. You can be, in fact, profoundly ridiculous. This risk seems to me something one owes to the filmmaker, who has, as is often pointed out, inevitably spent several months on a work that is reviewed in a day. Trying to draw on a wide field also leads to factual errors—which seem to me, in reviewing, less important than elsewhere. Errors in fact in writing are always appalling, but in reviews—unless the error occurs in the course of a pejorative argument—the

330

risk seems to me worth the try at the range.

There is the problem too of whom the reviewer is addressing. Nobody but a few studio people thinks a reviewer's job is to predict whether a film is going to succeed (i.e., make money), and to adjust his reviews to its possibilities for doing so. But whom is he speaking to: film buff, artist, posterity, other critics, literate twentieth-century person with a fairly broad range of contemporary experience, parent, man with $2.50 in his pocket and some time to while away? Ideally, to all of them—with special alerts for prudes and, more specially, a kind of salute to the artist. The moment a reviewer exists for, the one that justifies his existence at all, is when he finds something, when he notices something—a distinguished detail, a performance, a whole film—that somebody has fought for against all odds and that might otherwise have just gone by. It is like a little, recognizing wave of the hand.

This raises the question of praise. I am convinced that praising something not many people will like can actually hurt a film—which people might have discovered, against all odds, for themselves and liked better for it—and that it can create for the reviewer a distrusting audience. But it cannot be helped. The possibility that one person who belongs at the film will be drawn to it by praise, or even that a new audience will gradually be created for it, is too interesting. (This is why misleading or inadequate quotations in ads make any difference at all.) In the end, the review is a solipsistic job, addressed to someone very like oneself, with hopes that it includes enough to be interpreted by anyone.

Finally, there is the question of what to mention. There are always letters about not mentioning acting, photography, sets, costumes, music, choreography, titles, for any given film—as though a review were a checklist, on all these counts, every day. I think these are critical options. If the acting, or photography, or what have you are exceptional—exceptionally good, exceptionally bad, in any way distinct—then it is possible to characterize them. Saying they are good or bad, and no more than that, is like saying the same about candy bars. It is like saying nothing; it depends what you like. Often many elements of a film are competent and ordinary, and undistinguishing. In these cases, it seems to me, the tip-off is the dialogue. It is the thing closest to writing, and most self-evident when it is written out. It often characterizes a film as clearly as possible. I believe in quotes.

Failing everything else, one would like to have one thought, one sentence, one line, that shows a certain tension and effort, something worth reading after you have seen the film, or even if you haven't seen it and will never go.

One personal quirk: it happens that when I don't like the work of a given director or performer, but I admire what he is trying to do more than I have ever admired it before, I call it the best work he has ever done, and mean it. So much depends on mood. I try to say more with directors whose wavelength I'm on.

. . . . . . . . Euphemisms:
*The Impossible Years*

*12-6-68*

*The Impossible Years,* which opened yesterday at the Music Hall, is one of those peculiarly joyless, fumbling, dirty comedies that only Hollywood (and perhaps some small German filmmakers) would ever want to produce. The formula now is fairly clear. Take an actor with an English accent (in *The Impossible Years,* as in *Prudence and the Pill,* it is David Niven), who will give the whole thing an aura of cleanliness and respectability. Take some nubile actress (in this case, it is Christina Ferrare), who will speak in an intolerably high-pitched trill, and flounce. Make them father and daughter, to check in with the generation gap. And then take a string of euphemisms so nasty that they would occur only to an aging, isolated,

332

lecherous prig. A wholesome family comedy.

The taste level of the movie is set by Miss Ferrare's fifteen-year-old sister (played by Darleen Carr), who reads *Fanny Hill* while blowing bubblegum. A good part of the film is devoted to the question of what was the word Miss Ferrare was arrested for parading around a campus with. The actors are constantly on the verge of telling each other, and then can't bring themselves to say it, as though anybody gave a damn. The rest of the movie has to do with the question of how, why and to whom Miss Ferrare has lost her virginity—the circumlocutions for which are "having done the works," "having had her ribbons untied," "Her condition, or lack of condition" and "it."

"Doctor to doctor," Ozzie Nelson, as a friend, colleague, next-door neighbor and father of the seductor-apparent says to David Niven, "your daughter no longer qualifies to be a spinster." Other remarks are: "It's like the mumps, either you have it or you don't"; "It doesn't matter who it was. It's done"; "Linda's lost it and that's that"—and so on. In the midst of this disgustingly jaunty speculation, which goes on, with high righteousness, for hours, no one can even bring himself to use the word "pregnant." "Are you suggesting that she may be—oh, no"—and "oh, no" is the euphemism for pregnancy after that. Then, near the end of a plot that the writers (Bob Fisher, Arthur Marx, and George Wells) have not bothered to make consistent or even plausible, the script has the pious gall to blurt, "She is not indecent! She's married."

This movie makes clear something I had never quite realized—that dirty jokes between two generations of a single family are inevitably in the poorest taste imaginable. But to cap all its ugly, dreary innuendo (at one point someone actually suggests they dust the girl for fingerprints) with matrimonial pieties is like claiming altar status for a railroad station washroom.

*12-8-68*

A movie, like any other creative work that cannot be dashed off in a single stroke, entails so much effort over so long a period of time that a director's familiarity with his own material can get between his work and his audience. Working a long time on a film can cause a director to put in touches that an audience, in a single viewing of two hours, cannot be expected to notice, and these touches, the in jokes, the personal notes, the parallelisms, do not always enrich the material. Through overwork or just plain high spirits, it is possible to overload and jam your own broadcast.

The makers of *Joanna,* a long, rich, extremely uneven film about a mod girl who sleeps with a lot of people in a search for commitment, obviously knew what they were doing. The film is in no sense dry, as one would wish, say, a drink to be dry. It has stretches of archness, falseness and kitsch, in no way redeemed by the consciouness that the director, Michael Sarne, in his first feature film, has satire on his mind. Yet there are stretches of wit, power, old fashioned sentiment, and technical brilliance. There are fine, solid performances by Donald Sutherland as a young aristocrat dying—for a change, in films—of natural causes; Christian Doermer, as a cynical London art instructor; Calvin Lockhart, as a black nightclub owner from Sierra Leone; Glenna Forster-Jones, as his mod sister; and—more ambiguously—Genevieve Waite, as Joanna, a vacant, almost pre-verbal waif, with a baby-voice monotone, awkward in its contagiousness to the rest of the cast.

Joanna is a kind of plastic, arrested Juliet of the Spirits, or Cabiria—guarding the same romantic fantasies and undergoing much the same rudenesses at the hands of life as the other two, until she finds herself, in miscegenation (we are going to have to find a better word) and motherhood. Director Sarne is a great admirer of Fellini. It seemed that if Sarne ever did a film at his own highest level, it would be a very good film, and since Sarne, who is twenty-eight, is not a reticent man, *Joanna* seemed a good movie to go to see with him—asking him to talk, throughout the movie, about the little things he had put in it.

It began with the credits, which were in white except for the letters that occur in Joanna's name, which were, in all other names and words, red. There were opening shots of a London railroad station, which were meant to be in black and white, but which, since they were developed on color stock, came out blue. As an in joke, the man who appears underneath a station billboard that reads "Someone Must Lead" is Michael Sarne—who also appears in a later bedroom scene, who sings one of the movie's songs himself, and who receives a goodbye kiss, as the director, from Joanna when the film's whole cast is assembled on a railroad station platform at the end. (The entire cast is on that platform at the movie's beginning too, but since the audience has not been introduced to them yet, there is no way, on first viewing, of noticing that.)

When Joanna jumps off the train, the whole film jumps into color, and from that moment on, except for the zooms, the entire movie is shot through a fine gauze over the camera lens, to diffuse and soften the London light—in Sarne's word, "to pervert reality in a romantic way." The composition of almost every shot is deliberately off center. There are a lot of obvious references—posters of James Dean, Marlon Brando and Peter Sellers, a statue of Peter Pan, a man asleep in the park with an issue of *Cahiers du Cinéma* over his face, a running into each other's arms on the beach, cribbed and exaggerated from *A Man and a Woman*. "If you do something that has been done before," Sarne said, "you have to overdo, to do it satirically."

Musical themes are planted and recur, one for Joanna, a German waltz for Christian Doermer, a lovely sentimental song—set off, with a few guitar notes, when Joanna asks

"You're not very ill, are you?"—for Donald Sutherland. A lot of the ingenious cutting is musical, dissolving with the sound from sentiment into comedy. "Right after you've done the sentimental bit," Sarne said, "you have to stamp on it." When dialogue is meant to be ethereal, as when Sutherland has a fainting spell, it is post-synched.

There are a lot of games with lines of motion—Joanna getting out of bed and, in the next shot, getting out of a car, at the same spot and angle on the screen; Joanna walking down an art-school corridor and continuing, in the next shot, across a bedroom floor—which are matched with plot jumps, gaps in conversations closed by fantasy in retrospect, dialogue overlay from scene to scene, and real sounds in the street which impinge on dreams. There are also games with lines of sight—Mr. Lockhart, in his nightclub, catching the eye of girls, serially, all over the room. The music is stereo. "Music at the sides, dialogue straight down the middle," Sarne said. But not always. In party scenes, the peripheral dialogue is at the sides.

There is a short, key, art school lecture on the exuberance of the Baroque, and its quality as a rebellion against Neo-classicism. The shot freezes on the teacher and the word "Rebellion" on the blackboard beside her. There are equally obvious but less successful touches, like Joanna, on a particularly naive day, dressed all in green, with green shades and a green portfolio. Green for naive is very literary.

Michael Sarne describes his movie as by and about "a nonverbal generation, a generation that seems to be annoyed by words." He compares the making of a movie to the very careful and knowledgeable baking of a cake. "Of course, if you're saying something deep, it's a whole different bag. You're putting an idea in the cake." I'm not much for the ideas in *Joanna* and some of its cuteness may drive you up the wall. But a lot of its scenes are lovely, and a funeral—with a rose, black mourners in black, music and no words at all—is one of the few ineluctable weeping scenes of the year.

*12-9-68*

The failure of *The Fixer* seems simpler if you have not read the book. The triviality of the script by Dalton Trumbo, the old sentimental Hollywood formula (a few moments of mild happiness, an hour and a half of reversals and misery, with violins, a blitz happy ending with drums) applies, almost intact, to dog stories, horse stories, sports stories, love stories. It seems grotesquely inadequate when you apply it to a real drama on the moral plain that has virtually characterized this century.

"Yakov, what have they done to you?" "What have they done to you, Lassie?" In one case, they have probably clipped her ears, as in the other they have, inevitably these days, kicked him in the groin. The problem is that Yakov Bok represents a real Jew in Czarist Russia, persecuted for a ritual crime his religion made impossible, and that this irony, his oppression, suffering, and inexplicable secular courage, become demeaning and vulgar when they are drawn out with hack-plot fiction approximations of eloquence.

What is puzzling is that so much of the movie, as a movie, is on solid ground. From the first Isaac Babel-like pogrom, the direction, by John Frankenheimer, is powerful and discreet.

It averts its eyes at the easy, ugly consummations of violence—slashings, stabbings, the end of the hanging rope. It shows the stroke and the motion, and gives you credit for imagining the result. The acting, from Alan Bates, who plays Bok as a kind of healthy Beatle caught in maniacal historic forces (all the Jewish characters are cast as more healthy and Anglo-Saxon than their persecutors), through Dirk Bogarde as the cerebral, sympathetically homosexual interlocutor, and David Warner (of *Morgan!*) as an effete, pragmatic Count, is very fine.

So the problem, in spite of lines like "It's not madness

that turns the world upside down. It's conscience," cannot be entirely the film's. All the easy empathies, the cinema reflexes, break down, as Bok is simply tortured through most of the time *The Fixer* is on screen. The ordeal of sitting through these tortures becomes simply a disguise for lack of insight, lack of feeling—and in this case, where the subject is so ambitious and the text so ordinary, the ordeal becomes embarrassing. All that makes Bok's situation different from any cruelly treated horse's or Western hero's is some inverted sentences and some ritual allusions to indicate the man is Jewish. The reflexes of conventional sentimental movies have run straight into the reflexes of conventional sentimental Jewish fiction.

Because the book, too, does not account for anything. Bernard Malamud (who won the National Book Award and the Pulitzer Prize for *The Fixer* in 1967) is an infinitely better writer than Dalton Trumbo, and Trumbo's experience of McCarthyite persecutions has not made him equal to a subject as grand as this. Bok was an innocent man, who seems to have drawn his courage mainly from the injustice done to him (he had no family or beliefs to justify his love of life, particularly), but he did not yield. It is not enough to put him in a few cliché predicaments (an Old Testament Joseph situation, in which a rejected seductress accuses him of rape) with a few unresonating truisms ("I am a man!"), and hope that the context of Russia and anti-Semitism will explain something away.

We are just way beyond this. It's just not what it's about anymore. We are so accustomed, by the news and the screen itself, to the idea that innocent people suffer at the hands of other people, and sometimes prevail, that any individual case requires something more, some high eloquence or intelligence or note of particularity to have meaning or to register at all. Bok does not register. We know nothing about him except that he did not confess and did not die. Perhaps all cases of suffering and courage are on one level. The density of Mr. Malamud's prose, even when he is not at his best, covers this lack of insight into the particular. But the rhetoric is not the same; they are not the same morally or dramatically and a sign that

338

*The Fixer* is not equal to the dignity of the case is that the movie is such an unremittingly, unenlighteningly depressing experience.

......... *The Magus*

*12-11-68*

*The Magus,* which opened yesterday at the Festival Theater, is a fine adaptation of a strong, difficult novel by John Fowles, who also wrote the screenplay. In its style and ambition, *The Magus* is just the opposite of Mr. Fowles's other important novel, *The Collector,* which was stark, realistic, hermetically sealed—one obsessed, demented character exercising his power over another in a small, enclosed space. *The Magus* opens out, with many characters drifting in and out of time and place, possibly in one man's imagination, "to arrive where we started," in T. S. Eliot's line, "and know the place for the first time."

Michael Caine plays the young Englishman, Urfe, who, on a small Greek Island, meets Anthony Quinn, as the Magus, Conchis. (For people who don't read aloud in their minds, hearing the names first in the movie, before seeing them spelled, has the peculiar effect of turning the novel inside out.) Caine's special quality as an actor, the handsome, viable but essentially passive and bewildered hero, is just right for the kind of real unreal bargain he strikes with Conchis—never knowing whether he is part of a game, an experiment, a simple event, a madness or a fantasy, as the movie, like the novel, keeps inquiring of itself what its plot is going to be.

The director, Guy Green, is remarkable in knowing what to show, what to drop, what to put in relief. The camera picks up Empson's book, *The Seven Types of Ambiguity,* works by Auden, frescoes that are meant to be (and cannot, because of their location, possibly be) by Fra Angelico—but it does not dwell on them. You can see

339

the movie as just a dense, rather sexy story if you like. Candice Bergen, who is not a remarkable actress, is perfectly cast as a partly unreal character, some of whose essence is her artificiality. For a change, the work a character does to earn his living is shown with care, so that Caine's brief scenes as a teacher in a boy's school include a few classrooms and recesses as they actually are.

Occasionally the unreality, the voices drifting flatly from anywhere on the screen, gets in the way a bit, but there is some beautful cutting, some use of flashback that actually enriches the novel. And a scene in which Quinn faces the Hannah Arendt problem of whether a man has the right even to enter into a contract that entails sacrificing some lives to spare others (even when the murder of three might save eighty) ends with a Greek cry of *"Eleftheria!"* (Liberty!), which is as moving as anything on screen this year. It is surprising how the movie (which was shot, incidentally, in Majorca without the Greek crisis in mind) is not embarrassing, but actually dovetails with yachtings and oppressions in contemporary Greece.

Mr. Fowles lets the Magus describe the plot as "meta-theater—for the actors" and at another point, refers to the Nazis as "bringing order into the chaos of Europe." The implication is that natural life is chaos, and that order, even plotting, is an exercise of force, This is a highly doubtful point, but the movie, by following the disorder of the novel so faithfully, is, for a change, done just right to suit and complement the book. *The Magus,* of course, was a highly visual, movie-aware novel of ideas (it even included the screening of a pornographic film). On the screen, as in the novel, the ending, the arrival where we started, resolves nothing, but it is, mainly, a fascinating trip. The movie also stars Anna Karina, as Caine's original real girl.

The decline of narrative—the lapse of the story firmly grounded in specific persons and a shared sense of values—has had a particularly hard effect on movies. The theater has other options. It can become aggressive, can enter and force a reaction from its audience, as living, nontheatrical encounters do. The novel can lie low. But the movies, for lack of a story, are forced into decadent forms: events without persons—as in films of pure violence or poor pornography; science fiction; detective stories; spy stories; genre spoofs; archaisms, attempts to revive old forms like Westerns or traditional musicals. It is a question of keeping the genres intact until real events and persons come back again.

In the limited sense in which a movie is the shell of a performance, with live actors going on out of the celluloid to lead their lives (and the sense in which prose in print is the track of an idea), the shell of an argument or a moral question, in the media, can do enormous harm. It is possible, with the speed and reach of press or movies, to throw an audience entirely out of tune, to make a public inaccessible to a distinguished performance or a valid argument. Particularly the note of indignation, if sounded too often or too emptily, can throw the intellectual climate out of whack. At the smallest level, a wayward press column in a little city newspaper can point, time after time, to newspaper coverage of a given situation and claim that there must be another story there—with the same note of indignation as if the wayward press writer himself had bothered to find it, or even to find whether another story did exist. Insubstantial indignation kills the moral sense and leaves the shell of its vocabulary.

On a higher intellectual plane, there is the trick of taking an empty contradiction and treating it as a resonant profundity. A current one is "repressive tolerance," exactly on a par, intellectually, with the advertiser's slogan of

341

"fresh frozen orange juice." Frozen orange juice is never fresh, as tolerance has no repression in it, but put the words together often enough, and summon enough enthusiasm for the one and indignation for the other, and you have false deeps. In selling a product or a power elite, you've wrecked some minds and coined a household word or two. Intellectual confusion can drive you to the visual. At the approximate moment when children, turning on the schools, can say that they see no reason why the Board of Education should have the power to make decisions that regulate their lives (I suppose we shall soon be seeing the anti-spinach riots of 1969 and the nap confrontations of 1970), it seems clear that this is a time of misplaced or empty rhetoric. Yet, there are the movies, playing through, with the merest shell of an idea, and the terms of any argument go flat, or are ruined altogether.

In this context, *The Birthday Party,* an early Pinter play, superbly photographed and acted, seems positively warm, documentary and inhabited—although Pinter writes for characters as spare, unparticular, and allegorical as anything washed up on the beach. And John Fowles's *The Magus,* written as a novel or a screenplay almost in quest of itself, going constantly real and unreal, with characters inhabiting roles other than their own, seems as living, contemporary and grounded in what people actually go through as any piece of autobiography. Perhaps the movies, leaning on novels as they do, have pressured some writing toward emptiness—which seems all the more exposed on the screen—and others, as cinema-conscious, in the best sense, as *The Magus*, into going back in the shell where the living creature is.

## The Killing of Sister George:
## Not Much of a First

12-17-68

For the first few minutes of *The Killing of Sister George*, it seems the movie is going to be as viable as the play, by Frank Marcus, with Sister George—a motorbike-riding sister of mercy on a B.B.C. soap opera by day, a hard-drinking tweedy lesbian by night—about to be killed off in her TV role, and to lose her frilly roommate at home. Robert Aldrich (*Lylah Clare*) cuts cleverly around the ends of London brick walls from scene to scene, as Sister George, accompanied by a lot of bass music with a little thunder in it, makes her way home to where Childie, in a sort of tutu nightie, accompanied by a lot of treble music, waits. They discuss their day.

After that, the only nice things in the movie are a few solid Anglo-Saxon epithets ending in "off" and meaning "go away" and a scene in a London nightclub, where a number of real-life young ladies with short hair and field hockey player walks (shoulders down and forward with each step, like a rube high-school boy's feignment of non-chalance) give the only acceptable performances in the film. The scene of Childie eating George's cigar butt, for penance, does not work in closeup. All the speeches are slow, chirping and screamish; even Beryl Reid, as George, seems to have become, since the play, just a whinnying, hissing granny on a single unconvincing note.

Susannah York, as Childie, is disturbing, but seems, devoutly and understandably, to be wishing herself in some heterosexual part. Childie and George, for some reason, are not so much made up as oiled, as for a Channel swim. The prolonged, simultaneously serious and mocking treatment of homosexuals, I suppose, inevitably turns vicious and silly—as homosexuality itself inevitably has a degree of satire in it. But there is a scene between Coral Browne (the gossip columnist in *Lylah Clare*), playing a villainous lesbian studio executive, and Miss York's left breast,

343

which sets a special kind of low in the treatment of sex
—any kind of sex—in the movies now.

Miss York, whenever her face is in view, looks embarrassed. Miss Browne approaches the breast with a kind of
scholarly interest, like an ichthyologist finding something
ambivalent that has drifted up on the beach. The scene
goes on for ages (Mr. Aldrich's attempt, I suppose, to
gather some of the refugees from *Thérèse and Isabel*). It is
the longest, most unerotic, cash-conscious scene between a
person and a breast there has ever been, on screen and outside a surgeon's office. Not much of a first. The film
opened yesterday at the Beekman and Orleans theaters.

. . . . . . . . . . . *Candy*

*12-18-68*

*Candy*, which opened yesterday at the Astor, Baronet,
and Loew's Orpheum theaters, is faithful in dreary spirit
to the best-selling novel by Terry Southern and Mason
Hoffenberg, and also to the larger, more seriously received
schools of writing and cinema, which keep prolonging little trite, messy spasms of mediocrity and mistaking them
for the courage to go too far. In two hours of the picar-
esque story of Candy, an innocent high-school girl who
keeps being had in trucks, planes, hospitals and men's
rooms and on billiard tables (a kind of reversal of the old
Doris Day seduction comedies at exactly the same comic
level), there is not enough material for a two-minute
bawdy skit.

"He's leaking badly," somebody says of a man who's
bleeding. Or "Candy. That's a beautiful name. It has the
sound of the Old Testament." Or "Some of us haven't
had much dolce in our vitas." A Mexican lover, in the
course of making love, shouts, "Viva Zapata!" What's
supposed to be going on is an irreverent satire of sex,
police brutality, the medical, the military, film, academe,

the East, the Electra complex. One line, "It's not funny, Livia. It's not a funny situation," seems to sum the whole thing up.

The movie, directed by Christian Marquand, manages to compromise, by its relentless, crawling, bloody lack of talent, almost anyone who had anything to do with it. Richard Burton, as a poet-seducer, gives a firm, delighted, irrefutable demonstration of his lack of any comic talent whatsoever. John Huston and Ringo Starr look as though they had been drawn in by a regrettable, humorless beautiful people syndrome. Charles Aznavour performs uncrisply and badly as the hunchback. Marlon Brando, as a Jewish guru (the film has an ugly racialism and arrested development, frog-torturing soft sadism at its heart), is less unendurable, because one is glad to see him on the screen, in anything again. Rockefeller University, where some of the bumbling, fatuous assaults on Candy are set (and a pointlessly cruel brain operation, disgusting for its lack of comedy, is set as well) is hardly recognizable.

Only Walter Matthau manages to keep his comic professionalism intact, without going all over smug, out of control and self-amused—and his part, as a stock general from Central Satire, is one of the worst written of all. (In one of the film's comic climaxes, he parachutes from a plane, without his parachute. That's what it's like.) Ewa Aulin, as Candy, nude some of the time and mostly out of synch the rest, is a former Miss Teen Sweden, who seems not in great condition for eighteen.

... *Chitty Chitty Bang Bang*

*12-19-68*

In spite of the dreadful title, *Chitty Chitty Bang Bang*, which opened yesterday at the Loew's State Theater, is a fast, dense, friendly children's musical, with something of

345

the joys of singing together on a team bus on the way to a game. The film is based on a fantasy by Ian Fleming, and its violence level just after the credits is fantastically high (a car drives off the road and explodes, a child is nearly run over, the breaking of an adult bargain is treated as a desirable thing). After that it settles down and becomes a happy anarchical story within a story about cars, kids, adults, and candy.

Dick Van Dyke plays a gentle, nutty, apparently widowed father, who invents fine Rube Goldberg devices that serve eggs at breakfast. Heather Ripley and Adrian Hall are his two pleasant, unaccountable English children. Sally Ann Howes plays a Major Barbara-like candy tycoon's daughter, who ultimately marries him. Gert Frobe rather overplays a balloon-borne villain from the kingdom of Vulgaria—keeping one eye shut for most of the film in a physically disturbing, villainous way. Chitty Chitty Bang Bang is a car that swims and flies and finally rescues everyone.

The screenplay, by Roald Dahl and Ken Hughes (who also directs) is remarkably good. The music is not distinguished, but with lyrics (by Richard M. and Robert B. Sherman) like "Oh, what a lovely, lonely man," and "There's magic in the wake of a fiasco" and lines like "Zis is X speaking. X, as in X and pains," the movie, which accelerates, as a musical should, as it goes along, can hardly miss. The preoccupation with sweets and machinery seems ideal for children. There is a very jolly, well-done dance number in which Miss Howes and Mr. Van Dyke play puppets in Vulgaria, and another wittily choreographed (by Marc Breaux and Dee Dee Wood) vicious, patty-cake minuet.

The fantasy side of the movie is deliberately a little obvious technically—so that when Chitty Chitty Bang Bang flies or floats, in a kind of paper cut-out processing shot, it is just clear enough that what's happening is not real. The jokes and puns are fairly distributed among age levels. There are some subtle, intelligent concessions to a child's view of the absolute, unappealable arbitrariness of adult power—particularly the habit of replying to an absolutely

346

crucial question (some children, in this case, wanting to know whether they are going to get out of a dungeon or not), "Well, we'll see."

There is nothing coy, or stodgy or too frightening about the film; and this year, when it has seemed highly doubtful that children ought to go to the movies at all, *Chitty Chitty Bang Bang* sees to it that none of the audience's terrific eagerness to have a good time is betrayed or lost.

. . . . . . *Ice Station Zebra*

*12-21-68*

*Ice Station Zebra* is a fairly tight, exciting Saturday-night adventure story that suddenly goes all muddy in its crises, so that at two crucial points—when water comes rushing into a submarine under the polar ice cap, and when somebody is substituting something for the object everybody is searching for—it is very difficult to know what is going on, or who knows what about it. It doesn't make much difference, though. The story, based on a novel by Alistair MacLean (who also wrote *Guns of Navarone*) and directed by John Sturges (*The Great Escape*), has Rock Hudson, Patrick McGoohan, Ernest Borgnine and Jim Brown (one of them a spy) all rushing under the sea on a secret Allied mission to the North Pole. The special effects, of deep water, submarine and ice, are convincing enough—a special Super Panavision, Metro-color, Cinerama claustrophobia.

Rock Hudson, in his fifty-second picture, plays a submarine commander uncertain (until the puzzling second crisis) what his mission is. Mr. McGoohan, of TV's "Secret Agent," plays a laconic British intelligence agent. Mr. Borgnine is an agent too. Mr. Brown plays an embittered marine, and Tony Bill, a young actor with a clean-cut, troubled face, plays another intense, less important marine. They are all stock types, but the absolute end of the movie—when the press version of what happened at a Russian-American polar confrontation goes out to the world—has a solid, non-stock irony that makes this another good, man's action movie (there are no women in it) to eat popcorn by. The film opened yesterday at the Cinerama Theater.

........ The Ten Best
Films of 1968

*12-22-68*

In looking at what I take to have been the ten best films of this year, and perhaps, if we think in tens, the best ten after that, it strikes me how strongly movies are shifting from the sense of an audience as a huge, undifferentiated crowd to a sense of an audience as individuals who watch, not as we watch television, in national swarms, but as we read novels or short stories, in a kind of interior privacy. All the trappings of magnitude—the budget, the celebrities, the epic or grand-group themes—are gone. Not a single pure big-star film has made it this year; not a standard genre war, or Bond, or even horror film has been even fun this year.

It used to be that a talented director tried to sneak his talent through in a mass convention—Western, detective, tough guy, and so on. Now movies seem to be starting at the other end, something special, intense, even autobiographical, with the hope that from little solid audiences the grander commercial successes will follow later on. It has been a year not for the everybody film but for the serious, particular effort, which requires only a reasonable financial return to free the participants for future work. In a way, this is a loss. The old entertaining movies for Saturday night are dormant and not around, and people who have tried them this year wind up with depressing leviathans.

348

I guess what the ten best have in common are scenes that are memorable in a personal way—scenes that are clipped into one's mind almost autobiographically, so that the viewer has to deal with them ever after, as he would with an experience that is important to him, or a recurrent dream or a fantasy. In part, because movie advertising is often so inane that it positively interferes with a good film in finding its audience, in part because it takes a long time for certain kinds of work to build an audience, few of the films had long runs. Here they are, in no particular order:

*Charlie Bubbles,* screenplay by Shelagh Delaney, from an original story by Miss Delaney; directed by Albert Finney and produced by Michael Medwin, presented by Regional Film Distributors. With Albert Finney as a young celebrity, bored with himself and with the incredible, life-draining banalities people forever address to him. Billie Whitelaw, as his former wife, plays one of the few warm, exhausted, believable women on screen this year; Liza Minnelli is appalling and funny as a voracious, ambitious American child-woman abroad, who writes "contributions" for her hometown newspaper. I particularly remember a restrained, hilarious meeting in a diner late at night, with superb glances and innuendoes exchanged among Miss Minnelli, a soldier and a nurse. Also, Finney respectfully applying Miss Whitelaw's false eyelashes to the upper lip of his son, as a moustache; the perfect dialogue throughout; some exchanges with Finney's servants ("Mr. Noseworthy. . . and the worthy Mrs. Nose"); and the absurdist ending, when, if the story is not to continue into infinity, there is simply no other way out.

*The Two of Us,* screenplay by Claude Berri; directed by Mr. Berri; a co-production by P.A.C.-Valorie Films-Renn Productions, presented by Cinema V Distributing, Inc. Alain Cohen plays, with wonderful gravity and mischief, the Jewish child required to pass for gentile in occupied France. Michel Simon, as a lovable but anti-Semitic old Frenchman in the countryside, is still great, as he mutters, and harbors the child, and breathes in a slow, underwater sort of wheeze. The scenes are black-and-white elegiacal. The little boy, with shyness and humor,

349

forever unable to remember his assumed name; a little girl gravely chasing a goose; some men in a café urging the little boy to write a love note, which gets him in awful trouble at school; Simon arguing with a clandestine B.B.C. broadcast in his basement, or burying his dog. The gentle autobiography catches, in simple anecdote, the effects that war—even in a little pocket of peace—can have on the lives of children.

*Belle de Jour,* screenplay by Luis Buñuel and Jean-Claude Carriere, adapted from a novel by Joseph Kessel; directed by Mr. Buñuel; produced by Robert and Raymond Hakim; an Allied Artists release. Not at all characteristic of the dark mystic social dramas of decay and morbid eroticism by the great director, this highly elegant, smooth pornographic fantasy took a long time getting here but was a considerable commercial success. Catherine Deneuve, as the housewife submitting to various, beautifully directed, unspeakable practices in somebody's fantasies (I suspect they are mostly her husband's, as he sleeps in his chair), is fine, and so is the rest of the cast. Pierre Clementi, as a bucktoothed, swashbuckling gangster, is very funny; Geneviève Page is superb as a brothel owner, with all the firmness and insight of a humanist dietician in a boarding school.

*Faces,* written and directed by John Cassavetes; produced by Maurice McEndree; presented by the Walter Reade Organization. After the first twenty minutes or so, this film—acted with absolute naturalness by John Marley, as a middleaged husband; Lynn Carlin, as his wife; Gena Rowlands, as a young prostitute; Seymour Cassel, as a thirtyish hippie; Val Avery, as Miss Rowlands' client; Fred Draper, as his sidekick; and all the rest of the cast—becomes an incredibly compressed and powerful piece of eavesdropping on people in normal but absolutely desperate straits, laughing on the outer edge of an American hysteria. All the scenes of good-humored, helpless cruelties—as much as any epic, this film takes on the whole of an immense, demeaning American middle-class misery of aging, without grace and alone.

*Les Carabiniers,* screenplay by Robert Rossellini, Jean

Gruault and Jean-Luc Godard, from a play by Benjamin Joppolo; directed by Mr. Godard; produced by Georges de Beauregard and Carlo Ponti; presented by New Yorker Films. Not characteristic of Godard's style, this tight, spare, inspired fable shows that Godard can do just about anything anyone else can do, and do it better. Among other things, it is one of the strongest anti-war films ever made—without resorting in any way to sentiment. Four characters—all of them rather stupid, and spastic and nearly deformed—are drawn into the general "mozibilisation" for a war. I remember particularly the scrawled postcard message from Borges on "worn metaphors," which effectively preempts any possible criticism of the film; the car advancing, with one burning headlight, to pick the men up from their hut; Raoul Coutard's photography, conveying a war by the most economical means; and Godard's entire pictorial inventory of Western civilization—in postcard form.

*The Bride Wore Black,* adaptation and dialogue by François Truffaut and Jean-Louis Richard, based on a novel by William Irish; directed by Mr. Truffaut; a co-production of Les Films du Carosse, Les Productions Artistes Associés, Dino De Laurentiis, S.P.A.; distributed by Lopert Pictures Corporation. Somehow the story of Jeanne Moreau's serial murders becomes witty and romantic in a gentle Truffaut way. Miss Moreau plays an obsessed and unendearing character, quite unlike, say Hitchcock's kind Miss Froy, but the ending concludes a sweet, eccentric love story. The photography, again by Raoul Coutard, makes even a scarf flying through space remarkable, so that all the anecdotes spring visually to mind: Claude Rich's expression as he is about to be pushed off a balcony; Michael Lonsdale's minute, self-satisfied nod toward his Legion d'Honneur; a small, perfectly timed clapping of the hands in a game of hide and seek by a child actor, Christophe Brunot.

*The Fifth Horseman Is Fear,* screenplay by Zbynek Brynych, based on a story by Jana Belehradska; directed by Mr. Brynych; produced by Barrandov Studio, Prague, a Sigma III release. A story about physical courage, and moral honor, and one of the few films with real suspense all year. Miroslav Machacek risks his life to get morphine for, and ultimately to hide, a member of the Czech underground in World War II. These are the scenes of cobbles, streetcar wires and traffic in Prague; the Desperation Bar, a beautifully crowded Brechtian nightclub for the doomed; a brothel, with women in the showers, baroque music and a sense of the imminence of death; the expression of each of the beautifully characterized tenants of Machacek's building, as they file past his corpse.

*Petulia*, screenplay by Lawrence B. Marcus, based on a novel by John Haase; directed by Richard Lester and produced by Raymond Wagner; presented by Warner Bros.-Seven Arts. The film is nervous, jagged, very dense, as though the plot had broken and shattered through, but it has a fine cast, starring George C. Scott as a surgeon who ought to marry Julie Christie, and its fragments are simply brilliant. There are little sequences, which manage to imply everything: a hospital; the quality of a marriage conveyed when an orange is playfully thrown; a bedside visit, by Joseph Cotten, making clear a whole political cast of mind; a little, funny hippie conversation. Seed scenes that stay in the mind almost separately, quite a lot like gems.

*Rosemary's Baby*, screenplay by Roman Polanski, based on the novel by Ira Levin; directed by Mr. Polanski and produced by William Castle; presented by Paramount Pictures. One objection to this film—that it has a long dead part, in which Rosemary is simply obtuse about the coven—vanishes if one views it as a lapsed Catholic fable, not in the mind of the director (as I had originally thought) but in the mind of Rosemary herself. It makes absolute sense that Polanski (of *Repulsion*) should have directed the novel this way, and a lot of little clues fall in. In this view, the long static part becomes, not an infuriatingly slowly-burning revelation, but a gradual collapse, and the film, except in Rosemary's mind, is not a horror film. Miss Farrow and the cast are fine (one certainly believes that, either way, this sort of thing could have happened to her); and the scenes, particularly the closet door opening terrifyingly, to reveal a vacuum cleaner, are rather fun to screen in the mind at home.

*A Report on the Party and the Guests,* screenplay by Ester Krumbachova and Jan Nemec; directed by Mr. Nemec; produced by Barrandov Film Studios, Prague; distributed by Sigma III. This comic, infinitely menacing fable, directed, with a cast of Czech intellectuals, by Jan Nemec (who also did the beautiful, unsensational documentary *Oratorio for Prague*), was held up for two years by the pre-liberal Czech government. It concerns a party game that ends, through cowardice and lack of decency, in guns. One of the extraordinary things about the movie is its delicate, restrained and sophisticated treatment of fear. The beginning of the game, with a kind of conspiratorial dunce mock-trying and ultimately, with the merest touch of violence, torturing a guest; the scene at the party table, when people sit comically in the wrong seats at first, and then the expressions when it is realized that a guest has gone. The film is in beautifully lighted black and white, and one remembers most of it with the most peculiar combination of humor and a chill.

There are the second ten: Ingmar Bergman's *Shame,* not his best but still the master; on the subject of war, Jean-Luc Godard's *La Chinoise,* an unprecedented portrayal of young people through ideas; Milos Forman's *The Firemen's Ball,* one of the year's few laughing comedies, which is serious about stupidity, without being an example of it; Paul Newman's *Rachel, Rachel* (a bit like a young, poetic *Faces* in the absolute authenticity of its life, characterization and dialogue); Stanley Kubrick's *2001,* with its obsessional special effects; Marca Bellocchio's *Fist in his Pocket,* with an incestuous, demented family brought to a fugue of madness; the Beatles' *Yellow Submarine,* for one or two marvelous moments, as when the arrows, snails, and miscellaneous criss-cross through a corridor; *Romeo and Juliet* as an unreprehensible popularization of the play, which makes teenagers cry; *Bullitt,* as the one lean, straight, successful near-genre film of the year; and *Hot Millions,* with Maggie Smith and Peter Ustinov in pure, professional silly fun.

*12-24-68*

*Shame,* which opened yesterday at the Fine Arts Theater, is Ingmar Bergman's fable about war. Dry, beautifully photographed, almost arid in its inspiration, it concerns a couple of former musicians, Liv Ullmann and Max Von Sydow, who are caught on an island in the middle of an insurrection in 1971. They are not getting on well, they do not care who wins, and even the war fails to intensify anything about their lives. Von Sydow is a coward, increasingly debased as the film and the war go on by his completely unheroic, now virtually incomprehensible, determination to remain alive.

The "shame" of the title is God's. "What if that person should wake up one morning and be ashamed of what he had done?" one of the characters says. "That person" is God. The war is no longer a moral context. It is part of the order of things, the sides are not defined, no one is responsible for it. Bergman has moved, exhausted, straight out of the human condition to take on the universe again. He is getting to be the Job of directors, in the tired, outraged realm at the edge of things where there is nothing to be said.

Against the dull, authentic pounding of guns, Miss Ullmann and Von Sydow are rounded up, first by one side (for a dubbed, forged interview of solidarity), then by the other (to be abused for the interview). They become friends, for all the good it does them, with a colonel, Gunnar Bjornstrand, whom Miss Ullmann sleeps with, in a kind of tribute to his desperation. They take ferries on their nameless island very like—in their quotidian indifference to the soldiers aboard, the war around—the ferries in the delta of Vietnam.

Miss Ullmann, in her wish to have a baby, her impatience with her lover's lack of courage, her kindness to strangers, is the only one still grounded in any humanity at all. By the end, they set off in a boat through a sea littered with military corpses for the mainland or another island, where, presumably, there will be another war. *Shame* could be a film about the tenacity of civilians, but it is more like a document just before extinction. There is no strength in it. It is at Bergman's wits' end. Even the idea that a childless couple would go to such limits of energy simply not to die is not self-evident or even convincing any more.

. . . . . . . *Monterey Pop*

*12-27-68*

*Monterey Pop,* which was shown last night at Lincoln Center and which will open early in January at the Kips Bay Theater, is a contemporary music film—in the relatively fresh tradition of *Festival* and *Don't Look Back.* The movie filmed by Richard Leacock and D. A. Pennebaker, with the collaboration of Albert Maysles and other independent filmmakers, is an upbeat, color documentary of the 1967 pop-music festival in Monterey, California. It stars the Mamas and the Papas, the Jefferson Airplane, Ravi Shankar, the Who and other singing groups. From the moment Scott Mackenzie's "If you're going to San Francisco" comes onto the track and screen, it is clear that this is one good way to do a musical.

There is all that shiny hair, orangeade, beautiful hands, shades, watermelon, shoeless feet in tights, flowers, paper flowers, dogs, the wrinkled bottom of Ravi Shankar's tapping foot, psychedelic blobs behind the podium, smoke effects behind the infernal Who, mouths approaching microphones, eyes in all those various, distinct, serious young faces, which, ten years ago, before the seriousness of Vietnam began, we didn't seem to have. The photography is pretty well coördinated with the sound, sometimes blinded by strobe lights, so that the screen is absolutely white, sometimes shifting down lines of audience in a kind of *Rosencrantz and Guilderstern Are Dead* focus of attention on characters other than the main.

There are the lyrical songs, "California Dreamin' " and Simon and Garfunkel's "Feeling Groovy," Janis Joplin straining her voice and being to sing black. Then there is a kind of spot, purely visual interview—a beard and a cop laughing, wordlessly teasing each other; a girl from Champaign, Illinois, feeling lucky to be allowed to wipe the folding chairs between performances, a Hell's Angel arriving at the Shankar concert that is the long, wound-up climax of the film. There are rock violinists and young people dressed like pageant potentates.

"We all love each other, right?" Otis Redding shouts, half ironic, half intimidating. "Right," the audience replies. Jimi Hendrix goes through his thing of somersaulting, then being irreverently, frantically obscene with his guitar, finally destroying it—presaging in a fairly violent way, the quality of the kisses of Tiny Tim.

But the nicest thing about the movie is not its music or nostalgia, but the way it captures the pop musical willingness to hurl yourself into things, without all the What If ("What if I can't? What if I make a fool of myself?") joy- and action-stopping self-consciousness of an earlier generation, a willingness that can somehow co-exist with the idea of cool. Also, musically and photographically, the harmonies, the resolutions of chaos after everything looks as though it is going to fall apart.

"Once you leave here you may not re-enter," a guard at the festival says to some members of the audience at the gate. It is possible that the way to a new kind of musical—using some of the talent and energy of what is still the most lively contemporary medium—may begin with just this kind of musical performance documentary.

*12-29-68*

It is possible that television reporting and newspapers have almost completely exhausted the old dramatic possibilities of the arts. It is not just a matter of photography infringing on representational painting, so that people no longer require an artist to record their faces for posterity. It is that a lot of the traditional options of drama—a distillation of life into crises, speculations about the lives of the great, the simple transmission and preservation of news—have gone over into instantaneous documentary. The only point in a play or a movie about the funeral of James Chaney, in 1964, would have been to recreate in imagination that scene for people who were not there to see and hear it.

But we were all there, with television and the press, and the moment when David Dennis, a young black field secretary of CORE, said in a soft, breaking voice that he was sick and tired of funerals—when he enumerated Emmett Till, lynched, Mack Charles Parker, lynched, Medgar Evers, shot from behind, added "If you do go home tonight and take it, God damn your soul,"—and withdrew from the pulpit in tears, is there on film and in memory. It was one of the great, tragic scenes of our time. Before the media, people would have few, if any, such moments in their lives, and had to turn to literature and drama for the rest. Now we have them all, too many, in straight, fast transmission of events as they take place.

In trying to draw the emotional responses back, the most banal artists simply exaggerate, raising the threshold to extremes of misery or violence beyond what even reality has to offer. This doesn't work. You have to stylize. It is unlikely that a plain, "realistic" war or sentimental public film will ever succeed again. The ones that still work are films about private lives, essentially autobiography, that do not reach the media, good reporting, or

357

imaginative, undocumentary or absurdist breakthrough of various kinds.

*Up Tight,* a transposition by Jules Dassin of the plot of Liam O'Flaherty's *The Informer* to the black section of Cleveland, doesn't work, though the cast is black: Julian Mayfield, as an unemployed drunken steelworker who is expelled from the committee of militants; Raymond St. Jacques, as an intellectual militant leader; Max Julien, as a fallen hero; Janet MacLachlan, as his African haircut sister; Frank Silvera, as a believer in the system; Roscoe Lee Browne, as a homosexual collaborator with the police; Ruby Dee, as a desperate young woman on welfare; Juanita Moore, as the hero's dying mother. And the idiom seems solid and good.

Yet the film is never for one instant moving, never lives up even to its initial documentary footage of the voice and funeral of Martin Luther King. (This failure is complicated by the fact that the footage is hoked up with shots of cheese in front of a television set, which makes no point really and simply ornaments and artifies the event.) At its worst, when the characters are theatrically posed, it is as though everyone were about to burst into song and the film seems a drained, modernized *Porgy and Bess.*

The film's problems are complicated by the fact that it is not true, that the reality of the Negro movement in this country lies elsewhere. There is no black revolution so far in the Irish "troubles" sense. Negro heroes have not been killers, Negro militant meetings and Black Caucuses are much more complex than traditional party cells. It has not happened, and it does not make emotional sense to cast a black hero as a member of a violent revolution in progress and to star a discarded man who betrays him. It is not historically or foreseeably real. In fact, the whole black movement is too deep and complex to be treated —even in a first, and at heart admirable, effort to present some real Negro situation in a conventional film—in this particular way.

There is the nonviolence that swept out of the South. There is the movement in the North to educate the young, separately if need be, and create a historically unique intellectual community. There is the less dramatic effort to integrate with the white middle class. There are personal dramas unrelated to politics. There are all the manifestations of suffering, courage, achievement and despair. There are the Panthers, effective half at the level of fantasy, the black few's dream and the white few's nightmare. There just doesn't happen to be *The Informer*. All the tricky confrontations in front of distorting mirrors at carnivals, all the compressed, nearly balanced discussions of ideology won't make it fit. It fails in more than just being emotionally unequal to the documentary. It gets less audience response than *For Love of Ivy*. And yet, one can't help hoping that it has started something in films, and that truer versions will follow.

*Oliver!* although Carol Reed has directed it as a lovely, animated painting, is not, I think, a musical for anybody. Children are out. There are much too many threats of impalements on forks, confinements in coffins, insults to dead mothers and allusions to children being sold. While children go, with fascination and no demonstrable permanent harm, to horror films, I think the context is entirely altered when the horrors happen to a child. I remember, and other people seem to remember, Miss Havisham's scream, the graveyard scene and the paddle wheel from *Great Expectations*. I think the reason it haunted us, not briefly but for years, was the fact the hero was a child. The disproportion of the horror and the victim is too great.

As for adults, the music is mediocre, with endless reprises that stop the story cold. A yiddish accent that overcomes Fagin as he sings "You've Got to Pick a Pocket or Two" must have seemed funny at shooting time, but reflects a sensibility, or lack of it, one wants no part of. The scenes of old London are rich and convincing, the quality of the singing is quite good, but I can't imagine why anyone would have wanted to spend so much care and energy on a cast-iron pastry.

*1-5-69*

If there were a cinémathèque in New York City—and
now, with a lucky and imaginative combination of
publicity-shy American institutions, it seems that there
may be—it would be unthinkable without the collaboration
of Henri Langlois of France, and James Card of the
George Eastman House in Rochester. Mr. Card, who had
a private collection of 800 films in Cleveland until, in
1948, the Eastman-Kodak Company offered him a place
in Rochester to house and show them, is the closest thing
we have to an American Langlois. Eastman House, under
his direction, has expanded to become the finest film collection in the country. There are early, important silent
films from the Cecil B. DeMille estate; films starring Mary
Pickford, collected and donated by Miss Pickford; films
accumulated from everywhere (particularly from a New
Jersey scout, John Allen, who finds a lot of old movies in
the course of selecting clips for television). Original
camera negatives of American films going back to 1915
are still donated, in considerable numbers, to the Eastman
House. ("Well, if you think so much of it," Mr. Card
quotes studio donors as saying when they trade originals
for duplication in acetate, "then here it is.")

Mr. Card, whom I recently visited in Rochester, is a
tall, handsome man in his middle fifties, with that air of
modest, wry fanaticism that seems to characterize the true
film archivist. I asked him how, over the years, he has
continued to accumulate old films that were thought to be
unfindable. "You just smell the nitrate," he said. The
original nitrate versus safety-base copy controversy is one
in which Mr. Card, as in many other matters, sides with
Henri Langlois, and disagrees with many institutions
—among them the Museum of Modern Art, which will
be trading its original nitrates to the Library of Congress

for safety-base prints, on the theory that the nitrates are explosive and dangerous. Mr. Card concedes that nitrate is highly inflammable. But he points out that until 1950 nitrate films were carefully and safely transported everywhere and that, while valuable (particularly in circulating film libraries to local clubs, a practice begun by the British Film Institute and subsequently here), making copies is, for serious film students, comparable to Xeroxing, with infinite competence and care, the works in the Prado. "Up here, we can afford to be purists," he said.

The preservation of films has entailed, through the years, a lot of surprisingly violent and bitter controversy—with the purists, Card and Langlois, almost always on the same side. The International Federation of Film Archives, founded in the thirties by the Paris Cinémathèque, the British Film Institute, the Museum of Modern Art and the Berlin film archive, expanded rapidly to include institutions (among them, Eastman House) from many nations. Then, in the mid-fifties (under the leadership of its Polish president Jerczy Toeplitz), it turned in an absolute fury of cinema jealousies and politics upon its founding member, Henri Langlois, in a complicated lawsuit, which, if it had not ultimately been dismissed, could have had Langlois jailed for what amounted to idiosyncrasy. Only Mr. Card and the Japanese film archivists (whom Mr. Card describes as "anti-cabal") resigned to support the most important film collector of them all.

Langlois, of course, has been involved in countless controversies, among them the Paris demonstrations over his dismissal from the Cinémathèque (he has subsequently been reinstated), which most of his supporters regard as the forerunner of the national demonstrations in May. A pro-Langlois protest in winter certainly involved the first recorded public appearance, with megaphone, of Daniel Cohn-Bendit. James Card, like every other serious archivist and filmmaker, supported Langlois in that crisis too.

"Part of the genius of Langlois and the Cinémathèque," Mr. Card said, in the mansion with gardens, on a tree-lined street, which is Eastman House, "is not simply to be instructed by somebody else's taste. Save everything, the whole vast panorama on film, a mirror of times, places and moods, a person living. You don't have to convince anyone under thirty. Film is the most wanted art of all on the part of the young people. But if you ask older people for the $1,500 that it takes to save a film, they think you are some kind of crank." He said that foundation money is needed for research to prolong the life of camera negatives. "They are like human beings, everyone is different—experience, environment, life, prognosis.

"The British are very scientific about it," he said. "They punch out a little piece of film, like a biopsy, and then make a decision: destroy, retest in a year. The trouble is every part of an old film can be chemically different. A single film can be on variously printed stock, with varying degrees of decomposition. Sometimes you can save the film if you just excise five feet. To destroy the whole original is what studios did when film was held in infinite contempt. It is the essence of absurdity."

Since Rochester is not Paris, no school of filmmakers has grown around Eastman House as it has around the Cinémathèque, but Robert Youngson (*The Golden Age of Comedy, Further Perils of Laurel and Hardy*) spent a lot of time there, research for books goes on there, Langlois came to teach a course at the University of Rochester and there is a thriving film club (membership varies from 2,600 to 3,000) of buffs who pay ten dollars a year for a program of seventy-five films at the Eastman House. A recent program was Italian Cinema: 1908 to 1968. Mr. Card discussed the effect of the movie camera's having become a household thing. "I suppose I'm carping a little," he said, "but so far it hasn't been creative. Everybody out there pointing his camera at the family pet and thinking, Gosh, it's wonderful. There are images in apparent movement. It isn't the way it was when directors had to be able to do everything themselves, shoot, print, with all the care of a daguerreotype."

I asked what effect the American Film Institute was having on the work of Eastman House, and gathered it is not clear yet. The A.F.I. had offered to make safety-base copies of the Eastman House collection for deposit in the Library of Congress, but Mr. Card had not seen the advantages of that. A press release had implied that the A.F.I. was effecting a collaboration between Eastman House and the Museum of Modern Art, but the two institutions have often collaborated on programs in the past, and Mr. Card was not consulted before the press release. The people who prepared the lavish Stanford study, on which the structure of the American Film Institute is based, had not come to Eastman House at all. And the A.F.I. bulletin of missing films the Institute hoped to trace and accumulate included films that were not missing and films that had never been made. A "missing film" in the bulletin was, for example, a rare version of *Body and Soul,* in which Paul Robeson is supposed to have starred for MGM. But the film was not made for MGM, and a library positive of *Body and Soul* has been for years at Eastman House. Mr. Card and two other film experts had been consulted about the bulletin, but their corrections were not assimilated. Mr. Card said that he understood the A.F.I. was going to give some young filmmakers a little support, and that this might have a salutary effect.

Since old films have become a valuable property, there have been legally complicated and uncertain deals in which people go to the studios, buy the rights to an old film and then try to pry it loose from the museums. Since Mr. Card had mentioned that he often pays a producer for permission to make a print or a library positive—no rights, just the print—restoring the film to the producer afterward (and since there is a distinguished tradition of film-collecting piracy), I asked him whether, in those rare cases where a film is successfully pried loose, he doesn't save a print, quietly, for the Eastman House archive. He did not reply, had, in fact, an unmistakably archival smile. In the 400-seat screening room of Eastman House, as we left, some girls from a parochial high school were absorbed in watching a completely legal print of *Potemkin.*

*2-10-69*

*Havana*

In this year of severe rationing and shortages of nearly everything material, Cuban cultural life is particularly active, and under stress. With so little else available, Cubans spend a lot of what free time there is on the arts, and cultural priorities within the revolution have always been extremely high. Dance, writing, theater, painting, films and poster art travel in "itinerant exhibitions" to the remote provinces, Oriente and Camaguey. The jury for the Casa de las Americas prize in art and literature has gone this year, for symbolic reasons, to deliberate in an agricultural settlement on the Isle of Pines, where students from the Havana Art Institute are already spending their forty-five days cutting sugar cane.

Cuban art, conscious of the experience of socialist realism in the Soviet Union, appears relatively free so far of what the Cubans call *panfleto*, that is, flat propaganda work. But the arts in Cuba are, after all, administered by the Cuban Cultural Council, which is an agency of the government, and although its various bureaus—cinema, publishing, theater and so on—have so far determined on their own what degree of artistic freedom is admissible, there are forces gathering to suppress work that does not entirely reflect a propaganda line. At Havana's Teatro García Lorca, the Cuban National Ballet, directed by the internationally known choreographer Alberto Alonso, and starring Alicia Alonso and Maya Plisetskaya's brother, Azari Plisetski, is now staging a production of *Romeo and Juliet*. Set to electronic music and jammed even in rehearsal by enthusiastic crowds, the production ends with a little speech explaining the moral of the story: Two lovers

364

cannot oppose the system alone. It requires a united effort of the people.

A solid production with just a fillip of political commitment has become characteristic of much of Cuban art in the last ten years, and has developed certain stylistic values of its own. But some ideologues are beginning to demand a more thorough political orientation. A series of four pseudonymous articles last fall in the military magazine *Verde Olivo* attacked the "depoliticalization" of much of Cuban art, particularly two works, a book of poems, *Outside the Game* by Heberto Padilla, and a play, *Seven Against Thebes* by Anton Arrufat, which won the prizes of the Cuban Artists and Writers Guild, UNEAC, last year. The articles suggested worthy future subjects —heroism during Hurricane Flora, for example—for revolutionary art and deplored less committed work as counterrevolutionary. The attack went unanswered for three months. Mr. Padilla, whose poetry was denounced for its "pessimism" (his poems imply that individuals are inevitably crushed by historical forces), had already lost his job at *Granma*, a government newspaper, and has not been granted the trip abroad that is part of the guild prize. The contested book of poems also includes these lines: "I live in Cuba. Always/ I have lived in Cuba. These years of wandering/ through the world, of which they have spoken so much/ are my lies my falsifications./ Because I have always been in Cuba."

Mr. Arrufat's play, denouced for its "pacifist" elements (all war is depicted in horrible terms), has not been produced but both *Seven Against Thebes* and Mr. Padilla's *Outside the Game* have been published in a UNEAC edition—with two conflicting introductions. The first, by writers who belong to UNEAC, disclaims the poems and play but defends the freedom to publish them. The other, by members of UNEAC's international jury, defends Padilla's poems in the strongest terms. Earlier this month, Haydee Santa Maria, heroine of the revolutionary battle of the Moncada who is now head of the Casa de las Americas (an institute for Cuban cultural exchange with the rest of Latin America), suggested that the UNEAC jury consist only of Cuban writers in 1969.

Cuban filmmakers are now preparing to publish a position paper of their own—which will be the first public answer to the *Verde Olivo* line of attack. The six-page "Declaration of the Cuban Cineastes" will deplore equally the "clean hands" and "pure vocation" of liberal writers, who, in trying to prove their independence of ideology, produce "reactionary" art, and the "timid and bureaucratic" dogmatist, who, in trying to control development of the arts, occupy a "masked" counterrevolutionary position as well. The young filmmakers will advocate free artistic expression, not too "lazy" to take the aims of the revolution into account; their guardedly liberal statement is expected, in the intellectual community, to bring the controversy to a public crisis of some kind.

The last time the issue of artistic freedom arose in Cuba on a major scale was in 1961 when a documentary film, *P.M.*, which showed drunkenness and decadence in Havana nightclubs, was suppressed. Cuban artists and intellectuals protested vigorously, until Premier Fidel Castro, in a famous speech to the intellectuals, stated his position on freedom in the arts: "What are the rights of revolutionary writers and artists? Within the revolution, everything; against the revolution, no rights whatsoever."

Among the writers opposing the suppression of *P.M.* was Guillermo Cabrera Infante, then editor of *Lunes de Revolución*, a Cuban cultural journal. The journal was discontinued, and Mr. Cabrera Infante, who has since left Cuba, is now conducting an important correspondence in an Argentine periodical, *Primera Plana,* protesting Cuban censorship. It was after praising *Tres Tristes Tigres,* a book by the emigrant Cabrera Infante, as the best Cuban novel since the revolution, and after dismissing as unimportant a book by Lisandro Otero, vice president of the Cultural Council, that Mr. Padilla lost his job at *Granma.*

It might be assumed that artists who have not left Cuba after ten revolutionary years are demonstrably "within the revolution," but the present crisis seems a kind of testing of the still ambiguous and contradictory grounds, to determine whether Cuba is about to undergo what seems to many a historically inevitable tightening of control. The situation this year is different from 1961: Problems in the arts are ironically complicated by the fact that, except for the economic blockade—which many Cubans credit with having strengthened the country and unified the people—pressures from the United States have become less apparent. They appear, more subtly, as a Cuban internalization of the values of American culture itself. At every cultural level, for a newly literate people, past and present are learned together, and the weight of cultural history as well as the weight of contemporary art naturally falls on the side of peoples who have been literate for some time. A generation too young to remember Batista, the early struggles, illiteracy or real underdevelopment is growing up. And there exists a contingent of youth that Cuban intellectuals refer to as "snob"—bored with revolutionary discipline and fascinated by American life styles, American films, American rock (a Beatle-like group called Los Meme is greeted with screams; a Havana youth newspaper reports solemnly that the Mamas and Papas are breaking up), and what an official for Cuban television calls the American "Queen for a Day Psychology." Minor leanings in this line are tolerated, but students who drop out too firmly or too conspicuously are likely to be expelled from the schools and sent to the provinces for "agricultural re-education."

"In the early days of the revolution," a Havana University student said, "the important words were 'blockade' and 'imperialism.' People used to explain personal troubles, even nightmares, in terms of *imperialismo*." The crucial words now, he said, are "Third World" and "underdevelopment," with Cubans trying desperately to identify themselves with underdeveloped countries, to divorce themselves from the culture ninety miles away. It is out of lack of confidence that Cuban artists are developing in definably Cuban ways, he said, that a dogmatist approach takes form.

There are certainly fields in which Cubans are developing art and cultural dilemmas of their own. In the early days of the revolution the Cuban Institute of Film Art and

Industry, ICAIC, fought a battle over posters against bureaucrats who argued that representational, essentially socialist realist art was the only means of communicating to the people. ICAIC held out for art, and now professional and amateur artists in Cuba design posters with such style that even the political agencies are producing graphics of distinction and originality.

On the lawns of what was formerly the Havana Country Club, a Cuban architect, Ricardo Porro, has designed the Havana Art Institute (a school for children between twelve and seventeen), consisting of rounded structures, like Gaudí in brick, with bulbed dome windows on top and long columned walks along the windowed sides. It is one of the most pleasant, least institutional schools imaginable. The prefabricated houses replacing peasant huts all over the country, on the other hand, are flat, infinitely reduplicated rectangles. Cuban theater, since the Arrufat issue arose, has been largely limited to imaginative productions of Bertolt Brecht, or inventively staged choral readings from the Cuban poet and patriot José Marti. Vicente Revulta, one of the best-known theater actors and directors in Havana, has temporarily moved to the more liberal film institute.

Out of a concern about underdevelopment, a Youth Congress of Artists and Writers, which met recently in Havana, will meet again later this month, with delegates from all the provinces, in Camaguey. The young people want to discuss how, as active revolutionary workers, they can find time and access to materials, instruction and outlets for the art work they would like to do. A genuine cultural problem, acknowledged by the government, lies in bringing books, film, art and information to a generation of new intellectuals emerging from the schools, and being sent, for the most part, to settle in the provinces. The old propaganda vehicles, newspapers and television, are not suited to new sensibilities. Hard news of the outside world, even in Havana, scarcely exists.

The writer who introduced the word "underdevelopment" on the intellectual plane is Edmundo Desnoes, whose novel *Memories of Underdevelopment* (now a highly popular film in Cuba, and for some reason published in the United States as *Inconsolable Memories*) uses the word ironically to apply to a writer who is not entirely convinced by the revolution, who is not in fact entirely convinced by anything. Mr. Desnoes, a tall, blond man of thirty-eight, who worked until recently as an editor of books, now works for the Cuban propaganda agency COR in charge of coining slogans—rather like the poet Vladimir Mayakovsky in the Russian Revolution. Before the revolution in Cuba, Mr. Desnoes, who describes himself as having been for years completely alienated from society, lived on a boat in the Bahamas. In 1961 he returned to Cuba, expecting an invasion and expecting, he says, to die. Asked whether, as an intellectual, highly skeptical writer, he found that the revolution gave or cost him energy, he said, "For me, it is always an effort to remain alive." Asked whether he believed in progress at all, he said that formerly he did not, but that looking at Cuba fifty years ago, "a country of pimps and prostitutes," and looking at Cuba now, it is difficult to maintain his skepticism about it.

Mr. Desnoes, like nearly every other able-bodied Cuban, spends about a month each year cutting sugar cane. He acknowledges that he hates it. "As an intellectual, you have a certain idea of nature," he said. "Landscapes, something impressionistic. But the cane is alienating, overwhelming. Conversation becomes absolutely crude and elementary. Bending down to the coffee plants, I suppose, is physically more difficult. But the cane never seems to end." Mr. Desnoes, who has lived in the United States and who has traveled a great deal abroad, said he would not leave the country now until the sugar harvest of ten million tons, projected by Premier Castro for 1971, was in.

Before the revolution, books by Cuban writers were not published in Cuba except at the writer's own expense, and Mr. Desnoes published his own first novel, in an edition of 500 copies, himself. The Cuban bourgeoisie under Batista, he said, read mainly *Life* and *Reader's Digest*. "Now, for the first time, a Cuban writer has an authentic audience," he continued. "He does not have to look abroad for international acclaim. It entails certain responsibilities." Asked about the characteristics of that new audience, he said it was perhaps still too accepting, too uncritical. "The problem is to understand them, not to project," he explained. "In all the new education, we cannot be sure what the people know. It may be that with all the ideology about Latin America people have no idea what Latin America is. Or any country. Or a continent."

He said that the revolution had so far proceeded pragmatically, reactively, without any rigid ideological system, and attributed this to the instincts of Premier Castro. Asked how the revolution would go without Mr. Castro, he said, "Perhaps Stalinism, no? But it is not right to protect your ideas against the future. It might become a nightmare or a dream." In a late-night discussion between Mr. Desnoes and some friends in Havana's Hotel Nacional it was mentioned that the United States had not, after all, invaded Cuba, where it might once have succeeded, and had, instead, gone to Vietnam, where it had fewer interests and could not win. It was suggested that this might be construed as a colossal blunder of idealism. Mr. Desnoes said that in coming to grips with America, a colonial writer must also come to grips with the fact that it has also helped to form his own idealism. "If the country is so powerful that with a flick of its finger it could extinguish Che in Bolivia," he said, "one must also understand the things it has not done." On the subject of how the United States might react to a full recognition of its loss in Vietnam, Mr. Desnoes said, "I hope it will not be like Moby Dick. A bewildered monster who flicks his tail and wipes us off the island."

Humberto Solas, twenty-seven-year-old director of *Lucía*, the most popular film in Cuban history, works six months a year on films and six in the agriculture or at other jobs, which he does not mind. "The year has twelve months," he said, and when it was remarked that the content of the experience of American intellectuals is often only other intellectuals, he said he was certain his contact with the people in his months away from film helped in his work.

Mr. Solas, who is reading a Soviet polemical history of Stalinism distributed by the Cuban government to intellectuals (a few special books, called Polemical Editions, are occasionally circulated only among intellectuals, for discussion purposes), is very much concerned with the dogmatist position on Cuban art. "They do not understand the revolution," he said. "Now, after ten years, everybody is thinking. This is a popular revolution. We have a strong secret service to deal with real counter-revolutionaries. We don't need a populist-dogmatist bureaucracy."

Mr. Solas is also very much worried by a rumor that a book called *The Hard Years*, by Jesús Díaz, will become a reflection of a cultural line. "It is a study of the years before the revolution," he said. "But it is important to realize that 'the hard years' are now." He much admires a recent Colombian novel, *100 Years of Solitude*, by Gabriel García Marquez—"very revolutionary, very deep," he said. "The populist position is, 'I did not want to put the bomb, but I was told to, and I did.' The deep position is, 'I was told to, and then I thought, and perhaps I didn't put the bomb.' " Mr. Solas was convinced that young people "of talent and sensiblity" would not accept a populist approach. But if, as he thinks unlikely, the hard line should win out, he would stay in Cuba and wait for a better time. "If I could not make my kind of films, I would rest," he said. "In the end, the question is who is more revolutionary, which side of the controversy produces better art."

———

*2-11-69*

*Havana*

At the time of the revolution, Cuba's contribution to world cinema consisted mainly of cheap tropical locations, facilities for dubbing, and, in Havana's Chinatown, the three most famous pornographic theaters in the world. Starting virtually from nothing, Cuban filmmakers—most of whom are in their late twenties or early thirties—have now developed the most widely discussed, persuasive and controversial medium in the country. Films now reach far more extensively than television (which broadcasts mainly propaganda and old films monitored from stations in Miami) every place where Cubans meet.

In early 1959, three months after the revolution, the Cuban government founded ICAIC (Instituto Cubano del Arte e Industria Cinematográficos), a film institute instructed to form and document the revolutionary experience of people, while creating films as art. Under the direction of Alfredo Guevara, a former guerrilla, who, in exile in Mexico City, had served as an assistant to the Spanish director Luis Buñuel, the film institute took over all film production, distribution and collection in the country and began to move, rather like the new roads and schools, into the countryside. Since modern equipment was unavailable, the institute created a kind of spare-parts cinema, refurbishing the 100 commercial theaters in Havana and the 400 in the rest of the country, founding a 3,000-film cinémathèque, and sending all films, Cuban and foreign, to villages all over the country in mobile units, which show films in fields, community centers and schoolhouses. According to an official of ICAIC, every Cuban now has access to about two films a week. The pornographic film houses have been closed.

The budget varies considerably from year to year, but the government supplies the institute with what filmmakers call "means"—that is, props, locations, theaters, access to places, transportation, technicians, and actors temporarily released from national theaters. Since Mr. Guevara has long been a personal friend of Premier Fidel Castro, filmmakers are relatively independent of the national Cuban Culture Council, which nominally administers all the arts in Cuba. As a result, the film institute is regarded by Cuban intellectuals as one of the major sources of information and relative liberalism.

American films made since 1960 are not exported to

Cuba and, since the blockade, Cuban films have not been admitted to the United States. But among the most widely and seriously discussed foreign films in Cuba now is the Czechoslovak *Closely Watched Trains,* Jiri Menzel's story of a young boy who thinks himself impotent, sleeps with an older woman and, the next day, blows up a Nazi train. The crucial point for young Cubans is that the woman who brings the boy the bomb, and who sleeps with him, is an artist. "In any Russian film of the forties," Humberto Solas, a twenty-seven-year-old Cuban director, said over lunch in the Hotel Habana Libre (formerly the Hilton), "the woman would have brought the boy the bomb and sung him the Internationale. In Menzel's film, it is just as important for her to go to bed with him. It is something new. It is human."

Mr. Solas himself has just directed *Lucía,* the most popular and enthusiastically discussed film in Cuban history. Already seen by more than a million people, *Lucía* tells the story of a woman's problems in Cuba in three historical periods, 1895, 1932 and now. In the first episode, Lucía, played by Raquel Revuelta, falls in love with a Spaniard, who turns out to be married. She is persuaded to run away with him and reveals to him the location of the *cafetan,* the revolutionary headquarters. He turns out to be a Spanish spy as well, and brings the Spanish soldiers in. She murders him. In the next chapter, Lucía, played by Eslinda Nunez, is drawn by a boyfriend out of her rather F. Scott Fitzgerald set into guerrilla sabotage in which the boyfriend is killed. Both episodes are done with a remarkable sense of style and period, but it is the third, the contemporary, chapter that causes the greatest excitement in Cuba now.

Lucía, played by Adela Alegra, is young and married. She wants to work and to learn to read the country's alphabetization program, but her husband has the traditional Latin quality of *machismo.* His pride and his sense of manhood require that his wife be completely dependent on him and remain at home. He is enormously suspicious of anyone who wants to take her out of the house and into the revolution. A leader of the local agriculture settlement—a lovely, wizened, officious Negro woman who unconsciously imitates Premier Castro's mannerism of repeating an important sentence now and then, with bent knees and index finger pointing toward the ground— tries to reason with him. It is no use. Lucía leaves him. They have a sad and hopeless meeting on the beach, and the question of *machismo* is left unresolved.

Cuban audiences, whose members include even the most clearly *machista* men, adore the film, laughing at all the parodistic touches, particularly at the Premier Castro imitation and at elderly farmers being appalled by miniskirts. But young intellectuals tend to prefer the first two chapters for their style and to have reservations about the third for its simplicity, although they respect the sense of doubt and ambiguity at the end. Cubans acknowledge that *machismo* is a problem for the revolution—resisting the liberation of women and even affecting the use of modern machines. A man's pride in his strength and in the work of his hands can bring him into conflict with a tractor or a piece of factory equipment.

"Yet the problem is difficult," Mr. Solas, a tall, gentle young man, who became a guerrilla in the mountains at the age of fourteen, said of this chapter of his film. "It is, after all, the *machista* spirit that creates revolutionaries. *Machismo* is simply not suited to social relations. It can also be a factor in the government's relation to the people. Maybe it will be overcome now that everybody studies." Asked whether, for example, a *machista* spirit in government might be what inhibits young people in boarding schools (many of whom object to the system of fifteen days' confinement to school, with one day off) from registering any form of protest now, he said that it might. "For me, as a boy, fighting Batista was easier," Mr. Solas said. "He was hated. It was simple. Now the young have a complex of admiration and fear. The men of the revolution are Greek statues to them, and to say that the marble might be flawed or the statue might be missing one arm is difficult."

Mr. Solas described *Lucía* as an exercise in which he rid himself of the influence of international directors he admires—Luchino Visconti, Ingmar Bergman, Roberto Rossellini and Buñuel. His next film will be completely Cuban, examining in greater depth the problems of Cuba now, the contradictions, the people who have somehow been left outside the revolution. "It is important not to regard them as monsters," Mr. Solas said. "There is a tragic aspect. Even people who don't understand the revolution are giving everything." As examples, from his next film, he mentioned a guerrilla who, after the revolution has succeeded, becomes a functionary and misses the excitement of his life. Or a mother who is committed to the revolution because her sons are revolutionaries, but who secretly longs for them to become doctors or to have some other form of bourgeois success. Or an opportunist who becomes an interpreter for foreign visitors only to have contact with the products they bring in. Mr. Solas believes that these revolutionary dilemmas will disappear as the revolution develops.

Another vital and controversial film in Cuba now is *Memories of Underdevelopment,* directed by Francisco Alea, and based on a prize-winning novel by Edmundo Desnoes that was published in the United States as *Inconsolable Memories.* More than 600,000 people have already seen the film, which is a highly intellectual study of a writer living in affluence at the time the revolution comes. The writer's wife and friends leave Cuba, and he is unable to hear their voices when they step to the other side of the window in the airport waiting room. His life is full of Scarlatti, Botticelli, dry martinis and girls, and he has doubts whether his love of the revolution does not derive from an artist's hatred of the bourgeoisie. Mr. Desnoes himself appears in the film in a panel discussion, which ends when Jack Gelber, the American playwright, asks why, "if the Cuban revolution is really a total revolution," there should be a roundtable format "about issues with which I am familiar," instead of an open discussion with the people. "The American is right," the narrator says, a psychologically difficult sentence in Cuba these days.

The film is full of documentary footage, interior monologues, flashbacks, abrupt cuts and avant-garde touches.

Cuban audiences seem extraordinarily receptive to avant-gardism of every sort—electronic music, surrealism and absurdist comedy. Cuban intellectuals explain this in two ways: Before the revolution the masses in Cuba had not been exposed to art of any kind and, since tastes had not been "deformed" by popular art, avant-gardism seems quite natural. And most artists struggle consciously to keep the artistic and political vanguards together, against the "populist" idea that only representational art can reach the people.

In describing a fiction film in progress, a Cuban film-maker is likely to begin with an abstraction—and some-times leave it at that. Jorge Fraga, a twenty-three-year-old director, explained, for example, that his film *The American War* is about "two forms of violence, active and passive, generated in two brothers by the inevitable am-bience of colonial war." Pressed about the actual content of the plot, Mr. Fraga revealed an intensely dramatic story of rape, cowardice and murder, but the original equation was clearly uppermost in his mind.

While shooting *The American War*, Mr. Fraga's crew stayed at a former resort hotel, now a convalescent home, in the village of San Diego, which is in Pinar del Río, the nation's westernmost province. The home is near a spa, whose waters are still believed to be medically restorative. It was not a cheerful place—a murky swimming pool surrounded by plaster swans; eggs and an unidentifiable soup for lunch; people in ragged bathrobes wandering about; a salon whose furniture consisted of two facing rows of seventeen slatted rocking chairs. But the crew of fifteen actors and technicians did not seem to mind.

The actual shooting took place in a remote area at the end of a pitted road, on the Hacienda Cortina, the estate of a pre-revolutionary senator. This is near the site of one of the tourist resorts being built for Cuban workers, who, in their twenty days' yearly vacation, have no place out-side Cuba to go. The filming, like all filming, consisted mainly of waiting—for the sunlight to be right and for the old Zeiss 16-mm. camera to be properly set up. Vicente Revulta, the brother of one of the Lucías and himself one of the best-known Cuban theater actors and directors, was wandering about making jokes. Since the situation in Cuban theater is not just now as liberal as in cinema, Mr. Revulta has temporarily moved to the film institute.

A great many jokes were made about a truly hideous dog that was staggering around the crew. From the conversation, it was clear that the dog had nearly died in the night and that its owner, because of anxiety, had refused to eat. The dog, which was white, had a red band of what appeared to be medication around its neck, covering what seemed to be a hairless rash. It seemed for a moment to reflect all the misery of Latin America that such a repellent creature should exist, and that even its owner could care whether it survived. Then it suddenly became clear that the dog was in the film. There was no rash. The red band had been painted on because one of the characters in the film was supposed to strangle the dog. On the preceding afternoon, Mr. Fraga explained, he had injected the dog with a drug so that it would lie with its tongue hanging realistically out. Mr. Fraga had given the dog an overdose that had almost resulted in its death. The dog was fine, merely slightly looped, as it wandered about. It was still not handsome; its health still did not inspire much confidence, but it was waking up. The red band would be washed off when the shooting was done.

---

*2-12-69*

*Havana*

From the early days of the Cuban revolution, the priority of films, and particularly documentaries, has been so high that the government's first law dealing with cultural matters established a national film institute, ICAIC, in March, 1959. Film-projection crews began to move, in twenty-five-day trips, to the remotest villages. In addition, documentary filmmakers were instructed to overcome the influence of Western "films of a commercial nature which are ethically disgusting and artistically dull," to "serve as a narrator and protagonist of the revolution," and to bind city and countryside together in a revolutionary consciousness. Cuban television has never been of much importance, partly because the *campesinos* do not have sets and partly because it is not suited to public places, where people gather and discussion takes place. Television is still steeped in propaganda of the crudest sort. (A recent program reported that the reason Israeli forces were so strong in the Middle East was that they were led by Nazi generals.) Since television, which existed before Fidel Castro's revolution, is ideologically single-minded and technically archaic, it is films that are taken with the greatest seriousness as national sources of information and of art.

The quantity of propaganda in Cuban newsreels and documentaries is roughly comparable to the amount of advertising in American television, with the difference being that Cuban films advertise only one product, socialist revolution, and that propaganda is now integrated in what has become a distinctively Cuban style. Films characteristically cut, with great suddenness, from the pure study of a subject, with great respect for the quality of the subject's life, to an extremely blunt and remote political point. There is also a wider surreal and sometimes consciously comic conception of the relation between life and revolution. Cubans say that Cuba was the only socialist country to show *Morgan,* the irreverent English treatment of insanity and Marxism.

Among the most prolific, simultaneously folk and surreal filmmakers of ICAIC is Santiago Alvarez, who, since 1959, has made 437 newsreels and twenty documentaries. The forty-nine-year-old Mr. Alvarez now produces newsreels at the rate of one a week. At the time of the revolution, he was a music archivist for Cuban television who had never thought of making films. Asked how he happened to become a director, he said he had been caught up in creative revolutionary activism, "the same way Fidel became a *guerrillero.*"

Mr. Alvarez's films contain strong elements of what, to a foreign observer, seems absolute *panfleto,* that is, pure propaganda work. But Cuban filmmakers say that although in the present struggle over artistic freedom the socialist realist, "populist" forces will try to claim Mr. Alvarez for their side, he will place himself firmly on the side of relative liberalism.

An Alvarez documentary about North Vietnam, called *Hanoi: Tuesday, December 13,* is one of the most beautiful films ever made about Asia, capturing, with the delicacy of a scroll, the rhythm of Vietnamese life, the hats, nets, fish, rice shoots, rivers, water buffalo. But intercut with a kind of poem about patience and tragedy ("We turn our hatred into energy," a Vietnamese says, in preparing for a bombing raid), with a surprisingly contemporary narration from a children's book about Indochina, by the turn-of-the-century Cuban poet and patriot José Marti, are scenes of what seems like crude and dissonant propaganda. President Johnson is suddenly introduced with literal, breech birth scenes of a woman and a cow. Asked whether he had put these scenes in out of personal artistic necessity or for didactic reasons, Mr. Alvarez replied that his reasons were emphatically personal. "I have to put them in. They are what I feel," he said.

Except for *Lucía* and *Memories of Underdevelopment,* which are the most important of Cuba's few fiction films, the most distinctive films in Cuba are still documentaries—nearly all made with Alvarez-like juxtapositions of fact, with a strong, unpolitical sense of human misery, and the most blatant ideology. Looking at Cuba's documentaries is like watching ten years of Cuban history—the Bay of Pigs invasion, Hurricane Flora, the 1961 literacy campaign, speeches by Premier Castro, a film in which Major Ernesto Che Guevara appears, scarcely able to speak because of his asthma. ("We had to splice it together in a few days," Mr. Alvarez said, "to give the people something after the death of Che.") In the film institute's 1,500-seat cinémathèque, however, there are quantities of American films made before 1960, and subsequently nationalized. And there are frequent retrospective exhibitions of Hollywood films, including a recent retrospective of Marilyn Monroe.

The parodistic sense in Cuban films is so strong and so

deadpan that it is not always possible to tell when it unambiguously exists. There is a completely solemn film, for example, about the artificial insemination of cattle, with shots of three men at a kind of console behind a pane of glass, as a cow, flopping one idle ear, is inseminated with a single pill—coded blue, green or red, according to the breed of the bull. The seriousness of the Cuban cattle-improvement program seems here to run into a strong sense of ribaldry.

Another documentary, a kind of athletic *Potemkin* in style, shows Cuban athletes arriving by boat in Puerto Rico to protest being barred from the Central American games. (Acceptance in competition in capitalist countries or contexts plays a large role in many Cuban films.) They were ultimately admitted, and won many gold medals, but the film shows a Cuban athlete throwing up into the sea and another being cuffed on the ear by the coach for having responded to the jeers of the anti-Cuban crowd. The film called *Cerro Pelado*, after the name of a battle and the boat itself, shows streets of stores in San Juan, which audiences instantly and delightedly recognize as the stores of Cubans who fled. The climax of the film is a grand melee, in which Cubans tear down a Soviet flag that Puerto Ricans had run up a flagpole to mock the Cuban victories.

There seems also to be a sense if not of satire then at least of cheerful inconsistency, when—at a time of a virulent anti-Israel campaign—a film called *Now*, venomously anti-West, is accompanied almost completely by a rendition, set to Spanish words, of the Hebrew song, "Hava Nagila."

Two of the most moving and poetic documentaries in Cuba now were made by Octavio Cortazar, who is thirty-one, and who describes his films as "testimonies" to a Cuba that his son will never see. The first film, *About a Person Whom Some Call St. Lazarus and Some St. Babalou*, is about a pilgrimage that takes place each year on Nov. 16, near Santiago in the province of Oriente. The pilgrims are black, descendants of slaves from the Yoruba tribe in Dahomey; and the Christian St. Lazarus has merged in their beliefs with Babalou (of the song "Babalou Aye") in the voodoo cult of Santero. For twenty-four hours they crawl, either on their stomachs or backward, in sitting positions, some with weights dragging from an injured limb, some with sick children on their backs, many groaning, to the Lazarus-Babalou shrine. Mr. Cortazar interviews priests, psychiatrists, workers, students, the Tata Nganga (the local Santero leader) and the pilgrims as they crawl, about what can be the meaning of such a pilgrimage, in the middle of a socialist revolution, on the part of people who would otherwise consider themselves Marxist-Leninists.

"I was shocked when I saw them," Mr. Cortazar, a tall, sensitive man, who studied for two years at the film school in Prague, said of the pilgrims. "The contradiction, the superstition. I cannot speak for the new generation and say that they will not be religious. I cannot say that they will not believe in God. But I know that with literacy, in the new Cuba, this pilgrimage will not exist." The film ends with shots of some very healthy, modern schoolchildren doing exercises on a beach.

Mr. Cortazar's other testimony to a disappearing Cuba is *For the First Time*, a film about one of the film institute's mobile units bringing Charles Chaplin's *Modern Times* to villagers in the Baracoa Mountains of Oriente. Mr. Cortazar interviews the villagers, who had never seen a film before, about what they think film is. "It is like a party," one of them says, "with couples and beautiful girls." Another, an immensely dignified, wrinkled lady, wearing a handkerchief over her hair, says film "is something you show in a cinema—very important thing. Very good." A young woman gets frightened and bursts into tears. At night, carrying torches, a little audience arrives for its movie, and sits in folding chairs in a field. The faces are amused, not awed, and radiant. The children eventually yawn and go to sleep. ICAIC's directors say that film is one of Cuba's few windows to the outside world. *For the First Time* catches, simply and respectfully, a moment, the first viewing of film, that will probably never occur in Cuba again.

## ABOUT THE AUTHOR

RENATA ADLER was born in Milan, Italy, and grew up, mainly, in Danbury, Connecticut. She attended Bryn Mawr College, where she majored in philosophy and German; the Sorbonne, where she received a D.d'E.S. in philosophy with Jean Wahl and Claude Levi-Strauss; and Harvard, where she is still a student in comparative literature. In 1962 she became a staff writer-reporter for *The New Yorker*. From January, 1968, to March, 1969, she was film critic of *The New York Times*.